TRADE
IN STRANGERS

For the Flour[i]

PHILAD

The SN[O]

JOHN Mc. CA[

Burthon 2

Well known to be the[r]

place in a

A Stout Ve[ss]el and a

the 1[f]t,

ALL young Men and youg
their fortunes, will meet w[
ing to Mrs. *Mc. Donough* in
may be seen every Day.   For fr[e]
Lawton and Brown, near the Dra[

TRADE
IN STRANGERS

The Beginnings
of Mass Migration
to North America

MARIANNE S. WOKECK

THE PENNSYLVANIA STATE UNIVERSITY PRESS
UNIVERSITY PARK, PENNSYLVANIA

Library of Congress Cataloging-in-Publication Data

Wokeck, Marianne Sophia.
    Trade in strangers : the beginnings of mass
migration to North America / Marianne Wokeck.
        p.   cm.
    Includes bibliographical references and index.
    ISBN 0-271-01832-1 (cloth : acid-free paper)
    ISBN 0-271-01834-8 (pbk.)
        1. United States—Emigration and immigration—
History—17th century.   2. United States—
Emigration and immigration—History—18th
century.   3. Germany—Emigration and
immigration—History—17th century.
    4. Germany—Emigration and immigration—
History—18th century.   5. Ireland—Emigration and
immigration—History—17th century.   6. Ireland—
Emigration and immigration—History—18th
century.   I. Title.
JV6451.W64   1999
304.8′73043′09033—dc21   98-35716
                                                      CIP

To P. M. G. Harris

Contents

List of Maps and Figures

List of Tables

Preface

Research for this book began quite a while ago when interest in the patterns of cultural adaptation and persistence among German-speaking settlers in colonial Pennsylvania brought me to Philadelphia. For exploring the circumstances that shaped the "Americanization" of German immigrants in the New World, it soon became apparent that determining the flow and character of such migration to the American colonies was crucial in delineating the necessary framework for understanding how strangers adjusted to life in "the best poor man's country." This study of the characteristics of the colonial German migration and its Irish counterpart made it clear how important it was to assess the impact that the trade in immigrants had on the numbers, types, and experiences of its passengers. Unlike earlier flows of English and Irish colonists and servants, and also unlike the slave trade, the German trade in immigrants established a model for the mass migrations of free persons that have done so much to fashion the nature of America.

Expanding the story this way took longer than planned because of other opportunities that opened up for surviving a tight academic job market and for growing intellectually and professionally. One year as associate editor of The Papers of William Penn stretched into four. Directing the *Biographical Dictionary of Pennsylvania Legislators* consumed energy and resources well beyond the initial phase of getting started and achieving recognition. Most recently, the challenges of teaching at the urban campus of Indiana University in Indianapolis have been both demanding and rewarding. Along the way I incurred many debts of gratitude. They are gladly acknowledged here.

Archivists and librarians on both sides of the Atlantic provided crucial assistance in shaping search strategies and locating elusive records. Special thanks are due to the staff of the Historical Society of Pennsylvania, where I did most of my research over many years, and also to the staffs of the City Archives of Philadelphia and the Philadelphia Register of Wills; the American Philosophical Society; the German Society of Pennsylvania; the Lancaster County Mennonite Historical Society; the Library Company of Philadelphia; the Manuscript Division of the Library of Congress; the Maryland Historical Society; and the Pennsylvania Historical and Museum Commission. The Public Archives of Nova Scotia answered long-distance questions very efficiently before such inquiries could be handled over the Internet, and the staffs of the Public Record Offices in Kew and London produced unfailingly the many records I asked to see when doing research in Britain. In the Netherlands, the archivists of the municipal archives in Amsterdam and Rotterdam were particularly helpful in steering me toward useful materials in their rich collections, but the contributions of the archivist of the town of Arnhem and of Deana Sy-A-Foek in the Rijksarchief Gelderland (Arnhem), and especially of Cora Gravestijn in the Economic History Library of the university in Amsterdam, were truly outstanding and invoke fond memories of research trips to the Netherlands.

If librarians and archivists are the stewards of the materials from which the data were gleaned for my argument, the insights and critical reaction of others in the field have shaped and focused my interpretation. The circle of friends and colleagues whose opinions affected my thinking about this project include the participants of the Philadelphia Center for Early American Studies, especially Rosalind J. Beiler, Richard S. Dunn, Aaron S. Fogleman, Christine Hucho, Susan Klepp, Jane T. Merritt, William O'Reilly, George Rappaport, Stephanie Grauman Wolf, and Michael Zuckerman. In addition, I am grateful for special expertise, comments, and support received from Ida Altman, Annette K. Burgert, Leo Byl, Kathleen Conzen, Louis M. Cullen, Georg Fertig, David Fowler, Frank Fox, Hans-Jürgen Grabbe, Farley Grubb, Mark Häberlein, John Hollingsworth, James Horn, Owen S. Ireland, Henry Z. Jones, Catherine Keen, Hartmut Lehmann, John J. McCusker, Kenneth Morgan, Alison G. Olson, Philip Otterness, Sally Schwartz, Jean R. Soderlund, Hermann Wellenreuther, Renate Wilson, Klaus Wust, and Margaret B. Yergler. In addition, A. G.

Roeber, Billy G. Smith, and Peter J. Potter read the entire manuscript and offered sound and often detailed advice, for which I am thankful because their comments, together with the careful editing of Peggy Hoover, helped make it a better book. Support of a different kind came from the National Endowment for the Humanities; Indiana University–Purdue University at Indianapolis; the Philadelphia Center for Early American Studies; and the David Library of the American Revolution—all contributions that aided in the research for the project and that I gratefully acknowledge. The greatest debt of gratitude, however, I owe to my husband, P. M. G. Harris. He persuaded me, convincingly, to make my life with him in the United States and, as a result, suffered through the writing of each stage of the study. I dedicate this book to him with thanks.

Abbreviations

AHR	*American Historical Review.*
GAA, NA	Gemeente Archief Amsterdam, Notariel Archief.
GAR, ONA	Gemeente Archief Rotterdam, Oude Notariel Archief.
GSP	German Society of Pennsylvania.
Hallesche Nachrichten	W. J. Mann, B. M. Schmucker, Wilhelm German, eds., *Nachrichten von den vereinigten Deutschen Evangelisch-Lutherischen Gemeinden in Nord-Amerika, absonderlich in Pennsylvania.* 2 volumes. 1787; reprint ed., Allentown, Pa., 1886; Philadelphia, 1895.
HSP	Historical Society of Pennsylvania, Philadelphia.
ISHAW, 1996	International Seminar of the History of the Atlantic World, 1500–1800, Harvard University, Cambridge, Mass., 1996.
JAEH	*Journal of American Ethnic History.*
JAH	*Journal of American History.*
JEconH	*Journal of Economic History.*
JIH	*Journal of Interdisciplinary History.*
LC/MD	Library of Congress, Manuscript Division, Washington, D.C.
LC/MD, FCP: Germany; Great Britain; the Netherlands; Switzerland	Library of Congress, Manuscript Division, Foreign Copying Project: Germany; Great Britain; the Netherlands; Switzerland.

MPC

Minutes of the Provincial Council of Pennsylvania from the Organization to the Termination of the Proprietary Government. 3 volumes. Philadelphia, 1838–51. Reprinted with the binder's title Colonial Records of Pennsylvania in the first of the Pennsylvania Archives series. Harrisburg, Pa., 1851–52.

Passenger List [1768–1772]

Passenger List with Duties, 29 August 1768–13 August 1772. HSP.

Penrose Cashbooks

Thomas Penrose Journals (1738–51). 3 volumes. HSP.

Pennsylvanische Berichte

Der Hoch-Deutsch Pennsylvanische Geschicht-Schreiber [. . .] (1739–43); after 1743, Pennsylvanische Berichte, Germantown, Pa.

PMHB

Pennsylvania Magazine of History and Biography.

PRO

Public Record Office.

Record of Indentures [1771–73]

Record of Indentures of Individuals Bound Out as Apprentices, Servants, etc., and of Germans and Other Redemptioners in the Office of the Mayor of the City of Philadelphia, 3 October 1771, to 5 October 1773, City Archives of Philadelphia, Philadelphia.

"Redemptioners"

"Redemptioners, 1750–1830," Society Miscellaneous Collection, Box 7a, Folder 7, HSP.

Staatsbote

Der Wöchentliche Philadelphische Staatsbote (1762–67); Der Wöchentliche Pennsylvanische Staatsbote (1768–75), Philadelphia.

States General, Resolutions

Resolutien von den Heeren Staaten von Holland en Westfriesland and Resolutien von de H[oogh] M[ogende] H[eeren] Staaten General der Vereinigte Nederlandse Provincien.

Statutes at Large of Pennsylvania

James T. Mitchell and Henry Flanders, comps., Statutes at Large of Pennsylvania from 1682 to 1801. 18 volumes. Harrisburg, Pa., 1896–1915.

Tonnage Duty Book [1765–75]

Tonnage Duty on Incoming Vessels, 1 November 1765–30 August 1775, Cadwalader Collection, HSP.

Votes and Proceedings

Votes and Proceedings of the House of Representatives of the Province of Pennsylvania, 1682–1775. Philadelphia, 1753–75.

Votes of the Pennsylvania Assembly

Votes and Proceedings of the House of Representatives of the Province of Pennsylvania. 8 volumes. Reprinted in Pennsylvania Archives, 8th series. Harrisburg, Pa., 1931–35.

WMQ

William and Mary Quarterly, 3d series.

Introduction

A New Form of
Transatlantic Migration

The peopling of the English colonies of North America was becoming less and less English toward the end of the seventeenth century, in spite of the textbook images of Jamestown and St. Mary's and Plymouth and Massachusetts Bay, which present a more distorted picture. True, it was the offspring of these early settlers who contributed the most to the population increase in the colonies, but as word about the promise of the New World spread overseas, new immigrants came from increasingly diverse settings. In turn, their own children and grandchildren swelled, and diversified, the new society. In the South, African slaves were forcibly imported to replace English servants, the supply of which was not keeping up with demand. In European immigration, English adventurers, servants, and dissidents increasingly gave way to Irish, Welsh, Scots, Huguenot, and German arrivals. Of these newcomers, the large groups for the eighteenth century were the Germans and the Irish.

As new types of people sought relocation in the New World, a system evolved for bringing them over. It took advantage of increasingly sophisticated Atlantic trade and replaced what was haphazard transportation of predominantly English passengers in the seventeenth century with a specialized and profitable commercial operation. Emerging in the German emigrant trade of the middle of the eighteenth century, this system was then adopted for importing Irish immigrants in the last decades of the 1700s. Subsequently, the German immigrant trade became the model for how wave after wave of the forebears of modern Americans, from Killarney to Kiev, from Stockholm to Sicily, "crossed the water" in the nineteenth and early twentieth centuries. And it was the port of Philadelphia (only later replaced by New York) whose merchants helped invent and increasingly took over this trade in strangers, and through which the bulk of eighteenth-century German and Irish immigrants passed to fan out across the colonies.

This book tells the story of the fundamental changes in the process of populating America in the 1700s. New practices replaced the more simple and sporadic transplantations of the 1600s, when European settlers first landed in the English colonies in America. The ways of the immigrants themselves, of the merchants who shipped them, and of the employers and families who incorporated transatlantic colonists into New World life all became more sophisticated. In the eighteenth century, a system of migration developed that made immigrants and their diverse cultures a distinctive and integral part of the American fabric of life and that continued to shape the nature of American society on into modern times.

Such developments differed significantly from the circumstances of the previous century, when a mix of mostly English people had arrived. Among those earliest settlers were colonists of some means, who paid their own way in order to take advantage of the economic opportunity or religious and political liberty promised by various New World promoters. Others, mostly young men and women unable to pay for their passage, bound themselves in servitude to shipmasters and merchants through contracts that could be bought and sold in the labor markets of the colonies. With the exception of the Puritans of the early 1630s, both categories of immigrants usually crossed the Atlantic either as small organized groups or as willing individuals, but usually sharing the same ship. These "parcels" of both free passengers and bound servants were but a small portion of the cargoes that filled the modest vessels sailing the trade routes of the North Atlantic at the time.

By the late 1600s, a substantial degree of African slavery was spreading to mainland British North America from the Caribbean. After many decades of operating in the slave trade, Portuguese, Dutch, French, and English slavers had learned to build, outfit, and manage ships and to "recruit" and dispose of their human cargoes in ways that would maximize profits. By 1700, African networks for acquiring human freight had grown complex and far-reaching, vessels had become large and costly, internal space on ships was carefully arranged to pack in as many valuable pieces of property as possible on the westward voyage, new American markets for slaves were being constantly sought out, and ship owners wrestled with the problem of how to make the return trip profitable.[1] By the turn of the eighteenth century, two quite different systems for moving people to America were operating side by side.

Between the Peace of Utrecht in 1713, which ended a quarter-century of European and American war, and the outbreak of the Revolution in 1776, a third type of migration became increasingly important for the development of British North America. This new model established the pattern for the future: the repeated, diversified transatlantic flows to which most Americans can trace their origins today.

This new migration drew to the New World large numbers of people who were neither English nor African. While trickles of Scottish prisoners of war, dispossessed Irish, and religious dissenters from throughout the British Isles had added some variety to seventeenth-century English North America, major flows of other Europeans in the 1700s, particularly Germans and Irish, began to change the character of British American society. They helped make it more diverse in nationality, ethnicity, religion, and language, a diversity that modern historians take for granted as much as other present-day Americans.[2]

How these German and Irish immigrants, who began to play a significant role in eighteenth-century life, made their way across the Atlantic is not well known, for they did so in a way quite different from the immigrants of the seventeenth century. The trade in German emigrants combined some shipping technology of the slave trade, ethnic networking for recruiting and marketing, and more-efficient cargo planning, ship rental, and passage payment to bring approximately as many people from the Rhine lands to America between the 1720s and the 1770s as the total population of all the colonies together in 1713. The Irish trade subse-

1. The literature on the slave trade to the West Indies and Americas is extensive. Philip Curtin, *Atlantic Slave Trade*; Herbert Klein, *The Middle Passage*; Joseph Inkori and Stanley Engerman, eds., *Atlantic Slave Trade*; and early reports of results based on the ongoing Du Bois Slave Ship Data Project have been helpful for comparison with the North Atlantic trade in European passengers.

2. The conventional ethnic labels "German" and "Irish" are convenient but incorrect usage. In the context of the eighteenth century, "German-speaking" is a better but more cumbersome description for the migrants who left central Europe, and especially the territories bordering the Rhine and its tributaries—including Alsace, Lorraine, and Switzerland—collectively referred to here as the Rhine lands. "Irish" refers to "migrants leaving from Irish ports," and most of those were actually people from Scotland who had settled in northern Ireland, especially Ulster, before they migrated to the American colonies.

quently adopted features of the German experience to rival and replace that other ethnic migration in scale over the two decades leading up to the Revolution and in the years thereafter. These eighteenth-century changes established a model for the better-known mass migrations of the nineteenth and twentieth centuries.[3] Immigration to America was never the same again.

This exploration of migration shows how first the German system of immigration developed, and then how Irish immigration altered to adopt that same pattern. It focuses especially on the Delaware Valley because three-quarters of colonial Germans and about half the less-numerous Irish landed there. Many of these people settled in the greater Pennsylvania region (including down the Great Valley and inland areas of Maryland, Virginia, and the Carolinas). Ties among merchants in Philadelphia and in ports of England, the Netherlands, and Ireland are important, as are links that related passengers, recruiters, and New World employers. Together these bonds of connection formed networks that stretched across the Atlantic and set the pattern for the two great colonial migration waves that crested in the second half of the eighteenth century. Bridging the ocean— linking desire for a better life to its realization in the New World— became a distinct business that specialized in relocating people from one side of the Atlantic to the other, with forms that could be transferred readily from one group of potential immigrants to another. This replacing of the rather unsystematic "trade in strangers" of the 1600s with more modern methods promoted the vast and continuous transoceanic migration that did so much to make American society what it is today.

American historians have always recognized the importance of immigration, but few have examined early American migration at the time the seeds of modern immigration were being planted.[4] Most focus on the late

---

3. Marcus Hansen, Oscar Handlin, and John Higham described the features and consequences of these later mass-managed flows through ports like Liverpool, Bremerhaven, Le Havre, and Naples. Marcus Lee Hansen, *Atlantic Migration*; Oscar Handlin, *The Uprooted*; John Higham, *Strangers in the Land*.

4. Exceptions include David Allen, *In English Ways*; Ida Altman and James Horn, eds., *To Make America*; Bernard Bailyn, *The Peopling of British North America* and *Voyagers to the West*; Nicholas Canny, ed., *Europeans on the Move*; Aaron Fogleman, *Hopeful Journeys*; David Galenson, *White Servitude in Colonial America*; Henry Gemery, "Emigration from the British Isles to the New World"; Farley Grubb, "The Auction of Redemptioner Servants"; Mark Häberlein, *Vom Oberrhein zum Susquehanna*, partially published in English as "German Migrants in Colonial Pennsylvania"; and A. G. Roeber, *Palatines*.

nineteenth and early twentieth centuries, when many European populations were experiencing significant increases as mortality rates declined,
when emigration and immigration policies were liberal, and when steam-
ships and railroads could handle the large volume of transportation both
cheaply and efficiently.[5] The image of hundreds of thousands of people
moving each year from one country to another to form successive waves of
immigration to the United States during the era from the early 1800s to
World War I—the classic period of modern international migration—
has become a historical cliché. This image prevents many from recognizing that the several thousand immigrants a year who crossed the Atlantic
at certain times during the colonial period constituted a movement of
comparable magnitude relative to the size of the current American population.[6] Indeed, the transfer of more than 111,000 German-speaking settlers
to America between the 1700s and the 1770s constituted the first transatlantic mass migration of the modern type—that is, of non-English-
speaking alien—to become part of American society and culture.

Most seventeenth-century migrants to North America were English
people moving to English colonies, [7] so basic considerations of language,
culture, and citizenship were not at stake. Most of what we know about
this early movement of Europeans to America, moreover, indicates that
recruitment and transportation were not at all as large-scale, as concentrated, and as specialized as the eighteenth-century flow of Germans—
and, later, of northern Irish—across the Atlantic.[8]

5. This assumption is more often implicit than explicitly stated, as by Kristian Hvidt,
Flight to America; and by Kerby Miller, *Emigrants and Exiles.*
6. The scale problem affects pre-Revolutionary impressions as well. In his recent study
about the migration from England and Scotland to America (*Voyagers to the West*), for example,
Bernard Bailyn overemphasized the relative size of the migration from Europe to America in
the decade before the American Revolution.
7. The literature on the British migration to the West Indies and North America is
substantial and has yielded widely accepted estimates about the flow and composition of the
movement. See Russell Menard, "British Migration to the Chesapeake"; and David Cressy,
Coming Over, esp. 68–69, for estimates of the great migration to New England.
8. On the fragmented and small-scale form of the seventeenth-century shipment of
servants, see James Horn, "Servant Emigration to the Chesapeake." However, even in terms
of absolute numbers, seventeenth-century immigrants to the Chesapeake Bay alone well surpassed the eighteenth-century tide of German-speakers coming to colonial America, and in
proportionate terms the impact the early settlers had on American society exceeded any
imprint that latecomers left. Menard ("British Migration," 102) estimates that more than
123,000 immigrants landed on the tobacco coast of Virginia and Maryland in the seventeenth
century, while the number of German-speakers who arrived in North America before the
Revolution was about 111,000 (see Chapter 2, below).

Distinct national perspectives have traditionally shaped historical understanding of migration. Some scholars have emphasized the process by which Europeans were uprooted and transformed into migrants—in short, a focus on emigration.[9] Others have stressed the impact of such new populations on society in the New World—emphasis on immigration.[10] Increasingly, however, historians have been exploring the phenomenon of long-distance migration by integrating the ways in which conditions on both sides of the Atlantic have interacted simultaneously to move large numbers of people across three thousand miles of dangerous ocean and that include the business processes of locating, inspiring, collecting, transporting, and unloading large numbers of migrants year after year.[11]

Over time, official policies and popular attitudes about migration changed on both sides of the ocean and affected the process of relocation. In Europe, most seventeenth- and eighteenth-century societies had extremely restrictive—or at least highly selective—population policies that regulated both emigration and immigration. The basis for this policy was the mercantilist conviction that a vital part of a country's riches was the people. Many European governments subscribed to that view and curtailed emigration when they believed that there were not enough hands to work the fields for revenue, though they favored or even forced emigration when they feared overpopulation and mass poverty. The view from the American side, as a society receiving massive influxes of foreigners, has

9. Historians interested in migration commonly use the Latin prefixes "ex" (as in emigration—*Auswanderung* in German) and "in" (as in immigration—*Einwanderung* in German) to denote population movement in a particular direction and often over long distances. This usage is distinct from the terms "out-migration" and "in-migration," which simply describe the movement of people into or out of a particular locale. To complicate matters, the special use of those terms is neither uniform nor rigorous, and stylistic considerations and mannerisms can affect usage. Leo Schelbert, *Einführung in die Schweizerische Auswanderungsgeschichte* and "On Becoming Emigrants," and Andreas Blocher, *Die Eigenart der Zürcher Auswanderer nach Amerika*, are examples of scholars who concentrate mostly on aspects of emigration.

10. A. G. Roeber, "In German Ways?" and Allan Kulikoff, "Migration and Cultural Divisions" have noted this division of focus that tends to separate European and American scholars and have decried its negative impact on research agendas that have significant transatlantic components.

11. Philip Taylor, *The Distant Magnet*, summarized and synthesized many general aspects of the migration process shared by numerous immigration flows from different European backgrounds. Harald Runblom and Hans Norman, eds., *From Sweden to America*, is an example of a detailed, systematic, and comprehensive analysis of a transatlantic mass migration. Frank Thistlethwaite ("Migration from Europe Overseas"), building on questions first posed by Marcus Lee Hansen ("History of American Immigration as a Field for Research"), has been a forceful advocate for such an encompassing perspective for exploring all migration processes within Europe and overseas.

also changed, depending on the extent to which citizens viewed the new settlers and laborers as competitors for jobs and a threat to Anglo-American culture, or as an influx of newcomers who could help those already here rise in American life.

The flow of tens of thousands of Germans to Pennsylvania in the eighteenth century illustrates the kinds of challenges that a sudden influx of many aliens with a different language and culture posed for a receiving society. In terms very similar to today's debate over immigration, native-born colonists—and also earlier immigrants—argued about whether this flow of foreigners would be beneficial or harmful. On the European side, unlike later migrations of people largely regarded as "surplus," eighteenth-century Germans often had to slip out from under the rule of a territorial lord who was reluctant to have them leave. Irrespective of whether emigrants could relocate freely or whether newcomers were welcomed in colonial America, the mechanisms for moving these people to the New World previewed later experience.

The model most appropriate for comprehending early German migration across the Atlantic is similar to the models used for understanding more modern migrations. The networks that fueled mass migration in the eighteenth century combined forces of "push" and "pull."[12] Among the characteristics and circumstances that "pushed" emigrants to leave were harvest failure and indebtedness, while attributes and situations that tended to "pull" immigrants to start life anew away from home included promises of land or work. By now, students of migration generally agree on the kinds of "push" and "pull" factors that drive relocation over long distances, and they realize how important it is to explore the process by which particular elements at home and abroad are linked, especially the way information travels and how the costs and difficulties of transportation affect the movement of people. The newly revised "laws" of migration also emphasize the critical connection between "sending countries" and "receiving nations" and how the experience of relocation is linked to

---

12. Harry Jerome, *Migration and Business Cycles,* whose migration theory linked fluctuations in emigration to economic cycles and trends in the United States, was the first to talk of "push" and "pull" factors. Other important examples of theories of migration are Brinley Thomas, *Migration and Economic Growth;* Richard Easterlin, *Population, Labor Force, and Long Swings;* and Everett Lee, "A Theory of Migration." Examples of the applicability and usefulness of these theories include Sune Åkerman's "Theories and Methods of Migration Research" and "Towards an Understanding of Emigrational Processes"; and Allen Noble's *To Build in a New Land.*

success in adjusting to life in a new land.[13] With the exception of differences in scale and technology, which can be significant, it is important to
recognize that these characteristics of modern international migration also
applied in earlier times. Colonial transplantation must be approached with
these more general lessons in mind.

The "push" of economic change and hardship, the vicissitudes of
homeland politics, and issues of religious freedom and intercultural strife
may have taken somewhat different forms in the eighteenth century than
later. Still, from the early 1700s to the era of the American and French
revolutions, these forces caused many people in the Rhine lands to seek
new homes outside the region. Meanwhile, the "pull" of the demand for
rural settlers to make land speculation profitable, and of the need for more
labor in city and in countryside, opened the door for new Americans in
ways that are familiar to all who know something of nineteenth-century
history. Even the forces braking the flow of Germans across the Atlantic—namely, dwindling opportunities where immigrants had previously
gone, and changing conditions of transatlantic trade—should also not
surprise students of more recent periods. In short, as in modern analyses,
only a simultaneous view from these several different but connected perspectives—in Europe, in America, in the journey between—can properly
interpret the history of later colonial migration. Only within a comprehensive transatlantic framework for understanding transplantation into
New World life can bits and pieces, such as fragments of econometric
labor force analysis, localized studies of the growth in Pennsylvania, the
disrupting experiences of particular German lands, and genealogical detail,
fall into place together and make the best sense.

Finally, it must be remembered that the nature of the data available for
the eighteenth-century migration of German-speaking peoples to the
American colonies has stamped its own biases on the literature. Requirements that Pennsylvania established for registration, and oaths of allegiance for immigrant aliens, have allowed several generations of historians
and genealogists to outline the size of the migration involved and to iden-

---

13. Recent analyses of global migration are quite detailed in their descriptions of "push"
and "pull" factors, the micro level of the decision-making process that turns potential mi
grants into actual movers, and, on the macro level, the economic, social, political, and cultural forces that hinder or promote population movements. Gauging the success—and
costs—of integration into American society is an important focus for scholars interested in
recent international population movements, because much of their work is tied to shaping
immigration policies today. One such example is Elliott Barkan, *Asian and Pacific Islander
Migration*.

tify and trace particular individuals on both sides of the Atlantic. The data also form the basis for exploring other central issues, such as the ebb and flow of the migration over time, or changes in its composition in terms of sex, age, the balance of families to unattached individuals, and the ratio of free persons to bound labor. From the European side, growing state bureaucracies in German lands generated voluminous records in their efforts to regulate out-migration and curtail loss of population and capital. Scholars have begun to mine these sources profitably. Such treatments provide information about who left where, when, and under what circumstances, and by working with records on both sides of the Atlantic they are beginning to discover what kind of life the departing Germans found in the American colonies, and how they got there.[14]

Although the names of ships on which Germans arrived are available from colonial newspapers and the alien registration lists required in Philadelphia, little is known about the trade that brought German-speaking emigrants first down the Rhine to Rotterdam and thence via English ports of call to the Delaware and other American ports. These activities did not merely carry bodies from one side of the ocean to the other. It was, rather, in the end, through this trade that the dynamics inspiring Europeans to leave home for the New World interacted—through changes in information, shipping availability, cost, mercantile networking, and the like—with Americans' demand for more settlers and with the ways in which they came to be integrated into colonial society. A concerted business devoted principally to a transoceanic migration probably first developed in the middle of the eighteenth century to transport Germans to America. This system was then emulated for Irish relocation during the last third of the eighteenth century. In short, well before Cunard and other firms moved millions across the ocean in the second half of the nineteenth century, such a trade in emigrants was a distinct and important part of commerce across the Atlantic. The focus of this book is how such a transportation industry took shape in the middle decades of the eighteenth century to capture, service, and profit from migration flows from various European territories.

Chapter 1 examines German immigration to the British North American colonies—especially Pennsylvania—as part of a larger pattern of long-distance migration during the eighteenth century. America was not the

---

14. Häberlein's *Vom Oberrhein zum Susquehanna* marks the beginning of such exploration.

only destination for Rhineland emigrants. Many headed east. Although the flow to colonial America was indistinguishable from the other streams of international relocation in some respects, it differed in terms of its relatively small size, its westward direction and transoceanic nature, and, most important, the particular recruiting mechanisms that channeled Germans across the Atlantic to America. The forces of "push" and "pull" that led most migrants eastward to Prussia, the Habsburg Empire, and Russia, and only a small portion to America, are identified. The flow to the American colonies can be properly understood only as a secondary migration that attracted only some people with certain interests and capabilities—but not most emigrants from German lands, however overwhelming the influx through his beloved Pennsylvania might seem to a colonial like Benjamin Franklin.[15]

Chapter 2 surveys the large number of Rhineland migrants who were drawn to the American colonies in the eighteenth century. Once we know who these immigrants were, we can then find out how they were transported and how they adjusted to life in the New World. Then we can begin to compare them with other streams of newcomers, especially the Irish. German immigration to colonial America followed a distinctive pattern. In its initial phase, from the late 1600s to the 1720s, immigration was sporadic and light in numbers—mostly families traveling in groups, many of whom possessed considerable means. They often had religious motives and were aided by co-religionists. As the migration accelerated during the growth phase leading to its mid-century peak, the proportion of families (originating primarily from rural areas) continued to be high, but these migrants became increasingly younger in age, and more and more single people swelled the stream. At the height of the migration, in the late 1740s and early 1750s, immigrants were generally poorer, and families made up a relatively smaller proportion of the stream. More single, unconnected people were relocating. When German migration resumed after the Seven Years' War (1756–63), the number of immigrants declined significantly, and young men traveling alone made up the bulk of this transatlantic movement.

The chapter discusses the flow of German migration across time. How large was it at various stages? What do we know about the age, sex, family

15. Franklin had little sympathy for German immigrants and objected especially to settling in ethnic clusters. See Leonard Labaree et al., eds., *Papers of Benjamin Franklin;* Whitefield Bell Jr., "Benjamin Franklin and the German Charity School"; and Glenn Weaver, "Benjamin Franklin and the Pennsylvania Germans."

status, wealth, occupation, education, and regional background of the German newcomers? The chapter also looks at the kinds of vessels that carried German immigrants and at particulars of their voyages. As human cargoes changed in size and character from early to later phases of the migration, so did the shipping that brought that cargo.

Chapter 3 explores the business of transporting people from continental Europe to the American colonies and describes how networks of merchants in Rotterdam, London, and Philadelphia organized the passenger trade as a complement to their other overseas endeavors. For these merchants, shipping Germans was a way to make the westbound voyage more profitable. It is possible to see how mercantile interests influenced the timing, direction, size, and composition of the German immigrant flow. The operation of this trade in strangers is best demonstrated by examining the roles of the two most important ports: Rotterdam, the major harbor of embarkation in continental Europe, and Philadelphia, where the majority of immigrants landed. The organization of the business on each side of the Atlantic is a major focus; another is how the relationship between business partners in Europe and America altered over time.

In Chapter 4 the perspective shifts from the business of transporting human cargo to the people themselves. How did Rhineland emigrants experience the move from the Old World to the New? Unlike the slave trade from Africa, news about the ordeal of relocation had an impact on German migration. Reports about conditions of the move and how well immigrants established themselves ashore reached the Rhine lands, and such personal accounts did much to determine how potential migrants balanced risk and gain when thinking about coming to America. In the colonies, meanwhile, personal connections with and among those who had already immigrated did much to determine the demand for more Germans, where they would settle, and how successfully they would fit into American life.

The final chapter turns to the first major non-English immigrant group to follow the German model of mass migration in the eighteenth century: the Irish. An understanding of the transplantation of migrants from Irish ports makes our interpretation of what was happening in transatlantic relocation in the 1700s still more definitive. People from Ireland— Catholic and Protestant, from both northern and southern regions—were the second-largest immigrant group, and were among the new arrivals in the Delaware Valley, the gateway for most Germans. Fundamental new findings about this Irish migration both underscore what was distinctive about the German flow and show how the German immigration provided a model for the future.

Irish immigration in the 1700s has been overestimated. Before 1776, immigrants to the Delaware Valley included many more Germans than Irish. Not until the last decade before the Revolution did the Irish influx begin to increase rapidly. Actually, the peak phase of this transatlantic Irish movement was reached only in the 1780s and 1790s—almost half a century later than the German phase. In this surge, merchants once again exploited familiar strategies for maximizing profits that had first been developed at the height of the German immigration in the 1750s. In this new great immigrant wave—primarily from Ulster—how people were recruited, how they paid their passage, how ships were selected and outfitted, what the voyage was like, and how the immigrants adjusted to begin New World life all changed from earlier circumstances in the Irish trade (which had been going on since the later 1600s). Instead, it resembled the conditions established in German mass migration in the mid-1700s. Thus, the Irish experience before the Revolution confirms how the German migration to the Delaware Valley a few decades earlier established what would be the prototype for a lengthy series of later large-scale population movements across the Atlantic.

During the 1700s, the relocation of Europeans to the New World developed into a complex and sophisticated system. It became a business linking the personal objectives of a greater and greater variety of Europeans, an increasingly elaborate transatlantic shipping industry, evolving labor markets, and various ethnic networks to bring over more, and more diverse, new Americans. By the 1750s the system already presaged the characteristics of the better-known transatlantic mass migrations of the 1800s and early 1900s. A main feature of this "nation of immigrants"—the mass relocation of free peoples with distinct cultures—was born in this era.

German Long-Distance Migration

From the time Pennsylvania was founded and the Turks besieged Vienna at the height of their westward penetration—before falling back to open up land for settlement under the Habsburgs—until the American Revolution, hundreds of thousands of people left the German Rhine lands to settle in countries far beyond what had been their normal range of migratory experience. Most of the dynamics that led so many to venture over such extraordinary distances to foreign lands were common to life in preindustrial agrarian societies.

The balance between resources available to feed, clothe, and house people adequately, and the size of the population having to share those resources, was precarious at best. In southwestern Germany, the political system that regulated both the secular and the religious aspects of life was unbending, restrictive, and highly particularistic, allowing little room for innovation, individual action, or flexibility in response to crisis. Combined with the paternalistic and absolutist fashion in which most territorial governments ruled, including frequent rigidity in religion, the outdated feudal structure proved particularly harmful to the people who had to absorb the costs of increasingly bureaucratic and pretentious administrations in times of both war and peace. Farmers, tradesmen, artisans, and laborers carried a disproportionately heavy share of this burden, and consequently they or their children became indebted, impoverished, underemployed. Confronted by such prospects, people not only accepted the notion of migration in search of work and a different place to live—thus perpetuating the response to difficult circumstances that was already familiar to many residents of the Rhine lands—but also now embraced opportunities that were much farther removed from the places and ways of life to which they were accustomed. This desire to better their lives despite great risks and unknowns marks the migration to the American colonies as one that was characterized largely by a sense of hope and determination rather than desperation.[1]

Although German-speaking immigrants to the New World came from many different parts of the Holy Roman Empire, cantons of the Swiss Confederation, Alsace, and Lorraine, the majority departed from an area that, broadly, stretched along the Rhine from Basel to Cologne (see Map 1). This region generated successive migration streams that flowed mostly east to Prussia, Austria-Hungary, and Russia—but also west across the Atlantic to North America. Circumstances that threatened the livelihood of Rhinelanders, promises of a better life far away, some form of active recruitment, and a strong tradition of migration all combined to create substantial, recurring outflows from the territories along the Rhine.

Over the past century, fragments of this tale have unfolded in a growing literature on German-speaking immigrants in America, and recent studies of local and denominational migrations have added useful specifics. Several important points, however, are lost among the details: how much German and Swiss migrations were intertwined; how much continuing, connected migration was occurring; the ways in which recruitment mechanisms, and their repression, were or were not common from place to place; how relocation to America both resembled and differed from movements to Prussia, Hungary, Russia, Spain, and France, or other eighteenth-century migration to America, like that of the Irish. The dynamics of migration to the New World—its scope, its timing, its systems of recruitment and relocation—make most sense viewed within the context of general processes that in the seventeenth and eighteenth centuries were motivating German-speaking peoples to leave their homelands and making it possible for them to do so.[2]

---

1. Questioned about their reasons for leaving, emigrants answered that they wanted to make the move while their financial circumstances still allowed them to pay their own way, demonstrating that it was a reasonable and calculated move (Faust, *Guide to the Materials for American History*, 44–46). Häberlein (*Vom Oberrhein zum Susquehanna*, 209) came to a similar conclusion for the emigration from Baden.

2. The large evolving literature, the materials it has employed, and added documentation are presented in this book in the footnotes and Bibliography.

MAP 1   The Rhine lands

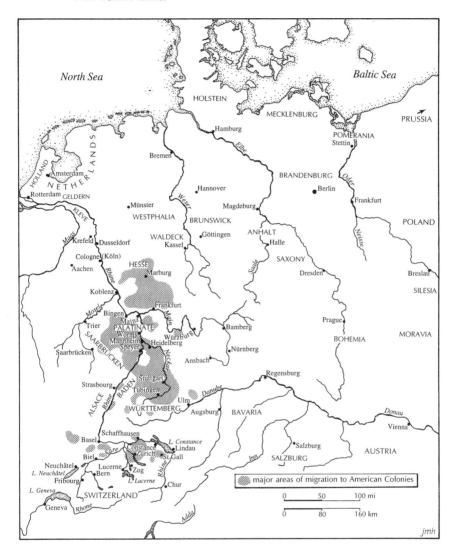

The Rhine lands shared many fundamental characteristics, but they were not a political entity. The many major and minor states and principalities involved were all pulled together by the Rhine River and its tributaries, especially the Main, Neckar, and Mosel. This riverine network was one of the chief arterial systems of Europe along which coursed traffic, trade, communication, and population movements.[3] The Rhine bound many dif-

3. Such main routes "helped form the streams and counter streams in which most migra-

ferent places together: poor mountainous areas and rich valleys; scattered farms, hamlets, and compact villages; and many towns and several cities. A patchwork of more than 350 distinct territories (*lehensrechtliche Herrschaften*) made up the greater Rhine valley, only some of which were part of larger political units under the rule of various councils and princes. This meant that the region was fragmented into many spheres of petty—and conflicting—interests.[4] Irrespective of the small size of most of the lands, and regardless of whether these territories were governed badly or well, in the seventeenth and eighteenth centuries their administrations were becoming increasingly bureaucratic, if not absolutist, in attempts to regulate virtually all aspects of their subjects' lives.

The overriding power of the territorial lords was especially strong in religious matters.[5] By the middle of the seventeenth century, divergent religious beliefs and practices within each territorial state were accepted, in principle, and subjects who held beliefs that were different from those of the official state religion (only Catholic, Lutheran, or Reformed churches were recognized) were not supposed to be at any civil disadvantage. In practice, however, the close ties between the established church and the state had an impact on most areas of education and work and did not allow for much religious toleration, even for adherents of the two other recognized creeds, let alone sectarians or separatists. Furthermore, it was not unusual for a state to use the official local church to proclaim, monitor, and enforce regulations governing many secular aspects of private and community life.[6]

The Rhine lands from which emigrants to the American colonies came

---

tory movements took place." See Horn, "Servant Emigration," 76–77. Fritz Trautz, *Die Pfälzische Auswanderung*, observed similar patterns for the eighteenth-century emigration from the Palatinate. Roeber again recently pointed to the importance of river and post routes for the network of German Lutheran emigrants (*Palatines*, 114–16).

4. There is no comprehensive treatise on southwestern Germany in the eighteenth century because the larger region was fragmented into a bewildering array of more-or-less self-contained units. Descriptions of individual lands, villages, and towns, and even larger territories, abound, but generalizing from such studies is difficult because most of the local in-depth treatments do not build on one another. The key to entering this vast literature is through the standard bibliographies of the states (*Länder*) of the German Empire and the present Federal Republic of Germany. The maps and accompanying texts of Willi Alter, ed., *Pfalzatlas*; *Historischer Atlas von Baden Württemberg*; and Eduard Imhof, ed., *Atlas der Schweiz*, are useful for locating specific places and territories.

5. The principle *cuius regius eius religio* (the lord rightfully determines which religion to establish in his territory) of the Religious Peace of Augsburg (1555) had been confirmed in the Peace of Westphalia following the Thirty Years' War (1648).

6. Thomas Klein, "Minorities in Central Europe," 44–45.

generally had a majority of Reformed or Lutheran subjects, and some territories were more restrictive with regard to religious dissent than others. The political fragmentation of the Rhine lands meant that many people lived close to territories that had a different established church. In other words, there was significant religious diversity within the region even though religious tolerance within specific territories was usually limited. People tended to move to locations where their particular religion received better treatment.[7]

Held in feudal bondage under different lords, and not always having the religious affiliation of their neighbors, most inhabitants of south-western Germany followed agrarian pursuits or practiced a craft that was tied closely to the agricultural sector. This dependence on the land and its products for a living left many farmers, artisans, tradesmen, and laborers in a vulnerable position during this period of recurrent agrarian crises. Moreover, the limited size of most of the territories contributed signifi-cantly to the prevailing inflexibility in responding to crop failure, high prices, or population pressures, because many territorial lords restricted the easy transfer of goods and people across their borders.

Most ordinary people living in the Rhine lands had to cope with polit-ical fragmentation, government regulation in the secular and religious spheres of life, and intermittent periods of economic and demographic instability, but some territories underwent more upheaval than others. The Swiss cantons, which as sovereign territories were not part of the Holy Roman Empire, did not participate in the lengthy religious wars and dy-nastic struggles that repeatedly engulfed the German Rhine lands, so the Swiss were spared the devastating effects of military action. Since the German territories along the Rhine north of Basel were strategically impor-tant in any confrontation that pitted France against the Habsburgs, how-ever, Rhenish territorial lords had to seek alliances that would protect their lands and particular interests. Nevertheless, the German Rhine lands repeatedly became involved in war, since their geographic location between hostile parties put them in a difficult and insecure position.

The difference between the Swiss cantons and German Rhenish terri-tories in terms of involvement in the European theater of chronic warfare largely determined the character of interaction between those areas. Dur-ing periods of fighting, neutral Switzerland acted as a supplier of goods to the Rhine lands farther north. In peacetime, Swiss laborers and settlers

7. *Pfalzatlas*, Textband 22:828, traces the changes in religion in the Palatinate from 1600 to 1790.

migrated to the war-torn and rebuilding regions of southwestern Germany—it was a welcome opportunity to relieve population pressures at home and to escape depressed economic conditions or religious persecution. The devastated German territories, for their part, eagerly tried to attract people and capital in efforts to foster recovery and prosperity. The Swiss were the most numerous among those newcomers; others came from many different parts of continental Europe.

The northward flow of Swiss emigrants had important consequences. Through continued family connections, it established a tradition of migration between the Swiss and the German Rhine lands that surpassed the usual links forged by regular trade and transportation. Furthermore, many of the people who were lured by the apparent abundant opportunities in the German territories were people likely to move again when reality fell short of expectations, when better chances were offered elsewhere, or when the stability of the land was seriously threatened.[8] Thus, southwestern Germany emerged both as a region of substantial and recurring immigration—coming mostly from Switzerland—and as the origin of repeated significant emigration streams. For these reasons, the Rhine lands were an area in which the migration tradition ran strong.

Population movements of the seventeenth and eighteenth centuries involving migrants from the Rhine lands attest to the readiness with which people from those territories relocated. The large-scale devastation and depopulation in the Rhine valley during the Thirty Years' War (1618–48) and the attendant damage to the economic infrastructure and social order is well known and was the source of the often stereotyped regional trait of "wanderlust."[9] The people who remained were not numerous enough to bring about economic recovery, so the territorial lords initiated liberal population policies to entice former citizens to return. They also extended an invitation to "all honest people of all nations" to settle in the depopulated areas.

The massive rebuilding program that many territorial lords undertook relied heavily on a variety of incentives to attract laborers, farmers, arti-

8. The likelihood and apparent ease with which people who have moved once will move again have been observed in a variety of European and American contexts. See, for example, Allen, *In English Ways*. Several examples exist of how local migrants from Switzerland to Germany later moved again to America. For instance, Annette Burgert traced some of those "stepped" movements (*Eighteenth- and Nineteenth-Century Emigrants from Lachen-Speyerdorf* and *A Century of Emigration from Affoltern am Albis*).

9. For a general description of the changing population of the German Rhine lands after the Thirty Years' War, see Karl Kollnig, *Wandlungen*, 13–20.

sans, tradesmen, merchants, and entrepreneurs to become new subjects. Tax incentives and favorable credit terms during the first years of settlement were important lures. Religious toleration, concessions to dissenting minorities, or protection of their separate status were other inducements. Exemption from military service was another powerful attraction. By the 1680s, the composition of the Rhenish population varied from settlement to settlement and had fluctuated considerably. The newcomers contributed significantly to recovery through the labor and the technologies they brought with them, and the personal stake these new settlers had in the region's development prepared them for assimilation despite privileges and customs that set them apart from the native population.[10]

During the 1680s and 1690s, however, before the Rhine lands had recovered completely and thorough assimilation of the newcomers could take place, Louis XIV sent his armies into the area. The "scorched earth" policy of the invading generals, the excesses of the soldiers, and burdensome contributions extracted from the populace to finance defense resulted in the flight of many inhabitants. Compared with the Thirty Years' War, when war-related famine and pestilence caused most of the population loss, the major reason for the demographic decline was now emigration.[11] Many former settlers believed that the region's instability was deepseated and the outlook for recovery bleak. To replace those who left, a new wave of Swiss emigrants settled in the rural environs of the Rhine, and to the cities flocked new citizens from many different backgrounds and countries.

By the beginning of the eighteenth century, conditions in southwestern Germany seem to have stabilized, although the threat of war persisted and the burden imposed by principalities in the form of taxes, compulsory labor, and military service became more oppressive. The negative effects of any crisis that emerged were increased by such political measures, because they aggravated the high level of poverty and indebtedness. Given such uncertain and deteriorating opportunities at home, reliable and promising

10. Estimates about their numbers vary, but by far the largest group were Swiss farmers from Basel, Lucerne, Bern, Solothurn, and Zurich, and, after 1664, also Anabaptists, especially from Bern. Groups of Huguenots expelled from France by the revocation of the Edict of Nantes (1685), and Walloons fleeing from persecution in the Spanish Netherlands, were small in number and settled mostly in towns and cities. See Kollnig, Faust and Brumbaugh, Blocher, Schuchmann, and Kirsten in the Bibliography.

11. Former French Protestants, who had been granted privileges protecting their religion, felt particularly threatened by the invasions of Louis XIV and left the Rhine lands—at a considerable loss to the territories in which they had settled.

news of chances for settlement elsewhere persuaded many inhabitants of the Rhine lands to migrate, in many directions, near and far, temporarily and permanently.

Distinctive and persistent migratory routes developed during the first decades of the eighteenth century, and it is not surprising to find that emigrants preferred to relocate in places where conditions were similar to those under which they had been living. The dominant or established religion in the area open for settlement was the most important factor. Overwhelmingly, Catholic emigrants chose to settle or find employment in territories that were under Catholic rule, while Protestants preferred countries with strong Protestant traditions and majorities.

The Rhine lands were the origins of several surges of religiously influenced emigration. One flow went to Hungary, where after the peace of Sathmar (1712) new areas opened up under Habsburg (Catholic) rule.[12] Another, much smaller but Protestant, flow was channeled to the American colonies, especially Pennsylvania, New York, and the Carolinas. It included the massive Palatine exodus of 1709, of which only a small portion eventually settled in North America, and it peaked around mid-century, when a substantial number of German immigrants landed in Pennsylvania, South Carolina, Nova Scotia, and New England. When the Prussian king offered entrepreneurs and private individuals an opportunity to claim and settle marshlands in Pomerania, Kurmark, and Neumark in 1747, there began a long-term, large-scale emigration that gained momentum and importance in the second half of the eighteenth century.[13] In the late 1760s and again in the early 1770s, settlements in the North American colonies, Cayenne (French Guiana), Prussia, Russia, Habsburg Hungary and Poland, and Spain attracted immigrants from far away. Only a small proportion—roughly 10 percent—journeyed overseas, a fact that German-Americans and some historians tend to forget. The vast majority relocated to eastern Europe, where the migration peaked impressively in the last two decades of the eighteenth century.[14] Locally, meanwhile, the

12. Werner Hacker, *Auswanderung*, 24.

13. Karl-Friedrich Hüttig, *Pfälzische Auswanderung*, 15–21.

14. All recent estimates about the proportion of emigrants destined for North America rely primarily on Fenske's findings. Differences in the specifics of the estimates—with the exception of the general magnitude of the flow—occur because scholars had different bases for their calculations. On balance, however, they agree that migration of all kinds was common in German lands and that long-distance migration was substantial and mostly to Eastern Europe. See Hans Fenske, "International Migration"; Marianne Wokeck, "Harnessing the

contribution that emigrants made to the population flow was uneven. Some villages sent large numbers to settle in distant places, others sent none or very few.[15]

Although prolonged instability of the Rhine lands made the area an important source of potential emigrants, the restrictions and other burdens imposed by the various government authorities in the region provided additional powerful motives for emigration.[16] Unemployment, high prices, and taxes, however, were in large part the result of an outmoded feudal system. Former emigrants made that connection indirectly when, in letters home, they extolled the freedom they found in the American colonies.

In southwestern Germany, the vast majority of the population was held in bondage—either because they had been born to a bondswoman or because they had bound themselves in the act of in-migration. In the feudal structure of the German Rhine lands, bondage was first to a specific territory and its lord, then to a sovereign, such as the Elector of the Palatinate or the Habsburg emperor. The feudal structure was complex and varied considerably from territory to territory, which makes generalization difficult and local studies enormously important.[17] However, it was

---

Lure," 208; Georg Fertig, "Transatlantic Migration from the German-Speaking Parts," 203 (table 8.1); and Aaron Fogleman, "Migrations to the Thirteen British North American Colonies," 698, 704.

15. Based on their work with particular localities, scholars found that more than 25 percent of villagers might emigrate, although most places lost between 5 and 10 percent of their residents. See Fertig, "Transatlantic Migration," 194–203; Fogleman, *Hopeful Journeys*, 163; Fogleman, "Review Essay: Progress and Possibilities," 325–26; and Häberlein, *Vom Oberrhein zum Susquehanna*, 9. Data from local sources, migration lists, and qualitative records confirm the high variability of emigration from place to place and over time.

16. In their petitions for manumission, emigrants did not cite government repression, but presented the most acceptable reasons for emigration. For examples, see William Hoffman, "'Palatine' Emigrants to America from Nassau-Dillenburg," 41–42; Faust, *Guide to the Materials for American History*, 4:44–46; and the results of a "questionnaire" that make up the primary data base in Blocher, *Eigenart der Zürcher Auswanderer*.

17. "Every village had its uniqueness." Rudolf Vierhaus, *Germany in the Age of Absolutism*, 45. At this point, the number of comprehensive local studies that focus on places from which people left for the American colonies is small and involves less than 10 percent of the migration flow overseas (Rosalind Beiler, "The Transatlantic World of Caspar Wistar"; Blocher, *Eigenart der Zürcher Auswanderer*; Georg Fertig, "Does Overpopulation Explain Emigration?" (paper presented at the meeting of the Social Science History Association in Chicago, November 1995); Fogleman, *Hopeful Journeys*; Häberlein, *Vom Oberrhein zum Susquehanna*; Hans Pfister, *Auswanderung aus dem Knonauer Amt*; Roeber, *Palatines*; Martina Sprengel, "Studien zur Nordamerikaauswanderung." In addition, however, many other studies with a distinct local focus,

common for territorial lords to manipulate ancient rights and privileges to
their personal advantage, both in this region and in the Swiss cantons,
where patrician oligarchies ruled the land the same way petty German
princes did.

The obligations of bondspeople were many, but they were primarily in
the form of taxes and services—continual reminders of their ties to the
land.[18] Each year was punctuated by seasonal feudal tributes; every stage or
change in the life of a bound subject was accompanied by acknowledg-
ments of the dependent status of dependency. Whether a man made his
living off the land or by pursuing a craft, everything was limited by
the rules that governed the communal use of fields, pasture, forest, water,
wood, and other natural resources. The increasingly bureaucratic way in
which even enlightened territorial lords stifled individual choice and action compounded any impulses to escape an already high degree of restric-
tiveness.[19]

Moving freely was not an option, however. In a political context where
everything was regulated and where the ruling powers were convinced that
it was people who gave value to their holdings, relocating across territorial
boundaries was a complicated process, even for subjects who were free
from bondage, though theoretically everyone had a right to migrate (*ius
destractus*).[20] It was important to comply with procedures for removal because through the Diet the imperial states had a reciprocal agreement not
to accept anyone as a citizen who was still under the bondage of another
territory. Therefore, bondspeople who were determined to relocate had to
apply for manumission—an act of grace (*ius gratiale*) of the landlord—and
subjects who were free needed a passport and an attestation that they were
not bound to a "pursuing landlord."[21]

---

especially extensively annotated emigration lists, have made significant contributions to our
understanding of emigration from the Rhine lands. The work of Annette Burgert, Werner
Hacker, Henry Jones, and Don Yoder (see Bibliography) stands out in this regard.

18. For a general description of bondage to the land, see Werner Hacker, *Auswanderer vom
Oberen Neckar*, 14–17, and Vierhaus, *Germany*, 45–46. The complexity of feudal ties and obliga-
tions is also apparent in the editorial comments about emigration lists—see, for example,
Don Yoder, ed. and trans., *Pennsylvania German Immigrants*, 8, 12, 159.

19. Beiler has demonstrated this in the case of Caspar Wistar.

20. Robert Selig, "The Idea and Practice of the *ius emigrandi*," 15–22; see also Vierhaus
(*Germany*, 28–29) on mercantilism, or cameralism, as the basis of state economic policy and
administration.

21. If the landlord and the territorial lord were not the same, it was the right of the
foremost landlord, not of the sovereign, to grant manumission. Hacker, *Auswanderer vom Oberen
Neckar*, 15.

Other manifestations of the state's authority caused hardship and distress too. The frequency and range of taxes and compulsory service were formidable.[22] Military service was especially burdensome, both to the large number of young men recruited by enterprising landlords or patricians (who supplied troops to warring European nations at a good profit) and to farmers, tradesmen, and artisans staying behind, who depended on the help of sons, apprentices, and laborers who had instead been called to arms—not to mention women in search of husbands.[23] All these requirements were costly to the farmers and artisans who were forced to contribute time, skills, resources, and perhaps even their lives, and when government authorities were also strict, and even arbitrary, resentment and despair increased.[24] The ostentatious and wasteful ways provincial courts that aped the splendor of Versailles made the lives of working men and women even more unbearable.[25]

Oppression through taxes, whether in fee, kind, or services, was not the only reason for a high degree of indebtedness in most of the Rhine lands and that was such an important impetus for people to emigrate. Emigrants seeking to settle elsewhere contended that their inability to make a living was also the result of farms that were too small to support their occupants and of unemployment or underemployment in trades.[26] Such circumstances were endemic in many territories, because efforts to balance limited communal resources with the number of people who had to share them were not sufficiently successful, despite restrictions in admission of new citizens, such as entrance fees and inheritance customs, aimed at keeping farms and homesteads economically viable.

Theoretically, migration became necessary whenever the population increased above the number of hearths or houses within a village that were

22. For examples, see Yoder, *Pennsylvania German Immigrants*, 156; Trautz, *Pfälzische Auswanderung*, 19; and Stumpp, *Emigration from Germany to Russia*, 25–29.

23. For the emigration of more than 300,000 Swiss mercenaries, see Leo Schelbert, "Swiss Emigration to America," 58; and Wicki, *Bevölkerung des Kantons Luzern*, 29. For the landgrave of Hesse's trade in soldiers, see Rodney Atwood, *The Hessians*.

24. This was the case in Württemberg in the early 1750s. See Yoder, *Pennsylvania German Immigrants*, 9.

25. Trautz, *Pfälzische Auswanderung*, 19. See also Beiler, "Wistar," chap. 2.

26. Recent case studies that build on older literature and explore local sources not only demonstrate the general concern about the ability to make a decent living under circumstances of acute population pressures on limited resources, but also show considerable variation in responding to the threat of such an imbalance between population and resources. Examples include Auerbach, *Auswanderung aus Kurhessen*, 65; Georg Fertig, "Um Anhoffung besserer Nahrung willen"; Roeber, *Palatines;* and Häberlein, *Vom Oberrhein zum Susquehanna*, 209.

economically viable. Only villagers who owned a proper house had the
right to use communally held land for grazing, and forest for firewood
and construction materials (and often also for pursuing a craft, as many
crafts relied heavily on wood).[27] In practice, however, the settlement of
cotters and the subdivision of houses and other rights that came with
ownership into halves and even quarters led to continuous economic instability, particularly unemployment. Small farms, especially when mortgaged
(as many of them were), forced their owners either to seek additional
income of some sort or to borrow more money to meet their many obligations.[28] As a consequence, economically strapped farmers made their own
tools and employed fewer laborers.[29] As the need for artisans changed,
competition in the trades, which were often overstaffed, increased so that
the future for artisans also looked dim.[30] Similarly, cotters and day
laborers (*Beisetzer, Hintersassen*) did not make enough to buy into any place
as full citizens and remained in a precarious situation that offered little
security and had no future.[31] It is therefore not surprising that small
means, large debts, and bankruptcies appear frequently as reasons for emigration.[32]

Inheritance customs contributed to the pressure on local resources.[33]
Families with more than one heir found it difficult to provide adequately
for all children. The son who took over the farm was heavily burdened by

27. Blocher, *Eigenart der Zürcher Auswanderer,* 71, 73, 106–13, discusses the effectiveness of
different strategies for controlling and regulating the increasing population in different regions
of Switzerland; see also Rudolf Braun, "Early Industrialization and Demographic Changes in
Zurich."

28. Bi-occupationalism was a widespread necessity—and custom—of peasants, who supplemented their livelihoods by pursuing rural crafts. Similarly, most rural craftsmen, and many
urban artisans too, were also involved in agricultural work. Wolfgang von Hippel, *Auswanderung
aus Südwestdeutschland,* 50–51.

29. Yoder, *Pennsylvania German Immigrants,* 157; Albert Faust, "Unpublished Documents," 14.

30. Faust, "Unpublished Documents," 14; Hacker, *Auswanderung aus Oberschwaben,* 37; Hüttig, *Pfälzische Auswanderung,* 15.

31. Hacker, *Auswanderung aus Oberschwaben,* 37; Auerbach, *Auswanderung aus Kurhessen,* 26–27;
Fertig, "Hintergrund," 115.

32. Leo Schelbert, "Von der Macht des Pietismus," 96; Adolf Gerber, *Die Nassau-Dillen-
burger Auswanderung,* 8; Albert Faust, "Documents in Swiss Archives Relating to Emigration";
Faust, "Unpublished Documents," 14; Werner Hacker, *Auswanderung aus Oberschwaben,* 36–37;
Yoder, *Pennsylvania German Immigrants,* 10.

33. Partible inheritance is usually blamed for the splintering of holdings, but even in areas
where the practice of impartible inheritance prevailed, small holdings became heavily indebted
in order to pay for shares for the siblings, who by custom had to move out of their parents'
house or farm—but not without some funding. See, for example, Häberlein, *Vom Oberrhein zum
Susquehanna,* 58–61; and Georg Fertig, "Household Formation and Economic Autarky."

a mortgaged house and substantial annual payments stemming from having to buy out siblings and their share in the inheritance.[34] Yet the portions of whose who were bought out were usually too small for them to find places of their own. Marriage too often depended on whether one could secure a permanent home, and that often curtailed the eligibility of men and women in search of marriage partners. Bondspeople needed official permission to wed (*Eheconsens*), which was granted for people who were marrying out, but rarely granted to newcomers unless they brought a certain amount of wealth to the territory with them.[35]

The effects of a restrictive political system that resulted in economic insecurity for many were compounded by the role of the established church, which in many respects was just another arm of the government. The secular authorities in most governments used the organizational structure of the church, and especially its clergy, as a convenient tool to publicize, implement, monitor, and enforce moral behavior in the interests of law and order.[36]

Extraordinary events, like war, contributed to already high levels of political and economic instability. In territories that were preparing for military conflict, caught up in it, or recovering from it, all spheres of life suffered from the extra demands on people and resources. Soldiers had to be recruited, outfitted, provisioned, quartered, and paid, and fortifications and roads required construction, maintenance, and repair. The propertied classes, mostly farmers and artisans, carried the heaviest burden under these conditions. Normality proved illusive in the presence of any army, whether it was fighting or merely stationed in an area. Beyond the ravages of war, there were the extra expenses needed to get life going again. Increases in already high taxes, and insistence on compulsory labor, had debilitating effects on the income and wage-earning capacity of citizens and thus led to more and more indebtedness and poverty. Even areas that were not directly touched by war experienced scarcity and high prices, as a consequence of dangerous and difficult travel and trading conditions during periods of military confrontation between some neighbor, friend or foe, and any of the leading European powers in the region.[37] Any confron-

34. For an example from Lucerne, see Wicki, *Bevölkerung des Kantons Luzern*, 268–69.

35. Hacker, *Auswanderung aus Oberschwaben*, 37–38; Auerbach, *Auswanderung aus Kurhessen*, 26–27.

36. Blocher's description of the interplay of church and state in Zurich is just one of many examples (*Eigenart der Zürcher Auswanderer*, 92–93).

37. Since tax barriers often impeded easy transfer of goods and people across territorial boundaries, neighboring villages and towns could have widely different experiences during

tation on the European continent that pitched the North Atlantic sea powers against one another also resulted in disruption of transatlantic trade. This had serious repercussions for migrants bound to the American colonies, because it reduced the number of ships that sailed, and their routes changed during periods of war between England and France.[38]

In an economy that was overwhelmingly dependent on agriculture, natural forces, such as weather conditions, were large and unpredictable factors. The weather affected the outcome and abundance of harvests, and in the Rhine lands the growing conditions were sufficiently marginal that climatic variations had repercussions for the people who directly or indirectly lived off the land. Good harvests and returns from farm products were the result not only of hard work but also of a delicate balance of natural forces over which human beings had little or no control. Extreme or persistent changes in the weather were likely to cause widespread scarcity, high prices, and famine.[39]

The vagaries of the weather and hostilities, then, generated periods of crisis. The War of Spanish Succession (1701–14) hindered recovery from the invasion of Louis XIV's troops into the Rhine lands.[40] The severe winters of 1708/9 and 1709/10, which destroyed many of the fruit trees and vines, brought famine and showed that the economic base in the German Rhine lands had been eroded so much that people had little hope for recovery—a decline that contributed to mass emigration.[41] The 1730s saw the War of Polish Succession (1733–38), the end of which was marked by two bad years that culminated in European-wide famine (1740–41). During the War of Austrian Succession (1741–48), Switzerland reported bad harvests in 1745 and 1749. In the Seven Years' War (1756–63), the European theater of fighting shifted east of the Rhine lands (to Silesia) and west to the American colonies, thus affecting areas of immigration more than areas of out-migration. Thereafter, harvests in many years were poor until

---

times of upheaval and also be of little help to one another. See Hacker, *Auswanderung aus Oberschwaben*, 36.

38. The ship lists (see Chapter 2) reveal the disruption and rerouting that occurred during times of war.

39. Wilhelm Abel, *Massenarmut und Hungerkrisen*.

40. Werner Hacker paid close attention to the connection between waves of emigration and adverse conditions at home; he chronicled such major events as war, bad harvests, and famines in certain areas of out-migration (Oberschwaben, Oberer Neckar, southeastern Schwarzwald, and Hochstift Speyer). I followed his basic chronology and added to it from studies of other areas.

41. Philip Otterness recently reexamined this large crisis migration of the early 1700s ("Unattained Canaan," esp. chap. 1).

the French Revolution, but from 1767 to 1773 weather conditions were especially cold and rainy, causing widespread famine in the early 1770s.

In addition to war and natural disasters, other extraordinary events, such as a change in government or policy, could create crisis conditions in the Rhine lands. For example, each time a new sovereign came to power, all customary rights and privileges had to be confirmed—a process that took time and money.[42] And as the cost of bureaucracy increased with each incoming government, the growing tax burden was a real complaint, since the tax base remained largely unchanged. Since knights (the lower nobility), the clergy, certain professionals, students, and others were exempt from taxes, propertied farmers and artisans were important for generating the revenues that financed the government. And when a new ruler also brought a change in the official religion, difficulties for citizens multiplied.

Religious minorities suffered especially from arbitrary rule and willful lords. Extraordinary hardships ensued when a shift from reluctant toleration to persecution occurred by governments that feared the influence the dissenters had on other subjects or were simply greedy for the property belonging to Nonconformists and Separatists.[43] Emigration was one way to get out from under the narrowly prescribed norms and escape punishment.[44] Although the right to emigrate was granted to religious dissenters in the Peace of Westphalia, government authorities tried repeatedly to curtail it, in spirit if not in fact, by prohibiting exportation of emigrants' possessions.[45] Immigrants to Pennsylvania who had left for conscience' sake often likened their situation to the Israelites' flight from Egypt—an image that occurred repeatedly in immigrant literature.[46]

The impact of political restrictions and economic instability in the Rhine lands in the seventeenth and eighteenth centuries was unevenly distributed. Impoverishment of large segments of the working and tax-paying

42. Groups dependent on special rights were in an especially precarious legal position, as the example of the Mennonites in the Palatinate shows. See Correll, *Das Schweizerische Täufermennonitentum*, 79–97; and the correspondence of the Palatine Mennonites with the Committee of Foreign Needs in Amsterdam (for example, AA nos. 1440, 1447, 2250, 2253, 2255).

43. In the late seventeenth and early eighteenth centuries, the persecution of Anabaptists in Switzerland was the most extreme and elaborate of similar incidents that occurred in many of the Rhine lands. Pietists of all kinds suffered especially from this intolerance.

44. Durnbaugh, "Radical Pietist Involvement," 30–31; Fogleman, *Hopeful Journeys*, chap. 4.

45. For example, decrees to that effect were issued in Württemberg (1709), Basel (1710), and Salzburg (1734).

46. See, for example, Francis Daniel Pastorius's report to the Frankfort Company, 7 March 1684, published in Jean Soderlund and Richard Dunn, eds., *William Penn and the Founding of Pennsylvania*, doc. 89; and Leonard Melchior's "Advice to German Emigrants, 1749" (ed. Hannah Roach), 237.

population resulted from a precarious balance between limited communally held resources and the relatively large number of people who had to share those resources. Both the division of land into marginally economical farms and the overstaffing of the traditionally organized trades led to underemployment and unemployment, which eroded the economic infrastructure even further.[47] Geographic mobility became almost a necessity for a majority of villagers and townsfolk who were seeking employment and a home, and this mobility took place not only in reaction to immediate crises but also as a strategy for avoiding future difficulties that Rhinelanders anticipated and feared.

A serious imbalance between people and resources did not exist everywhere in the Rhine lands at the same time, however, so the intraregional and interregional effects evened out somewhat, despite policies that restricted movement across territorial boundaries. Hard hit, and therefore most apt to move away, were the "lower sort," who owned some property, but not enough to support their families or to make it through occasional hard times without accumulating more debt.[48] In any place, this was the largest group. The poorest people could not move because they were too destitute and dependent on public assistance, and the well-off—usually a small proportion in any locale—had little need to relocate, because they were secure in their station in life and not as easily caught up in the vicious cycle of indebtedness and unemployment.

In such widespread but irregularly occurring circumstances of political and economic uncertainty, it was not unusual for a substantial portion of eighteenth-century Rhinelanders to leave their birthplaces in pursuit of temporary as well as permanent employment and settlement—even if the majority of citizens and many residents stayed put.[49] Most of the migration that did take place was by young people and extended over large parts of Europe. Servants walked in their seasonal search of masters, ranging

47. Local studies demonstrate the delicate balance between population pressures and resources. They also show the diverse official reactions to diminishing opportunities in their territories, and the many different ways in which residents reacted to increasing economic difficulties. Fertig, "Hintergrund" and "Household Formation"; Fogleman, *Hopeful Journeys*, 24–25, and "Auswanderung aus Südbaden im 18. Jahrhundert"; Häberlein, *Vom Oberrhein zum Susquehanna*, 42; von Hippel, *Auswanderung aus Südwestdeutschland*, 37.

48. Vierhaus distinguishes three groups of peasants: large farmers who had income beyond their cost of living; those who did not always have enough; and peasants who were forced into a secondary occupation (*Germany*, 46). For high levels of indebtedness and the tax burden in Baden, see Häberlein, *Vom Oberrhein zum Susquehanna*, 46–54.

49. In areas of the canton of Zurich, for example, half the men left their place of origin to look for work and residence elsewhere. Blocher, *Eigenart der Zürcher Auswanderer*, 80.

progressively farther from where they had grown up as they became older and gained more experience.[50] Large numbers of laborers went north regularly to work in Holland in the summer months, where some signed on as sailors or servants in the employ of the Dutch seaborne empire.[51] Journeymen often wandered far in their mandated quest for experience—and for a permanent position—in their crafts and trades. And soldiers were marched over long distances whenever armies gathered or transferred troops. For those who stayed behind, the departure of substantial numbers of villagers meant that the scarcity of resources was eased at least temporarily. Local land markets reacted favorably to the redistribution of property that ensued when citizens who left converted their real and mobile estate into cash—most of it to satisfy creditors and pay taxes.[52] Yet this process often marked only the beginning of a new cycle of precarious indebtedness for those who could consolidate their holdings in that fashion, because they continued to be threatened by an unstable economy, high taxes, many obligations, and an uncertain future.

As a result, trickles, rivulets, and streams of migrants developed, made up of young men evading the draft, farmers and artisans determined to escape near certain poverty and dependency, religious minorities who had resolved to flee unbearable intolerance, youths and adults forced to seek their fortunes elsewhere, and others who were either willing or pressed to move for want of work and a home.[53] Out of these disparate springs of dissatisfaction, however, there arose a major flow of out-migration that did much to people in both North America and Eastern Europe.

Given these many reasons for moving out of the Rhine lands, and the long-established practice of migrating among Rhinelanders, the actual decision to move on was made most often in response to particular oppor-

50. For a brief summary of the literature on servants in Germany, see Marianne Wokeck, "Servant Migration." The best account of servitude in England is Ann Kussmaul, *Servants in Husbandry.*

51. Jan Lucassen, "The Netherlands, the Dutch, and Long-Distance Migration," 161–65, 172–73, 182; see also Johann Carl Büttner, *Büttner, der Amerikaner* and *Narrative of Johann Carl Büttner.*

52. Häberlein details this important development for Baden (*Vom Oberrhein zum Susquehanna,* 61–63).

53. The loss of a parent who had provided economic support seems to have been a powerful inducement to migrate. See Horn, "Servant Emigration," 83–84, for seventeenth-century England; and Blocher, *Eigenart der Zürcher Auswanderer,* 121–26, for eighteenth-century Switzerland. Examples of the emigration of religious minorities are especially numerous and well documented. See Durnbaugh, "Radical Pietist Involvement"; Brecht, "Schwenkfelder Families"; and Fogleman, *Hopeful Journeys,* chap. 4.

tunities that opened up elsewhere.[54] In addition, interests of kin and friends, masters and employers, creditors and debtors, neighbors and co-religionists commonly defined deliberations about relocation, and often determined whether people actually left, and if so when they left, under what circumstances, and for what destinations.[55] Planning was essential in this process, and the choice of destination was paramount. Potential emigrants had some choice when relocating to foreign lands, because the Rhine lands were fertile ground for promoters of many schemes and settlement projects that were searching for laborers and settlers.

The Rhine lands welcomed recruitment of emigrants, because such relocation endeavors often fit the interests of the territorial lords. Large-scale, government-sponsored, and government-supported settlement projects attracted the greatest number of migrants, and their operations served as models for other, smaller, public and private recruitment efforts. Under the best of circumstances, the cooperation between governments that sought settlers and those that used such offers to set or realize their own population policies served both parties well. More often, however, the complexities of organizing emigration, even in regions with high levels of potential recruits, resulted in less-than-ideal conditions and repeatedly set the concerns of local and foreign lords at odds.

Ideally, a well-planned and well-executed campaign to attract emigrants included the following components, collectively, each building on the others: Effective advertising, which was essential to publicize the scheme and let people know what types of emigrants would be accepted as colonists or laborers. Pamphlets, newspaper articles, and handbills that detailed opportunities in remote lands, as well as printed transportation contracts that doubled as promotion and subscription lists (most alluring

54. In discussing the literature on the causes of German emigration, Fogleman concluded that the structural and acute circumstances of adversity in the Rhine lands were not what caused people to move. They emigrated, instead, in response to the promotion of settlement projects ("Hopeful Journeys" [diss.], 84–91). However, Fogleman does not consider the general literature on migration, which has found that, with the exception of unusual crisis migrations (such as the Irish exodus because of the potato famine), long-distance flows are most likely to develop when there is already a strong tradition of moving in reaction to difficult circumstances and when a concrete offer for improving one's lot elsewhere comes along in conjunction with one or more immediate reasons for emigration. That model, not Fogleman's, best fits the situation in the Rhine lands in the eighteenth century (see the Introduction).

55. Häberlein demonstrates such a "collective" decision to emigrate for Baden (*Vom Oberrhein zum Susquehanna,* 77). For a more general summary of migration patterns, see Leslie Moch, *Moving Europeans.*

when embellished with fancy seals and titles) were standard.[56] Support from territorial lords to solicit emigrants among their subjects secured cooperation from local authorities and eliminated competitors.[57] An efficient network of agents was imperative for recruiting and arranging transportation.[58] Persuading well-known and respected citizens, especially ministers, to become emigrants provided critical endorsement.[59] Good reports about the transport and conditions in the new situation from the initial group were necessary to win over relatives, friends, and neighbors to follow in the steps of the pioneers. All serious recruitment efforts that counted on large numbers of settlers over an extended time had a vital interest in creating this self-generating effect among the settlers who were the vanguard. When such first efforts failed, further recruitment was called into serious question unless it could shift to groups of people or territories that were not affected by negative reports from trailblazers.[60]

In practice, competing interests, incompetence, impatience, and greed hampered even well-conceived and well-organized recruiting efforts.[61] The

56. Examples of recruiting efforts for New England and Nova Scotia show that titles and other symbols of authority carried weight with German citizens who were considering emigrating. See Rattermann, "Geschichte des deutschen Elements," 15:349, 357; Stumpp, *Emigration from Germany to Russia*, 15–19.

57. For example, the Council of Bern actively backed the ventures of Georg Ritter and Christoph von Graffenried and therefore had no interest in allowing Jean Pierre Purry to solicit Bernese emigrants for his endeavor. See Leo Schelbert and Hedwig Rappolt, *Alles ist ganz anders hier*, 425, n. 20; and Schelbert, "Swiss Emigration to America," 156. In an effort to eliminate competition Ehrenfried Luther, advocate for the New England settlement projects, succeeded in obtaining official decrees restricting "free agents" from soliciting in a number of territories. See "Geschichte des deutschen Elements," 14:432, 15:105–9.

58. Luther, who came up with a recruitment campaign for the New England settlement project, recognized the need for reputable, locally known agents but failed to see the importance of winning respectable and relatively well-to-do local individuals as emigrants. See Rattermann, "Geschichte des deutschen Elements," 14:430–32, 16:13.

59. The critical role of religious leaders in spearheading pioneering settlement efforts is evident in the examples of Kocherthal leading a band of Palatines to New York in 1708 and of Purry winning the support of clergyman Bartholomus Zuberbühler for his South Carolina venture in the early 1730s, not to mention the Pietist and Separatist groups who relocated under the guidance of their respective leaders. For later examples in the nineteenth-century migration from Sweden, see Sten Carlsson, "Chronology and Composition of Swedish Emigration," 116–20.

60. Recruiting efforts for Samuel Waldo's patent in Maine failed in part because letters from emigrants to relatives and former neighbors in the homeland told how difficult both the journey and the land, climate, and farming conditions were. See Rattermann, "Geschichte des deutschen Elements," 16:72–76.

61. On the extensive advertising war between Captain Heerbrand, the recruiting agent for

more complicated the operations, the more room there was for misman-
agement, self-interest, and fraud. Unscrupulous agents undermined efforts
on behalf of reputable ventures, created widespread suspicion, and encouraged the imposition of harsh measures against emigrant recruiters. Temporarily, however, such deceptive practices served well enough to impress and
confuse uninformed and uneducated prospective recruits. They also satisfied many local officials who did not mind profiting from questionable
recruiting activities in exchange for leniency concerning rules and regulations governing emigration procedures, or by condoning actions that ran
counter to the interests of the emigrants.[62]

In addition, many private and public promoters, developers, and speculators found it difficult to tap the volatile migration potential of the
Rhine lands effectively, because their projects vied simultaneously for settlers from the same pool of prospective emigrants without being truly
competitive. More important, only some of the promoters were able to
come up with the substantial capital that was necessary—often in cash—
to launch a project that would pay off only in the long run. The Austrian,
Prussian, and Russian governments put much of their own funds toward
their respective colonizing efforts, but the results seemed to justify the
investment. They succeeded mainly by offering colonists land at no cost
or on very reasonable terms, by granting tax exemptions, and in some
cases by assuming or contributing to the migrants' transportation costs.
Others, offering comparable terms, often fell short in delivering what they
had promised. This prevented even well-conceived projects from being
realized at all, or at least from becoming profitable.

Samuel Waldo's scheme for settling one thousand families in Massachusetts Bay is an especially interesting example. In 1757, after considerable
experience—and frustration—with soliciting colonists in previous years,
Waldo approached the count of Neuwied with a settlement plan that not
only included a detailed budget of projected expenses but also contained
an ingenious way to distribute much of the start-up and operating costs of
the project among the emigrants. He suggested to his prospective invest-

a group of four English merchants in Rotterdam, and Joseph Crell (Crellius), agent for the
New England settlement projects backed by Luther, and Gottlieb Tobias Köhler, agent for
John Dick who was commissioned by the Board of Trade, see Rattermann, "Geschichte des
deutschen Elements," 14:464–68, 15:174–82, 16:12–13.

62. On the cooperation between recruiting agents and local officials, see Rattermann,
"Geschichte des deutschen Elements," 15:352. However, the report in *Pennsylvanische Berichte* (16
October 1753) tells of harsh, official treatment in reaction to the misconduct of newlanders.

ment partner that the importation of settlers be staggered and that the pioneering group should be financed well. He made the point that positive reports from the pioneers would be critical in stimulating additional emigration among kin and friends—a lesson Waldo had learned from earlier failure. According to this plan, the transportation and settlement of the second group of emigrants could then be paid for with funds the investors received from debt payments of the pioneering settlers. All subsequent groups of colonists were to be paced in this fashion too, essentially recycling the initial start-up costs and thereby keeping the promoters' expenses fixed. Waldo also suggested that the count bind all underage emigrants as servants to himself, so that he could use them as servants or apprentices in any business or sell their indentures to people who needed labor (and presumably could afford to pay for it). The latter option would give him a quick return on the monies advanced on behalf of those youths. Although Waldo's elaborate and clever investment proposition was never implemented, it survives as a contemporary reflection of the dynamics that were in fact successfully at work generating lasting immigration to Pennsylvania.[63]

Like Waldo, many other speculators short of capital and settlers approached the territorial authorities in the Rhine lands with projects for granting them support in soliciting emigrants from among local subjects. In their appeals to the various governments along the Rhine, the promoters of foreign settlements counted on the desire of the lords to control the population of their lands. Seizing such opportunities for getting rid of undesirable residents made the territorial lords active, if mostly silent, partners in those schemes. Such partnerships, however, were usually short-lived; they often turned sour when the promoted colonies attracted too many emigrants or citizens who were valued for their contributions to their Rhineland home territory.

The decrees that many territories issued concerning emigration reveal that their highly selective population control policies were fiscally motivated.[64] The policies and related regulations were usually couched in the

63. Fürstlich Weidsches Archiv, Neuwied, Schrank VI: 5:2; 30:3: 1, fols. 34, 69–77 (1757), LC/MD, FCP: Germany. Waldo's earlier attempts to attract settlers are detailed in Rattermann, "Geschichte des deutschen Elements"; see also Schoff, "Descendants," 12–30.

64. The following incomplete list provides a typical cross section of government reaction to legal and illegal emigration: decrees forbidding Nassau Dillenburg residents to leave (18 May 1709; 28 February and 12 April 1764; 3 June 1766; 26 June 1773), Hoffman, "'Palatine' Emigrants to America," 42; Gerber, *Nassau-Dillenburger Auswanderung*, 7–8, 30–33, 37; decrees against emigration in Württemberg (16 January 1700; 25 June 1709; 8 September 1717; 28 Febru-

language of paternalistic concern, but they were designed above all to discourage or prohibit propertied subjects who were of value to the community from emigrating. Consequently, many territories likened illegal emigration to desertion.[65] Poor emigrants, however, were rarely hindered from
leaving, and some governments even provided active encouragement and
travel money to facilitate their departure.[66]

    When loss of emigrants—or, more precisely, loss of their wealth and
earnings potential—became a major concern, official steps to limit the
number of residents leaving involved increasingly restrictive measures to
prevent the exportation of personal property.[67] By 1763, every detail concerning emigration was regulated. Those who emigrated without *dismissoralis* would lose their property as punishment; those who received permission to move had to leave for good, taking their entire family, so that
unruly children did not become a burden to the country. Regulations concerning the sale of property and the process of dismission required a list
of the property to be sold, including mortgages and the name of the
prospective buyer, which were to be handed to the appropriate official for
inspection. The inspector, the emigrant, and the buyer then came to an
agreement on a price, which the latter had to pay, mostly in cash. Only
then could the *dismissoralis* be granted—if it was considered not harmful to

---

ary 1750; 18 January 1753; 27 January 1764; 25 March 1766), Karl Arndt, *Rapp's Separatists*, 5, 11, 14–
16, 25–42, 49–50, 59–60, 60–61; decrees against emigration from the Palatinate (21 June 1752; 3
March; 26 and 29 May, and 20 November 1765), Häberle, *Auswanderung und Koloniegründungen der
Pfälzer*, 5–6; decrees hindering or prohibiting emigration from Wertheim (1752–54), Yoder,
Pennsylvania German Immigrants, 184–89; and, in Faust's *Guide to the Materials for American History*, 3,
15–17, 23, 29, 47–48, 58–59, 109, 112, 129, decrees against emigration from Zurich (3 November
1737; 29 January 1735; 3 February 1736; 13 May 1739; 4 February 1741; 18 March 1744; 10 December 1767; 29 November 1770); decrees prohibiting emigration from Bern (1720, 1735, 1736, 1738,
1742, 1749, 1753, 1754, 1771, 1773); attempts to control emigration from Basel (30 April 1735; 13
August 1749; 1750; 25 March 1771; 30 January 1773). See also Faust, "Documents in Swiss
Archives," 128–31; decrees to prevent emigration for Lucerne (1767, 1770–71), Wicki, *Bevölkerung
des Kantons Luzern*, 29; and decree of the "Chur-Rheinische Crayss" (2 April 1766; imperial
decree against emigration, 7 July 1768), Stumpp, *Emigration from Germany to Russia*, 29–31.

    65. Gerhard Kaller, "Archivalien zur Auswanderungsgeschichte der Pfälzer," 3.
    66. Among the many examples are Nassau-Dillenburg (Gerber, *Nassau-Dillenburger Auswan-
derung*, 8, 16–18) and Bern (Faust, *Guide to the Materials for American History*, 3, 40–44; see also LC/
MD, FCP: Switzerland; and Schelbert, "Swiss Emigration to America," 156); Basel (Albert
Faust and Gaius Brumbaugh, eds., *Lists of Swiss Emigrants*, 95, 113); Zurich (Blocher, *Eigenart der
Zürcher Auswanderer*, 13); and Clausthal (Andreas Brinck, *Deutsche Auswanderungswelle*, 150).
    67. For example, Württemberg regulated the sale of emigrant property (Arndt, *Rapp's Sep-
aratists*, 5, 14. 60); Nassau-Dillenburg raised the removal tax (Häberle, *Auswanderung und Ko-
loniegründungen*, 92); and Basel stopped the exportation of inheritances (Faust, "Documents in
Swiss Archives," 130–31).

the country. In any case that circumvented these regulations, the property would be confiscated and the noncompliant buyer would be forced to emigrate too. Court officials had to verify with the local officials that the prospective emigrant's wealth had been estimated correctly. Other creditors had two months in which to stake their claim, and the buyer had to wait—under threat of punishment—until then and had to obtain permission from the relevant official before the emigrant could receive the agreed-on payment. The *dismissoralis* decree was amended to allow an arbitrary removal tax to be set in each case.[68] Territorial lords imposed other measures to enforce any decreed prohibition of emigration. The loss of citizenship or right to reside in the land was a standard final consequence of most emigration procedures everywhere in the Rhine lands. Emigrants who had been denied passports could travel only illegally and could therefore be denied passage.[69] Ironically, however, the intense efforts to control migration ensured awareness about settlement opportunities in distant lands and made those opportunities even more attractive.

In competition for colonists from the Rhine lands, the projects for settlement in the British North American colonies differed from those organized by Prussia, Austria, Russia, France, and Spain in two fundamental ways. First, the campaign for settlers involved many different interests that were not ultimately defined and funded by the authority of one particular government. Transatlantic recruitment efforts were not concerted drives. Second, promoters depended in large part on colonists who were able to pay the substantial costs of relocating overseas, because most settlement projects did not assume transportation expenses. Both characteristics meant that the common promotion and recruitment methods needed to be modified, and it was these modifications that shaped the migration flow across the Atlantic.

Promoters ranged from European and colonial governments to small-scale operators with interests in a wide geographical area, from Nova Scotia to Georgia and including coastal regions, as well as areas along the frontiers of European settlement. (See Map 2.) In their quest to turn vast

---

68. Gerber, *Nassau-Dillenburger Auswanderung*, 16–18, 30–32. This procedure was typical for many territories, with some local variations. A detailed and complete record is Höchst, Bestand IX, 5, Amt Höchst § 11/12, Title, no. 3 (1723–84). Others are, Kurpfalz, no. 35/I (1685–1779), 14–16, 19, 20–22, LC/MD, FCP: Germany; and Faust, "Documents in Swiss Archives," 128–30.

69. Faust, *Guide to the Materials for American History*, 32–34, 46, 112.

MAP 2   The British colonies in North America

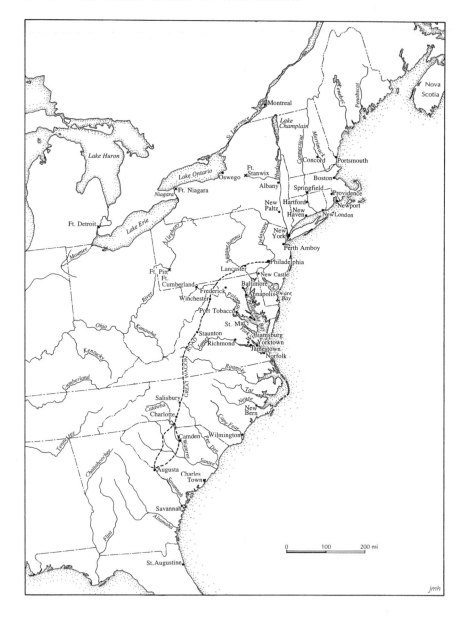

areas of New World land into profitable ventures, American landlords and speculators made use of any connections they had or could readily establish in the Rhine lands, in order to tap the reservoir of potential emigrants.

William Penn, proprietor of Pennsylvania, was in the forefront when he advertised among co-religionists on the continent to win settlers for his "holy experiment."[70] The success of German settlement in Pennsylvania inspired others to adopt and improve on features of the project that fit their own situation. Impoverished landed gentry in the Rhine lands, as well as would-be landlords and speculators in America, approached both the Board of Trade and colonial proprietors and governments with offers to settle their lands in return for property and a title of their own. Conversely, provincial governments and many different kinds of private developers in North America sought "foreign Protestants" in order to secure title to their lands, gain protection against Indians and other enemies, and improve the value of their holdings or operations.[71] Each of these schemes, big or small, started in the homeland of its European promoter or the continental agent employed by its American developer. As a result, communities with especially close connections to American settlements could be located quite close to each other in the Rhine lands, so competition for emigrants could be fierce. Such competition led recruiters to tap new sources and branch out into other territories.[72] Whether these points of origin became sources of emigration over time, forming well-established and long-term networks linking German homelands with the American colonies, depended on how effectively a project could be promoted and the types of settlers it could enlist.[73]

70. Richard Dunn and Mary Dunn, eds., *Papers of William Penn*, 2:591–97; 5:264–69, 276, 302–7, 320–23. The letter of the Franconia Mennonites in 1773 showing the reasons Mennonites came to Pennsylvania is a testimony to the success of Penn's strategy. See *Mennonite Quarterly Review* 3 (1928): 228.

71. Among the many developers were Wistar, who established glassworks in New Jersey (Beiler, "Wistar," 290–330); Peter Hasenclever, who sought labor for ironworks in New Jersey (Bailyn, *Voyagers to the West*, 249–51); Georg Ritter and company, who set up a silver-mining scheme in Virginia (Klaus Wust, "Palatines and Switzers for Virginia," 45–48); and a Virginia land speculator named George Washington who sought settlers for his lands in Ohio (Washington Papers, LC/MD, reel 33; J. C. Fitzpatrick, ed., *The Writings of George Washington*, 3:185–96).

72. The expansion of recruiting networks into new areas (Hanover, Kassel, and the Harz) and solicitation of criminals are examples at the height of the German immigration to the American colonies. For details, see Brinck, *Deutsche Auswanderungswelle*, 116–29, 151. Lowell Bennion has described this expansion of recruitment areas beyond the Rhine lands ("Flight from the Reich," figs. 5–7).

73. For example, statistics on emigration from the *Ämter* in Württemberg show that some

Advertising and recruiting were critical in disseminating information about faraway places to those who had already decided to leave the homeland, and were crucial in preparing the way for those who were still uncertain or not yet interested in relocating. In the long run, successful colonization schemes—public or private—depended on persuading large numbers of people to relocate, not just the much smaller number of people who had few options besides to leave the homeland. American settlement projects, in particular, offered potential colonists no financial support, so only emigrants who had some property could even contemplate a move overseas. Advertising was often the important first step in making known the opportunities available in a specific unfamiliar place. Effective techniques for soliciting settlers for distant locations included both skillful use of the media and the face-to-face persuasion by recruiters, selectively targeting the types of emigrants most desired or needed for a particular settlement. Personalized enlistment efforts by people who were known and trusted locally were especially convincing and most likely to transform potential emigrants into actual colonists. Private letters or visits from former emigrants who had succeeded in the New World were other powerful means for persuading Rhinelanders to leave home for America.

Promotional literature acquainted large numbers of people with settlement opportunities. Despite great variation in composition, length, and style, a glowing account of the geographical features, climate, animals, plants, and other notable characteristics of the colony was standard.[74] The lack of accuracy, common to most such early descriptions, usually gave way to a more realistic outline of settlement conditions, including advice on how to prepare for the journey and what to take, leave behind, or acquire along the way.[75] As migration to America increased, more let-

---

successful migration streams that were distinct in their direction formed, most commonly to places to the east (von Hippel, *Auswanderung*, 300–305). Close scrutiny of migration lists and local records on both sides of the Atlantic reveals that repeated contacts between America and the Rhine lands over the long term were essential for stable and reliable transatlantic migration networks. This is particularly evident in the genealogically grounded work of Burgert, Hacker, and Wust: emigrant begat emigrant.

74. The description of Pennsylvania by William Penn in 1682 was in many respects prototypical of the promotional efforts to win settlers that followed in the eighteenth century. See Soderlund and Dunn, eds., *William Penn and the Founding of Pennsylvania*, 58–66; Hull, *William Penn and the Dutch Quaker Migration*, 329–35.

75. No systematic survey and analysis of the promotional literature in the Rhine lands in the eighteenth century exist. Faust, *Guide to the Materials for American History*, 29–31 (somewhat abbreviated also in Faust and Brumbaugh, *Lists of Swiss Emigrants*, 22), lists fourteen books and pamphlets that were widely circulated in Switzerland in 1684–1754; a greater selection is provided in Julius Sachse, "Literature Used to Induce German Emigration," 175–98 (facsimiles of

ters, reports, and advice were made public and circulated in the Rhine lands.[76]

If promotional pamphlets and tracts planted the idea of residing and working overseas, newspapers helped bring people into direct contact with real possibilities for emigration.[77] They accomplished this by publishing specific information about arrangements for relocation and by printing reports from and about successful immigrants with whom the reader could identify.[78] Since not everyone could read or had ready access to printed material, personal letters would reach a greater variety of people and were much better targeted. Everyone agreed that a positive letter from America had a tremendous impact and was likely to prompt emigration.[79]

Whether a particular settlement in the American colonies fizzled or thrived depended in large part on its reputation in the Rhine lands above and beyond the propaganda. Only migrants who had undertaken the move across the Atlantic could convincingly convey to relatives and former neighbors whether the promises about settlement in the colonies held up or fell short.[80] Positive news meant that others would follow, creating a chain of migration. Negative reports had a detrimental effect on migra-

---

title pages, 201–56), the most important of which are also in Albert Dyers, ed., *Narratives.* Klaus Wust has collected material about the many settlement projects and development schemes seeking emigrants from the Rhine lands. So far, only some of his findings have been published.

76. Francis Daniel Pastorius and Christopher Sauer were early pioneers whose letters became part of the widely circulated canon of American lore. Melchior's "Advice to German Emigrants, 1749" (ed. Roach) and Gottlieb Mittelberger's *Journey to Pennsylvania* (1756) were published in reaction to the large exodus from German lands and to the exploitation of emigrants at the height of the migration around mid-century; see Donald Durnbaugh, "Christopher Sauer," *The Brethren in Colonial America,* and "Radical Pietist Involvement," 36–37. See also Melchior's "Advice to German Emigrants, 1749"; and Mittelberger, *Journey to Pennsylvania.* In general, propaganda about emigration to the American colonies—both positive and negative—was widespread. See Häberlein, *Vom Oberrhein zum Susquehanna,* 86–88.

77. One such example is a letter praising Georgia published in the Leipzig newspapers (25 December 1733), which influenced the Moravians who did emigrate to Georgia later (Herrenhut, Rep. 14 A [Georgien Rechnungen & Quittungen, 1735 etc.], LC/MD, FCP: Germany).

78. For example, Caspar Wistar's report (8 November 1732) about the limited opportunities available in Pennsylvania. *Leipziger Post Zeitungen* (21 May 1733). The New England settlement project (Broad Bay, Maine) is well documented and reveals the heavy use of newspapers in its campaign. See Rattermann, "Geschichte des deutschen Elements," 14:345, 15; 15:4–82, 109–13; 16:12–13. William O'Reilly was kind enough to lend me a copy of the microfilmed document collection in the Massachusetts Archives, which was the basis of Rattermann's description and extensive document selection.

79. There is no systematic collection of eighteenth-century immigrant letters. Much of the discussion here is based on letters that have been published in many different places. (The migration lists in the Bibliography often include letters.)

80. Häberlein demonstrates how important the question of trust was in such communications (*Vom Oberrhein zum Susquehanna,* 89–92).

tion and forced recruiters to find settlers elsewhere.[81] This is in part why some villages and areas participated in a particular migration flow repeatedly and in substantial numbers, while other places contributed only limited numbers or only once.[82]

The practice of writing to relatives and friends left behind in the homelands was widespread and had been established early. These communications were clearly intended to be read to kin and neighbors, as is evident from the prominent part given to "family news" on both sides of the Atlantic—sometimes in connection with inquiries and instructions concerning inheritance matters.[83] The letters that survive vary a great deal in content and style.[84] Not all writers were happy in the New World.[85] Others, although content with how things had turned out for them, were cautious in recommending such a move to friends and former neighbors because they did not want to be blamed for any difficulties that might occur if those back home decided to undertake the long and dangerous journey.

The letters that directly or indirectly advocated immigration had certain recurrent themes. Most immigrants first wrote home when they could

81. " . . . their Report to their Friends in Germany who only send them for an essay of the Country & usage: the rest who are the chief & Substantial persons all declare that they will follow next year on being satisfied of the Solidity of the undertaking. . . ." Sebastian Zuberbühler to Samuel Waldo, London, 5 July 1742, cited in Rattermann, "Geschichte des deutschen Elements," 14:56–57; see also Faust, *Guide to the Materials for American History*, 112; and Gerber, *Nassau-Dillenburger Auswanderung*, 19. In some instances, such chains of migration were strung out over considerable periods of time. Lutheran and Reformed emigrants from Freinsheim, as well as those from Wolfersweiler Parish, displayed such behavior. See Annette Burgert, *Colonial Pennsylvania Immigrants from Freinsheim; Pennsylvania Pioneers from Wolfersweiler Parish.*

82. For example, emigration from Hochstadt was substantial. It started in 1732 and continued for twenty years (Burgert, *Hochstadt Origins*). Fogleman (*Hopeful Journeys*, 62) shows a quite different pattern of emigration across the villages of the Kraichgau.

83. For an example of this interaction between the completion of family migration and the settlement of financial affairs connected with it, see Fritz Braun and Friedrich Krebs, "German Emigrants from Palatinate Parishes," 256.

84. Roeber described those letters as always focusing on household, family, food, drink, and land (*Palatines*, 23), although a substantial number of letters also discussed religious matters. Those themes show what was most important to Rhineland immigrants in the American colonies: the community of kin and neighbors, the ingredients necessary to make a decent living, and justification for moving to the New World.

85. Esther Werndtlin-Göttschi is one woman who, together with her children, encountered unanticipated hardships when her husband died on arrival in the new land (see Schelbert and Rappolt, *Alles ist ganz anders hier*, 113–18). Another example is the anonymous author of *Sendschreiben aus Philadelphia* (15/25 September 1728), who believed he had been lured to Pennsylvania under the false pretense that life was easy there; he later found that applied only to people who were willing to earn a living with manual labor.

impart positive news, but difficulties encountered during the journey and in the early years of settlement figure large in such reports. Pride in subsequent achievements, especially acquisition of property and all the basics for making a decent living, temper this impact of initial hardships, however. Most immigrants found that they missed the people who remained behind, but they expressed no desire to return. Many immigrant letters mentioned that the country was free of all German taxes (*Auflagen*), had no tithe and no compulsory service, had free hunting and fishing, and had a yearly tax so low that some people spent the same amount during one visit to the tavern.[86]

What stands out in letter after letter is the strong lure of a "free country," a characteristic that set relocation in the American colonies apart from settlements established eastward by the governments of Prussia, Austria, and Russia.[87] Other positive features were added, although one must allow for some bragging. Descriptions of America as a land with enough bread and work and plenty of wood—where one could "buy, settle, and borrow without restrictions," where "all trades and professions are free," where chances for women to marry were good, where "whoever works hard can make a decent living," where "it is not like at home that the lord pesters the subjects to the utmost with taxes and compulsory service, for we sit . . . quiet under our government, who govern no longer than a year, then they or others are elected by the subjects . . . ," and where all religious groups were tolerated de facto, if not de iure—carried a good deal of weight with those who knew the writers and their circumstances in the Old World.[88]

Yet most immigrants who had become successful settlers were realistic about the difficulties that later emigrants would face, and they repeatedly warned that people who do not want to work should stay at home. In the words of a settler in South Carolina, "As attractive as this country is, as difficult and expensive is it for everybody to reach it; only untiringly ac-

86. Letter quoted in Gerber, *Nassau-Dillenburger Auswanderung*, 14–15. For an early letter (Cornelius Bom, 12 October 1684) very much in the same vein, see Hull, *William Penn and the Dutch Quaker Migration*, 318–22.

87. Letter from a settler in Lebanon, Pa. (23 August 1769), in Faust, "Unpublished Documents," 37–39.

88. Letter from a settler in Lebanon, Pa. (23 August 1769), in Faust, "Unpublished Documents," 37–39; letter by Elisabetha Strohmann (1768), in Faust and Brumbaugh, *Lists of Swiss Emigrants*, 121–22; letters by Johannes Hayn and Daniel Becker (12 November 1752), quoted in Gerber, *Nassau-Dillenburger Auswanderung*, 20–21; letter by Antony Gondy (Charleston, 28 May 1733), in Faust, "Documents in Swiss Archives," 115.

tive and strong people who have money can eventually become rich and happy."[89] A reluctance to advise others to relocate was counterbalanced by few indications of any desire to return and by offers to help those who did come.[90] The letters that offered advice about preparations for the move included some quite specific recommendations, ranging from where to buy provisions cheaply to warnings about certain agents.[91]

Receiving news from a relative, friend, or former neighbor who had settled in the distant "islands" of Carolina and Pennsylvania was in itself a major event. Being able to seek confirmation from the mail-carrying "new-lander" and to ask questions was also highly conducive to emigration. At a time when regular postal service over long distances was not available for ordinary people, personal letters from the American colonies to the Rhineland were often carried by people who were traveling that route anyway and offered to carry messages for a fee.[92] The difficulties and expense involved in sending news may help explain the long periods of time that elapsed between emigration and the first letters home.[93] Over the course of the century, however, it became easier to find Germans who were willing to carry letters back home, because more were returning to Europe more often, and even regularly, and because those who crossed the Atlantic

89. Schelbert, *Einführung in die Schweizerische Auswanderungsgeschichte*, 335.

90. Johannes Tschudi (1749) warned not only those unwilling to work to stay home but also those "who like to drink wine because there is only small beer and cider" (quoted in Faust, *Guide to the Materials for American History*, 112). The letter by Christen Engel (Carolina, 1711) contains the typical wish that his neighbors could be with him to share a life that was better than life at home (quoted in Faust, "Graffenried Manuscripts," 296).

91. Heinrich Näff to Hansz Jacob Müller, Purrysburg, S.C., 18 August 1735, in Schelbert and Rappolt, *Alles ist ganz anders hier*, 63; letter by Johann Henrich Schmitt, quoted in Krebs, "Emigrants from Baden-Durlach," 31–32. See also Braun and Krebs, "German Emigrants from Palatinate Parishes," 256; and Yoder, *Pennsylvania German Immigrants*, 168.

92. Letters could be sent along commercial routes—that is, from the American ports to a major English port, usually London, and from there to Rotterdam or Amsterdam and on to Frankfurt am Main or Basel. Letters from immigrants telling correspondents in the homelands about reliable ways to route letters and goods thereby revealed intricate networks of communication back and forth across the Atlantic. For instance, John Theobald Endt, a Brethren-affiliated merchant in Germantown, recommended relying on John Wister, David Däschler, and Christopher Sauer in Philadelphia; Richard Neave, the correspondent of Israel Pemberton and Philip Benezet in London; and Zacharias Hope in Rotterdam. (See letters to Arnold Goyen [10 May 1758 and 10 February 1759], in Durnbaugh, *Brethren*, 56–57.)

93. An enterprising newlander, Hanna Regina Ruhstein, carried nine letters when she returned home to the Harz mountains, all of them addressed to people who could not pay the fee she asked. Although she succeeded in persuading the government to cover her expenses, she failed to initiate a substantial emigration. See Brinck, *Deutsche Auswanderungswelle*, 91.

eastward often advertised their services as couriers in the newspapers.[94] Yet Germans on both sides of the Atlantic harbored suspicions that letters could be intercepted, confiscated, or tampered with by people who had vested interests—such as merchants and their agents, who feared the effects that negative reports would have on their reputations and business, and also territorial officials, who had the power to censor all mail from foreign lands. Consequently, some immigrants and letter-carrying "newlanders" took precautions, such as using codes, to assure the addressee that the message was authentic, or they took measures to conceal letters from the authorities.[95]

Return visits of newlanders had an even broader and more immediate impact than letters, because, having already made the journey, they could help others arrange to relocate.[96] The most common such visitors were those who came but once to fetch family members left behind or to settle inheritance matters—both powerful incentives to brave the Atlantic again.[97] Since immigrants connected by bonds of kin, friendship, or former place of residence tended to keep in touch in the New World, any one member of such a network could significantly serve all its members when visiting the homelands. Those links broadened the range of the visits by "newlanders"—those who had successfully completed the trip earlier—beyond their own places of former residence and gave to their reports and advice a

94. See, for example, the advertisements in the *Pennsylvania Gazette* and in *Pennsylvanische Berichte*. Fertig, "Migration," 320 (map 8.1) plotted them by destination in the Rhine lands. Roeber has traced some of the German Lutheran communication networks in the American colonies (*Palatines*, 123–24, 249).

95. For example, Johannes Hayn, in his letter of 15 October 1752, used a special signal that identified his message as genuine. See Gerber, *Nassau-Dillenburger Auswanderung*, 19. Brinck showed that some quite sophisticated recruiting operations made use of fabricated and forged letters (*Deutsche Auswanderungswelle*, 101–3).

96. Newlanders received much press—mostly bad—in the eighteenth century, especially at the height of the immigration, when their numbers proliferated. By now, there is a considerable body of literature, although it is scattered and often builds on the same cases. Brinck recently added to our understanding by detailing the recruitment operations in northern Germany, especially the mining areas of the Harz mountains (see Brinck, *Deutsche Auswanderungswelle*, 88–111); and William O'Reilly is working on a dissertation that focuses more generally on the role newlanders played in emigration from Germany.

97. Häberlein, who distinguishes between casual newlanders and professional recruiting agents, found both types from Baden operating in their homeland (*Vom Oberrhein zum Susquehanna*, 92–97). Roeber, who explored the settlement of inheritances in some detail, found about 10 percent of cases of inheritance recovery among emigrants from the electoral Palatinate east of the Rhine (*Palatines*, 263–65). In Baden the proportion was smaller (2 to 3 percent), but not without impact (Häberlein, *Vom Oberrhein zum Susquehanna*, 173–77).

special weight. Locally known newlanders often played the crucial role of catalyst in transforming potential emigrants into voyagers to the west.[98] As a result, emigration from certain areas often peaked in response to the visits of such trusted emissaries, because people took the opportunity to make the transatlantic move in the company of an experienced traveler who was on the way back.[99]

Another kind of newlander operation developed not as a service to relatives and friends but as a business enterprise.[100] As some newlanders found out that the money with which they were entrusted in Germany could be invested in goods for resale in the colonies, the collection of inheritances attracted people who wanted to exploit the profit potential of this highly specialized international banking function.[101] In addition, newlanders who organized and led groups of emigrants acted as transport leaders who could invest any funds their fellow travelers might have and wanted to import profitably to the American colonies.[102] A system of transferring capital and goods across the Atlantic built primarily on personal contact and trust, it was easily abused by some who faked concern for emigrants for their own personal gain.[103] Still another way for a newlander to profit from emigrants was to agree with a Rotterdam merchant to recruit passengers for his ships. Free passage, payment of some expenses, and a small fixed sum per passenger delivered into the hands of the merchant were common rewards in small-scale recruiting contracts.[104]

A third category of newlanders consisted of professional agents whose

98. Blocher observed the recruiting mechanisms at the local level in Zurich in some detail (*Eigenart der Zürcher Auswanderer*, 46–47, 114). See also Brinck, *Deutsche Auswanderungswelle*, 88–111; and Georg Fertig, "Migration," 229–31.

99. It is possible that the large number of young men in the 1744 emigration from Baden followed the lead of Sebastian Neff, who had returned to recover an inheritance and recruit others. See Häberlein, *Vom Oberrhein zum Susquehanna*, 93.

100. Some of these ventures were operated out of inns and taverns that catered to a largely German clientele in Philadelphia. See Roeber, *Palatines*, 249, 254.

101. Caspar Wistar did not return to the Rhine lands as a newlander, but he used commercial contacts in his homeland for recovering inheritances as part of his business (Beiler, "Wistar," 241–44). Most inheritance recoveries were valued between £10 and £30 (Roeber, *Palatines*, 276).

102. For details, see Chapter 3.

103. German settlers in the American colonies who gave unscrupulous newlanders powers of attorney in order to collect their inheritances would lose their inheritance if such agents absconded with it or reinvested it at a loss. For an advertised warning against untrustworthy newlanders in the colonies, see *Pennsylvanische Berichte*, 16 May 1755.

104. The interest of Rotterdam merchants in channeling the migration flow onto their ships is discussed in more detail in Chapter 3.

interests were tied to large-scale enterprises run by foreign governments, private developers, or merchants of substantial stature and resources. Of a different caliber, this group of recruiters included newlanders of various types, skills, and motivations and operated on a regional and interregional scale.[105] These agents normally used a number of recruiting techniques to lure potential emigrants and drew much attention from competitors, imitators, and officials.[106]

Few of the profit-hungry newlanders maintained a reputation that was good enough for them to work the same area repeatedly. As competition among recruiters grew, and as more territories prohibited soliciting emigrants from their subjects, agents who moved into areas hitherto untouched by overseas emigration were likely to make little headway because they had to share a declining market with other competitors. By mid-century, when emigration from the Rhine lands to the American colonies peaked, the ranks of recruiters had swelled substantially and included many disreputable characters who were in the business for quick and easy profits.[107] Collectively and somewhat stereotypically, their mode of operation became symbolic of the ruthless exploitation of naive emigrants that marred the years of heaviest emigration. Success in the business of recruiting emigrants depended mostly on a good name, so exploitive newlanders could harm or ruin a considerable number of emigrants who had trusted them, but they would stay in the business only until the true nature of their enterprising ways became known. Although each of the "bad apples" had only limited effects, there were always others who copied and per-

105. In fact, agents promoting private or official projects for settlement overseas were the first to lead emigrant groups down the Rhine and across the Atlantic. Entrepreneurs like William Penn employed agents—often friends and associates—to recruit settlers and to organize the transportation. See Hull, *William Penn and the Dutch Quaker Migration*, 325, 327–28; and Schelbert and Rappolt, *Alles ist ganz anders hier*, 33–40, 65–67, on the schemes of Francis Louis Michel, Georg Ritter, Christoph von Graffenried, and Jean Pierre Purry. See also Bern Immigration Records, 1705–49, LC/MD, FCP: Switzerland. A different example is Caspar Wistar, a successful German merchant in Philadelphia who linked up with a newlander to further his business interests (Beiler, "Wistar," 278–80). Waldo's New England settlement project and John Dick's operations to gather and transport settlers for Nova Scotia are especially well documented. See Rattermann, "Geschichte des deutschen Elements"; Erna Risch, "Joseph Crellius, Immigrant Broker"; Brinck, *Deutsche Auswanderungswelle*, 109; and *Journal of the Commissioners of Trade and Plantations*, January 1749/50–December 1753 (1732).

106. For examples of deceptive practices, see Mittelberger, *Journey to Pennsylvania*, 30–31; and Brinck, *Deutsche Auswanderungswelle*, 101–2.

107. Sauer estimated that more than 100 newlanders were ready to fan out of Pennsylvania in 1753 (*Pennsylvanische Berichte*, 16 December 1752); that is about one newlander for every 50 immigrants shipped to Philadelphia at the time.

fected disreputable methods of operation and thereby continued to cause much misery among travelers and to contribute to the strong reaction against newlanders in general.

Overall, agents were an integral part of the emigration process that they exploited to their advantage, although the many honest and responsible newlanders among them provided important and even indispensable services for emigrants. Occasional and small-scale recruiters were often successful in converting potential emigrants into prospective emigrants, but the catalytic role they played could produce a lasting and increasing emigration flow only if the new land continued to be attractive and affordable.[108]

To understand the dynamics that set long-distance migration into motion and kept it fueled over time, it is first necessary to comprehend the diverse forces that impelled people to relocate. Several kinds of circumstances that diminished prospects for a decent or acceptable living at home were crucial. So were the nature and the appeal of opportunities—real or perceived—in foreign lands. Especially important, finally, was how active promotion and recruitment for distant settlement projects triggered or curbed various types of long-range moves.

While, to contemporaries, the decision to emigrate seemed reasonable and acceptable for Rhinelanders who had no place or little stake in the community—such as orphans, children from large families, and men and women who were unable or unwilling to conform to prescribed norms—the relocation of people who were respected, integrated, and useful members of their communities caused official alarm. For such wealthier and well-adjusted subjects to overcome the threshold of inertia and investment that tied them to their homes, there must have been something acutely wrong to impel them to leave, or a very strong lure. Still worse, these influential people not only took their families with them, but also inspired friends and neighbors to leave too.

Emigration from eighteenth-century Germany reflects both kinds of dynamics. Those who felt they had to leave in swift reaction to conditions at home could only choose from currently available terms of settlement and conditions of transportation that seemed best suited to their personal aspirations and particular circumstances or resources at that moment.

108. When German immigrants to Spain found settlement conditions unsatisfactory in the 1760s, a number of them moved on to Pennsylvania, which they knew as a well-established and popular destination for many of their former neighbors in the Palatinate.

Those who were attracted primarily by enticing news from relatives, friends, and former neighbors, or by promising offers from private speculators or foreign governments, were likely to schedule and organize their departure more deliberately. Consequently, the overall pattern of migration from the Rhine lands peaked repeatedly to reflect both incidents of major upheaval and adversity at home and the availability of significant settlement opportunities abroad.

On the local level, such historic waves of emigration were not always discernible, because many territories contributed large numbers of emigrants to those major emigration flows only once or twice during the eighteenth century, while others lost subjects whenever emigration peaked. Bursts of large-scale emigration from particular territories that did take place tended to follow a certain pattern: On the initiative of an entrepreneur or religious leader, a group of colonists explored a new migratory route and found a hitherto unknown place to settle in a foreign land. If settlement conditions in the new area seemed to be satisfactory and continued to be promising, letters to home attracted a wave of relatives, friends, and former neighbors eager to join the pioneering emigrants. This second, substantially larger outflow usually occurred several years after the initial one and then peaked quickly, after which local emigration "fever" subsided, until it resurfaced in a neighboring Rhine territory in the same sequence, with similar results and with some possibility that it would also rekindle emigration where it had occurred before.

Such local waves formed the great overall tide of relocation from the Rhine lands to colonial British North America. The flows and ebbs reflected both the forces that drove inhabitants from the Rhine territories and the appeal of relocating to the New World compared with other resettlement options. These interacting dynamics are familiar to scholars of modern migrations. Throughout the eighteenth century, they also shaped a significant Irish transplantation to America, the dynamics of which, in a less restrictive society that had closer contact and more regular commerce with the colonies, resembled the German pattern in certain ways. Very generally, it was the fit between these repelling and attracting forces, interacting with each other through communication and transportation systems that bridged the Atlantic, that shaped the immigration flow that was so important to the colonies of British America.

CHAPTER 2

The Flow and Composition of German Immigration to the American Colonies

Before 1776, about 111,000 German-speaking immigrants arrived in the American colonies. Like other pre-Revolutionary migrations, this influx of Germans was unevenly distributed. Pennsylvania was the most popular destination for colonists from the Rhine lands, and Philadelphia received the core of the German migration to America. Settlement projects in New England and Nova Scotia created clusters of Germans in those places too, as did an early settlement experiment in New York. Many Germans also went directly or indirectly to the Carolinas. While backcountry counties of Maryland and Virginia acquired substantial German populations in the colonial era, most of these people had entered through Pennsylvania and then moved south.[1]

This first large influx of free white political aliens unfamiliar with the English language occurred in three stages. From sporadic beginnings in the late seventeenth century, the flow gathered considerable strength in the

1. The literature on German migration to the American colonies is neither well defined nor easily accessible. Pertinent materials have to be culled from a large number of often obscure publications that deal in one way or another with German settlements in British America. Emil Meynen's *Bibliography on German Settlers in Colonial North America* is still an indispensable general starting point because it lists the older literature, which provides valuable information even though much of the explanation and interpretation is dated.

The colony of New York was unpopular largely because of the miserable experiences of the Palatines who settled along the Hudson in 1710, as described in Walter Knittle, *Early Eighteenth-Century Palatine Emigration;* and Philip Otterness, "The Unattained Canaan." Klaus Wust's *The Virginia Germans*, and in parts also Robert Mitchell's *Commercialism and Frontier*, are two recent studies that focus on the Germans in the Shenandoah Valley.

second quarter of the eighteenth century, peaked impressively around mid-century, and declined in the two decades before the Revolution. An outstanding characteristic was the large proportion of families immigrating, especially in the early phases of the migration.

Concerns about possible ill effects from an unchecked immigration of strangers led provincial governments to devise measures for controlling foreigners, and such administrative actions make it easier for us to trace the movements of migrants. All colonies required German settlers to register and qualify in some form before they could legally acquire property and pass it on to their children, and the extant registration records allow us today to determine with some accuracy the number of Rhineland immigrants who settled in a given colony and the approximate date of their arrival.[2]

Since Pennsylvania was thorough in monitoring the immigration of non-English-speaking people, the flow of Germans into the Delaware Valley is well documented. When foreign Protestants began to arrive by the hundreds in 1717, Governor William Keith suggested a qualification procedure for registering aliens that became law in 1727 and remained in force throughout the colonial period. Every white male over sixteen years of age entering the province was required to sign oaths of allegiance and abjuration. The resulting lists of immigrants are known as "ship lists," because the names were listed according to the name of the ship on which they arrived.[3] Such lists, however, survive only for Rhinelanders who entered Pennsylvania through the port of Philadelphia on ships whose captains complied with the prescribed procedure.

The importance of the ship lists as sources for information regarding immigration becomes particularly apparent in the literature on English and Irish immigration to colonial America. The size and the composition of these groups of the very earliest English settlers of most colonies is

2. James Kettner, *Development of American Citizenship*, chaps. 4 and 5, discusses the legal aspects and implications of the registration procedures for each colony.

3. Only German immigrants seem to have been registered with some degree of regularity. The ship lists include some non-German names, for example, a number of French immigrants on the ship *Princess Augusta* in September 1736. Since there were so few non-Germans, though, those names were subsumed under Germans; for a case of German names rendered in Spanish, see the ship *Patty & Peggy* for October 1774 (the Appendix to the present book includes a list of all known German immigrant voyages). Only a few of the lists for other, non-German-speaking immigrants from Europe survive. Most important of those is the "Passenger List [1768–72]," HSP.

fairly well known, but the subsequent, larger waves of immigrants from the British Isles generally become apparent only on tax lists, rent rolls, or similar sources—unless the migrants could be easily distinguished because of their particular religion, such as the Quakers, or had a special legal status as servants or convicts. Lists of bound laborers have provided valuable information about the composition and flow of this particular type of immigration and its effect on the development of colonial society.[4] They have also, however, significantly biased what we know about the kinds of people who came to America

Yet such detailed sources exist only for selected British ports of embarkation for occasional periods of time, or in early court records in a few places in the colonies. In contrast, surviving ship lists give the names of all immigrant men on the vast majority of ships that arrived carrying German settlers and often supply additional information that allows us to estimate both the number and the composition of Rhineland migration through colonial Philadelphia.[5] They provide basic information about German-born arrivals in the port of Philadelphia that can be fleshed out with details from other sources.[6]

The first step in analyzing the flow and ebb of German immigrants to Philadelphia is to determine the number of ships that arrived annually with German passengers (see Table 1). Including vessels known to have landed before ship lists were initiated in 1727, German immigration to colonial Pennsylvania can be divided into four distinct periods, across

4. Timothy Breen and Stephen Foster, "Moving to the New World"; Mildred Campbell, "English Emigration on the Eve of the American Revolution"; Gemery, "Emigration from the British Isles to the New World"; Horn, "Servant Emigration"; Galenson, *White Servitude;* and Bailyn, *Voyagers to the West,* are a few examples of the literature on emigration from the British Isles. For a discussion of Irish immigration to the Delaware Valley, see Chapter 5 in the present book.

5. For a detailed discussion of the ship lists, see the introduction in Ralph Strassburger, *Pennsylvania German Pioneers,* ed. Hinke, which is the only complete and reliable edition of the lists and supersedes all other editions for scholarly use (vol. 1: *Introduction and Lists;* vol. 2: *Facsimile of Signatures* [the original lists are in the State Library in Harrisburg, Pa.; this volume was not included in the first reprinted version, which is used for citation here]; vol. 3: *Lists, 1785–1808, and Indices*). Additional details about the ship lists can be found in Marianne Wokeck, "The Flow and Composition of German Immigration," esp. 255–63.

6. The most important of these include: the customhouse notices in the *Pennsylvania Gazette;* Lloyd's Lists; the contracts that bound merchants and captains of German emigrant ships that survive in the notarial archives of Rotterdam and Amsterdam; merchants' accounts in Philadelphia; and immigrant letters. The Appendix summarizes some of that information.

TABLE 1   German immigrant voyages to North America, 1683–1775

	Philadelphia	Nova Scotia	New England	New York	Md./Va.	N.C./S.C.	Ga./La.	Uncertain Destination	Total
Pre-1700	3								3
1700–1709				1					1
1710–1719	5			10					15
1720	2								2
1721	2						7*		9
1722	3			2					5
1723	1								1
1724	2								2
1725	1								1
1726									
1727	5			1					6
1728	3								3
1729	2								2
1730	2								2
1731	4								4
1732	11			1					12
1733	7								7
1734	2			1			2		5
1735	3			1		1	3		8
1736	3			1		1	2		7
1737	7			2		1	1		11
1738	18			1	1		1		21
1739	8			1			1		10
1740	7								7
1741	11					1	2	1	15
1742	5		1						6
1743	10			1	1				12
1744	6			1		2		1	10
1745	1							2	3
1746	3						1		4
1747	8					2			10
1748	9			2		2			13
1749	30	1		1		1	1		34
1750	15	3	1	3		1	1		24
1751	17	4	1	2		1	1		26
1752	27	6	5	5	2	14	2	1	62
1753	21		2	6	2	1		1	33
1754	18			6	1	1		1	27
1755	2				1				3
1756	1			2					3
1757									
1758	1								1
1759									
1760	1								1
1761	1			1					2
1762									
1763	4			1					5
1764	12			1		1			14
1765	7					1			8
1766	5			1		2			8

TABLE 1   (*Continued*)

	Philadelphia	Nova Scotia	New England	New York	Md./Va.	N.C./S.C.	Ga./La.	Uncertain Destination	Total
1767	7								7
1768	4								4
1769	6								6
1770	7								7
1771	9								9
1772	8					1			9
1773	16					1			17
1774	8								8
1775	2								2
Totals	382	14	10	55	8	36	25	7	537

SOURCE:
Appendix.

*Ships with German settlers to French Louisiana.

which the number of arrivals first rose and then declined.[7] In the first period, which lasted from 1683 until the mid-1720s, about 20,000 settlers of German descent had taken up residence in Pennsylvania, likely consisting of some 5,000 immigrants, their American-born offspring, and early migrants who had come from New York.[8] There was a small peak in 1717, when three ships with 363 passengers arrived.[9] The second segment of the migration stretched from 1727 to the peak in mid-century, a period during which the numbers of ships and immigrants increased rapidly. A third and

7. Aaron Fogleman proposes a chronological division of the German flow to colonial Pennsylvania, according to what he sees as the causes of emigration from a European point of view: 1683–1709, 1709–14, 1717–75 (Fogleman, *Hopeful Journeys*, 2). However, the periodization I use here better reflects both the dynamics of the trade that helped Rhineland emigrants relocate to the American colonies and the number and kinds of people coming, including shifts in family status, age, prosperity, and servitude.

8. This is in agreement with Kuhns's summary assessment (Oscar Kuhns, *German and Swiss Settlements of Colonial Pennsylvania*, 52–55). Stephanie Wolf's study of Germantown (*Urban Village*) and James Lemon's analysis of the advancement of settlements in southeastern Pennsylvania, differentiated by national origin and based on the number of taxables (*Best Poor Man's Country*, 42–49), corroborate the notion that before 1727 relatively few Germans came to Philadelphia. For other partial estimates of early immigrants' arrivals, see C. Henry Smith, "The Mennonite Immigration to Pennsylvania."

9. This cluster of alien arrivals triggered the administration's first attempt to ensure that foreigners were properly integrated into Pennsylvania society (*MPC*, 3:29). The proportion of religious dissenters and Separatists was relatively large among these early immigrants, which was a direct result of the difficulties these groups encountered when Karl Philip became Elector of the Palatinate in 1716 (see Chapter 1).

short but important phase consisted of the six successive peak years of 1749–54. From the mid-1750s to the Revolution, the flow of Germans through Philadelphia declined. The number of German immigrant ships reflected the levels of the 1730s and 1740s, but the ships carried fewer passengers, and total migration generally shrank in the period 1755–75 (see Figure 1).[10] Short-term fluctuations around these movements reflect demand for transatlantic passage and the availability of transportation, which in turn were shaped by the ways in which wartime and peacetime affected the safety of travel across the Atlantic.[11] Such fluctuations should be viewed as secondary movements to the principal upward-then-downward trend of German immigration to Pennsylvania.

The numbers and dates of arriving ships are only crude measures for estimating the number of German immigrants entering Philadelphia, for, among other things, they do not reflect the different sizes and capacities of vessels. Fortunately, however, the ship lists provide a reliable count of adult males reaching Philadelphia,[12] and that data can in turn be used to estimate the total number of German passengers, including women and children.

Trends in the numbers of German immigrant men generally resemble patterns in the ships (see Table 1 and Figure 1), and the numbers of women and children immigrating largely followed the basic pattern for German men, although the decrease in numbers in the decade preceding the Revolution was even more dramatic than that for the adult male fellow

10. Figure 1 shows the number of ships in semi-logarithmic scale (Figure 2 displays the number of immigrants in similar fashion).

11. For details, see Chapter 1.

12. The names in the surviving lists are the basis for all calculations here. Additional information about particular voyages in the headings or endorsements of those lists or from other sources has been added. Men whose names were crossed out, those with distinct excluding designations (such as Britons, resident Pennsylvania Germans, or "newlanders"), and those who had died are not included. Boys who had signed but were under sixteen years of age are also omitted. As a consequence, there are differences between my count of German immigrant men and Hinke's count (summary total of the lists [Strassburger/Hinke, *Pennsylvania German Pioneers*, 1:768–76, cols. A, B, and C]). For one brief period in the declining phase of the migration flow, the "Passenger List [1768–72]" provides a record of immigrants into Philadelphia that parallels those published in Strassburger/Hinke. The high degree of agreement between the two listings indicates the accuracy of the ship lists, undoubtedly in part because of the need to calculate and account for the fee collected for the importation of immigrants and servants. Wokeck, "German Immigration to Philadelphia," 266 n. 34, discussed earlier estimates. Table 2 here includes more recently collected additional information in the annual totals. See also the Appendix.

FIG. 1   German immigrant voyages to North America, 1710–1775

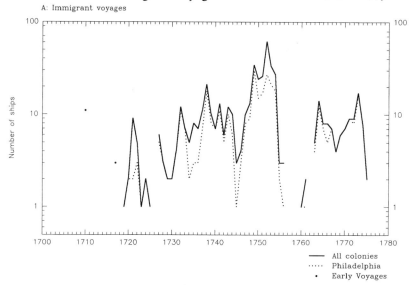

A: Immigrant voyages

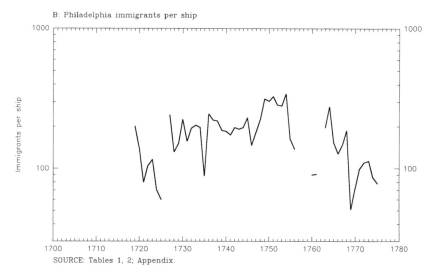

B: Philadelphia immigrants per ship

SOURCE: Tables 1, 2; Appendix.

travelers.[13] When estimates of women and children are combined with the count of men, an overall migration pattern of first rise, then decline is apparent (Table 2 and Figure 2). During the expanding and peak years, 1727–54, the number of arriving immigrant vessels grew steadily, and their passenger-carrying capacity increased too (see Figure 1B). The result was an even greater increase in the flow of immigrants than the number of arriving ships suggests. The yearly influx of Germans began in the late 1720s and rose steadily until immigration was temporarily halted during the Seven Years' War. When German immigration resumed in 1763, it was at a declining rate.

The estimate of 80,969 Rhinelanders entering the port of Philadelphia (Table 2, column 1) serves as an important benchmark for understanding the migration of German-speakers to colonial America and its significance; the calculations of the number of women and children arriving yearly, and the pattern of the German immigration flow over time, provide still more insights. The vast majority of Germans (about 58,000) arrived before 1755, and well over half of those (close to 35,000) arrived during the peak years 1749–54. The individual maximum year, 1749, reflects the end of the War of Austrian Succession, when German immigration could flow freely and safely for the first time in almost a decade. The peak of German immigration passed in the early 1750s, and thereafter decline was an underlying trend, not just the impact of the Seven Years' War. Previous interpretations have based their estimates mainly on the number of ships mul-

---

13. Women and children on arriving vessels can only be estimated, because precise information is scarce. The most complete data available are for 1727–38; a decade of hardly any information follows. From 1749 on, most figures for the number of women and children are provided only indirectly, as part of a ship's total number of "freights" or full fares. A suitable conversion factor can translate the total number of passengers expressed as "freight" into reliable estimates for men, women, and children. Establishing an appropriate way to convert freight into women and children involved several considerations. First, wherever possible, the relationship of the number of freights to the number of women and children had to be established. Freights for women and children before 1749 were calculated on the basis of the average fare structure that pertained through the half-century before the Revolution: half fare for children between five and twelve years of age, and full fare for women and children above twelve years old. After 1749, the ratio between the known number of freights and the known number of women and children was stable. Since the ratio of freight charged for women and children remained about 69 throughout the period 1727–75, a conversion factor of 1.69 or 1.43 for translating the known number of freights into the probable number of women and children on a ship is justified. A reliable estimate for years for which we have no totals for passengers or freight (1739–48, 1752–53, and 1774–75) could be obtained by interpolating the number of women and children for these years according to what is known about the ratio of men to women and children before and after.

TABLE 2 Estimated numbers of German immigrants to North America, 1683–1775

	Philadelphia	All Other Ports	All Colonies
Pre-1700	153		
1700–1709		41	41
1710–19	646	2,335	2,981
1720	242		242
1721	161	1,300*	1,461
1722	314	305	619
1723	116		116
1724	170		170
1725	60		60
1726			
1727	1,198	240	1,438
1728	395		395
1729	300		300
1730	447		447
1731	628		628
1732	2,133	80	2,213
1733	1,431	50	1,481
1734	392	397	789
1735	268	517	785
1736	736	642	1,378
1737	1,553	805	2,358
1738	3,919	822	4,741
1739	1,499	409	1,908
1740	1,288	184	1,472
1741	1,916	222	2,138
1742	981	150	1,131
1743	1,907	291	2,198
1744	1,182	385	1,567
1745	230		230
1746	441	222	663
1747	1,451	374	1,825
1748	2,019	470	2,489
1749	9,435	926	10,361
1750	4,552	2,190	6,742
1751	5,560	1,926	7,486
1752	7,677	8,998	16,675
1753	5,894	2,551	8,445
1754	6,139	1,823	7,962
1755	324	200	524
1756	138	19	157
1757			
1758	90		90
1759			
1760	90		90
1761	91	44	135
1762			
1763	789	10	799
1764	3,298	418	3,716
1765	1,068	200	1,268
1766	641	328	969

TABLE 2   *(Continued)*

	Philadelphia	All Other Ports	All Colonies
1767	1,028	283	1,311
1768	744		744
1769	309		309
1770	505		505
1771	889		889
1772	881	32	913
1773	1,808	53	1,861
1774	686		686
1775	157		157
Totals	80,969	30,242	111,211

SOURCE:
Appendix.

NOTE:
Some estimates for entry ports other than Philadelphia are quite rough: based on annual averages of the total number of immigrants to a particular colony—Georgia, for example—and based on the assumption that the average number of emigrants loaded on ships to South Carolina in the early 1750s was comparable to that on ships to Halifax and Philadelphia.

*German immigrants to French Louisiana.

FIG. 2   **Estimated numbers of German immigrants to North America, 1683–1775**

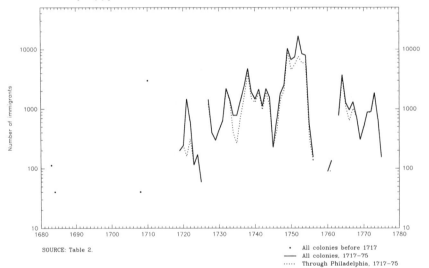

Number of immigrants

SOURCE: Table 2.

•   All colonies before 1717
——   All colonies, 1717–75
·····   Through Philadelphia, 1717–75

tiplied by an average number of passengers per ship. This led some to hypothesize that the Seven Years' War had temporarily dammed the flow of immigration, which became substantial again from the peace until a few years before the American Revolution. More careful analysis, however, shows that fewer men, and still fewer women and children, arrived per ship from the mid-1750s through to the 1770s, despite little decline in the number or carrying capacity of vessels transporting immigrants.

Given these changes in the size and composition of the flow of German immigration to colonial Pennsylvania, one would also expect to see changes in the proportions of settlers who came with families and as individuals, as well as shifts in the age structure. Indeed, the age distribution of German immigrant men did vary significantly over time.[14]

A survey of ship lists that include the ages of passengers reveals fluctuations and variations from ship to ship throughout the period. The age profiles from almost all lists display clustering around ten-year intervals (ages twenty, thirty, forty, and so on) an "age-heaping" that is familiar to scholars of early censuses too.[15] Furthermore, men in their early and mid-twenties consistently outnumber those in their late twenties and older. However, important trends over time provide insights into how the flow of Germans into Pennsylvania swelled then shrank. The age distribution was relatively more balanced in the 1730s, when both proportionately and absolutely more men over the age of fifty immigrated than in the 1740s. The age groupings became especially lopsided in the peak years of the 1750s, when hardly any man older than fifty appears in the lists. This observation supports long-standing descriptions of the German immigration to Pennsylvania that characterize the earlier arrivals as belonging in large part to sectarian minorities, like the Mennonites and Schwenkfelders, who tended to emigrate in congregational groups and extended families, and to other pioneering groups interrelated by familial and communal ties.[16] These tight-knit groups with middle-aged leadership, however, were not very numerous relative to the passenger capacity of most ships. Their numbers were augmented considerably by young men between twenty and twenty-

14. Sixty-three ship lists included the ages of male passengers over sixteen years old, and thirteen of these ship lists gave the ages of all passengers. The information is most abundant for the years 1730–43, although some lists for 1748 and 1753–54 also include this detail.

15. T. Lynn Smith, *Demography*, 152–57.

16. C. H. Smith, "Mennonite Immigration to Pennsylvania," 1–169; Samuel Brecht, *Genealogical Record of the Schwenkfelder Families*.

five years of age and also by some men around thirty who headed very young families.[17]

The relative increase of younger males is quite noticeable during the early peak years of 1732 and 1738, when the largest or most crowded ships transported disproportionately high numbers of twenty-year-old men. Yet increasing proportions of young men, combined with a decline in the number of men over age fifty, became even more typical in the 1740s. At the same time, the number of eighteen-year-olds increased greatly, quite unlike any other phase of the migration. The most likely reason for this was a new conscription law in the Palatinate that did away with the traditional exemption from military service for men engaged to be married or newly wed, allowing only rich young men to buy out of the draft.[18]

The age patterns that survive for the peak years 1753–54 differ from those of both previous decades—significantly so if the ten ships that listed the ages of male passengers then are representative for the years of greater migration. At the point when German immigration to Pennsylvania reached its pre-Revolutionary high, the age profile for men showed a large proportion in their early twenties. Nonetheless, the group of men age twenty-five to thirty gained proportionately, while the number of men over forty is comparable only to that of men in their fifties in the preceding decade. Evidence from individual ships suggests that, by the 1750s, a few vessels specialized in transporting large numbers of men between the ages of twenty and thirty, while others continued to carry immigrant men whose ages were more evenly distributed.

Such shifts in the age structure of arriving German immigrant men provide important information about the process of change in the overall composition of the immigration and the manner in which numbers increased to the 1750s. Unfortunately, the only complementary data on the ages of women and children are for the period 1730–35 (and for one additional ship in 1738), when the age structure of the men was most balanced and atypical, compared with the pattern that prevailed during later, peak years. The distribution of the ages for women in the early 1730s parallels that of men on corresponding ships, although the general level of the

17. For examples, see ships no. 42 and no. 43 in 1736. Fogleman estimates the number of "radical Pietists" (among which he includes the Amish, Dunkers, Mennonites, Moravians, Schwenkfelders, and Waldensians) to be between 3,100 and 5,550 (*Hopeful Journeys*, 103–5, tables 4.1, 4.2). That is less than 5 percent of the total German immigration to the American colonies. Ever since the eighteenth century, these groups have received a disproportionately large share of "the press."

18. *Pennsylvanische Berichte*, 16 December 1747. See also Chapter 1.

women's ages is slightly below that of the men. In particular, most of the names of women in the twenty- to twenty-five-year age-group can be matched with at least one other man's name in the same list. This indicates that many young women traveled as members of family groups, although nothing more specific can be said about the nature of those family ties—for example, whether the women were with husbands, fathers, or brothers.

The distribution of the recorded ages for children shows high clustering in the one- to-four-year age-group, and a pronounced low at five years. This last is almost certainly a result of shipping policies that required half fare at that age. The highest clustering occurs at age eight, and then there is a steady decline until age thirteen. The very few names in the fourteen-to-eighteen age-group are mostly girls' names, because boys over the age of sixteen appear as signers in a different category of passengers. In all, a substantial presence of young middle-aged couples and their children is indicated.

If after 1735 the age distribution of women continued to parallel that of men, the range of their ages would have contracted significantly further, the number of middle-aged women would have declined, and the number of young women in their twenties would have risen proportionately. It seems reasonable to assume that up to the early 1750s many women in the migration were wives and mothers of children. Between the 1730s and 1750s, then, older women and their children, as well as middle-aged men, no longer constituted a substantial portion of the migration.

The decreasing ratio of women and children to men after the 1750s indicates that as the size of the total immigration decreased, its composition shifted significantly. The change in age structure helps establish why the numbers declined: first, immigrants became younger, then they were more likely to be single men. Middle-aged couples became less important and less numerous as the tide of Germans coming to Pennsylvania crested in the late 1740s and early 1750s. Then, as immigration ebbed before the Revolution, Philadelphia became even less attractive as a gateway for settlement in America.[19]

Numbers, sex ratio, and age structure are important factors in establishing a demographic profile of the German migration through Philadelphia determining the impact of this migration on the development of the population of greater Pennsylvania, and for understanding where and how immigrants were likely to fit into their new society. These demo-

19. This can be deduced from the declining ratio of women and children to men, because no data on ages are available for the period after 1754.

graphic indicators, however, can shed little light on the occupations and former residence of the newcomers.[20] The rate of literacy among the men, however, provides an intriguing clue to the general level of education among German immigrants. Judging from the proportion of marks instead of signatures among the names on the ship lists, most men coming from the Rhine lands who were sixteen years or older had had some schooling.[21] In the beginning phase, the percentage of men who could sign their name was relatively the lowest—about 60 percent in the 1730s and 1740s. When the immigration surged about mid-century, the rate of potential literacy increased to more than 70 percent, and in the dozen years before the Revolution it reached a level of about 80 percent for German immigrant men. This suggests that in many of the Rhenish territories the training of a large proportion of young men included some instruction in writing and presumably reading, and that such practice had been widespread for some time and was increasing in the eighteenth century. (A change from a 60 percent literacy rate in the 1730s to an 80 percent rate in the 1770s suggests that some sort of schooling for boys had become much more widespread.) However, it also might mean that, as the tide of immigrants ebbed, the single men came most often from places that provided schooling and were young people with some skill who believed they could succeed in an established labor market.

The lack of comprehensive data about the geographical origins of German immigrants is especially unfortunate because other information contained in the ship lists provides strong but indirect support for a migration in groups. Students of migration, and especially genealogists, have uncovered many intricate and long-standing networks of kin, co-religionists, and neighbors stretching from the Rhine lands to the American colonies. How these various groups were channeled across the Atlantic and then distributed among New World settlements is a story that is still unfolding through painstaking study of local sources that complement the

20. The ship lists contain occasional references to occupations, and several list headings indicate the regions from which the passengers originated, but all such information is rare and not at all systematic.

21. As the lists clearly show, the ease with which newly arrived Rhinelanders affixed their names to the oaths and abjurations varied greatly, ranging from those who labored much over their signatures to those whose penmanship reveals much experience, even flourish. Although the ability to sign one's name has traditionally been considered proof of at least some literacy, the crude nature of some of the signatures suggests that this measure represents the upper bounds for literacy. For an economic interpretation, see Farley Grubb, "Colonial Immigrant Literacy."

ship lists, instead of starting with information provided directly by the ship lists.[22] What the lists do show is a high degree of kinship among German immigrants. About 17 percent of all men who arrived between 1730 and 1750 had the same last name as at least one other man next to theirs on the same ship list. Although the frequency of such relatedness— a very crude measure of family connections among passengers—varied considerably from ship to ship and fluctuated from year to year, before 1750 the trend declined only gradually from its peak in the early 1730s. Because of the patrilineal principle by which German last names are passed on, family connections are only partially evident in simple listings such as these. It is therefore reasonable to assume that between 1730 and 1750 relatives among passengers probably constituted between one-third and one-half of all German immigrants.[23]

A relationship between the high incidence of kin groups among a ship's passengers and the increasingly young age at which men in the 1740s migrated to the American colonies makes it possible to be more specific about changes in migratory dynamics as the flow intensified. While the proportion of men who were related to each other remained relatively stable from the early 1730s through the end of the following decade, the character of those relationships changed from intergenerational to intragenerational. Fathers and sons had predominated in the early periods, but later, as the flow of Germans approached its crest around mid-century, the related males were younger and more likely to be brothers or cousins. On the other hand, the years after 1750, when no ages were recorded, show a different pattern: a marked decline in recognizable kinship ties among German immigrants. This further demonstrates a change in the composition of the flow. There were now more young, single, unconnected individuals who had been gathered independently to form immigrant cargo. From about 1750 on, families and middle-aged people from German-speaking parts of Europe were no longer immigrating to Pennsylvania in increasing numbers, as had been the case in the growth era of the 1730s and 1740s. What immigrants there were tended to be younger, single persons.[24]

22. Recent examples include the work of Annette Burgert (see Bibliography); Fogleman, *Hopeful Journeys*; Häberlein, *Vom Oberrhein zum Susquehanna*; and Roeber, *Palatines*.

23. Three examples demonstrate this: Raymond Bell, "Emigrants from Wolfersweiler Parish"; Hans Pfister, *Zürcher Auswanderung*; and Alfred Kuby, "Die Leute von der Snow 'Ketty'," in Karl Scherer, ed., *Pfälzer—Palatines*, 79–95.

24. Recent studies by Burgert, Häberlein, Fogleman, and Roeber that focus on the importance of networks among settlers, migrants, and place of origin underscore this development; the links between Germans on both sides of the Atlantic were disproportionately anchored in

The ship lists are a unique source of data for determining the kinds of Germans who came to colonial Pennsylvania and when they arrived. There is no comparable information on any other major group of immigrants to any other colony, with the exception of the short passenger list for ships from all European ports unloading in Philadelphia in 1768–72 and the rich record on emigrants from the British Isles just before the American Revolution—which is the foundation for Bailyn's *Voyagers to the West.* The German lists show a migration of just under 80,000 passengers arriving in the Delaware Valley from 1727 to 1775 (indicating that altogether there were about 84,000 from the time Pennsylvania was founded), and a pattern of German immigration that first rose and then fell during the eighteenth century. As the numbers of immigrants climbed, even into the crest of the early 1750s, the ratio of women and children to men on registered ships remained relatively constant, and at the least one-third of all immigrants were related to someone else on the same vessel. To a considerable degree, the flow consisted of settlers who came as families, not just single persons seeking their futures in the labor force of the New World. At the beginning, there were more intergenerational family ties among parents, their grown children, and their grandchildren than during the peak years of German migration through Philadelphia in the 1740s and 1750s. That pattern then was supplanted by a pattern of more family bonds within the same generation or between younger parents and their children. When the number of immigrants was largest, the number of young men and women in their twenties was highest. Thereafter, unrelated single men became more predominant in the migration.

The patterns that can be determined from the ship lists delineate a migratory group that "discovered" Pennsylvania in the early 1700s but then became relatively less attracted to that part of the New World after mid-century. Indeed, more than 80 percent of all German immigrants who came by ship through Philadelphia arrived before 1755, about 50 percent of them during the peak years of 1749–54. The basic qualitative changes apparent in those who continued to arrive after that time show that war was not the factor that slowed the pace of arrivals in Philadelphia during the two decades before the Revolution. Instead, it is evident that the immigration came to a peak in a relatively short period of time in the mid-

---

the 1730s; they were less frequent in the 1750s and rarely demonstrated after the Seven Years' War.

eighteenth century because of more long-term processes in Europe and America.

How much do the flow and composition of the German immigration through Philadelphia reflect the movement of Germans to all the North American mainland colonies? In sheer numbers, the stream to the Delaware Valley represents roughly three-quarters of the total flow, or about 81,000 immigrants through Philadelphia, compared with an estimated 111,000 German newcomers before 1783 (see Table 2 and Figure 2). This important and reasonably accurate benchmark is derived from combining Philadelphia ship list evidence with a wide variety of sources bearing on relocation to other colonies.[25]

Even this best estimate, however, is somewhat misleading for emigration, because the number of people destined for the American colonies was even higher, although it is impossible to gauge just how much higher. Quite a few potential immigrants never actually embarked for America, because they changed their minds and went elsewhere or returned home; others, less fortunate, died en route. Eighteenth-century travel was almost always stressful and hazardous, but it posed additional risks for emigrants who might spend several months in cramped quarters with many fellow travelers and only marginal provisions. Under such circumstances, accidents and disease increased, threatening especially children and people who were already frail or had impaired health. Mortality aboard ship was even higher than during the trip to the coast or while waiting to embark in port, because at sea there was no way to escape infection and other health-

25. The overall estimate is built on Strassburger/Hinke's *Pennsylvania German Pioneers* for Philadelphia and, for the rest of the colonies, on the relevant secondary literature on immigration, systematic gleanings from colonial Pennsylvania newspapers, details of the charterparties registered in Rotterdam, shipping information published in *Lloyd's Lists*, entries in English port books, and incidental information from merchants' accounts and immigrants' letters that add to and corroborate details from those sources about ships and the passengers they carried. Contemporary estimates and listings of ships or passengers provided additional evidence. Drawing an all those sources, I compiled a master list of ships that carried Germans across the Atlantic to calculate the numbers of passengers they carried. The Appendix contains a summary of that list; see also Table 2 and Figure 2.

Since the foundation for this total of 111,000 German-speaking immigrants to the American colonies is new and better data, not just different assumptions about already existing information, it should be preferred to the estimates of Fogleman (*Hopeful Journeys*, 2, table 1.1, 177 n. 5) and of Georg Fertig ("Transatlantic Migration," 202). It also supersedes my own earlier calculation in "Harnessing the Lure of 'the Best Poor Man's Country,'" 104–43, which neither Fertig nor Fogleman considered in their respective discussions of the size of the German immigration flow.

threatening conditions. It is therefore surprising that on some voyages the rate of mortality was actually low—even comparable, it can be argued, to what emigrants would have experienced had they stayed home.[26] Yet many other voyages were unexpectedly long, lacked good or sufficient victuals, or experienced outbreaks of acute and contagious illnesses. Whenever such a disaster struck, many passengers died. Misfortunes of any kind were more likely to occur in years when there was increased migration, when there were more passengers per ship than usual as inexperienced captains and merchants tried to make a profit from the trade. Such misfortunes had a negative effect on the overall rate of mortality. In the single worst year, 1738, the death rate was as high as 35 percent—well beyond the 15 percent average for slave ships.[27] Several spectacular incidents of shipwreck, foremost among them the sinking of one immigrant ship off the Dutch coast in 1754 in which all 468 souls on board perished, demonstrate how variable and unpredictable sea-voyage survival rates could be.[28]

Disaster at sea could strike any ship, and misfortunes did affect how the estimated 30,000 immigrants who landed in colonies other than Pennsylvania in the eighteenth century were distributed. Nonetheless, the pattern of German immigration to colonies north and south of Pennsylvania was distinctive. It reflects the strong lure of the initial settlement, which for some reason failed to generate continuing immigration over the long term. The first such experiment occurred in 1710 and involved the settlement of "Palatines" from the 1709 mass exodus in New York and North Carolina. The second surge, around 1720, which includes the migration of about 2,000 Germans to French Louisiana, basically falls outside the parameters of the German immigration to the British North American colo-

26. Farley Grubb estimated an overall mortality rate of 3.8 percent on ships arriving in Philadelphia with German immigrants from 1727 to 1805—about four and a half times the three-month crude death rate for places in Germany at mid-century ("Morbidity and Mortality on the North Atlantic Passage"). Fogleman, in contrast, found that only one of about 800 Moravian immigrants (or 0.13 percent) died during the voyage—a testament to good planning that minimized risk factors associated with mass travel—and that 1.6 percent of the immigrants in the northern Kraichgau cohort died "at sea" (Hopeful Journeys, 126, 209 n. 38). This compares with a three-month death rate of about 0.8 percent in five German communities in 1750–59 (33 per 1,000 per annum). See Robert Lee, "Germany," in W. Robert Lee, ed., European Demography and Economic Growth, 182, table 4.5.

27. Klaus Wust, "Emigration Season of 1738." In the slave trade, a 15 percent mortality rate for the middle passage seems to be an accepted estimate; an additional 15 percent for the journey to the ports and while in holding for sale and shipment must be added when calculating the risks slaves encountered in their transportation—not counting losses through seasoning in the Americas. Patrick Manning, "The Slave Trade," 115–41, 120–21.

28. Known shipwrecks are included in the Appendix.

nies but conforms to the model of unsustained flows outside the Delaware Valley.[29] In the 1730s, Germans arrived in a variety of ports to settle in Georgia, the Carolinas, and New York.[30] As these pioneers explored widely scattered settlement opportunities outside Pennsylvania, their combined numbers in some years almost equaled the number of immigrants headed for Philadelphia. In the boom around 1740, sporadic direct migration to Georgia and the Carolinas was renewed, and New England too tried to lure foreign Protestants, but overall the numbers were small. When German migration to America peaked between 1749 and 1755, the "spillover" effect in ports of entry other than Philadelphia was most pronounced. During that period, almost 2,400 Germans landed in Nova Scotia; 1,500 in New England; 1,700 in New York; 600 in Maryland and Virginia; 4,300 in the Carolinas; and 500 in Georgia.[31] When migration resumed in 1763, after the Seven Years' War, South Carolina attracted the most immigrants outside of Philadelphia, but in the mid-1760s these arrivals numbered only in the hundreds, rather than the thousands of the peak in 1752.[32] After 1720, Pennsylvania's increasingly numerous and prosperous population of ethnic Germans, and the success Philadelphia merchants had in establishing a profitable trade in German passengers to the Delaware Valley, made Philadelphia the dominant port of entry over other ports.[33]

In comparing the entire transatlantic German migration flow to America with the portion that came through Philadelphia, we see that the attraction of the Delaware Valley clearly dominated the pattern of immigration in terms of both numbers and composition. This is true even though there were some years (1710, 1720, 1735, 1752, 1766) in which other colonies successfully attracted German emigrants, probably mostly families eager to pursue agricultural settlement opportunities that were no longer available in Pennsylvania.[34]

29. Hans Fenske, "International Migration," 344n; Lowell Bennion, "Flight from the Reich," 196.

30. George Fenwick Jones, *Georgia Dutch*, xiii; Robert Meriwether, *Expansion of South Carolina*, 19–26, 34–35; Klaus Wust, *Guardian on the Hudson*.

31. See Appendix. An additional 1,400 emigrants are known to have left Europe, but their ships encountered disasters along the way and few of those migrants made it to America.

32. Janie Revill, comp., *Compilation*; Meriwether, *Expansion of South Carolina*. The ships that carried those settlers could not be identified and therefore are not included in Table 1 and Figure 1.

33. For details, see below, Chapters 3 and 4.

34. Reports about the declining availability of land, especially affordable land, in Pennsylvania began to reach the Rhine lands in the 1730s. Evidence for the preponderance of families among immigrants to colonies other than Pennsylvania is often indirect. For example, adver-

Since Philadelphia played such a dominant role, it is important to know how complete and how accurate the ship lists, arranged by ship and date of arrival in Philadelphia, were. Gleanings from a variety of sources ranging from shipping contracts registered in Rotterdam to Philadelphia newspapers reveal that few ships carrying German passengers escaped Pennsylvania's registry procedure, especially after the trade was well established and the routines had been standardized.[35] For the period covered by the ship lists (1727–75), only thirty-one ships (8.3 percent) were not listed, mostly because they arrived with many sick passengers on board or with too few immigrants to submit to the normal registration procedure.[36] Other ships escaped being included because they were misrouted, wrecked, or encountered other serious problems during the voyage.[37]

As for the question of whether the ship lists were accurate with respect to the number of migrants who actually left southwestern Germany for America, the answer is more complicated. Nevertheless, evidence suggests that a fairly high percentage of the emigrants who arrived in Pennsylvania do in fact appear on the ship lists. The most fruitful and precise approach to matching emigration records with immigration lists is to painstakingly review local records, particularly church records, and that has been done for several areas in Germany.[38] The results show that 90 percent of emigrants headed to America who appear as such in the records of the northern Kraichgau and the western Palatinate can be traced to the Philadelphia ship lists.[39]

---

tisements for settlement projects, such as those in Nova Scotia and New England, solicited families to develop land; lists of applications for headright land in South Carolina include heads of households more often than single persons.

35. See the Appendix for all immigrant voyages to Philadelphia. In 1768, when customs officials kept a list of all the immigrants who landed in Philadelphia as a way to record the duties levied on, and paid for, such newcomers, the clerk first included German immigrants by name in the same manner as for colonists arriving from Irish ports. He soon discontinued the practice, though, noting the total on board each ship according to the lists submitted for the registration of German immigrants. This was a strong indication that contemporaries who had an interest in the revenue generated by immigrants themselves considered the ship lists complete ("Passenger List [1768–72]").

36. For the longer period 1683–1775, some 48 ships (12.9 percent) do not appear among the 324 ships whose immigrant lists did survive, but that number covers four decades of arrivals before registration became mandatory. See, for example, the ships *Rachel*, and *Francis & Elizabeth*, Strassburger/Hinke, *Pennsylvania German Pioneers*, 1:409. See also the Appendix in the present book.

37. See, for example, the arrival of the survivors of the ill-fated ship *Love & Unity* wrecked off New England. Strassburger/Hinke, *Pennsylvania German Pioneers*, 1:57.

38. Notably, the northern Kraichgau and the western Palatinate have been examined by Burgert, *Eighteenth-Century Emigrants* (1983), vols. 1 and 2.

39. The majority of ship lists omit the names of women and children.

Although local records are superior to regional compilations for such searches for German emigrants, documents for the larger geographical units also provide an important, though flawed, collective perspective. Cross-referencing the migrants who are listed in the regional records of Baden and Breisgau as destined for the colonies with the Philadelphia ship lists has identified almost two-thirds as newcomers to the Delaware Valley, and that percentage is probably substantially too low because the names of women and children are greatly underrepresented on the ship lists.[40] Based on the regional records of the Rheinpfalz and Saarland, only one-third of the emigrants who indicated they were going to America are positively known to have taken the route through Philadelphia.[41] The reasons for such regional distinctions may simply reflect differences in record-keeping, but they also remind us that Philadelphia, though the predominant choice, was not a uniformly popular destination.[42] Following the lead of successful local pioneers, certain areas in the Rhine lands exhibited distinct preferences for a particular American colony or settlement, such as the emigration from the Canton of Zurich to South Carolina.[43] However, aside from the approximately one-quarter of the migrants who went elsewhere, the percentage of relocating men who disembarked in Philadelphia and appear in the ship lists is high. Consequently, the ship lists can reveal much about the nature of the total eighteenth-century German flow across the Atlantic and its changes through time.

The composite picture based on the German ship lists for the Delaware Valley, along with comparable and complementing information about Rhineland immigrants at other North American ports in the eighteenth century, reveals a significant flow of foreigners seeking to capitalize on opportunities to work and acquire land in the New World. Although the influx of German immigrants from 1683 to 1783 was considerably less than the seventeenth-century population movement of mostly English people across the Atlantic, and substantially less than the importation of enslaved

40. Hacker, *Auswanderungen aus Baden und dem Breisgau.*

41. Hacker, *Auswanderungen aus Rheinpfalz und Saarland.* Again, the percentage of Pennsylvania immigrants may also be too low because women's and children's names were underrepresented on the ship lists, but the difference between results for the two regions remains significant.

42. Bureaucratic requirements about recording the planned destinations of migrants varied from region to region and across time; individual officials interpreted such requirements differently; and migrants could be vague, if not untruthful, about their intentions.

43. In the 1730s and 1740s, the emigrants from Zurich were drawn to Carolina, not Pennsylvania. See Andreas Blocher, *Die Eigenart der Zürcher Auswanderer;* and Pfister, *Auswanderung aus dem Knonauer Amt.*

Africans to North America in the colonial era, the 111,000 colonists from the Rhine lands constituted the first large wave of free political aliens unfamiliar with the English language and customs who made a lasting impact on American society and culture. This flow of immigrants was uneven in its intensity across time and in its distribution among the ports of the eastern seaboard. After slow beginnings, it gathered strength in the 1730s and 1740s and flowed most forcefully around mid-century, when more than half the transplantation occurred, ebbing thereafter. The flow was most concentrated to Pennsylvania and to the inland areas for which Philadelphia was a gateway. The substantial proportion of families among the newcomers provided Rhineland immigrants with a strong base from which to grow and become American. Kinship and familiarity were also links that kept immigrants connected to their homelands. Such ties led to a marked local clustering of German-speaking settlements across the American colonies.

The significance of Philadelphia as the most popular port of entry for German immigrants to the American colonies is twofold. First, after a slow start, Philadelphia's dominance in the German passenger trade remained unsurpassed for five decades, from the 1720s to the 1770s. Although William Penn's successful promotion of his province in the 1680s had stimulated similar approaches in several other colonies, only Pennsylvania succeeded eventually in drawing a steady and growing number of Rhineland immigrants. Second, Pennsylvania's solid reputation for opportunity, the willingness of those already settled to help newcomers start their new life, and the ability of some Rotterdam merchants and their Philadelphia "correspondents" to adapt the English system of transporting indentured servants to fit the distinctive characteristics of the German migration to make it a profitable part of their complex trade all came together to create a system that allowed large numbers of emigrants of limited means to move to the New World.

CHAPTER 3

The Trade in Migrants

For the most critical part of the journey to the New World, German emigrants bound for the American colonies had to rely on merchants who could provide transportation across the Atlantic. Over the course of the eighteenth century, arranging such transatlantic passage developed into a highly specialized business. Shipping emigrants was a complicated endeavor that involved many different interests on both sides of the ocean. The focus here is on the organization of this trade, from its incidental beginnings to a standardized and routine service that merchants offered as one part of their diverse commercial ventures. Merchants devised this service as a profit-making venture, but emigrants from the Rhineland also benefited, because it enabled many ordinary people to come to the New World.

Organizing the trade in German emigrants required the cooperation of merchants in the ports of Rotterdam, Amsterdam, and Hamburg; in London, the center for English trade and credit; and in the ports of the American colonies, especially Philadelphia, New York, and Charleston. It developed in three distinct phases. Through the first third of the eighteenth century, much of the trade was casual, but in the late 1730s and 1740s transporting passengers across the Atlantic became commonplace and regular—especially in the late 1740s and early 1750s when it became a large and competitive enterprise. After the French and Indian War, that trade continued to be regular but was reduced in scale. Throughout, merchants in Rotterdam helped shape the business by providing the human freight.

They also arranged for the outfitting and provisioning of the ships and managed the voyages from the continent via England to American ports of destination. Their partners and "correspondents" (informal trade partners, which whom merchants corresponded in order to conduct their business, such as handling cargoes or ships, usually on a commission basis) on the other side of the Atlantic, especially in Philadelphia, were responsible for defining and overseeing procedures for unloading ships freighted with immigrants and their baggage. As the trade matured, settling accounts with passengers, captains, and shippers became increasingly complex, and many responsibilities that were critical for the success of the business shifted to the ports of debarkation.

Merchants in London, Rotterdam, and Philadelphia worked together to make the voyages of vessels sailing between Europe and the American colonies more profitable. Since their interests were primarily in other commercial activities—most often trade in provisions or dry goods, or general investment in ships and shipping—they shared a desire to benefit more from the westward run of ships and from transporting emigrants to the New World. In managing these voyages from Europe to America, however, each of these merchant communities had distinct interests and tasks, and over time the significance of each merchant community changed.

Arranging voyages for passengers from continental Europe to North America was complicated business involving many different people and including many steps. Of the four European ports from which German emigrants regularly left to settle in the New World—Amsterdam, Hamburg, London, and Rotterdam—the latter was by far the most common place of embarkation. Rotterdam dominated the trade because its port was relatively easy for emigrants from the Rhine lands to reach and in part because several Rotterdam merchants had connections in Philadelphia, where most German migrants wanted to go. London was an alternate point of departure for Germans and also played a significant role in the passenger trade. The constraints of the Navigation Acts, which stipulated that only British-owned and operated vessels could engage in the trade between England and her overseas colonies, ensured that London would be important as a ship provider and broker. "Ships are commonly hired here for the voyage from London to Holland, New England, Philadelphia, New York, and Nova Scotia," wrote Samuel Waldo from London in the 1750s.[1] Amsterdam and Hamburg too were ports of embarkation for em-

---

1. Waldo, a New England merchant and land speculator who had an interest in a ship

igrants, especially those from territories in northern and eastern Germany, such as the Schwenkfelders, Moravians, and miners from the Harz mountains. Compared with Rotterdam, however, few passengers left from those ports.[2]

The trade in German emigrants evolved in three phases. In the early years, from Pennsylvania's founding in the early 1680s through the early 1730s, almost all Germans bound for the American colonies traveled in organized groups. These groups often consisted of co-religionists following the lead of a pioneering settlement promoter who made the arrangements for the voyage. The first organized transport group of colonists from the Rhineland, who had taken William Penn up on his invitation to settle in his province in 1683, availed themselves of the network that linked Quaker merchants on the continent, in England, and in the Delaware Valley. Francis Daniel Pastorius and the Krefelders negotiated with James Claypoole to carry them and—their families, servants, baggage, and household goods from London to Philadelphia.[3] The transportation contracts that survive for the first two decades of the eighteenth century provide evidence that this was typical.[4] The contracts (or, to be more specific, the charterparties) entered into the records of the Rotterdam notaries over the course of the century also show the many details involved in negotiating and arranging for transatlantic passage to suit each situation. Many contracts involved emigrants and shippers who belonged to religious minorities, mostly Quakers and Mennonites. And in the early 1700s there was considerable variation in destination, fare price, number of passengers, and victualing.[5] As increasing numbers of German emigrants sought trans-

---

involved in the German immigrant trade, gave this characterization of the practice of chartering vessels to transport emigrants in 1752 (quoted in Rattermann, "Geschichte des deutschen Elements").

2. Lisbon, Le Havre, and Marseille were other European ports from which Germans emigrated to the New World, but that traffic was never a regular part of the German migration flow westward. The list of immigrant voyages in the Appendix includes the ports of embarkation and arrival.

3. Marion Balderston, ed., *James Claypoole's Letter Book*, 196–201, 210–33; see also Craig Horle and Marianne Wokeck, eds., *Lawmaking and Legislators in Pennsylvania*, 1:586–92.

4. Transportation contracts, or "charterparties," were commonly registered with a notary, a municipal official. The records of Amsterdam and Rotterdam notaries have survived in the massive archival collections of the respective municipalities. In Amsterdam, Samuel Hart identified and indexed the records that pertain to the British North American colonies; in Rotterdam, the old notarial archives are indexed (by notary, contracting party, vessel, destination, and cargo). This description of the organization of the trade in German emigrants is based largely on records in the notarial archives and on merchants' letters and accounts. The list of immigrant voyages in the Appendix includes information uncovered about charterparties.

5. Examples are GAR, ONA, 2090/316 (13 July 1719), *Royal George*; 2095/445 (21 July 1721),

atlantic transportation in the 1730s, this early, incidental way of procuring ships for emigrants for some merchants in Rotterdam evolved into a regular business activity, for which those shippers established standards and routines.

During the beginning phase of the trade in emigrants, the usual ways of finding ship passage for Germans intent on settling in the American colonies proved inappropriate or inadequate on at least three occasions. The first and most serious deviation from the typically casual pattern occurred in 1709, when thousands of Palatine Protestants streamed into Rotterdam expecting ready, and free, passage to America. Overwhelmed by this large influx of German emigrants, municipal officials turned to the States General of the United Provinces of the Netherlands and the English authorities for help in dealing with the refugees. As a result of the difficulties and expenses arising from trying to meet the needs of those in transit to England, Rotterdam authorities took steps to prevent poor German emigrants from being stranded in and around the port and becoming a burden to Dutch taxpayers.[6]

A dozen years later, in 1722, several "transports" of German emigrants ("transports" was the term used to describe those groups at the time) again overtaxed normal business procedures for transatlantic passage, because some had left Koblenz to relocate in the American colonies without making sufficient preparations or having the means for the move. This time the English envoy refused support for emigrants who did not have an invitation to settle in the American colonies and who were not welcome in Holland because they were impecunious from the start or had become impoverished on their way to Rotterdam.[7] Circumstances were different for emigrant transports that enjoyed government backing and whose plight caught the public's compassionate eye. The Protestant refugees from Salzburg fell into that category; Dutch authorities granted them free passage through the Netherlands on their way to embark for Georgia in 1733.[8]

Such support and generosity did not extend to more ordinary emigrant

---

John & Catherine; 2096/333 (2 July 1722), 2316/169 (14 July 1722), *Greyhound;* 2098/232, 233 (9 June 1723), *Weerelkloot* (Globe); 1529/53 (20 June 1725), *York of Bristol.*

6. Copies of the complaints and negotiations in Rotterdam are included in the Dutch West India Company Records, Dutch Copies of Letters, 1678–1792, HSP.

7. Archief Hof van Gelre, Memorie- en resolutien boeken, no. 34, 555 (20 July 1722); Archief Staten Veluwe, Kwartiersrecessen, no. 80 (1 July 1722).

8. Archief Hof van Gelre, Memorie- en resolutien boeken, no. 37: 316 (22 January 1733), 369 (7 May 1733). See also application for passports for Salzburger emigrants in 1735, 38:28–29 (6 April 1735); and Jones, *Georgia Dutch.*

groups from Switzerland and Germany, although merchants Archibald and Isaac Hope received a government subsidy to ship Swiss emigrants stranded in Rotterdam to Pennsylvania.[9] By 1735, the local authorities in the Netherlands could see that the existing regulations needed tightening. The states of the United Provinces that bordered German territories, and those from which German emigrants left for England on their way to North America, instituted measures that barred poor emigrants from entering the Netherlands—a clear message that Dutch resources were not to support indigent foreigners trying to reach overseas destinations.[10]

The States General, in cooperation with provincial and municipal governments that had a vested interest in protecting their citizens from potential problems and costs arising from the transit of emigrants from Germany, passed laws regulating the transfer of German migrants bound for America. These regulations were first systematically implemented in 1735, then reiterated and refined in 1739 after a year of heavy emigrant traffic that caused many problems. They were reissued essentially unchanged in 1764, adjusted to include pedestrian border crossings in 1765, and remained in place until the migration flow to the American colonies came to a halt in 1775 with the outbreak of the American Revolution.[11]

The regulations were simple. At Schenkenschanz, the fort on the Rhine that guarded the Dutch border, and at other crossing points, only travelers who presented valid passports could continue their journey, and only emigrants who could present positive proof of arrangements for transatlantic passage were allowed to board boats to Rotterdam. All boats transporting German emigrants had an escort of two to four soldiers to keep immigrants from running off or being left behind. Merchants in

9. The Hopes received Fl 2,000 for this service. Benjamin Furly, long a supporter of William Penn and Pennsylvania, had vouched for the Hope company when it entered the business of providing transatlantic transportation for German emigrants. Archief der Gemeente Rotterdam (s.v. *landverhuizers; emigranten*), microfilmed as LC/MD, FCP: Netherlands, reel 2:4–26, 38–42, 57 (20, 24, and 30 December 1734, April 1735). The organization and fate of the transportation of emigrants—mostly from Zurich—under the leadership of Moritz Goetschius is detailed by Pfister, *Zürcher Auswanderung.*

10. *Resolutien von den Heeren Staaten van Holland en Westfriesland* and *Resolutien von de H[oogh] M[ogende] H[eeren] Staaten General der Vereinigte de Nederlandsche Provincien* (published annually with the names of the petitioners indexed) (hereafter *States General, Resolutions*); Archief Hof van Gelre, Memorie- en resolutienboeken, no. 38: 27–28 (6 April 1735), 29–30 (10 April 1735).

11. *States General, Resolutions* (29 April 1739); Archief Hof van Gelre, Memorie- en resolutienboeken, nos. 38: 27–28 (6 April 1735), 29–30 (10 April 1735), 39:76–77 (27 May 1739); 50:261–62 (10 July 1764); Oud-Archief van Arnhem, inv. no. 3672; Archief der Gemeente Rotterdam (LC/MD, FCP: Netherlands, reel 2:1 [3 July 1764]); College of the Admiralty of the Maas (4 and 6 July 1764; 28 October 1765), Algemeen Rijksarchief, The Hague.

Rotterdam and Amsterdam had to apply to the States General and to regional and local authorities for permission to "transship" emigrants from the eastern border to their respective ports. Permission was granted when the necessary fees were paid and the required bond was posted. Merchants also had to guarantee that the emigrants would be taken directly to vessels ready to sail and had to vouch their person and goods (that is, were personally liable) if they did not comply with the required measures for preventing delayed or stranded emigrants from becoming a problem for local authorities.[12]

The legal constraints on transporting emigrants from the German border to Rotterdam or Amsterdam had far-reaching consequences for the organization of transatlantic passage. During most of the first four decades of the eighteenth century, merchants, Rhine shippers and boatmen, emigrant transport leaders (persons in charge of organizing and guiding groups of emigrants), and individual migrants headed for the North Sea ports in Holland and applied for and received free passage through the Netherlands, providing always that they could present the requisite papers and guarantees, and arrange and pay for the military escort that the law demanded for travelers in transit.[13] After 1738, when German emigration had soared and strained resources and patience in several of the United Provinces, the regulations were enforced more strictly and the procedures became more complex.[14] Expecting more and more emigrants, and seeking ways to streamline procedures, the firms of Francis Trimbel, Ward Stanton, and John Stedman followed the example of Archibald and Isaac Hope and began to petition the states and provincial governments for free passage through the Netherlands by thousand.[15] Merchants who entered the busi-

12. Petitions for transshipment of German emigrants have survived in *States General, Resolutions;* Archief Hof van Gelre, Memorie- en resolutienboeken, Geemente Archief Arnhem; Gemeente Archief Rotterdam (LC/MD, FCP: Netherlands); and Oud-Archief van Arnhem, Commissie- en politieboeken der Stad Arnhem, Gemeente Archief Arnhem. They form the basis for discussing the procedures that prevailed for the journey from the Dutch border to the port of embarkation.

13. For an example of a petition by Archibald and Isaac Hope for free passage of 300–400 well-to-do Swiss emigrants and for a transit application by Willem van Walsem, captain of a flat-bottom Rhine boat, see *States General, Resolutions* (20 April 1735).

14. Many of the German emigrants who crowded into Rotterdam to await transportation to the American colonies found temporary shelter in Kralingen under cramped and unhealthy conditions. For details, see Wust, "Emigration Season of 1738"; and *States General, Resolutions* (13 May 1738—Kralingen), and the resolution about a new burial place for emigrants who died en route (microfilm, "Emigranten," reel 2:6, 61, LC/MD, FPC: Netherlands [20 June 1737]).

15. Contrary to the views of some contemporaries, no company had a monopoly in transporting emigrants, as the records in Rotterdam and Amsterdam clearly show. Farley Grubb

ness later joined them in applying for transshipment of such large numbers of migrants. By the middle of the century, some merchants were applying for free passage for as many as 3,000 emigrants at a time, although the Rhine boats employed to carry migrants to Rotterdam did so in much smaller increments, in groups of forty, fifty, sixty, or more per boat.[16]

The flow of German emigrants across the border can be traced in part through the careful records made by officials at Arnhem, who tallied the number of passes each merchant who had established an "account" of one, two, or three thousand passes had used.[17] They also kept track of the payments merchants had made to defray the costs of providing the military escort that accompanied each boat carrying emigrants in transit.[18] Since the transshipment of German emigrants required considerable planning and expenses, merchants focused on three strategies to help them secure as many migrants as efficiently as possible for their ships in Rotterdam. They used recruiting agents and such incentives as credit to purchase passage and to get a competitive edge, and they relied on their representatives in Gelderland to expedite bureaucratic requirements at the border.[19]

reached the same conclusion indirectly from evaluating much more limited evidence that survives for Philadelphia ("Market Structure").

16. The Hopes had received permission to transship 1,000 German emigrants in 1735 (Oud-Archief van Arnhem, Commissie- en Politieboeken der Stad Arnhem, 55:394–95, Gemeente Archief Arnhem). *States General, Resolutions* (13 May 1738: Francis Trimble, Rotterdam merchant—free passage for 1,000 migrants; 3 February, 29 April, 16 June 1739: Ward Stanton, Rotterdam merchant—free passage for 2,000 [in the later petitions 1,000] migrants; 29 July, 17 August 1739: John Stedman—free passage for 1,000 migrants).

17. The "List of Palatines Who Left Rotterdam to the Various Destinations (in the English Colonies of America)" is another tally, although it shows some rounding of the numbers (Minutes of the Council, Archieven der Admiraliteitscolleges 31, no. 239:5–18, Algemeen Rijksarchief, The Hague, LC/MD, FCP: Netherlands).

18. For example, see the entry that lists the transports of one merchant, probably for Daniel Harvart, in 1751–53 (Oud-Archief van Gelre, inv. no. 3672). The Commissie- en politieboeken der Stad Arnhem, 55–67 (1736–73) (Oud-Archief van Arnhem, Gemeente Archief Arnhem) are rich sources for the particulars of the transshipment procedure. Although the entries vary considerably over the decades, a typical entry may name the shipper who brought emigrants from Germany to Schenkenschanz; the merchant who applied for the emigrants' free passage, including the date(s) of the petition(s); the name(s) of the merchant's commissioner(s) who appeared before the town's council according to the requirements of the 1735 resolution; the name(s) of those who posted bond for the merchant in compliance with the 1739 resolution; the amount paid to defray the costs of the military escort of the boat(s) through the Netherlands; the number of boats; and the number of immigrants.

19. For example, Nicolas Oursel, a Rotterdam merchant, advanced money to emigrants (GAR, ONA, 2699/175 [26 September 1752]; power of attorney [folio]); and John Dunlop & Company and John Dick, both English merchants in Rotterdam, made recruiting contracts (GAR, ONA, 2698/210–12 [4 December 1751]; 2698–225 [27 December 1751]).

By contrast, one-time or small-scale operators found it difficult to enter or stay in the business, because they lacked the necessary capital and connections.[20]

The requirements regarding transit through the United Provinces favored merchants in Rotterdam and Amsterdam whose network of correspondents included contacts not only in London and the English Channel ports but also in the principal towns of the inland province of Gelderland, and they benefited those who maintained regular dealings with Rhine shippers.[21] Applications for free passage across the Netherlands cost money, required familiarity with federal, provincial, and local bureaucracies, and entailed a considerable amount of bookkeeping. Providing security in compliance with the law required ready access to financial and legal resources, and to post bond in the western border province called for associates who could deal with the local authorities. Moreover, the logistics of transporting emigrants through the Netherlands depended on the agents at the border stations, who facilitated communications and hence planning. These agents supervised the loading of boats with emigrants and their baggage, the provisioning of the travelers during transit, and delivery of the human freight to oceangoing vessels at Amsterdam or Rotterdam. Rhine shippers and boatmen who regularly conducted business with the Rotterdam and Amsterdam merchants involved in the emigrant trade often provided those specialized services.[22]

At the height of the emigration flow in the middle of the eighteenth century, however, competition among merchants was stiff, and that led them to engage additional recruiting agents to procure passengers and ensure smooth operations when transferring migrants from the German border onto their ships.[23] When German emigration resumed after the end of

20. Heinrich Keppele, a German immigrant and merchant in Philadelphia, and Captain George Parish, of the *Queen of Denmark*, circumvented shipment through the Netherlands by using Anthony Simpson, an English merchant in Hamburg, as their contact and correspondent in seeking and freighting German emigrants. See Brinck, *Deutsche Auswanderungswelle*. On Keppele's mercantile networks more generally, see Roeber, *Palatines*, 123–24, 248.

21. On the importance of correspondence networks, see Jacob Price, "Transaction Costs," 279–81.

22. In addition to the entries about the boatmen who delivered parcels of emigrants into the hands of Amsterdam and Rotterdam merchants in the Arnhem Commissie- en politieboeken, evidence for this connection has also survived for Amsterdam—for instance, in GAA, NA, 10305/317 (9 July 1737), *Townshend, Molly;* 10305/339 (18 July 1737), 10310/402 (18 July 1737), *Anna Galley;* 10306/390 (4 June 1738), *William*.

23. The most comprehensive was an arrangement between Jacob Frederic Curtius and John Stedman and Hope Company (GAR, ONA 2779/108 [14 May 1751]). John Dunlop &

the Seven Years' War, effective networks for handling the administrative side of transshipping migrants were already in place, and the logistics had been worked out and had become routine.[24] What did change during the dozen years preceding the American Revolution was that a smaller number of emigrants sought transshipment and that the migration flow was temporarily rerouted through the Netherlands in response to Prussia's policy of closing its Rhine territories to all emigrants.[25]

If money, connections, and organization made for success in the border operations of the emigrant trade, those characteristics were also critical in loading emigrants onto ships bound for the American colonies. Merchants in the Dutch ports played that crucial role in the trade. Three very different components were required for a profitable voyage: a suitable ship, the proper outfitting and provisioning of the ship, and freighting the ship with passengers. Arrangements for a mandatory stopover in England and for unloading the ship in the colonies were extensions of plans freighters made in Amsterdam or Rotterdam in concert with their correspondents in England and America. As with procurement and transshipment, established and well-connected firms had an edge in the freighting portion of the business. Good management and good timing were crucial. Most merchants who were involved in regularly providing passengers with transatlantic transportation started out with interests and experience in shipping, most often in the provisions trades. As ship owners and freighters, their business was to carry cargo that would earn them a profit, and the same ships they used for transporting tropical woods, tobacco, rice, indigo, and flour eastward were used again to carry German emigrants westward, as supplementary cargo to fill space on ships that otherwise would have sailed in ballast or perhaps with only a partial load of dry goods.[26]

Company contracted with three different agents (GAR, ONA 2698/210–12 [4 December 1751]), while John Dick, the British agent for the Nova Scotia settlement, agreed with Gottlieb Tobias Köhler as his recruiting agent in Germany (GAR, ONA 2698/225 [27 December 1751]).

24. Some merchants who applied for free passage in the 1750s did not deplete their "accounts" of transit passes by the time German emigration virtually came to a stop in the later 1750s. For example, the "account" of the Hopes carried over well into the 1760s before the firm had to apply for additional passes (*States General, Resolutions* [15 and 29 May 1765]).

25. Kleve (Cleve), the territory bordering the Netherlands to the east, belonged to Prussia at that time. Archief der Gemeente Rotterdam, OSA (1769), College of the Admiralty of the Maas.

26. The charterparties registered in Rotterdam, as well as the entries in the port books in England, provide ample evidence of the merchants' interests in the provisions trade and of the varied uses of ships they owned or managed. GAR, ONA 2334/137 (28 June 1740), *Bolton;*

As businessmen, the merchants in Holland pursued the trade in German emigrants for profit, and as the emigration flow swelled and the business became more regular, certain features of the operation became standardized. Merchants could use their experience in business both to address—things that went wrong and to capitalize on situations and procedures that proved profitable.[27] The basic formula for success was simple. The more emigrants that could be shipped per vessel, the greater the profit for the freighter, so merchants expanded and intensified their efforts to attract emigrant cargoes, streamlined their operations, and guarded against competitors and circumstances likely to reduce profits. In the late 1740s and 1750s, business soared and attracted several newcomers seeking to share in the profits. When immigration to the American colonies resumed at reduced levels in the 1760s, however, the trade was dominated by a handful of merchants, who even in the face of scaled-back demand for passage continued to profit from transporting German emigrants to North America as part of their shipping operations. (See Table 3 [A] and the Appendix.)

In the early years of the German trade in emigrants, most vessels were chartered in London, although later a substantial proportion of passenger ships were Philadelphia built, owned, and operated. This meant that merchants based in Rotterdam or Amsterdam had to have regular business connections in London and Philadelphia if they were to arrange suitable ship charters. More important, they needed reliable information about the availability of ships in order to arrange to have vessels arrive in Holland in time to make proper preparations for the embarking Germans. Without suitable vessels, they could not load and thereby recoup the expenses in-

2335/59 (17 July 1741), *Thane of Fife*; 2335/158 (14 July 1741), *Margarett of Aberdeen*; 2720/42 (25 April 1744), *Aurora*. Cust(oms) 61/1 (reports/accounts to commissioners of ships, Cowes, December 1749–July 1754, PRO, London [28 March, 10 April 1751]); Cust(oms) 61/2 (Cowes, July 1753–March 1759 [25 July 1753], *Two Brothers*; licenses for rice [1 February 1755], *Rowand*; *Friendship*; *Patience*; *Neptune*); Cust(oms) 61/4 (Cowes, 1769–74, especially the entries dealing with George and James Mackenzie, rice merchants). Evidence for merchants' interest in the dry-goods trade is in port books for Deal, Dover, and Plymouth, E(xchequer) 190, PRO, London (Chancery Lane), where a typical entry for dry-goods merchant Isaac Minet Jr. reads: "arrived from South Carolina with rice, barrel staves, planks; continued to Amsterdam; returned to England to clear large quantities of cloth, thread, paper, wrought iron, brimstone, brass wire, glass, millstones, cordage, chimney backs, passengers' baggage" (6/9 July 1737, *Molly*).

27. For example, Thomas Clifford, a Philadelphia merchant who wanted to fill cargo space on the westward voyage with immigrants and servants from England, corresponded with the Hope Company of Rotterdam and took their advice about how to recruit German emigrant craftsmen for the Philadelphia labor market. See Grace Larsen, "Profile of a Colonial Merchant," 111–24.

curred from collecting and transshipping emigrants from Germany. And if the emigrants could not embark, the merchants would incur costs for housing and feeding them. Furthermore, the regulations that governed shipping and transferring goods between the American colonies and England required that most of the vessels stop in an English port before anchoring in Rotterdam or Amsterdam to be readied for the embarkation of passengers.

Activities of the London-based firm of John Hunt & Isaac Greenleafe, both of whom were Quakers who maintained close relations with the Pembertons, also Quakers, in Philadelphia, provide some details about the supply of ships for transatlantic passage at the height of emigration from Germany.[28] During the winter of 1748/49, news circulated in London that large numbers of German emigrants would be seeking transportation from Rotterdam to Philadelphia in the coming spring. Hunt, who had never before transported German immigrants, acted on this information and contacted John Stedman, an English merchant residing in Rotterdam, offering to provide him with a suitable ship if he could procure enough full-fare paying passengers (referred to as "freights"). Soon after, Hunt followed up on his initial offer, assuring Stedman that he was "fully determined in the affair," especially since he had found another ship that he could hire at the reasonable rate of seven pounds per ton and that, in his judgment, met the trade's specifications even better than the first ship. At the same time, Hunt inquired about the advantages and practicalities of an early departure date, even if it was not the earliest departure of the season. That would mean scheduling the vessel's dispatch to Rotterdam for arrival by the end of March or the beginning of April. Providing his correspondent in Rotterdam with information about the size and build of the ship,

28. The following description is based on letters in John Hunt & Isaac Greenleafe, London, Letter Book 1747–49, HSP (John Hunt to John Stedman, 3 January, 14 and 24 February 1748/9; to John Pemberton, 27 February 1748/9; to John Crell, 28 February 1748/9; to John Stedman, 3 March 1748/9; to Israel Pemberton, 6 March 1748/9; to John Stedman, 10 March 1748/9; to Isaac & Zachary Hope, 20 March 1748/9; to John Stedman, 20 March 1748/9; 7 April 1749; to I. & Z. Hope, 7, 13, and 18 April, 23 May 1749; to Captain Michael James, 13 April, 9 May 1749; to I. & Z. Hope, 9 and 23 May 1749; to John Pemberton, 30 May, 1749; to George Mackenzie (Cowes), 30 May 1749; to Capt. James, 30 May 1749; to I. & Z. Hope, 30 May 1749; to John Pemberton, 28 May, 6 June 1749; to I. & Z. Hope, 9 June 1749; to John Pemberton, 2 July 1747) and in the Pemberton Papers, 5:96, 102, 127, 154, 150; 6:28, 67, 162; 7:7 HSP (James Pemberton to John Pemberton, 24 and 30 May, 5 and 6 June, 8 July 1749; John Hunt to James Pemberton, 11 and 24 July 1749; John Hunt to Israel Pemberton Jr., 5 May 1750; James Pemberton to John Pemberton, 17 August 1750; John Hunt to James Pemberton, [5 May 1750]; 15 December 1750). These letters tell us much about how the trade was organized, but information about the final accounting did not survive.

TABLE 3   Merchants involved in the German migrant trade to North
America, 1730–1775

A. Merchants in Rotterdam and Amsterdam involved in the German emigrant trade, 1730–1775:					
Name of Merchant or Firm Appearing More Than Once[a]	Year(s) of Operation	Known No. of Ships Freighted	Percentage of Ships Freighted	Estimated No. of Emigrants Loaded	Percentage of Emigrants Loaded
Benezet, Pierre [Amsterdam]	1754	5	3	1,646	4
Clarkson, Levinius [Amsterdam]	1737	3	2	630	2
Crawford (James & Patrick)	1764–73	24	16	4,427	11
Curtius, Jacob Frederic	1751–52	2	1	1,330	3
Dick, John	1750–52	9	6	2,259	5
Dunlop (John & Robert)	1750–53	8	5	2,002	5
Harvart, Daniel	1750–54	6	3	1,653	4
Hope (Archibald; Isaac; Zacharias)	1722–63	20	12	4,072	10
Oursel, Nicolas	1723; 1752	8	5	2,709	7
Rocquette & van Teylingen	1752–54	6	3	1,953	5
Stedman, John	1736–54	47	27	12,572	31
Stewart, Alexander	1745–47	4	2	790	2
Wilson, William [= captain]	1743–44	2	1	526	1
Subtotals		145		36,572	
		(171)		(40,780)	

Hunt was also eager to find out from Stedman how many passengers the
ship could transport and how much each freight would pay for passage.
His determination in the matter was further evident in a letter he wrote to
Joseph Crell, a German shopkeeper and printer from Philadelphia who
had a keen personal interest in promoting German settlement in the
American colonies.[29] Crell had been a fellow passenger of Isaac Greenleafe
on a memorable voyage from Philadelphia to Europe in 1748, during
which the ship was captured by a French privateer and payments for
Greenleafe's release were transferred with the help of John Stedman. Hunt
acquainted Crell, who was traveling in Europe as a newlander, with his
plans and urged him to recommend this ship to any of his friends and
compatriots who wanted to go to Philadelphia. Better still, Hunt suggested, the German shopkeeper might set an example by choosing this
ship for his own return voyage.[30]

Being new to the emigrant trade, Hunt also consulted knowledgeable
people in London about the number of passengers the ship could conveni-

29. John Hunt to Joseph Crell, 28 February 1748/9, Hunt & Greenleafe Letter Book. Crell
appeared as principal agent for the New England settlement project in Maine, documented at
considerable length in Rattermann, "Geschichte des deutschen Elements."

30. Crell's interests, however, had shifted from Pennsylvania to New England, where he
became involved in recruiting German Protestants for settlement in Maine. See Risch, "Joseph
Crellius, Immigrant Broker."

TABLE 3 *(Continued)*

B. Merchants in American colonies involved in the German immigrant trade, 1730–1775[a]		Immigrant Ships Belonging/Consigned to Merchant/Firm		Immigrants on Ships Belonging/Consigned to Merchant/Firm	
Name of Merchant or Firm Appearing More Than Once[b]	Colony and Year(s) of Operation	No.	Percent	No.	Percent
Andrew, Alexander	Pa. 1738–43	4	1	944	2
Austin & Laurens	S.C. 1751	2	1	650	1
Benezet, Daniel	Pa. 1753–54	6	2	1,970	3
Christie, James	Md. 1771–73	2	1	236	<1
*Curtius, Jacob Frederic	Pa. 1751–52	2	1	930	1
*Fisher, Joshua	Pa. 1753–74	6	2	763	2
Gray, Thomas	Pa. 1765–71	2	1	197	<1
Howell, Samuel	Pa. 1752–74	14	5	3,176	5
Inglis, Pickering & Wraxall	S.C. 1752	2	1	500	1
*James [& Drinker & Warder]	Pa. 1756–64	2	1	250	<1
*Keppele [& Steinmetz]	Pa. 1752–75	12	5	2,258	4
Lawson [& Johnson]	Md. 1752	3	1	900	1
McCall, John	S.C. 1752	2	1	625	1
Pemberton, James & John	Pa. 1749–70	5	2	1,565	
Penrose, Thomas	Pa. 1738–41	4	1	695	1
Ritchie, Robert	Pa. 1773–74	2	1	616	1
*Ross, John	Pa. 1766–73	3	1	103	<1
Ruecastle, Robert	Pa. 1764–65	6	2	1,582	3
Searle, James	PA. 1764	2	1	216	<1
*Shoemaker, Benjamin & Samuel	PA. 1734–70	54	21	15,804	27
*Stedman, Charles & Alexander	PA. 1736–53	44	17	11,097	19
Strettle, Robert (& Amos)	PA. 1742–49	6	2	1,457	2
*Warder [& Parker]	Pa. 1755–73	5	2	164	<1
*Willing [& Morris]	Pa. 1753–73	22	9	4,168	7
Wolstenholme	Md./Pa. 1752–53	2	1	600	1
Subtotals		217 (255)		52,167 (58,339)	

SOURCE:
Appendix.

NOTE:
The subtotals in parentheses include the number of voyages and passengers, respectively, of the merchants who engaged in the German immigrant trade only once.

*Firms owning vessel(s) that were registered in Philadelphia and that carried German immigrants at least once.

[a]In addition to the 11 merchants who are known to have freighted ships with German emigrants more than once, 26 other merchants could be identified as shippers (see Appendix). Moreover, other Dutch listings concerning the German emigrant trade attest to the involvement of other firms that could not be connected with the freighting of particular ships: Ward Stanton, Francis Trimble.

[b]The total of 255 ships that had identifiable importing merchants does not include ships consigned to the colonial governors of New York and Nova Scotia or ships chartered or owned by the Moravians to organize their own transatlantic transportation. Some 6,072 immigrants traveled on the 38 ships that carried German settlers for a particular importer only once (10 percent of the total number of immigrants on ships whose importers are known).

ently carry and how many provisions would be necessary. He then based his computations for provisions on current Rotterdam prices for "rice, beef, butter, oatmeal, bread etc." After receiving the comparable calculations from Rotterdam, Hunt made his offer more specific, stating which provisions he would provide directly from London and which items Stedman should acquire on the continent, where such goods were customarily purchased with cash or on short credit and where the commission for such services was 2 percent.[31] Dispatch of the vessel depended on agreement about all relevant terms of the venture by both merchants. In this particular case, Hunt was unwilling to accept Stedman's terms regarding consigning the ship to Stedman's brother in Philadelphia. He himself was committed to James Pemberton, who was visiting in London at the time and was a partner in the ship's run. Consequently, Hunt dropped Stedman and approached another well-established merchant house in Rotterdam, Isaac & Zachary Hope, whose interest in emigrant transport was already documented as early as 1721, when Benjamin Furly stood security for the Archibald Hope firm.[32] Hunt used a mutual business partner for introduction and recommendation. Isaac & Zachary Hope agreed to procure the desired freight, and the ship, laden with tobacco, was sent to Rotterdam, where it was supplied with 330 immigrant freight and all provisions except bread, water casks, and medicines. The captain, Michael James of London, had instructions to follow the directions of the Hopes in all matters concerning the German passengers, and then to proceed to Cowes,[33] where he was to make contact with one of Hunt's business partners to get his final instructions before setting out on the ocean crossing. Upon arrival in Philadelphia, the captain was to take the medicine chest and all other

31. The tabular listing of the provisioning of the Palatines in 1751, 1752, and 1753 (Archieven der Admiraliteitscolleges XXXI, no. 239:9–23; on microfilm, LC/MD, FCP: Netherlands) gives a good idea of the kinds and quantities of victuals that were involved. See Price, "Transaction Costs," 279, 292, on the payment for goods and commissions customary in the Netherlands.

32. Charterparty of the *John & Catherine* (GAR, ONA 2095/445 [21 July 1721]). In the early years of the trade, when demand for transatlantic passage was low and sporadic, Hope was the only merchant firm in Rotterdam that provided such services for German emigrants—a monopoly more defined by little need for transportation than the firm's dominance of the trade. John Stedman entered the business when the numbers of emigrants seeking passage increased.

33. The charterparty between the Hopes and Michael James could not be found, but three other agreements between the firm and captains in that year indicate similar terms, although those ships were smaller than the *Crown* (*Good Intent*, GAR, ONA 2745/147 [5 June 1749]; *Reinier*, GAR, ONA 2745/154 [16 June 1749]; *Patience & Margaret*, GAR, ONA 2144/124 [28 August 1749]).

items belonging to Hunt off the ship and report to the Pembertons for further orders.

Hunt's experience shows how the terms set by the Rotterdam merchants could complicate and frustrate operations for owners or lessees of vessels intended to carry emigrants. In 1737, a Mr. Bragg wanted to send his ship freighted with German emigrants to Carolina, where he had interests, but the Hopes insisted that Philadelphia was the only acceptable destination—not because they had no business connections in Charleston but because only their Philadelphia correspondents were set up to handle the unloading of immigrant cargoes.[34] Sebastian Zuberbühler, a professional emigration agent who conducted German migrants to the Carolinas in the 1730s and to New England in the 1740s, was forced to pay a high price to provision and outfit a ship to transport German passengers to Maine, because it was late in the season and he was dependent on the services of the English commission merchants in Holland.[35] Although John Hunt was able to negotiate with the two major firms in Rotterdam in the first year he was involved in the trade, dissatisfaction with the services the Hopes provided, and disappointment with the way they did business with him, caused Hunt in the following year to decline any offers from fellow London merchants concerning another German immigrant shipment.[36]

The Rotterdam merchants were in an ideal position to impose their terms on nonresident ship owners and merchants who wanted to fill their vessels with profitable freight for a route on which cargo space was often underutilized. Many of the goods carried from London to the American colonies were dry goods of considerable financial value but relatively little bulk.[37] Also, as Hunt put it, the profits from the transportation of Palatines seemed particularly promising when the Philadelphia market was glutted with dry goods.[38] Many other ships destined to load tobacco, rice, or flour in the American colonies normally left England in ballast and

34. "Report on the Petition of Kieffer and Others, 9 September 1737," PRO, London, SP 42/138, published in part in Elizabeth Kieffer, "The Cheese Was Good," 28.

35. Sebastian Zuberbühler to Samuel Waldo, 5 July 1742, in Rattermann, "Geschichte des deutschen Elements," 14:57; for the charterparty for the *Lydia*, see GAR, ONA 2336/149 (25 July 1742). See also *Journal of the Commissioners of Trade and Plantations from January 1734/5 to December 1741* (London, 1930), 8 February 1736/7; 3 and 5 May 1737; 17 and 31 August 1737; 12 and 21 April 1738.

36. John Hunt to James Pemberton, 15 December 1750, Pemberton Papers, 6:162, 7:7.

37. Thomas Doerflinger, *A Vigorous Spirit of Enterprise*, 82–97.

38. John Hunt to John Pemberton, 27 February 1748/9, Hunt & Greenleafe Letter Book.

would therefore profit from taking on cargo for the westward voyage. Especially at times when there was consistently high demand for transatlantic transportation, Rotterdam merchants sought to capitalize on their middleman role in manipulating the supply of shipping, in procuring a desirable but limited cargo, and in providing other services in connection with outfitting and loading ships on a commission basis. The advance knowledge they had about the demand for transatlantic passage, and their exclusive access to the German emigrants, was crucial in this respect. The Holland merchants received information about the flow of emigrants—such as how many people wanted to go, when, and what types of migrants were involved—from their own agents in Germany, foremost among whom were the Rhine shippers with whom they maintained regular communication networks. Profits for the Rotterdam merchants were almost guaranteed, as long as the supply of vessels was plentiful and competition among freighters was limited.

The gradual increase in the demand for immigrant transportation to the American colonies before 1749 allowed two Rotterdam firms and one Amsterdam firm to dominate the trade. None of the merchants held a monopoly on the trade, however, as the charterparties recorded by the cities' notaries, and the records detailing the transshipment of emigrants through the Netherlands, clearly indicate; there is even evidence that the merchants cooperated when it suited them (see Table 3[A]).[39] The Hope merchant house (Archibald, Isaac, and Zachary combined into different companies that constituted the firm over time) provided passage for German emigrants from the early 1720s well into the 1760s.[40] Before John Stedman moved from London to Rotterdam in the late 1740s to engage heavily in the trade as a merchant, he was involved in transporting migrants as captain and part-owner of emigrant vessels in the 1730s. His

39. Some contemporaries mistook the regulations that governed the transshipment of emigrants from Germany through the Netherlands to be exclusive authorizations for the transatlantic transport. One such misinterpretation of procedures occurred in 1736 ("Petition of Kieffer," 27), and Christopher Sauer perpetuated and populated that misconception in his letter to Governor Robert Hunter Morris about the abuses in the trade in the 1750s. Quoted in Frank Diffenderfer, *German Immigration*, 240. See also Wust, "Emigration Season of 1738," 24–25; and Grubb, "Market Structure."

40. The duration of the Hopes' involvement in the immigrant trade is evident in the Dutch records (*States General, Resolutions;* charterparties and other legal records in GAR, ONA; transshipment records in the Gemeente Archief Arnhem) and also in mentions of the firm in immigrant letters. For a description of the Hope family and firm up to the 1770s, see Marten Buist, *At Spes Non Fracta*, 3–13; for their ties to the Quaker merchant elite, see Jacob Price, "Emergence of the Great Quaker Business Families."

career in the immigrant trade can be directly traced through his appearance as a captain in the ship lists (see Appendix, ships no. 15, 20, 32, 36, 47, 62) and as a part-owner of immigrant vessels built and registered in Philadelphia. His brother Charles had been a captain too, before he, together with yet another brother, Alexander, settled as merchants in Philadelphia in the late 1740s. Portions of the Stedmans' business activities are evident in their appearance as consignees of immigrant ships, as owners of immigrant vessels registered in Philadelphia, and as investors in Stiegel's furnace in Lancaster County, for which they procured German immigrant labor.[41] After the hiatus in the trade forced by the French and Indian War, Charles Stedman no longer invested in German emigrants, instead taking up insuring ships in this and other trades.[42]

The merchant houses of Hope and Stedman set the tone in the emigrant trade and provided the bulk of immigrant shipments to the American colonies, mostly to Philadelphia. In the 1730s and 1740s, they first established and then streamlined procedures for managing passenger ships, which included granting credit on some fares. Those operations are well illustrated in the contracts the shippers negotiated with captains of vessels they chartered when the number of ships they owned and managed regularly was not enough to satisfy the demand for transatlantic passage. They can also be traced, at least in part, through accounts of the merchants who received the cargo in the ports of the American colonies. The typical sequence for managing emigrant ships began with preparations for readying and loading the vessel. Outfitting and provisioning were the shipper's responsibility, as was filling the ship with emigrants—the last a prerogative meant to discourage competition from other, new merchants, captains, and recruiting agents working for their own accounts.[43]

The Rotterdam merchants and their counterparts in Amsterdam provided two kinds of services for their London and Philadelphia correspondents or partners and for landowners and speculators—and their agents—who were eager to win settlers for their patents and projects. One service was securing human cargo for a ship's run; the other had to do with the final outfitting and provisioning of the vessel according to the agreement, with adjustments for the actual number of freights procured.

41. John McCusker, "Ships Registered at the Port of Philadelphia."
42. Edwin Perkins, *American Public Finance and Financial Services*, 289.
43. Charterparties with captains who owned part or all of their vessels differed from those who did not, as the example of Robert Brown of the *Albany of Glasgow* (GAR, ONA 2344/63 [30 May 1749]) shows.

Obtaining the desired number of passengers for a ship depended largely on a merchant's ability to predict realistically his share of the supply of emigrants during that season and to time the flow from the Rhine lands. Ships that were idle in port drained merchants' resources, as did emigrants awaiting departure, because they consumed provisions planned for the voyage and yet might leave to sail on another ship.[44] As a result, clauses regarding the number of days allowed in port for loading and unloading—and the fines in case of time overruns (demurrage per diem)—were an important component in the contracts merchants made when chartering ships, engaging a captain, and signing up passengers. As in other trades, merchants became increasingly interested in shortening the turnaround for ships and therefore raised the penalties for time wasted.[45] In response to this pressure to increase efficiency, merchants, masters, and emigrants used all possible, and sometimes unfair, means to avoid late fees—or, worse, charges arising from breach of contract.[46]

Arrangements for water, sleeping spaces, fireplaces, kettles, and other necessities for the emigrant ship were contingent on the availability of these items in the desired quantity and quality at or near the port, and on whether delivery and loading could be accomplished on relatively short notice. The logistics of outfitting emigrant ships were quite formidable, because they required subcontracting for many different services that involved a variety of people, each striving to make a profit in a market niche that was not regulated and that therefore tolerated—even encouraged—

44. Transshipment regulations required that passengers be provided with food and drink once they had arrived in port. The notarial archives include a number of protests that charge emigrants with breach of contract because they left or signed up with another freighter (GAR, ONA 2325/174 [18 July 1731], *Britannia*; 2326/147 [8 July 1732] *John & William*); as a consequence, the Hopes' transportation contract released emigrants from their commitment if they paid for expenses they had incurred up to that point.

45. Economic historians have observed this measure of increased productivity in other trades over the course of the eighteenth century: Gary Walton, "Sources of Productivity Change"; Ralph Davis, "Maritime History," 180; Richard Dell, "Operational Records of the Clyde Tobacco Fleet," 5. The charterparties reflect this trend for the German migrant trade. Port time was cut from ten weeks in the 1730s to four to five weeks before 1775. Shortening the time it took to load and unload passengers meant that the preparations for embarkation and debarkation had to be well planned and well coordinated, and that added to the responsibilities of freighters in the European ports and their correspondents in the American ports.

46. For example, Sebastian Zuberbühler saved his employer, Samuel Waldo, from having to pay demurrage money to emigrants when, at their expense, he deliberately delayed transporting them from Germany because he had heard that the ship he expected had not yet arrived in Rotterdam (Rattermann, "Geschichte des deutschen Elements," 15:110).

cutting corners, exploitation, and outright fraud.[47] Many merchants undoubtedly tried to keep provisioning costs low by calculating tightly the
amount of daily rations for each freight as well as the projected length of
sailing time for which victuals were required.[48] Providing low-quality food
and drink was another way merchants could, and did, economize, as passengers and other contemporary observers noted.[49] Inferior provisions and,
especially, bad water could have devastating effects on the health of the
passengers, however, and were therefore not in the interest of shippers,
who relied for profits on landing with immigrants alive and healthy.

The profits of merchants involved in transatlantic emigrant transportation
increased proportionately with the number of freights per ship—that is,
the number of full-fare passengers, which was the unit used for most calculations in this trade. Whenever the flow of Germans swelled to fill more
than just a few ships per season, but particularly during the emigration
peak of 1749–54, all Rotterdam and Amsterdam merchants with either an
established or a new interest in the trade strove hard to attract as many
emigrants as they could in order to increase not only their profit margin
but also their shares in this valuable market. The result was growing competition among merchants, which in turn influenced business practices
regarding how emigrant vessels were freighted and the way in which recruiting was conducted.

The size of vessels employed in this trade had direct bearing on the
number of freights that could be shipped. The first vessel John Hunt
described as suitable for carrying German immigrants measured 64 feet
long at the keel, 10½ feet wide in the hold, and 44½ feet high between
decks and was judged to be a ship that had excellent accommodations for

47. John Dick's account of preparing vessels for transporting immigrants to Nova Scotia
provides some good illustrations. See *Journal of the Commissioners of Trade*, January 1749/50–December 1753 (June–July 1751).

48. According to some early charterparties, provisions were calculated on the assumption
that they had to last for fourteen weeks (GAR, ONA 1529/53 [20 June 1725] *York of Bristol*;
2325/174 [18 July 1731] *Britannia*). Later contracts stipulate that leftovers be delivered to the
merchants' correspondents in the American ports, which suggests that not all shippers
skimped on the amount of victuals (for example, *Friendship*, GAA, NA, 10269/471 [2 June 1754];
and *Good Intent*, GAA, NA 10269/490 [5 July 1754]). See also Penrose Cashbooks for provisions
received from German immigrant ships (15 January 1750/51).

49. Attesting to this custom are "The Case of the Palatine Protestants who are ship'd from
Rotterdam to Philadelphia and Carolina in America in the Months June and July [1750],"
Pennsylvania Miscellaneous Papers, Penn & Baltimore, 115, HSP; and "Petition of Kieffer," 28–
29.

passengers.[50] However, the *Crown*, his later charter, a strong ship built on
the Thames River and a prime sailer—was even more suitable for the
trade and appreciably larger in dimensions: 103 feet long between decks, 4
feet 10 inches high between decks fore and aft, 25½ feet wide with cabin
and steerage 50 feet long and 5 feet 10 inches high, and a quarter-deck of 50
feet. It was calculated that the *Crown* could carry more than 400 freights
easily, which puts that ship among the 10 percent of ships known to have
arrived in the colonies with that many German passengers.[51]

All ship owners and freighters wanted to fill their ships, so passengers
were usually crowded together, along with their baggage, victuals, and
other goods, often far beyond the well-being and even the sensibilities of
eighteenth-century people who were already accustomed to cramped spaces.
During the peak emigration period, and to a lesser extent also in the peak
years of 1738, 1764, and 1773, all merchants practiced tight packing. There
were, of course, differences in degree, even at the height of German immigration to the American colonies, when virtually every merchant accepted
relatively large numbers of passengers per ship. For example, John Hunt
instructed his captain and crew to vacate their usual quarters and live in a
shack on deck to make room for more passengers. Other merchants did
not even provide each full-fare passenger with a bunk space, so that passengers had to sleep on deck or wherever they could find room. Whatever
the methods of crowding, such practices were possible only when the actual number of emigrants awaiting shipment at a given time was sufficiently large enough to put pressure on available space. With many prospective passengers standing by for transportation, it was easier to induce
passengers to accept crowded conditions on board. The average numbers
of passengers per ship follow the now-familiar division into three distinct
periods of German migration. The ratio of passengers per ton indicates
that the increased number of emigrants during the peak years were mainly
handled not by providing more ships but by squeezing more immigrants
into each ship.

During the early years of steadily increasing German immigration, an
average of five passengers filled every four registered tons. Although registered tonnage is a poor measure for the cargo stowage-capacity of a vessel,

50. The *Good Intent* of London measured 75 feet from stem to stern; 22½ feet from out to
out; 9 feet deep in the hold; 4 feet high between decks before the main mast; and about 34 feet
abaft length of the quarter deck (GAR, ONA 2745/147).
51. The ship *Crown* probably registered around 220 tons. See John Hunt to John Stedman,
24 January, 14 and 24 February 1748/9, Hunt & Greenleafe Letter Book.

it is the only available consistent measure of ship size that can be used to detect at least relative change over time. Cargo capacity was typically at least twice the registered tonnage.[52] Using this measure, British troop transports during the Seven Years' War allowed considerably more room per soldier and gear (2⅔ cargo tons) than the German immigrants were granted in the 1730s and early 1740s.[53] The optimum rate figured by slave-ship owners was two-thirds of a cargo ton per slave, which was less crowding than German emigrants experienced at the height of the immigration, when two passengers might be squeezed into the cargo space each registered ton provided.[54] It is important to remember that although German immigrants were not in chains they did travel with children and baggage, and that slave ships, on the other hand, carried a relatively small number of children, so storage space for personal belongings was not as important.[55] In the peak immigration years (1749–54), merchants practiced very tight packing in order to maximize profits from transporting human cargo. Conditions for emigrants improved considerably, however, during the twelve years before the Revolution, when the number of German emigrants seeking transatlantic transportation declined significantly.

The arrangement of passenger accommodations was the basis for all calculations concerning a vessel's capacity for human cargo. The bunk space for each full freight was commonly specified to be 6 feet long and 1½ feet wide. A ship of the *Crown*'s dimensions would yield a maximum of a little more than 200 such spaces between decks—regardless of whether the bunks were arranged lengthwise or crosswise—with just enough space between them to allow passengers to get in and to reach the hatchways. The actual arrangement of sleeping platforms took advantage of and worked around the ship's interior structural elements, such as support beams and masts. On the same principle, the cabin and steerage could provide room for about another 100 comparable spaces. Additional berth space could be obtained by constructing an upper tier of bunks in the cabin and other areas of the ship that offered sufficient headroom. Freighters gained additional space by making use of the space normally occupied by the captain's

52. John McCusker, "Tonnage of Ships Engaged in British Colonial Trade," 90.
53. N. A. M. Rodger, *Wooden World*, 60–61.
54. Herbert Klein, "Economic Aspects of the Eighteenth-Century Atlantic Slave Trade," 2:304–5; and "New Evidence on the Virginia Slave Trade," 873, table 1; Du Bois Slave Ship Data Set, preliminary presentation of selected findings at the annual meeting of the Social Science History Association, Chicago, September 1995.
55. The tonnage figures for this comparison are given in McCusker, "Tonnage of Ships," 94.

and crew's quarters. In 1765, Pennsylvania legislation against abuses in the immigrant trade required that a bunk be 3 feet 9 inches high (2 feet 9 inches in the steerage), to clarify an earlier law that had stipulated only the length and width of each berth.[56] The lodgings on some ships were fitted out to accommodate two passengers in an "apartment" or "cabin," with hammocks for beds.[57] Others offered firm sleeping platforms constructed of removable boards in a loose lattice pattern for four, or even more, full freights.[58]

Although careful refitting of a ship to carry emigrants could increase cargo capacity significantly, and although merchants in their quest for profit were usually guided by their most immediate vested interest, it was good practice to use some restraint in packing passengers. Not only would healthy immigrants be much more likely to complete deferred passage payments upon arrival in the American colonies, but they would also find masters more easily, should indenture be the way fares were paid for.[59] Simply put, live, healthy cargo was worth more. It was therefore also good business for the freighter to construct privies and ventilation pipes as part of refitting vessels for passengers; those improvements were considered indispensable on naval ships and hence became standard around mid-century.[60] However, not all merchants had a strong interest in delivering German immigrants alive and in good health in the American colonies. Shippers whose primary goal was to deliver a contingent of freights for a price arranged in advance had little reason to be choosy about the kinds of emigrants with whom they contracted for the voyage, the quality of provisions they gave them, and the arrangements on board ship. The situation was different for merchants who freighted their own ships or expected to participate repeatedly in the emigrant trade, and for American land developers and promoters, all of whom gained if they could land immigrants in good financial and physical shape.

While calculations concerning cargo capacity for emigrants were negotiated between merchants in Holland and nonresident ship owners or other

56. James Mitchell and Henry Flanders, comps., *Statutes at Large of Pennsylvania from 1682 to 1801*, 5:94–97, 6:432–40.

57. Charles Baird, *History of the Huguenot Emigration*, 1:186–87.

58. Passengers' financial accounts, arranged by cabin, on board the ship *Nancy* (see "Redemptioners," HSP).

59. Heinrich Melchior Muhlenberg made this observation in *Hallesche Nachrichten*, 997–1012.

60. For example, GAR, ONA 1529/53 (20 June 1725), *York of Bristol*; 2747/147 (20 June 1752), *Kitty/Catherine*; see also Rodger, *Wooden World*, 106–7.

investors interested in the trade, the actual procurement and loading of emigrants from Germany were usually the prerogative and responsibility of the freighter.[61] Essential for a profitable run was a filled ship, and because a reliable supply of emigrants was critical for their business, merchants in Rotterdam and Amsterdam turned to active recruiting to secure cargoes for the vessels they owned or operated, especially at the height of the emigration in the mid-eighteenth century, when many newcomers to the trade vied aggressively to obtain a share of the emigrant market.[62] Competition for German emigrants arose from many different quarters. It included merchants like John Hunt and his American partner, James Pemberton, who were interested in obtaining cargo from firms already established in the trade; entrepreneurs like John Dick, who secured a government contract for the transportation of German emigrants to Nova Scotia; the Rotterdam company of Rocquette & van Teylingen, which counted on gaining a share by winning settlers for South Carolina; Henry Keppele of Philadelphia, who banked on success in the business by circumventing the Dutch Channel ports altogether in favor of Hamburg as the port of embarkation for emigrants from newly opened areas of recruitment in northern Germany; and captains like George Parish, who had gained experience in the service of the Stedmans but could arrange more favorable terms for himself with another shipper.[63]

61. In a few instances the merchant contracted with a shipowner, investor, or captain who could load passengers on his account (for example, GAR, ONA 2747/97 [18 May 1752], *Rowand*).

62. Brinck's study of the peak of German emigration describes many of the manifestations of this competition but it does not uncover the nature of the divergent business interests that developed from the surge in the demand for transatlantic transportation and that pitted established merchants and newcomers against one another in the rush to profit from it.

63. John Dick's operation to recruit and transport emigrants for settlement in Nova Scotia is especially well documented. See *Journals of Commissioners of Trade and Plantations*, January 1749/50–December 1753 (multiple entries between 22 December 1749/50 and January 1752/53); GAR, ONA 2693/87 (1 May 1751), *Speedwell*; 2693/90 (5 May 1751), *Gale*; 2698/119 (19 June 1751), *Murdock*; 2698/120 (19 June 1751), *Pearl*; 2699/100 (13 May 1752), *Gale*; House of Lords Library (Correspondence about Settlements, 1749–52), LC/MD, FCP: Great Britain: Nova Scotia. See also Winthrop Bell, *The "Foreign Protestants."* Jacques Rocquette and Peter Theodorus van Teylingen established connections to South Carolina and were also prepared to transport emigrants to other colonies (GAR, ONA 2747/107 [26 May 1752], *Nancy*; 2747/123 [12 June 1752], *Neptune*; 2747/135 [20 June 1752], *Kitty/Catherine*; 2747/154 [26 July 1752], *John & Mary*; Walter Dulany to Rocquette & van Teylingen [29 December 1752], Dulany Papers, MS 1265, Box 2, Maryland Historical Society). Heinrich (Henry) Keppele established connections in Hamburg (Brinck, *Deutsche Auswanderungswelle*, 39, 151; see also Appendix). Captain John Mason, who contracted with Rocquette & van Teylingen, had sailed for the Hopes before and came recommended by them (GAR, ONA 2747/123 [12 June 1752], *Neptune*).

Established merchants adopted two primary strategies in their quest to get more emigrants to choose to travel on their ships. One was to expand an already established network of business contacts with boatmen of the Rhine waterway system; the other was to engage recruiting agents to solicit emigrants for transportation on ships belonging to a particular merchant. The overseas merchants' close cooperation with the Rhine boatmen paid off, because the latter provided reliable information, had experience with the critical transportation routes, and had ample opportunity to steer emigrants in the direction of a particular merchant. The boatmen could easily access and operate at the major collecting points along the Rhine and its tributaries and, especially after 1738, at the customs and inspection station at the Dutch border. Rotterdam and Amsterdam merchants therefore began to arrange with the boatmen to provide emigrants with river transportation on special terms. Although this service added to the merchants' cost, it may have been considered a relatively small expense if it could generate or guarantee a desirable number of emigrants ready for transport at the right time.[64]

The boatmen's interest in recruiting emigrants for travel on their river crafts was fueled by the price set for each freight delivered to a particular merchant. As in the case of the port merchants, the profits of the Rhine boatmen rose in proportion to the number of emigrants they could sign up to make the trip down the Rhine with them. Johann Philip Buch, a Wertheim boatman, received just over nine pounds sterling (Fl 100), or not quite five shillings per head, in return for soliciting thirty-eight well-to-do emigrants for the Hope company in 1754.[65] Other shippers and recruiting agents were said to be compensated at a rate of eight or nine shillings, and sometimes even more, for each passenger who could pay the fare for transatlantic passage.[66] The rate merchants paid for the emigrants delivered depended on two factors: the degree of competition among merchants, which varied considerably from year to year and fluctuated during each season, and the quality of the prospective passengers—those who could pay for their fares were usually more valuable to freighters than those to whom they had to extend credit to enable them to make the voyage.

When the Rotterdam merchants decided to employ recruiting agents in addition to the Rhine boatmen with whom they were already cooperating, they knew that the successful immigrant who returned to his former

64. A late example of such cooperation includes GAA, NA 13500/801 (2 June 1764).
65. Yoder, *Pennsylvania German Immigrants*, 168–70.
66. Rattermann, "Geschichte des deutschen Elements," 14:324, 346; *Pennsylvanische Berichte* (16 September 1749).

place of residence to fetch remaining family or friends, to settle inheritance matters, or simply to visit and brag was most persuasive and effective in drawing others to follow in his steps. The merchants therefore tried to take advantage of the newlanders' power to entice emigrants by offering free return passage to those who would convince their relatives and former neighbors to take passage on a specified ship. Daniel Harvart's proposal to newlander Johann Christian Schmitt, and John Hunt's suggestion to Joseph Crell to direct his friends onto the *Crown*, are two such examples.[67] Most of those arrangements, however, seem to have been informal and on a case-by-case basis.[68] Evidence of this recruiting practice indicates that it was valuable to the Rotterdam merchants, despite the irregularity and unreliability inherent in a system that made use of largely incidental business contacts.[69] An added bonus for the merchants who hired newlanders was the fact that these agents could be called upon to act as transport leaders and interpreters. Such services could be especially valuable in negotiating contracts and explaining unfamiliar procedures on board ship. At the height of German emigration, some merchants new to the trade, such as Dunlop Dick contracted with professional recruiting agents.[70] A most ambitious and elaborate arrangement of this kind was a contract that John Stedman and Hope Company made with Jacob Frederic Curtius, a newlander who had become a professional agent and investor in the emigrant trade. In a partnership arrangement that was to last two years (1752–54), the Rotterdam merchants agreed with Curtius that he would procure emigrants—in return for a share of 400 passengers for his own ship, one-eighth of the profits, and one-third of the commission in Philadelphia—while Stedman and Isaac Hope would obtain and pay for "the needful Dutch and Prussian passes for the passengers."[71]

67. Gerber, *Nassau-Dillenburger Auswanderung*, 22. John Hunt to Joseph Crell, 28 February 1748/9, Hunt & Greenleafe Letter Book; Curtius, owner of the *Duke of Württemberg*, advertised in *Pennsylvanische Berichte* (16 November 1752) that he would credit any newlander's passage until his return to Philadelphia.

68. The notarial archives contain no evidence of formal agreements between merchants and newlanders, with the exception of those who had turned professional agents.

69. The ship lists occasionally identify such newlanders, and in some merchant accounts they were carried without price or fare debt next to their names. Account Book, Richard Neave Jr., 1773–74 (concerning ship no. 304), HSP; see also financial accounts concerning passengers on the ship *Nancy* (Appendix, ship no. 155), "Redemptioners," HSP; Penrose Cashbooks.

70. Dunlop & Company, for example, made agreements with local merchants and officials at critical points on the emigrants' trip to Rotterdam (GAR, ONA 2698, 210–12 [4 December 1751]); John Dick contracted with Gottlieb Tobias Köhler in Frankfurt (GAR, ONA, 2698/225 [27 December 1752]).

71. GAR, ONA 2779/108 (14 May 1751). See also the Penrose Cashbooks for portions of

Direct incentives to emigrants—in the form of credit for the fare—
were yet another way for merchants to augment the pool of potential
passengers. Already in the 1730s, merchants familiar with the trade and the
consistent demand for labor in Pennsylvania had devised a system that
suited this purpose. Based on the experience that successful former immigrants were often inclined to assist relatives and friends with the relocation
by advancing their transportation costs when they arrived, freighters
agreed to accept payment *after* arrival in Philadelphia, although this was
possible only for a limited number of fares. They could provide this service in the knowledge that, if the relatives who were already settled in the
province did not pay the fare they could count on employers being willing
to pay the outstanding fare of the German newcomers in return for an
agreement of servitude. In effect, then, the demand for bound labor became the security on which Rotterdam merchants extended credit for passage—in part or for the full amount, first to single men and women, and
eventually to entire families. That way, also, German emigrants who were
eager to go to Pennsylvania but had insufficient funds to do so on their
own could afford to relocate.

Once merchants discovered that advancing passage money to prospective New World settlers with limited financial resources would work to
their advantage, the practice became widespread, as a way to win more
emigrants. This critical step for broadening the base from which passengers were recruited helped to ensure a high passenger-per-ship ratio,
which made the business of transporting Germans even more attractive.[72]
By the 1730s, merchants had determined that a ship's run was profitable
when two-thirds of all passage money for a fully freighted vessel due could
be collected in advance, to cover expenses already incurred from transship-

the accounting in Philadelphia. Evidence that Curtius made agreements with other Rotterdam
merchants indicates that the partnership agreement was short-lived and not very successful.
Other partnership arrangements included John Dunlop, Alexander Symson, and Robert
Ritchie of Rotterdam and Alexander Ray of Philadelphia (GAR, ONA 2698/152 [3 August
1751], for shipment of "dry goods and Palatines"); and Nicolas Oursel and John Archdeacon
of Rotterdam, who consigned their German emigrant freights to Pole & Howell in Philadelphia (GAR, ONA 2699/175 [26 September 1752], folio).

72. "Case of the Palatine Protestants"; Isaac & Zachary Hope to Thomas Clifford et al.,
20 October 1761, Pemberton Papers, Clifford Correspondence, 3:248, HSP. Surviving fare accounts for about half the passengers on the ship *Nancy* (1750) show that only 23.4 percent of
the freights were paid in advance. Entries in the Penrose Cashbooks about payments received
from passengers on a particular ship (compared with the fares still outstanding) range from a
high of three-quarters of the expected total to a low of half within about two months after the
ship's arrival, with the exception of ships on which many passengers had died.

ping emigrants and in outfitting and provisioning the vessel.[73] In the early 1750s, at the height of the immigration, merchants regularly involved in the trade still seem to have considered this the customary basis for their calculations. Newcomers to the trade, however, not only imitated those practices but also sometimes pushed the limits, which meant that they could not always realize the profits on which they were counting. For example, the Rotterdam firm of Rocquette & van Teylingen shipped German emigrants on credit to South Carolina in the expectation that the provincial government would pay their transportation costs. Since their knowledge of the local situation proved insufficient, however, they eventually had to write off a considerable amount of passage debts, because immigrants who were unable to pay their fares were neither redeemed by their former compatriots nor able to be sold as servants to German or other settlers.[74] Even in Pennsylvania, where the market for redemptioners and servants was generally strong, merchants had to devise methods to offset losses from the increasing number of passengers who defaulted on the credited portion of their fares. By the time the tide of immigration ebbed over the two decades before the Revolution, freighters and their correspondents had implemented a variety of procedures that protected their investment in advanced fares.[75]

As the transportation of a growing number of emigrants required more ships, the Rotterdam merchants found it increasingly difficult to meet the various initial costs involved in chartering and provisioning immigrant vessels.[76] Advance payments of passage money covered a smaller proportion of their expenses, especially because a larger absolute (if not relative) number of German emigrants chose to take advantage of the opportunity to

73. Transportation contracts in the early years of the emigration from Germany already indicate that not all passengers paid the fare in advance but instead agreed to remit what they still owed within three weeks or one month after arrival in Philadelphia. At this time, however, the proportion of the payments due after arrival was small, and at least in one case merchant and passengers pledged their respective persons and goods as security (GAR, ONA 2096/333 [2 July 1722], *Greyhound*).

74. Advertisement for payment of fares by emigrants who arrived on the ship *Anne* (23 October 1751); Henry Laurens to Foster Cunliffe & Sons (15 November 1755; 24 February 1756); Henry Laurens to James Rocquette (6 March 1757); Philip Hamer et al., eds., *Papers of Henry Laurens*, 1:242, 2:9–10, 106, 485.

75. Accounts of the ships *Nancy* (1750), *King of Prussia* (1764), and *Catherine* (1772), John Steinmetz Papers, Jasper Yeates-Brinton Collection, HSP; *Dolphin* (1773), Accountbook, Richard Neave Jr., 1773–74; and *Britannia* (1773).

76. Jacob Price pointed out that, in the Netherlands, payment for such goods as provisions was expected in cash or short credit at cash prices ("Transaction Costs," 292).

postpone paying the fare at least until arrival in Philadelphia. This opportunity to pay for the passage later helped increase the number of emigrants substantially and was largely welcomed because of its potential for continuing high profits. On the other hand, the practice also led to prolonged and more complicated lines of credit, and accounting, among those who participated in the trade.

The increasing practice of credited fares made it necessary for the merchants to amend their transportation contracts with the passengers to include the price of the passage and the payment requirements and options for settling accounts upon arrival in the American colonies. This was added to the standard contract the merchants utilized to prove to local and regional authorities that they were prepared to ship "their" German emigrants out of the Netherlands with proper dispatch. This agreement also set down the shipper's conditions for providing passage to the emigrants.[77]

Every contract for passage across the Atlantic included three parts. The first had to do with the preliminaries of embarkation, the second detailed particulars concerning provisions, and the third focused on the fare price and any payment options. The merchants designed their agreements with the emigrants to ensure that those who signed to be transshipped through the Netherlands followed through with their plans for migration to the American colonies and honored the contract, and therefore a down payment was often required.

An enumeration of the types and quantities of food and drink passengers could expect on board ship, including how they would normally be distributed over the days of each week, usually constituted a significant portion of the agreement. There being no constraints imposed by regulations, the merchants' concerns about food and drink for the passengers usually reflected only their interest in the bottom line. They merely calculated quantities needed to last for the entire voyage—usually fourteen weeks—with little or no regard to quality or palatability.

The payment part of the contract stipulated the fare, which ranged from five to eight pounds sterling, and the terms and payment schedule for those who did not pay in advance. It also protected the shipper from losses from defaults on fare debts. In case emigrants died en route, the shippers charged the relatives with the debts the deceased had incurred. In the early decades of the eighteenth century, when organized groups or

---

77. A number of these contracts have survived. One late example is the contract for passengers on the ship *Pennsylvania Packet* (1773), "Redemptioners," HSP.

their leaders paid the fare for everyone in advance, such protection had been unnecessary.[78] However, at the height of the emigration, when mortality was high, this practice was exploited and merchants required the payment of fare debts of those who died during the voyage not only from kin but also from unrelated fellow passengers—a practice that was eventually prohibited. At the same time, renegotiating contracts during the voyage—that is, under pressure or duress—was also forbidden. Such regulations indicate that passage agreements were not always honored.[79]

For most of the period, passage agreements stated that baggage transportation was included in the fare price, but loading baggage could lead to problems. In the early years of the immigration, most emigrants were relatively affluent and brought a variety of household goods, clothing, tools, and farm implements, both for their own use and for sale in the American colonies. Regardless of weight or bulk, these "Palatine household goods" were brought on board the immigrant vessel, declared and cleared as such in England, and carried ashore in Philadelphia, where their owners could do with them as they wished. The transfer of large quantities of trade goods this way—mostly in relatively small, individual parcels—was the source of many problems because it attracted the common thief both at sea and ashore. It also invited elaborate schemes of deception by merchants and customs officials, and tempted captains, crews, and both former and current emigrants to exploit the system for their own advantage.

The many formal agreements between merchants, captains, and passengers that included clauses about the loading of baggage and goods attest to the importance of this issue.[80] Telling insights into the procedures and conventions surrounding the transportation and importation of immigrants' goods can be found in surviving records of three cases in which ships or their cargoes were seized in Philadelphia under suspicion of illegal importation. From the court proceedings on the ships *Princess Augusta*, *Sandwich*, and *Brotherhood*, respectively, it is clear that immigrant ships habitually carried improperly declared cargo in addition to passengers, their provisions, and "Palatine household goods," and that was in violation of

78. The charterparty of the *Weerelkloot* (Globe) made a special point of saying that "survivors need not pay for those who die during the voyage" (GAR, ONA 2098/232 [9 June 1723]).

79. *Statutes at Large of Pennsylvania*, 5:94–97; 6:432–40, 437; *Pennsylvanische Berichte* (16 September and 16 October 1749).

80. For example, one charterparty allowed "no extra goods on captain's account" (GAR, ONA 2748/114 [17 May 1753], *Edinburgh*).

the law.[81] Those who were caught argued that a liberal interpretation of "household goods" was customary, sanctioned by little or no enforcement.[82] That excuse did not hold up in admiralty court, but it was widely considered an invitation to import wares illegally. Immigrants who brought trade goods with them were expected to observe the English laws that regulated such imports and were therefore required to inform the captain about the exact nature of the items. The captain could then declare them properly, to avoid risking seizure of the ship and its cargo for carrying contraband.[83]

The imprecise definition of household goods and the often cursory and superficial inspection of emigrants' belongings by customs officials were temptations to many. Shippers and captains stretched "Palatine household goods" to include items transported on their own accounts, or used German emigrants' chests containing used household wares to hide goods from customs officials.[84] Such goods were rarely itemized in the vessel's docket (the official list of items declared and cleared by customs) and presented a relatively small risk to illegal importers because the emigrants could be blamed for violating the law. In addition, meticulous searches of immigrant ships in Philadelphia were apparently rare, in part because customs officials accepted bribes to look the other way—as Israel Pemberton hinted in his report about the seizure of the ship *Sandwich* (1750).[85] Merchants, captains, and newlanders, and even some enterprising immigrants, therefore took advantage of a system that enabled those who had experience in the business, some help and connections, and luck to trade on their own account with untaxed goods that almost guaranteed immediate and very profitable returns. This opportunity was nearly irre-

81. Records of the Vice-Admiralty Court Held at Philadelphia, 2 vols., LC/MD; Philadelphia Custom House Papers, 1:4; Pemberton Papers, 13:112–13.

82. Some of the entries in the English Channel port books illustrate that impression. Cust(oms)/61/1–4 (Cowes 1749–73): 1 July 1751; 2 February 1754; 19, 23, and 30 June 1764; 11 January and 6 July 1766; E(xchequer) Plymouth (1754): 1 and 26 August 1754 (*Adventure, Halifax*).

83. *Statutes at Large of Pennsylvania*, 6:436; Philadelphia Custom House Records, vol. 1, Cadwalader Collection, Thomas Cadwalader Section, HSP; Israel Pemberton to (Henry Blommart?), 22 November 1759, Pemberton Papers, 13:112–13; *Pennsylvanische Berichte* (1 January 1751); proceedings pertaining to the ships *Princess Augusta* (1736) and *Sandwich* (1750), Records of the Vice-Admiralty Court Held at Philadelphia, LC/MD.

84. Charge by Sauer in his letter to the governor, May 1755, quoted in Diffenderfer, *German Immigration*, 240.

85. Pemberton Papers, 13:112–13. The refusal of one tide surveyor in Cowes to accept ten guineas for not reporting the discovery of linen handkerchiefs and silk thread hidden in two casks of peas gives the impression that bribery was customary and widespread. See Cust(oms) 61/3 (Cowes [30 June 1764] *Charlotte*).

sistible to people seeking quick profits, so loading passengers' baggage—and goods—became an important part of the embarkation procedure.[86]

Readying ships for transporting passengers required certain contacts. Carpenters were needed to outfit the ship with bed platforms, privies, and ventilators. Although only the ventilators required specialized knowledge and work, time was a critical factor in all the carpentry work. Keeping idle time in port to a minimum reduced costs significantly and was especially valuable when competition for emigrants to fill available cargo space was stiff—most often toward the end of the season, when it became difficult to load vessels fully. Victuals had to be located, purchased, and stowed. Providing medicines for sick passengers, or even engaging a physician for the ship's run, were, in addition to installation of privies and ventilation pipes, measures taken to reduce the risk of disease and death among passengers while maintaining a high passenger-to-ship ratio. Such measures became standard practice, even though the steps taken to improve the passengers' well-being would be judged quite ineffective by modern standards.[87] Most important, however, captains had to be engaged, and instructed in the particulars of the voyage, which meant drawing up contracts that detailed the respective obligations of captains and merchants and having such agreements officially notarized, to avoid future conflicts.

The contracts that the merchant houses of Hope and Stedman negotiated with captains of vessels they chartered set the standard in the trade. For the emigrant ships, the first step was preparations for loading the vessel. Outfitting and provisioning were the responsibility of the shipper, as was loading the ship with emigrants. In the interest of expediency in completing those preparations, the time spent in port was often limited by contract. If a freighter was tardy in preparing for and loading the cargo, he had to pay penalties; if the captain failed to ready the ship for departure on time, the negotiated fines were charged against his account. Such payments for overruns were standard in all charterparties, not just in the emigrant trade. Demurrage was usually assessed by the day, and only "running" days (normal working days under regular weather conditions) counted.[88]

86. The prevalence of "mixed" cargoes of trade and household goods on immigrant ships is evident in many charterparties. Some examples are GAR, ONA 2338/203 (7 July 1744), *Musclift Galley;* 2344/63 (30 May 1749), *Albany* of Glasgow; 2344/78 (9 July 1749), *Isaac* of London; 2747/97 (18 May 1752), *Rowand;* 2747/107 (26 May 1752) *Nancy.*

87. John Hunt to John Stedman, 28 February 1748/9, Hunt & Greenleafe Letter Book.

88. In the emigrant trade around the middle of the eighteenth century, fines for detaining the loading of the ship amounted to 2 pounds sterling a day but were often double that if time

Since vessels were refitted to accommodate passengers and their baggage, space for cargo was at a premium. In an effort to load as many
emigrants as "the ship can conveniently stow and carry," captain and crew
were usually asked to vacate their regular quarters so that passengers could
use them—an inconvenience for which the freighter rewarded the captain
with a bonus at the end of the ship's run, when the shipper also removed
any additional platforms, roundhouses, or huts he had constructed to
accommodate more passengers with sleeping places. In most cases, the
shipper held exclusive rights for loading provisions, emigrants, passengers'
baggage, and trade goods, leaving no doubt about who had final responsibility for managing the voyage.[89] Other terms common in contracts were
payment of port charges, pilotage, and similar expenses in connection with
clearing and making port, and arrangements pertaining to the mandatory
stop in England and the ship's destination in the American colonies.[90]

Agreements concerning the price for transporting German emigrants
were a crucial part of each charterparty between merchant and captain.
Captains either received a lump sum for their services or, more often, a
fixed amount for each full freight loaded, usually payable at the end of the
run together with a bonus, or "hat money," which ranged from five to
fifty guineas. When merchants paid the ship's captain a lump sum, the
actual number of emigrants the ship's master carried had no effect on his
return from the voyage, but when the price was calculated on a unit basis
for each full-fare emigrant, ranging from twenty-nine shillings (sterling) at
the height of the emigration to forty-five shillings at other times, the
captain had a vested interest in carrying as many passengers as possible in
order to increase his profit. Since he was paid for the number of passengers taken aboard in Europe, he had no special incentive to preserve the
health or well-being of the passengers. Therefore, when emigration peaked
around mid-century when many ships were competing for emigrants, and

was an important factor—as at the end of the season, when there might be too few emigrants
to fill ships and when late arrival in Philadelphia might mean that ships could not leave until
the next spring, because the Delaware River often froze in winter.

89. Less often, the captain was responsible for some of the outfitting, provisioning, and
loading. Examples of such practices include charterparties John Dick made with captains
transporting emigrants to Nova Scotia.

90. Captains traditionally paid part of their ships' port charges and pilotage. Most contracts included procedures that captains were to follow when stopping over in England and
upon arrival at the final destination in the American colonies; particulars often centered on
terms of demurrage. For a description of procedures for ships that "touch from Holland &c
to Clear for the Plantations," see Cus(toms) 61/2 (Cowes [25 February 1754]).

prices per freight were low, freighters and captains both had an interest in packing as many passengers as possible on board and taking chances with the consequences of that.[91]

Captains were professionals in a tough and demanding business. In the vast majority of cases, they had little or no control over their cargo or the conditions under which they would live for many weeks, yet had a vested interest in managing both the ship and its cargo well, because the ship master's reputation depended on it. Emigrants were a demanding load that required constant attention to ensure their well-being and, most important, the safety of the ship. This task was particularly difficult if the freighter had loaded the vessel to capacity and calculated provisions for the passengers tightly.[92] Captains got the blame for crowded conditions, as well as for inadequate and insufficient food and drink, even though the merchants were responsible for those conditions. Some merchants seem to have been aware of the extra strain under which captains of emigrant ships labored, and therefore rewarded good treatment of the passengers at sea with extra pay by raising the bonus customary at the end of the voyage.[93] A number of masters were part-owners of the ships they commanded and had therefore a vested interest in all aspects of the vessel's management (see Appendix for owner-operated ships). There is no indication, however, that captains who owned shares of the shipping were particularly profit-oriented or more tyrannical than those who were merely in the employ of a merchant and had no investment in the ship. John Stedman was obviously very successful as a merchant who specialized in transporting passengers, yet his advancement from captain to merchant did not seem to have been based on exploitation of German emigrants.[94]

Contrary to the prevailing popular image of the tyrannical captain, then and now, in retrospect and after acknowledging the dangers of the voyage, many immigrants attested to genuine concern that captains showed

91. The Appendix identifies the ships for which a charterparty could be located.

92. The best arrangement for life on board was a regular and regulated organization of daily activities that involved preparing and distributing provisions and maintaining rudimentary hygiene and cleanliness. According to observations based on the much larger number of slave ships, mortality tended to be low on vessels that were kept clean and on which passengers had good provisions and water. See Klein, "Economic Aspects," 304, 306.

93. As a "further Encouragement and with a Proviso the said Master Theophilus Barnes do treat the Passengers with the utmost humanity in order to preserve their Lives, he is to receive 20 guineas for the use of the Cabin by way of Hattmoney" (GAR, ONA 2747/135 [20 July 1752], *Kitty/Catherine*).

94. On the contrary, his passengers described him as a competent and caring commander. See Wust, "Emigration Season of 1738," 29.

for their charges.[95] Still, the very real stress, hardship, and difficulties of the voyage often negatively colored passengers' perceptions of the ship's master. Unfamiliar with the harsh realities of life at sea, emigrants were apt to view a captain's insistence on authority and discipline as cruelty and tyranny. Not all captains, however, handled their human cargo well, as is evident from several contracts that specify that the ship's master would receive a bonus for treating passengers well.[96]

There were two steps in loading emigrants: final contracting for passage, and then actually bringing passengers on board and allocating space for them and their baggage. Once a vessel was cleared, it could proceed—with the help of a pilot—from the Dutch port into the North Sea and then through the Strait of Dover into the Channel. In the English stopover port, most often Cowes, the correspondents of the Dutch merchants in Holland supervised customs procedures and any additional provisioning. Debarkation procedures were largely determined by local circumstances and merchants, though merchants in Europe sent instructions for consignees and partners in the American colonies.

It is worth remembering that human beings were not the only factor affecting the outcome of the adventure of crossing the Atlantic. Eighteenth-century vessels were extremely fragile and vulnerable in face of the forces of wind and sea. This does not, however, diminish the achievements of those who provided and operated the shipping that braved ocean and nature to establish a reliable link between Europe and America, but rather reminds us of how much they accomplished in adversity.

Whether the Rotterdam merchants only monitored the German emigration flow as it came their way, or channeled it actively in various fashions, their main function in the emigrant trade was to provide transportation on vessels dispatched from British ports and destined for America, and for the most part Philadelphia. Their profits depended on their role as middlemen in manipulating the supply of shipping to meet, and perhaps encourage, the demand for transatlantic passage and on commissions they received for outfitting and provisioning any ships they did not themselves own. The size of their profit was closely linked to the ratio of passengers per ship. Under normal circumstances, the larger the number of emigrant

---

95. That is, on balance, the impression after reading many accounts.

96. Such a clause was first included near the end of the peak in emigration, most likely in reaction to complaints from preceding voyages. At the same time, some contracts began to emphasize that payment of a bonus "is left to the freighter's generosity and liberty" (GAR, ONA 2148/128 [12 July 1753], *Eastern Branch*).

freights on a vessel, the greater the return. The magnitude of the emigration flow—and, to a lesser extent, the degree of competition among merchants involved in the trade—determined size of the profits. By the second quarter of the eighteenth century, whether those profits were realized
depended more and more on how successful the consignees of the merchants in Holland were in handling the unloading of the ships in the
American colonies, and especially how they settled passengers' accounts.

Since the majority of all vessels carrying German emigrants from Rotterdam were destined for Pennsylvania, the role the Philadelphia merchants
played provides important insights into the procedures that were common
in the port of debarkation. As the trade matured, the merchants there
evolved from passive to active participants in the network that connected
correspondents and partners that had interests in the passenger trade.
Philadelphia's part in this specialized business can be seen in the procedures for admitting aliens into Pennsylvania. In particular, the ship lists
name many of the merchants who were in the trade.[97]

The Philadelphia merchant community that handled German immigrants was divided into those who participated only occasionally and
those who had regular involvement. Beyond that, merchants handling the
arrangements before the French and Indian War differed from those con-
ducting the business after the war. At first glance, the fifty-eight Philadelphia merchants or firms that can be identified as dealing with immigrants seems like a large number. (See Appendix.) A closer look at the
distribution across the different stages of German movement to America
in the eighteenth century, however, puts this number in a different perspective (Table 3[B]).[98] During the early years and the peak period (1727–
55), twelve different merchants handled affairs connected with German

97. The ship lists provide the basis for much of the information about German immigrant
ships and the Philadelphia merchants who were connected with the trade. Merchants' correspondence and financial accounts; immigrants' letters home; reports in the German-language
press in Pennsylvania; and records of the lobbying and relief efforts of the GSP (founded
1764)—all contributed specific aspects of a description of the German immigrant trade.

98. For the first two decades after the beginning of the ship lists (1727–47), however, there
is available only scattered information on this matter. Charterparties in Rotterdam and Amsterdam, merchants' correspondence, and *Lloyd's Lists* provided additional information (see the
Appendix). Philadelphia merchants involved in the German immigrant trade can be identified
systematically only for the time after 1750, by which time the ship lists headings were including
the name of the merchant to whom the immigrants were consigned. Further information
concerning the consignment or ownership of immigrant vessels is contained in two kinds of
port records—the ships registered in Philadelphia, and the account of duties collected from
all incoming vessels. See "Tonnage Duty Book [1765–75]"; and McCusker, "Ships Registered
at the Port of Philadelphia."

immigrant vessels in some significant way, compared with thirteen during the twelve years preceding the Revolution (1763–75). Except for six firms (Shoemaker, Fisher, Howell, Pemberton, Warder, Willing), however, there was no overlap between the two periods. Throughout, most merchants engaged only once in the German immigrant trade. Collectively, these "dabblers" made up 7 percent of all voyages and transported a comparable portion of the German immigrants landing in Philadelphia.[99] In contrast, the merchants who emerged repeatedly as consignees or owners of more than half of immigrant shipping to Philadelphia took responsibility for over two-thirds of the immigrants (Table 3[B]; Appendix). Up to the year 1755, the Stedmans and the Shoemakers alone were recipients of the majority of vessels arriving with German immigrants whose consignees were known. This largely reflects the dominant market shares captured by John Stedman and the Hopes in the departure port of Rotterdam (the Shoemakers were the Philadelphia correspondents of the Hopes). After 1763, more merchants participated regularly in the lessening immigrant trade, accounting for most of the German arrivals. Yet in this period too, four merchants outperformed the rest by considerable margins, with Willing & Morris being responsible for the largest share of German immigrants who came to Philadelphia.[100]

The growth of Philadelphia merchant participation in transporting Germans to the Delaware Valley is even more dramatic than this broadening of local responsibility after the era of the Stedmans and the Shoemakers indicates, because more and more ships that carried immigrants were now owned by Philadelphia merchants. (The Appendix provides ship ownership and registration information.) Until 1748, only a few ships were registered in Philadelphia, and of those only two were at least partly owned by a Philadelphian, and four of them clearly belonged to Londoners. The dominance of London ship owners among vessels employed to transport German emigrants is corroborated by the prominence of London over Philadelphia as the home port of the captains who commanded German immigrant vessels.[101] In contrast, by the peak period of

<hr />

99. In the British slave trade, one-time voyages were the norm; the German immigrant trade was more like Scotland's tobacco trade, in which regulars dominated. See Walter Minchinton, "Characteristics of British Slaving Vessels," 72, table 16; and Dell, "Clyde Tobacco Fleet," 3.

100. It was no accident that George Washington was advised to consult Robert Morris about how to procure German Protestants as settlers for his Ohio lands. See James Tilghman Jr. to George Washington, Philadelphia, 7 April 1774, Washington Papers, LC/MD, reel 33.

101. During the first two decades, a number of the ship list headings included the master's

1749–55, when many more of the merchants to whom the arriving German immigrants were consigned or belonged could be identified, the percentage of immigrant shipping built and registered in Philadelphia had more than doubled, and the balance between owners in London and Philadelphia had shifted; more of the ownerships now included at least one investor who resided in Philadelphia. Two of the three ships belonging to Londoners named John Stedman as part-owner. Although from London and later living in Rotterdam, Stedman had strong ties to Philadelphia through his brothers Charles and Alexander, who resided there as merchants. After 1763, half of all the ships arriving with German immigrants on the Delaware were registered in Philadelphia, and only three had no Philadelphia owners (the residence of the owners of two ships is not known). The majority of the merchants who engaged more than once in the German immigrant trade in this later period, after the transatlantic flow had peaked, owned at least part of a ship transporting German immigrants, and one-quarter of all German immigrants arrived on vessels owned by Philadelphia merchants—a clear indication that merchants who already had interests in shipping sought extra profits from transporting passengers. The shift toward concentration of the business in the hands of a few large firms that invested heavily in shipping was a developmental characteristic for Philadelphia merchants operating in other trades too.[102]

The same pattern of increasingly active participation by local merchants is evident in the distribution of ships that carried German immigrants to Philadelphia more than once. Just over half the immigrant ship arrivals were repeat voyages.[103] In the early years (1727–48), some 51 percent of the arrivals were repeats, while during the peak period (1749–55) 58 percent of all ships landing Germans had previously been to Philadelphia with immigrants, or would return again. Then, during the years of declining immigration before the Revolution, no less than 67 percent of voyages with Germans were by repeating carriers. In other words, the degree to which the transportation of German immigrants to Philadelphia was provided by ships already experienced in the trade increased significantly over

---

home port. Altogether forty-five ships (36.8 percent) carrying German immigrants were commanded by captains with European home ports. In addition to London, four captains (3.2 percent) were from other English ports, four were from Dublin, and three (2.5 percent) were listed as from Amsterdam or elsewhere in Holland.

102. Doerflinger, *Vigorous Spirit of Enterprise*, 78, 86, 97, 99–100, 109, 179.

103. The figures are based on the first 324 voyages listed in the Appendix. For all the colonies, 44 percent were repeat voyages.

time as the number of freights first peaked in the 1749–54 era and then
waned. Meanwhile, the role of Philadelphia ownership in this more regular
and reduced immigrant trade after the 1750s increased decisively. Local
merchants on the Delaware both managed and owned a larger share of the
business to be had from transporting aliens along with other cargo.

The change from being predominantly merely consignees of German
immigrant shipments to becoming actual owners of the ships that provided transatlantic transportation made it necessary for Philadelphia merchants who were involved more regularly in the German immigrant trade
to change how they managed ships and cargo. In the earlier years, most of
the concern of Philadelphia merchants centered on collecting unpaid passage money from the German immigrants sent over by Rotterdam merchants. In this opening phase of the trade, the majority of the German
immigrants arrived with at least part of their fare paid in advance. Any
differences that passengers still owed were either paid in cash on arrival by
the immigrant himself, his relatives or friends, or his employer or—upon
sufficient security—agreed by note or bond to be paid later at a specified
time.[104] Squaring these accounts turned out to be an increasingly complicated and tedious business for the Philadelphia merchant. Successful remuneration for immigrant freights and a speedy and advantageous dispatch of the vessel to the next port depended on a well-coordinated
partnership between the merchant in Holland and his Philadelphia correspondent.[105]

As Philadelphians became more interested in the German immigrant
trade, as their investment in vessels suitable for transatlantic transportation expanded, there emerged a more equitable distribution of the responsibility (and presumably the profit) among the partners. In particular, existing ties were strengthened between Rotterdam and Philadelphia at the
competitive height of the German immigration to America (1749–54); it
was newcomers to the trade who tended to explore opportunities in other
colonies or linked up with merchants in other continental ports.[106] Then,

104. For a description of the different credit instruments, see Perkins, *American Public Finance
and Financial Services*, 65–67; on the system of credit more generally, see Brewer, *Sinews of Power*,
186–89.

105. It also required extensive bookkeeping. The Cashbooks of Penrose, who was Stedman's
Philadelphia correspondent, demonstrate the many tasks related to this part of the voyage. It
was important to keep good records, which were the basis on which merchants figured their 5
percent commission.

106. Rocquette & van Teylingen, for example, established links with South Carolina and
were willing to take their business to any colony. John Dick transported German migrants to
Nova Scotia. On the other hand, adversarial actions by competitors discouraged Pemberton,

after 1763, the strong interest of the Philadelphia merchants in providing transatlantic shipping more generally reversed the direction of the passenger trade. Instead of serving as a first port of arrival for London ships that carried German immigrants to the New World, Philadelphia became home port from which ships in the provisions trade were dispatched to Europe. For their return to Philadelphia, these ships filled their unused cargo space with German immigrants.[107]

Increased ownership of vessels involved in the emigrant trade combined with effective management of the complex tasks of unloading and accounting for the ships' human cargo to give Philadelphia merchants a critical edge in the passenger trade, especially once the custom of extending credit for the transatlantic fare had been firmly established.[108] The diverse activities that went in to disembarkation involved not only logistics and bookkeeping but also a knowledge of the regional market for German immigrant labor and wares. Three major steps were involved in the process of ending an immigrant ship's run in Philadelphia. Compliance with the registration requirement for German immigrant men, and the unloading of passengers and goods, constituted the first component of debarkation. The second component centered on settling immigrants' accounts. The final balancing of the books for the voyage was the third step, which often took place long after the ship had been turned around in port and sent on to its next destination.[109]

---

who tried to branch out from regular interests he already had in the Philadelphia dry-goods market, from pursuing the business on a long-term basis.

107. Philadelphia's emerging role as the most important point in the German emigrant trade, based on owning and controlling more shipping, is in accord with studies of Philadelphia's commercial community showing increased investment of Pennsylvania merchants in ships. See John McCusker, "Pennsylvania Shipping Industry"; John McCusker and Russell Menard, *The British Economy of British America*, 196, table 9.2; and Doerflinger, *Vigorous Spirit of Enterprise*, 179.

108. Services and expenses connected with debarking immigrants in Philadelphia are listed in the Penrose Cashbooks: doctor's expenses; qualifying fees; interpreter's fees; pair of shoes for boy; advertisement, porterage, and storage of chests; appraising of goods at vendue; liquor for people at vendue; nursing Palatines; payment for the sick on Providence Island; provisions and medicines for the sick; beets and greens for sailors and Palatines; wood; clothing and coffins for dead immigrants; fees for customs (collector and comptroller); naval office fees; pilotage; wharfage; light money; actions in court; writs; attorney's fee; prison fees; payments and fees for sheriff; riding into the country after sundry people; insurance; ship chandler; steward's wages; putting up the cabin; administration fee (stamping of papers with the great seal).

109. Only some parts of such final balancing has survived, so it is impossible to assess the profitability of the business from actual accounts. Some merchants clearly considered it profitable, because they stayed in the business for extended periods of time; others, like Pemberton, were frustrated with it and did not continue.

Registering immigrant men from Germany before the magistrates in Philadelphia was simple. With the exception of people who were too sick to leave the vessel, the captain or consignee presented a list of passengers to the local authorities and saw to it that the men signed the requisite declarations of abjuration and allegiance (see Chapter 2). Like many administrative procedures, the registration of immigrants and the inspection of the vessels on which they arrived required the payment of fees. Most merchants charged those expenses as "city dues" or "head money" to the outstanding accounts of the immigrants.[110]

Unloading goods from immigrant vessels presented mostly a logistical challenge in terms of the sequence in which goods, leftover provisions and equipment, and the belongings of the immigrants were to be removed. Three general considerations affected the order for emptying the ship. Prompt removal of any illegally imported goods took absolute precedent over all other steps, in an effort to avoid detection and escape any punitive measures—notably seizure and forfeiture.[111] Properly registered trade goods, however, could be brought to land depending on where they were stowed and how urgently they were needed. The unloading of passengers' belongings usually took place only after accounts had been settled, because merchants had learned to hold baggage as surety until they received outstanding fare payments from the immigrants. Victuals and medicines, kettles, and any other utensils or equipment belonging to the freighter in Rotterdam were usually removed last.[112] That way such leftovers could serve the passengers whose debarkation was delayed, because the merchants were required by law to provide immigrants with food and drink for at least two weeks after landing in Philadelphia—the time most transportation contracts stipulated for paying fare debts.

Settling outstanding accounts was central to the operations of the Philadelphia merchants and their commissioners.[113] It was a complicated procedure, because the passage debts that had to be squared were variable

110. The different way of charging immigrants on prepaid passages is apparent in the surviving account of the ships *Nancy* (1750), *King of Prussia* (1764), and *Britannia* (1773). See "Palatines and Servants Imported on the *King of Prussia*," *Pennsylvania Genealogical Magazine* 27 (1971): 54–61.

111. *Princess Augusta*, Records of the Vice-Admiralty Court Held at Philadelphia, LC/MD.

112. Provision for such removal was a standard feature in agreements between shippers and captains.

113. Penrose provided John Stedman with many of the services involved in unloading German immigrant vessels, at the usual rate of 5 percent, and continued to do so even when Stedman's brothers operated as merchants in Philadelphia. See Penrose Cashbooks.

and because immigrants had a number of options for making payment. When merchants in Rotterdam first offered credit for part or all of the fare, Philadelphia merchants were not prepared to handle the complicated accounts of variable debts accumulated by German newcomers efficiently and effectively. The consignees of German immigrant vessels in Pennsylvania simply trusted the informal or even formal promises of immigrants to settle their accounts once landed; but this resulted in lists of outstanding debts that would probably never be paid.[114] The poor prospects for recovering long-term passage debts gave the merchants a strong incentive to distribute such anticipated losses among the parts of the fare they could legitimately charge beyond the base price. When they calculated the rates for "fees" or "head money" charged to each passenger, and when they determined the interest for any credited portion of the fare or monies advanced before embarkation in Rotterdam, merchants could make up some of the costs that resulted from defaults on passage debts.[115]

In addition, merchants took measures to prevent immigrants from disappearing without settling their accounts. In particular, passengers who vanished into the interior of the province or across the border to Maryland were impossible to track down and legally out of reach.[116] Therefore, preventing immigrants who were traveling on credit in any amount from leaving the ship until payment, or dependable arrangement for it, was made became an integral part of the landing routine. As the proportion of passengers traveling on credited fares grew, and as merchants depended increasingly on exploiting the market for indentured servants in order to be repaid promptly for outstanding passage debts, more and more immigrants were restricted in their travels ashore.

The need to settle variable accounts of passage money still owed became the basis for negotiations for indentured servitude and the distin-

---

114. Except for the entries in the Penrose Cashbooks, all evidence about outstanding debts is for the later period, see: "List of Outstanding Debts on Sales of Palatines on the Ships *Pennsylvania* (1755) and *Chance* (1756), 9 February 1761"; "Lists of Promissory Notes and Bonds" on German immigrant ships *Crawford* (1768), *Minerva* (1770), *Minerva* (1771), *Recovery* (1771), *Tiger* (1771), *Minerva* (1772), *Crawford* (1772), *Hope* (1772), *Hope* (1773), *Crawford* (1773), in "Redemptioners," HSP. See also ads urging immigrants to pay outstanding debts in *American Weekly Mercury* (26 December 1732), *Pennsylvania Gazette* (16 April 1739), and *Pennsylvanische Berichte* (16 May 1748, 16 May 1751).

115. Some of those charges were required and fixed, like that for registering the men, and the duty Philadelphia levied on all immigrants. Others were very much at the discretion of the importer, such as rolling over expenses for the mandatory health reports to passengers who still had open accounts.

116. *Votes and Proceedings*, 6:4732; *Statutes at Large of Pennsylvania*, 4:339–44, 370–75.

guishing mark of the German servant trade, as opposed to previously known service for passage, in which fixed terms had been the rule.[117] Only one "mustering book," itemizing the accounts of each passenger on board, survives in its entirety; that of the ship *Britannia* (1773). Several others are incomplete or are presented in part as items in merchants' accounts pertaining to shipment of passengers and servants.[118] Fairly typical in this respect is the tabulated account of the passengers on the ship *Nancy* (1750). A main entry identifies the head of each party or travelers by name and cabin number ("bed space" or "berth" was closer to reality) and gives the number of persons per party (ranging from one to eight) with the corresponding full fares (which were calculated according to a variable fare structure that allowed infants to travel free and half-price for children). The amount of money paid in advance is listed, as well as the amount still owed—including itemized charges other than the passage money or authorized reductions of the regular fare price. Values are in European currency; and the outstanding debt was also converted into Pennsylvania money to speed and simplify transactions upon arrival in Philadelphia. Clearly, the basic information was compiled in Rotterdam, but it was solely for the use of the captain and Philadelphia merchant; who used it when settling accounts and who added to the original entries such information as the date, form, and amount of payments received. Accounts were generally kept in English, and immigrants rendering them legally binding with their signatures may not have fully understood what they signed, which could result in misunderstandings upon arrival.[119]

Once the custom of coordinating the passage debt with the time of service had been established, merchants began to exploit the potential of the continued strong market for German servants aggressively. They did so by first liberalizing their credit policies upon embarkation, and then by tightening their standards for granting long-term credit upon arrival, thereby encouraging an increased flow of immigrants but ensuring prompt returns on their investment by encouraging immediate indentures as a form of debt settlement. With the exception of immigrants who had problems, such as unusually large amounts of debts, being handicapped by

117. This was also the custom in the early years of German immigration to Pennsylvania.
118. Penrose must have had such mustering books to keep track of fare payments he received and entered in his cashbooks.
119. See Muhlenberg in *Hallesche Nachrichten*, 461, and also entries concerning the account of the Widow Martin in the Beamtenratsprotokoll, 24 October and 21 November 1772; 16 January 1773, GSP, Philadelphia.

illness, or being burdened with a spouse or small children—none of the sources ever mentions sluggish market conditions for German servants. However, repeated notices advertising the sale of German immigrants, in which merchants offered increasingly liberal credit policies to prospective purchasers, indicate indirectly that at least some immigrants had difficulty in finding employers.[120] As part of the change, increased dependence of merchants on returns from the system of indentured servitude actually brought about more considerate treatment of passengers during the voyage, because dead or sick immigrants cut down the returns to be had from the servant market in Philadelphia.[121]

Merchants, who were required by law to provide immigrants who could not pay up with food and shelter for thirty days, at the immigrants' expense, found that there was little they could do to force payment from destitute people.[122] Although the number of immigrants in this group was relatively small, their debts collectively could form a substantial proportion of the total fares credited on a given vessel. Similarly, expenses of caring for sick passengers, which was required by law, could be added to the passengers' accounts. That meant an increase in already-existing fare debts. Merchants commissioned special boardinghouses for such cases on a for-profit basis rather than as a charity.[123] In response to the increased expenses they incurred after immigrants had landed, merchants redistributed the amount they expected to lose from such uncollectable debts as extra or hidden charges onto accounts that they had reason to believe would be paid off.

In efforts to ensure a return on their investment, the merchants made all payments on the American side of the Atlantic, however prompt, subject to interest charges. Some began to require interest on credited fares even before the height of the German immigration. In the two decades before the Revolution, this became a firmly established custom among importers of German immigrants. Immigrants were also jailed for nonpay-

---

120. For example, *Pennsylvanische Berichte* (1 December 1768; 24 January 1772; 19 October 1773; 14 December 1773).

121. See also the expenses listed for medical care (on the ship *Britannia* [1773]), for the fare of J. D. Roth, a physician who traveled on discount, and for outlays for clothing for servants on the *King of Prussia* (1764) and the *Dolphin* (1773).

122. Stedman provided those services before they were required by law. See Penrose Cashbooks.

123. The health report by Drs. Graeme and Bond, November 1754, Ferdinand J. Dreer Autograph Collection (Physicians, Surgeons & Chemists, vol. 2), HSP, also in *PMHB* 36 (1912): 476–79, 476.

ment, but the wisdom of such action seems questionable, unless it was a legal prerequisite for gaining access to property held as bond, or as an example, to pressure others from whom there was some way of extracting payment.[124] Money advanced in Rotterdam was expensive; it drew a flat interest of 20 to 25 percent for a lending period of about three months.[125] Manipulating exchange rates, from florins into Pennsylvania currency or from pounds sterling into Pennsylvania money, was another way of over-charging successfully, because most immigrants were not sophisticated in those types of business practices and were easily confused about how merchants calculated prices in different currencies.[126]

Merchants expanded such creative accounting ingeniously by keeping the basic fare within customary limits but swelling the actual price by charging for every service along the way, including interest for each item on the account. And for their own benefit, they billed those extra charges in some European currency that could then be converted into Pennsylvania money—a step that ensured still further profit. The account for Sophia Leonora Heistrigen on the ship *Britannia* (1773) is a typical example: one "freight," £16.10.0 (Pennsylvania money); head money (including a variety of fees, taxes, and so on), £1.0.0 (Pennsylvania money); proportion of bed space, Fl 1.0; money advanced, Fl 28.0; 20 percent interest on the items charged in, Fl 5.6 (the subtotal of Fl 34.16 was then converted—at a very disadvantageous rate of Fl 6 per £1—into Pennsylvania money and added to the freight and head money), resulting in a grand total of £23.6.0 (Pennsylvania money) owed on the passenger's account, compared with the nominal base fare of £16.10.0 or a 41 percent increase in the initially apparent cost.[127]

The evidence demonstrates that the Philadelphia merchants were skillful, and successful, in profitably balancing customary business practices with taking full advantage of opportunities in the local market. Since they

124. Beamtenratsprotokoll (December 1770 and 5 January 1771); *Votes of the Pennsylvania Assembly*, 7:5719–20.

125. See Sauer's report in *Pennsylvanische Berichte* (16 December 1746) and his letter to the governor, 1755 (Diffenderfer, *German Immigration*, 241–42). On the other hand, see also accounts charging no interest on the ship *Nancy* (1750). In 1754, Willing & Sons charged interest on fares credited until arrival in Philadelphia, as did James and Drinker (*King of Prussia*) in 1764, and Fisher & Sons in 1773 (*Britannia*). See also Beamtenratsprotokoll (31 October 1772).

126. Beamtenratsprotokoll (24 and 31 October 1772).

127. Over the course of the century, the price of the voyage fluctuated considerably, partly because the cost of providing transatlantic transportation changed and partly because of different methods of calculating those costs and the various ways in which they were passed on to passengers.

assumed many of the additional responsibilities that arose from the wider use of deferred payment for passage—services for which they charged a commission—their involvement in the trade in German emigrants increased.[128] Their expanded part in the credit chain that connected the partners, their growing expertise in gauging the market for German settlers and servants in America, and their increased investment in the shipping that provided the transportation, contributed to strengthening the role of Philadelphia merchants.

Success in the "trade in strangers" varied and depended much on the situation of each merchant and the particular goal he set for the endeavor.[129] Most of the casual participants in the trade expected to make an easy profit from such ventures. They entered the business at the height of the emigration around mid-century, when competition from regular shippers and other newcomers was high. Some could exploit that situation to advantage, others were greatly disappointed in the returns. These onetime or sometime participants included merchants in London, such as John Hunt; commercial firms in Rotterdam, such as Harvart & Company and John Dick; and traders in the American colonies, among them Jacob Frederic Curtius, James Pemberton, and Samuel Waldo. They differed from companies that were regularly involved primarily in that they could not, or would not, absorb the fluctuations common in this business. Ironically, it was they who were largely responsible for attempts to regulate the trade against abuses that resulted from unusual greed and extraordinary competition.[130]

The laws that were finally passed in Pennsylvania in an effort to protect passengers without cutting too much into the profits of freighters in effect favored the merchants who could compensate for having fewer passengers per ship over the long term. The legislation discouraged shippers who were dependent on immediate returns. In general, merchants who had interests in ships or who profited from commissioned services were more

128. The firm of Pole & Howell entered into an agreement that detailed their role as consignees of Nicolas Oursel of Rotterdam (GAR, ONA 2699/175—folio [26 September 1752], *Phoenix, Louisa, Rawleigh*).

129. Accounts and letters of Philadelphia merchants in the immigrant trade include some tantalizing evidence about receipts and expenses for ships making the transatlantic voyage loaded with emigrants, but the surviving records are scattered, making it impossible to come up with a complete set of business records that would allow us to figure actual profits in the trade.

130. The best summary of the diverse interests in the debate about regulating the German emigrant trade to Pennsylvania is in Schwartz, *A Mixed Multitude.*

likely to persist in the business, because they could more easily apply gains and losses from the emigrant trade to other parts of a ship's run or to their other ventures, especially if such operations were reasonably large and diversified. In particular, they avoided the costs of having ships that were underutilized on the westward leg of the voyage.[131] Some long-term partnerships in the business of transporting German emigrants speak to the success of such strategies.

A few examples illustrate the great variety of interests in this specialized business and the diverse approaches to making a profit from transporting German emigrants to the American colonies. John Hunt of London and James Pemberton of Philadelphia were merchants regularly engaged in the dry-goods trade who branched out into the passenger business when the dry-goods market became unpromising. They did not own a vessel, so they chartered one and contracted with shippers in Rotterdam for the freight. In order to make a profit, they had to collect enough money from the passengers they transported to Philadelphia to pay for the *Crown*'s charter, the commission of Hope & Company, and any other charges they had incurred through buying additional provisions in England, bringing the ship to port, and unloading its cargo. They were disappointed in the returns they realized from the venture. Pemberton ended his foray into the business with German emigrants after the ship *Sandwich* was seized for transporting illegal goods, probably because of a tip-off to customs from a fellow merchant trying to limit competition in the trade.

John Dick, an English merchant in Rotterdam, fared much better. When German emigration peaked, he seized the opportunity by proposing to the Board of Trade that he recruit and transport settlers for Nova Scotia. His proposal was in effect modeled on the contracts that merchants made with the government for transporting prisoners to the American colonies.[132] Dick was able to persuade the Board of Trade to underwrite his operations by granting him a fixed sum per settler. Like Hunt and Pemberton, however, he was not a ship owner, so he had to charter vessels. Since he was the freighter, unlike Hunt and Pemberton, he saved on commission and could therefore spend considerable funds on recruiting emigrants for Nova Scotia. Based on the accounts Dick presented to the Board of Trade—undoubtedly padded to maximize his returns—the

131. John McDonald and Ralph Shlomowitz could explore these issues in much greater detail for the Australian passenger trade ("Passenger Fares on Sailing Vessels").

132. Roger Ekirch, *Bound for America*.

government spent an average of £6.7 per immigrant.[133] Thanks to these generous subsidies, Dick had little need to build a good reputation in the business, and he could count on the Nova Scotia governor to bind immigrants who were too poor to pay their fare to labor in public works projects. Although Dick continued in the business in order to capitalize on his recruiting efforts even after completion of his commission for the Board of Trade, he soon left Rotterdam and became consul at Leghorn.[134]

Jacob Frederic Curtius and Samuel Waldo too had specific interests in seeking to enter the business of transporting German emigrants. Waldo needed settlers for his lands in northern New England, while Curtius wanted passengers for his account and his ship, the *Duke of Württemberg*. Both established extensive recruitment operations in the Rhine lands, but neither could ship emigrants across the Netherlands to Rotterdam. Curtius solved this problem by going into a partnership with Stedman and Hope in an arrangement designed to guarantee him a fully loaded ship as freighter. Under normal circumstances, the voyage was likely to yield a good return: it was big. Curtius had first choice among the emigrants he recruited for his own account and his partners. As a newlander himself, he could negotiate effectively with his passengers. And his contacts among Germans in Pennsylvania assured him reasonable speed and success in settling passengers' accounts after landing.[135] Waldo depended on Rotterdam merchants to provide ships to transport the emigrants he recruited. That involved considerable commission charges, as in the case of Hunt and Pemberton, in addition expenses for recruiting. Had Waldo managed to attract mostly settlers who could pay their way, and to make his a successful settlement that would then lure additional immigrants for further development, his investment would have paid off. It is unlikely, however, that the transportation of German emigrants brought him any immediate profits. Yet Waldo's continued interest in perfecting an investment strategy that would work for his situation indicates that his losses must have been only moderate and did not completely discourage him from continuing in the business.

133. House of Lords, Correspondence About Settlements, 219, 191:1438.

134. In 1752, John Dick chartered the *Oldbury* to sail to the Carolinas or Georgia (GAR, ONA 2699/99 [30 May 1752]).

135. Curtius apparently advanced the fare of quite a few passengers on the *Fane*, probably for redemption by the immigrants' relatives or by others who had "ordered" immigrants from him. See Penrose Cashbooks (5 January 1749/50).

The case was quite different for partnerships that were in the business for the long term. The Stedman brothers, formerly of London, who had established residences in Rotterdam as well as in Philadelphia, seem to have focused more exclusively on providing passage for German emigrants than any of the other firms, possibly as a result of their experience in the trade as captains in the 1730s. Their prominent shares in the Rotterdam and Philadelphia markets are a reflection of their success in the trade. Part of their strength came from their combined ownership of seven vessels registered in Philadelphia. As ship owners, they could use profits realized on the eastward voyage to offset expenses on the outward leg of the run. Moreover, losses that occurred occasionally—such as very high mortality rates on some of Stedman's ships in 1738 and 1749—were blunted in their effect if most other voyages progressed normally and brought reasonable returns. Extended lines of credit that developed as fewer passengers paid their fare in advance were also easier to handle for a firm that had a comfortable market share in a business in which they engaged over a number of years.[136]

In contrast, the firm of Benjamin & Samuel Shoemaker appeared only once as part-owners of an immigrant ship registered in Philadelphia; they too fared well in the Philadelphia German immigrant market. Their strategy for success was to run a more diverse business operation than that of the Stedmans. Their close connection with the Hopes in Rotterdam extended well beyond the shipping of emigrants and sustained their participation in the passenger trade well into the 1760s. Like the Stedmans, they accumulated considerable experience in the business, which helped them weather competition, regulation, and fluctuations in the flow of emigrants and shipping. Profits for them came less in spectacular returns for a particular voyage and more in the steady and reliable gains the business provided over the long term, as a supplement to other commercial activities on which the partners on both sides of the Atlantic could bring to bear trust in one another's sincerity and reliability in business dealings, as well as specialized knowledge.

When Thomas Willing's company became involved in the German migrant trade in Philadelphia after the wave of immigrants had crested, it combined the strategies on which the successes of the Stedmans and the

---

136. Entries in the Penrose Cashbooks show that some payments for particular voyages stretched over many years. However, many of the very late payments were small and the bulk of the accounting was completed within months of the ship's arrival—no doubt in part because Penrose was interested in receiving his commission.

Shoemakers had rested: interest in shipping, diverse operations, reliable overseas connections, and a good knowledge of the local market.[137] Similarly, the Crawford merchant house, which included the transportation of emigrants as a minor component among its interests and services, became the major exporter of German emigrants in Rotterdam after the end of the Seven Years' War. The Crawfords cooperated closely with the Hopes, and that put providing passage for Germans into the hands of very large and influential firms. In contrast, most of the merchants who had entered the market at the height of the migration flow discontinued active participation after the war, in part because the colonies with which they had established connections in the business no longer attracted the remaining Rhinelanders who sought to relocate in the New World.[138]

Providing passage for German emigrants was at all times firmly embedded in the prevailing overall structure of ties among business partners on both sides of the Atlantic. Participants in the trade simply took advantage of that structure for their own use, to develop a highly specialized business by shifting and balancing in order to capitalize on current opportunities for carrying passengers. Most important, they developed a way to profit further from underutilized shipping on the westward leg of transatlantic trade, or at least to cut their losses in bringing vessels back for American cargoes.

At the beginning of regular German immigration to Philadelphia, when London provided the bulk of all shipping to the American mainland colonies, German immigrants took passage to Pennsylvania on London-owned and -operated ships, which then proceeded on their way from Philadelphia to the southern colonies and the West Indies, or both, and from there back to England. At the height of the German immigration wave, most immigrant vessels still followed the same itinerary, but other destinations in the American colonies were included, and the number of ships owned in and operated out of Philadelphia had increased. This trend to greater colonial ownership continued after the disruption of the Seven Years' War. As a result, the destinations of immigrant vessels after pas-

137. Thomas Willing was one of those merchants. Part of his operations was the sale of servants he imported, for whose indentures he accepted cash or bonds. See Robert Wright, "Thomas Willing," 527.

138. After 1763, most of the shippers in Rotterdam and Amsterdam had "open accounts" for the transshipment of German emigrants, but when the emigration flow resumed in the 1760s and early 1770s, only some of those accounts were activated.

sengers were unloaded also changed. More went straight back across the Atlantic, reflecting Philadelphia's expanding role in overseas shipping that now involved more direct links with Great Britain and southern Europe. Until 1755, some 40 percent of those vessels continued to the southern mainland colonies, especially South Carolina—a clear indication of the importance of the rice trade that drew ships to Charleston; after 1763, only 7 percent gave that colony as their next destination.[139] Overall, 14 percent of the ships sailed on to the West Indies, and 4 percent went to England and Scotland (an additional 4 percent to Ireland). Mediterranean ports accounted for 12 percent of destinations and were heavily clustered in the last decade before the Revolution.

These sailing patterns observed for the ships engaged in the German immigrant trade reflect a shift from the dominating impact of the rice trade out of South Carolina to an expansion of Philadelphia's trade, but especially flour and shipping.[140] It also underscores that transporting emigrants depended not only on well-established trade connections but also on the reputation of particular destinations in the colonies. South Carolina had several promising starts in drawing settlers from the Rhine lands: in the 1730s, 1750s, and again after the French and Indian War. None of those beginnings, however, developed the kind of migration networks that forged regular and long-term connections and generated extensive flows. In the long run, the southern colonies, and also New York, New England, and Nova Scotia, lacked the opportunities for work and settlement that sustained the migration flow from the Rhine lands. Access to Pennsylvania, Maryland, and the Virginia and Carolina Piedmont through Philadelphia and the Great Valley did offer those opportunities. Conversely, transportation on less popular routes allowed passengers and shippers to avoid some of the negative conditions that had become common, if not customary, in the trade that centered on Philadelphia.

The dynamics that shaped the transatlantic transportation of German

139. From the customhouse notices published in the *Pennsylvania Gazette,* one can determine the next destination of three-quarters of all listed German immigrant vessels that had entered Philadelphia; supplemented from *Lloyd's Lists.*

140. McCusker, "Pennsylvania Shipping Industry." Evidence from the surviving port books in England and from the notarial archives in Rotterdam suggest close links to the rice trade in particular. Vessels that carried German emigrants loaded rice at other times, and the correspondents and partners on whom Rotterdam merchants could count for customs and inspections procedures in the English Channel ports tended to be those with whom they were already connected through the rice trade. See Kenneth Morgan, "Organization of the Colonial American Rice Trade."

immigrants to the American colonies depended on merchants involved in British overseas trade who tried to take advantage of profits to be had from carrying passengers as one part of their diversified operations. That commercial opportunity was larger at some times than at others, and the flow and then ebb in the numbers of Germans seeking transportation to North America helped change which companies carried passengers, and in what manner, through the three successive phases of the history of the German migration from the early 1700s to the Revolution.

Throughout, providing overseas passage for German emigrants always depended on the cooperation of merchants in three different ports. The relationship among business partners in London, the Dutch ports, and in North America changed over time, however, in response to the relative strength of each merchant community's interest in transporting Rhineland immigrants to the American colonies.

London was always a strong focal point in the relationship among merchants who had interests in the immigrant trade, because of the city's dominating role in England's trade with all the overseas colonies. The city was the financial center and source of much credit in the colonies, and it also played many ancillary roles. Most important for the trade in German emigrants were insurance and ship brokerage services. As the center for trade in general, London was then called on over and over again to cope with or take advantage of underutilized cargo space on ships sent with dry goods from England to the American mainland colonies, or going in ballast to take on rice in Charleston. That was what made the transporting German immigrants across the Atlantic so attractive for merchants involved in overseas trade. In 1736, one London merchant and ship owner explicitly sought to take advantage of the demand for transatlantic passage from German immigrants by offering them transportation on his vessel bound for the colonies where he had interests and would otherwise go mainly in ballast.[141] In 1748–49, when John Hunt expected the Philadelphia market to be glutted with dry goods, he chartered a larger ship than he would have otherwise under those conditions, in order to transport German immigrants—admittedly a complicated and at times bothersome business—because it seemed much more profitable than just sending more dry goods on his own account.[142]

141. "Petition of Kieffer," 27. On the difference in shipping rates for vessels in the tobacco trade destined for Europe and on the outward voyage to the Chesapeake Bay colonies, see Jacob Price, *Capital and Credit in British Overseas Trade*, 40.

142. John Hunt to John Pemberton, 27 February 1749/9, Hunt & Greenleafe Letter Book.

Although London never lost its dominance in the exchange of goods between England and the American colonies before the Revolution, ownership and control in the shipping employed in one facet of this exchange, the German immigrant trade to Philadelphia, shifted significantly during the third quarter of the eighteenth century—away from London. In the early years, London merchants with interest in Philadelphia utilized unfilled cargo space on London-owned vessels to transport immigrants—supplied through the services of English merchants in Rotterdam—to Philadelphia. During the peak years of German immigration, providing transatlantic passage became a profitable end in itself, not simply a supplementary activity for filling vessels, and attracted newcomers to the business, who challenged customary practices and pushed the limits of the market by drawing emigrants from hitherto untapped territories in Germany and by importing them into colonies other than Pennsylvania. Both strategies had only limited success because they could not replicate the dynamics that fueled the flow from the Rhine lands to the Delaware Valley. After 1763, as the number of Germans seeking to go to Philadelphia subsided, carrying Germans once again became a supplement to other transactions. Now, however, the immigrant ships were owned in and operated out of Philadelphia. London's particular role in the immigrant trade largely changed from direct supplier of shipping with vested interest in the vessels, to that of ship broker for Philadelphia business partners who wanted to use their tonnage more fully.[143]

The progressive phases of the German immigrant trade through three distinct periods are most evident and revealing in Rotterdam's relations with London and Philadelphia. During the early years of regular and increasing emigration from Germany, the English merchants in Rotterdam—and to a lesser degree in Amsterdam—applied their special expertise and position as middlemen to coordinate the demand for transatlantic emigrant transportation with the supply of shipping from England, mostly London. In this they were crucial mediators between participants in different and not otherwise directly linked spheres of European trade. This mediating function intensified dramatically when German emigration

---

James Pemberton expressed the same conviction to John Pemberton, 5 June 1749, Pemberton Papers, 5:102.

143. For example, Keppele & Steinmetz contacted their English correspondent in 1772 to find out the chances of securing a German emigrant cargo for their ship on the return voyage from Europe to Philadelphia. See Joseph Banfield to Keppele & Steinmetz, Falmouth, 5 December 1772, Steinmetz Papers, Jasper Yeates Brinton Collection, HSP.

peaked between 1749 and 1754. At that time, considerably increased profit margins through high passenger-ship ratios influenced many of the practices in the trade. The virtual monopoly the Rotterdam merchants had over the supply of passengers guaranteed the merchants as a group decisive manipulative powers over profits that would be gained from any supply of shipping beyond the transatlantic transportation requirements of the preceding more normal years.

A decided shortage in transatlantic shipping would have diminished Rotterdam's powerful role in freighting vessels with desired emigrants, but throughout the peak period offers by merchants to transport passengers were plentiful. John Hunt's venture in the business demonstrates this point. His Rotterdam partners, Isaac and Zachary Hope, were unable to obtain what he considered a full load of emigrant freights, even though his ship was in Rotterdam at the beginning of the busiest season of the colonial period. Yet the Hopes themselves sent an agent of their own to London to obtain suitable shipping. In turn, some ship owners and ship-owning captains were lured by the prospective profits and dispatched their vessels directly, apparently without previous arrangement, to Rotterdam.[144] Others decided to circumvent competition with merchants already established there and tried to tap into the passenger market by setting up partnerships in ports from which few German emigrants had embarked before. Hamburg was especially attractive in that regard, because it drew on a different hinterland and because freighters could operate there without the constraints that the transshipment requirements posed for merchants doing business out of Holland. The boom in potential passengers not only brought about an increase in the demand for the regular services of the Rotterdam merchants—at a price set largely by them—but led also to a heightened interest in how their business partners managed the American end of the voyage, because high mortality at sea and poor recovery of fare debts cut into profits.

At the height of the immigrant trade (1749–54), when large profits were being made, the most effective and concerted effort of all three ports demanded close ties between Rotterdam, which provided the substantial numbers of German emigrants necessary to ensure continued large profit margins, and Philadelphia and the other ports in the American colonies, which received and placed the human cargo and guaranteed their payment to make the venture profitable. London was playing a more diffuse role as

144. John Hunt to I. & Z. Hope, 9 and 23 May, and 7 June 1749, Hunt & Greenleafe Letter Book.

recipient of American cargoes and clearinghouse for additional ships requested by or offered to Rotterdam.

After 1763, however, Philadelphia merchants gained in relative importance because of their increased interest in providing transatlantic passage on vessels they now owned and operated, and also because merchants in other ports of the American colonies could not draw on, let alone rely on, the same circumstances that allowed traders in Philadelphia to shift the risk of extending credit for the transatlantic fares to residents of the greater Pennsylvania region primarily through the market for labor. Profits from transporting emigrants remained attractive for Philadelphia merchants as long as they could count on the willingness of settlers to redeem immigrants who were still indebted for their fares or to purchase them as servants. As the German emigration flow subsided, after its peak years, English merchants in Rotterdam returned to their role as middlemen in simply coordinating the emigrants' demand for passage with shipping that was available in the various trades for which they routinely managed freight. This meant now, in most cases, that ships owned by Philadelphians and operated out of their port would make an additional stopover in Rotterdam on their return voyage from England to pick up passengers to supplement their cargoes. And toward the end of the colonial period, the Rotterdam merchants even sent emigrants to London, where regular and more frequent transportation to Philadelphia was available and more efficiently handled, given the now relatively small numbers of passengers available per ship. In the last few years before the Revolution, more and more immigrant ships listed Hamburg and Lisbon, besides London, as ports of embarkation, which is another indication that transporting what were now relatively small numbers of immigrants was no longer so profitable for many English merchants in Rotterdam.[145] The trade in German emigrants, whose flood had crested in the early 1750s, was now in full ebb as fewer and fewer of the disappointed and disaffected chose America over eastern Europe when they relocated, and as transatlantic traders saw less profit to be gained in the business.

145. Strassburger/Hinke, *Pennsylvania German Pioneers*, 1:xxxiv.

CHAPTER 4

The Ordeal of Relocation

If transportation across the Atlantic provided a business opportunity for merchants, it posed a formidable obstacle for the emigrants who were relocating. Yet the long, difficult, and expensive journey from the Rhineland to the American colonies was the one component of the migration experience that all the more than 111,000 German immigrants who arrived in the New World before 1776 shared. For every immigrant it was a complex move, from preparations for leaving the homeland, to taking the first steps toward making a new home in America. Success in this challenging undertaking depended both on the circumstances under which emigrants left their homelands and on their experiences along the way. At all times, good planning was essential for coping with the problems of the journey; but in some years the dangers inherent in the enterprise were much more threatening to the well-being of emigrants than in other years, and affected the lives of some people more than others. How the nature of the journey shaped the immigrants' prospects for achieving their goal of a decent life in America needs to be examined carefully to be truly understood.

So far, a handful of travel accounts have provided much of the information we have about the trip.[1] The descriptions in those accounts form

1. Gottlieb Mittelberger's diatribe on a poor voyage, *Journey to Pennsylvania*, Heinrich Muhlenberg's observations on immigrants and the trade in his reports to Halle (*Hallesche Nachrichten;* and Christopher Sauer's extensive comments in *Pennsylvanische Berichte* are the most prominent eighteenth-century sources. Numerous other accounts of the journey—mostly in

the basis for the popular image of the transatlantic voyage as one of physical, emotional, and financial suffering aboard overcrowded ships, where exposure to the unpredictability of the sea and the winds was compounded by the greed of the merchants involved, the tyranny of captains, and the irresponsibility of newlanders. In reality, the true picture is complex and more subtle.[2] The hazards of the journey were undoubtedly many and real, and the trip was always a stressful experience that required extraordinary endurance, patience, reserves, and resourcefulness—quite unimaginable to people with late twentieth-century sensibilities. A broader reading of travel accounts reveals the wide array of reactions people had to the difficulties of the voyage, and the role of former emigrants and compatriots in helping—and exploiting—those who followed in the footsteps of the pioneers. Most important, not all migrants were victims of circumstances beyond their control; more often than not, they took an active role in shaping what happened to them on the way to settle in America.

When migration from the Rhine lands to the American colonies began in the early 1680s, arrangements for overseas transportation were made on a case-by-case basis. Passengers made agreements for the transatlantic voyage with merchants in London, and occasionally in Amsterdam, or used the services of a merchant in Frankfurt am Main, who—through his correspondents in Holland—acted as a broker for passage. This method of contracting for passage remained an option throughout the colonial period.

Rotterdam became the predominant port of embarkation for Rhinelanders seeking transatlantic passage in the late 1720s, the time the number of German emigrants began to increase significantly. Located at the western, Atlantic end of the complex Rhine estuary, it was a natural choice, even in competition with Amsterdam, the great commercial hub of the Netherlands. Rotterdam was the port of departure for three-quarters of all

immigrant letters home—have survived, but these are widely scattered, and systematic gathering and publishing efforts have only just begun. Schelbert and Rappolt, *Alles ist ganz anders hier,* is one example. These letters represent a wealth of material for illustrative purposes, even though they cannot yet be analyzed in a systematic fashion. The older literature on German immigration usually includes descriptions that detail the perils of the voyage.

2. Descriptions of the journey, mostly in immigrants' letters home, have added much detail to the story. More particulars come indirectly from mercantile records and administrative sources, which are listed in the Bibliography, and from illustrations in the footnotes.

vessels carrying migrants to the American colonies.[3] Since the overwhelming majority of German overseas passengers came from areas directly and conveniently connected with the extensive and heavily traveled Rhine waterway system, they could take advantage of boat service to Rotterdam—an important consideration for those who traveled with baggage, as many apparently did. Also, the mass migration of Palatines to England in 1709 had taken its route via Rotterdam, setting a precedent for later emigrants and their shippers to begin the voyage to the American colonies there. Although Amsterdam was the center of Anglo-Dutch financial dealings, Rotterdam actually received more British shipping.[4]

After departure from Rotterdam, all immigrant ships had to stop in one of the coastal ports in England, or—during times of increased danger from French and Spanish warships and privateers—in Scotland. There they completed provisioning, paid customs duties on wares other than used household goods, and waited for favorable wind, and sometimes for a convoy to be completed, before starting across the ocean. The southwestern coast of England was the last land most German immigrants sighted before reaching Cape Henlopen at the mouth of the Delaware, or comparable landfalls on their way to destinations other than Philadelphia. Some ships, however—especially when England was at war with France—like the ill-fated Spanish Armada sailed more northerly along the eastern coast of England, and rounded Scotland and the Hebrides. Several others took a southern route, more like that of Columbus, across the Atlantic, stopping over at ports like Madeira for additional cargo and provisions.[5]

Sailing times varied considerably. Different routes and stopovers accounted for some of the differences, but the dependence on the wind for propulsion resulted in some very good times—a number of ships made the voyage from land to land in about four weeks—and some catastrophically long ordeals that lasted three months and more. The expected sailing time from England to Pennsylvania ranged from eight to ten weeks,

3. The immigrant voyages listed in the Appendix note the port of embarkation.

4. Charles Wilson, *Anglo-Dutch Commerce and Finance*. For the organization of the transfer of Palatines from Rotterdam to London in 1709, see Knittle, *Early Eighteenth-Century Palatine Emigration*.

5. The ship lists give the location of the last stop in the British Isles for all but thirty-seven of the reported vessels carrying German immigrants to Philadelphia. Cowes alone harbored 47 percent of all listed vessels, Portsmouth 11 percent, Deal 7 percent, Dover 3 percent, and Leith 2 percent; Gosport, Porte, Plymouth, Falmouth, Berwick, Orkney, Teignmouth, Shields, and Aberdeen all harbored 1 percent or less. See Strassburger/Hinke, *Pennsylvania German Pioneers*, 1:xxxiv. See also Appendix.

with a normal variation of two weeks in either direction.[6] The wrong abnormality could be disastrous.

When the vessel reached the mouth of the Delaware, a river pilot guided it upstream to Philadelphia. Occasionally, stops provided opportunities for relatives, friends, and vendors to meet the ship along the way up the river. In Philadelphia, the ship was inspected by a health official to be sure no infectious disease was present before passengers and goods could be landed. Usually within a day or two of arrival, all German immigrant men age sixteen and older were led to the courthouse, where they swore allegiance to the laws of the province and to the English king in an oath or affirmation that included testimony against the Pope. In ports of debarkation other than Philadelphia, landing procedures for immigrants and their baggage varied. Most often the people who had strong vested interests shaped the process. If provincial or local governments did not regulate the influx of immigrants, the merchants and their assigned partners or factors in effect directed the debarkation of passengers. If local merchants and captains lacked clear instructions about, or personal interests in, unloading the human cargo, the immigrants were left to make their first steps in the New World on their own. How well they fared depended to a large extent on the resources they had to draw on at this stage. Life in the New World looked bleak for poor and impoverished colonists, especially if they could not count on support from family, friends, co-religionists, or compatriots. For immigrants of some means, or those who could link up readily with already established settlers, prospects seemed more promising.

For many emigrants from the Rhine lands who had little direct knowledge of the Atlantic and seafaring life, the ordeal of even a smooth ocean crossing must have been an extraordinary experience. Since, however, many of the immigrant letters and reports that survived in German archives did so because local authorities used them as anti-emigration propaganda, the apparent emphasis on the difficulties connected with the relocation may not be totally representative of information that circulated at the time. While such tales of misfortune may have dissuaded some potential emigrants from leaving, they were generally of little practical use to those

6. The immigrant voyages listed in the Appendix include the times of departure and arrival in port whenever they could be ascertained (the charterparties in GAR, ONA, *Lloyd's Lists*, the customhouse notices in the *Pennsylvania Gazette*, and the lists in Strassburger/Hinke provide most of the information). Sailing times are difficult to compute; especially before 1752, when England and the continent reckoned by different calendars, mistakes are likely because sources did not always indicate whether they measured times at sea or in port in the old-style calendar or the new-style calendar.

who had already decided to make the trip. For the latter, concrete advice about how to plan for the relocation was most useful.

What follows is a presentation of typical aspects of the journey that focuses on the options available to the emigrants along the way under various conditions and at different times. This is not to downplay the extreme hardships of wrecks and other disasters that could and did occur on some voyages under extraordinary circumstances.[7] The intent is to underscore what was in fact a wide spectrum of individual opportunities and experiences, and to comprehend the various processes or conditions that could make the relocation either easy or difficult.

Whatever motivated individuals to leave their homelands, the majority of all emigrants began their journey in the spring, when the rivers were more easily navigable after the winter's ice had broken and when dangers from the rapid runoff of melting snow had subsided. The seasonality of the emigrant trade seemed to be determined largely by the weather; inland travel in Germany during fall and winter was uncomfortable, time-consuming, and cost-consuming—and often hazardous. Yet the availability of suitable shipping, which was dictated by the requirements of other overseas trades—such as provisions, especially rice—may well have played even more of a role in the time frame. This can in part be inferred from the way any seasonal pattern became less obvious toward the end of the colonial period, when transatlantic shipping of German emigrants was taking place virtually year-round and was no longer channeled almost exclusively through Rotterdam. The actual date of departure from home depended also on the time it would take to complete the bureaucratic procedures required for permission to move legally from the territory and to gain manumission from feudal bondage.[8] For those who had planned the move and finally had all requisite papers in hand, taking leave was

7. Accounts of voyages gone wrong also help us gauge what was considered a normal Atlantic crossing. Examples of disastrous voyages include those of the *Love and Unity* in 1732; the *Oliver* and several others in 1738; and the 1754 wreck in the coastal waters of Holland. See Wust, "Emigration Season of 1738"; "Eine Leyder Wahrhaffte Traurige Geschicht und Beschreibung," Broadside Collection, HSP.

8. For details, see Chapter 1. Migrants found only three of the official documents useful in their journey: the passport for the trip to Rotterdam; the minister's certificate attesting to the Christian behavior for those who wanted to get married after they left home and before they embarked for the American colonies; and the baptismal certificate of children, as proof of their age, in order to determine the correct fare and when young immigrants bound out as servants would reach the age of maturity and therefore freedom. *Rundbrief* ("circular letter") from a settler in Maryland, 17 September 1750, Faust, "Unpublished Documents," 30.

often a momentous event that brought out not only family and friends but also many curious onlookers.[9] There were no such good-byes for the emigrants who left illegally.[10]

The choice of transportation to the port of embarkation—usually Rotterdam—depended on many factors. The prospective emigrants' financial situation was the most important and determined many of their choices later in the journey as well. Emigrants who had adequate funds for the whole trip generally traveled with luggage, containing bedding, clothing, cooking utensils, provisions, and a variety of other items. This made river transportation desirable because it minimized the number of transfers and reduced the heavy cost of overland hauling; haulage was usually charged according to weight and bulk. When emigrants seeking passage through Prussian territories along the Rhine refused to follow the king's settlement offer to populate his eastern provinces instead of going to America, and were consequently denied river passage, they were forced to travel from Cologne to 's Hertogenbosch over land. "To have our goods hauled all that distance cost us 3¼ kr (about 6½ shillings) for each hundredweight."[11] Singly or in small groups, those emigrants of more comfortable circumstances preferred to travel down the Rhine as it suited them.

Emigrants with restricted travel funds had to be more selective in their choice of Rhine passage. The number of people in a given party often determined the actual cost per person. Calculated for one hundred emigrants plus baggage in 1710, the most economical way was to charter and outfit one's own boat at the expense of thirteen shillings per head (without food). This meant hiring an experienced helmsman and at least four rowing servants, plus a "director" (or "leader") whose job it was to deal with customs, present passports, provide victuals, wood, coal, straw, and other necessities, and generally manage the transport.[12] This was cheaper

9. The chapter-opening vignette of the young men of Schwaigern boisterously celebrating the immanent departure of four of their group in 1743 is one example. See Fogleman, *Hopeful Journeys.*

10. One emigrant who had left clandestinely later wrote a letter (July 28, 1752) in which he told of his regrets about leaving his family and friends without saying good-bye, and of his concern that his secret departure might have hurt their reputation. See Faust, "Unpublished Documents," 31–34.

11. Gerber, *Nassau-Dillenburger Auswanderung.*

12. The calculations are in a report by Johann Ludwig Runckel to the (Mennonite) Committee of Foreign Needs in Amsterdam. The boatmen were hired at a fixed daily rate for the length of the trip plus the same number of days for the return trip. See "European Mennonites, Amsterdam Archives" (microfilm, Lancaster Mennonite Historical Society).

than chartering a boat from Rhine shippers already established in the trade, who charged about eighteen shillings per head from Basel to Rotterdam in 1711, and up to one pound sterling (excluding baggage) by mid-century. None of the quotations for Rhine transportation included food. The cost of transportation down the Rhine varied, of course, according to the distances from Rotterdam.[13]

Since many German emigrants traveled in groups of family, friends, and neighbors, they were advised to "keep in a group and appoint three or four of your number to contract for Rhine transportation," because that enabled them to travel at a lower price than Rhine passage secured with the help of an agent, who would make all the necessary arrangements but whose quotation of the fare would include his own profit.[14] Competent leadership paid off for the travelers, but not all leaders of emigrant transports were good tour managers. The group headed by Moritz Götschi, a clergyman from Switzerland, did not fare well because of his shortcomings in holding the transport together and arranging affordable and efficient Rhine travel.[15] Emigrants who were unwilling or unable to make their own arrangements for the trip down the Rhine had to engage the services of an agent, most likely a recruiting agent or boatman working for a Rotterdam merchant, who could offer terms agreeable to the emigrant, such as "charging" the expenses of the trip to the passenger's account for deferred payment. These services, however, invariably raised the cost and curtailed flexibility for the emigrant in arranging the rest of the long journey.

Since food was not included in the fare, any extra delays on the way down the Rhine—a trip that normally lasted anywhere from about two weeks to two months—could swell the account considerably, upsetting calculations of expected expenses. In 1735, a group of emigrants from Bern spent three times as much money on the trip down the Rhine as they had originally calculated.[16] The relative duration of the Rhine trip from any of the major collecting points (Basel, or Bingen on the confluence of the Ruhr) varied according to weather and traffic conditions and according to

13. The citations used here represent a range of fares; a precise fare scale according to relative distance and type of service cannot be established. Mittelberger reported a fare from Württemberg of a little over 3£ (Fl 40) for the Rhine passage per person, which is in line with other known prices for the trip (*Journey to Pennsylvania*, 17). See Schelbert and Rappolt, *Alles ist ganz anders hier*, 101; contract of Dunlop & Company; Rattermann, "Geschichte des deutschen Elements," 14: 354–57; Melchior's "Advice to German Emigrants, 1749" (ed. Roach).

14. "Advice to German Emigrants, 1749," 232.

15. Pfister, *Zürcher Auswanderung nach Amerika*.

16. *Bernisches Avis-Blättlein*, no. 22, quoted in Faust and Brumbaugh, *Lists of Swiss Emigrants*, 25.

the skill of those in charge of expediting arrangements at the many toll stations. This required planning, experience, money, and the ability to deal effectively with customs officials and other government authorities at many territorial border stations. There, insufficient documentation for passengers and their goods, especially on boats with unusually large numbers of emigrants, could result in lengthy inquiries and searches. The proverbial tyranny of customs officials along the Rhine had its foundation in the dependence of petty territorial lords and their administrations on the revenue extracted at those toll stations, which usually represented their largest single tax source. Much of the collection was farmed out and well regulated and documented, because the lords of the tolls wanted to guard their privileges against any form of circumvention and smuggling, while the profits for customs collectors depended on their contracted percentage of the tolls. Each required the keeping of good accounts.[17] Under such circumstances of tight control, it was advisable for emigrants and their agents to notify the various Rhine principalities in advance of any large emigrant movement, to be certain to have all the required travel documents, especially the necessary customs papers (*Zollbrief* or *Freischein*), and to be prepared to line the right pockets to ensure speedy and lenient clearance.[18]

The need for timely progress at each toll station was dictated not only by the desire to keep travel costs low but also by the sheer number of toll stops, which forced considerable delays along the way. Emigrants who started out in Strasbourg had to pass ten toll stations before they arrived at Mainz; they had to stop at eleven between Mainz and Cologne; and at another nine before they reached Schenkenschanz, the station at the border of the United Provinces of the Netherlands, at which the Dutch authorities required security in order to ensure that their country would not be burdened with poor Germans stranded on their way to the American colonies. From there, migrants on their way to Rotterdam encountered three more toll stations, while the journey of those who opted to follow the river Waal to Amsterdam had to make stops at four additional points.[19]

Those who were willing and able to travel on foot could escape the

17. For examples of lists of tariffs and instructions for collecting tolls from Jülich and Berg (1763) and Cologne (1764) and several accounts of collected tolls, see Alfred Engels, *Die Zollgrenze in der Eiffel*, 104–18.

18. Report of Runckel to Committee of Foreign Needs, AA no. 1321; Mittelberger, *Journey to Pennsylvania*, 17.

19. W. F. Leemans, *De Groote Gelderse Tollen en de Tollenars*, 7–8.

heavy fees imposed on passengers and wares shipped down the Rhine, but they were still vulnerable to the whims of the border authorities, whose responsibilities included checking emigrants and transients and their goods carefully and who could thereby run up costs and delay emigrants unduly. The only way to avoid all the toll stations along the Rhine was to walk through France, but the length of that journey was about the same as the Rhine trip, and the cost—including food and lodging—was not any cheaper. In any case, this alternative route was suitable only for those who traveled without baggage.[20] Embarkation from Hamburg could also save emigrants the trip down the Rhine, but the miners from the Harz found the overland trek difficult in 1752, especially for women and children, who could not keep up the pace of the long daily marches.[21]

Most emigrants traveled as part of a group, and most relied on agents of different kinds to help them in their journey. Single young men and women were generally least dependent on those services, because they traveled light and often had previous experience with walking the roads as journeymen or laborers in search of seasonal work far from their homelands.[22] Irrespective of emigrants' confidence and experience as long-distance travelers, most preferred to follow the lead of someone whom they considered knowledgeable and trustworthy, rather than travel alone. For those who could make a conscious choice about joining a particular group, the presence of a newlander—someone who had already completed the trip successfully—seemed to promise significant assistance in negotiating travel arrangements that lay ahead. Such reliance on the travel services of newlanders, however, was fraught with potential difficulties. Not all made good guides just because they had once made the trip themselves, and adversities that emigrants experienced because they placed too much trust in their assistance were equally devastating, whether these stemmed from incompetence or from fraud.[23]

Contemporaries therefore warned that it was best to avoid all contact

---

20. Schelbert and Rappolt, *Alles ist ganz anders hier*, 96.

21. Brink, *Deutsche Auswanderungswelle*, 189–91.

22. Many Germans labored as migrant workers in Holland and were known as *Hollandgänger*. Moch, *Moving Europeans*, 41–43; see also Lucassen, "The Netherlands, the Dutch, and Long-Distance Migration," 161–65.

23. Newlanders repeatedly left their charges stranded and in dire straits—for example, the emigrants abandoned in London in 1764 by their recruiter Johann Heinrich Christian von Stümpel. See Robert Selig, "Emigration, Fraud, Humanitarianism, and the Founding of Londonderry"; and the letter by Philipp Jacop Irion, 9 May 1766, in Fritz Braun, *Auswanderer aus Kaiserslautern*, 14–15.

with newlanders. If that was impractical, however, it was possible to guard against unfair or bad practices by comparing contract offers and heeding the advice of experienced and well-informed former emigrants. At the height of the German immigration to the American colonies many recruiting agents competed to win colonists or passengers. Emigrants therefore had a number of choices and seemed to have taken advantage of this situation.

> Take one or two, three or even four—the fewer the better—of the newlanders that are abroad, whether good or evil, praised or blamed, whether provided with letters of recommendation or not, if he can purchase much goods abroad, or gained it through that useful trait of his—take him before a sworn notary and make a contract with him that he will truly keep all the promises he makes you, pledging to you as security the goods he has with him both at that time or later, and agreeing that they shall not be delivered to him from the ship until he has kept his word. . . . All other agreements and arrangements you make with newlanders must be in writing and with the foregoing conditions. Should you lend them money or buy anything with them on a fifty-fifty basis, have it put down in writing and have their goods, wares, etc. pledged to you until the things are unloaded, until they find bail for you in Philadelphia in order that no one can steal both you and your effects away, as often happened.[24]

The value of these instructions for keeping a check on exploitative and fraudulent practices must have been far superior to mere lamentations about abuses in the trade, yet it is not known how many emigrants fared better than their less well advised companion travelers because they had followed such instructions. What this advice does demonstrate, however, is the business nature at the heart of the relationship between emigrant and newlander. Since opportunity to do better in the American colonies than at home persuaded many emigrants to leave, it is not surprising that they were receptive to promises of deals that could minimize relocation expenses and ease startup costs in the New World. The cautious tended to stay home, while the more daring not only took the chance of emigrating but also seemed willing to put critical resources into ventures that carried considerable risk. Careful reading of the accounts that describe the opera-

24. "Advice to German Emigrants, 1749," 235.

tions of newlanders, and the laments of those who lost their investments, indicate that the outrage at the newlanders often reflected indignation at shady and fraudulent business practices that had soured endeavors that promised rich returns. Emigrants who banked on risk-free, high-yield investments were likely to be disappointed. Those who used some caution and care in their dealings, and who followed established business practices, faced better prospects. It is clear that the advice literature for emigrants supported, even recommended, the purchase of goods for resale in the American colonies. In this process, greed on the part of the emigrants prompted impulsiveness and disregard for common business sense. Both could have disastrous results for investors. Greed on the part of the newlanders invited deception and outright fraud, which could enrich the schemer but harmed lasting success in a business that depended on a good reputation.

Circumspect emigrants could protect themselves and their belongings and investments by making legally binding contracts with newlanders and with all others they did business with on their way to the American colonies. When German emigrants arrived in Rotterdam, they made agreements with merchants and captains, either for the first time or when finalizing contracts they had signed earlier in Germany. In this matter, it was crucial to observe certain guidelines that not only determined much of the quality of life at sea but also ensured that the contract was legally binding if it proved necessary to seek redress after arriving in the colonies. Without a valid contract, recourse was impossible for the immigrant; and without a clause that stipulated the right to withhold payment of the fare until all promises were met, any suit brought by a passenger against a merchant involved in the trade was likely to fail. In Philadelphia, no direct evidence of immigrants suing merchants for breach of contract survived. However, Christopher Sauer reported in *Pennsylvanische Berichte* (16 December 1746) about a suit concerning fare-charging practices pending in court. In the 1760s and 1770s, one of the declared goals of the German Society of Pennsylvania was to assist newly arrived immigrants in cases of justified redress against their importers—if necessary, with the help of their attorney in court.[25]

When contracting for transatlantic passage, it was especially useful to have advice from experienced travelers concerning particular features that regulated the quality and quantity of provisions, their distribution, the

25. Preamble to the Beamtenratsprotokoll, GSP.

shipment of luggage, and general procedures to be observed on board
during passage. From what the merchants or their agents or employees
chose to tell them, most emigrants could not realistically anticipate what
the voyage was like, apart from hearsay about its dangers. Yet attention to
the right detail could mean surviving the ordeal in reasonable physical and
financial shape. It is not surprising that taking advantage of useful contract options required the financial independence of the emigrant. Other
terms of the passage may have already been set by some earlier commitment to which travelers had subscribed when they contracted for transatlantic transportation in Germany. Some characteristics of the voyage depended on a well-informed choice when negotiating for passage.

Whether traveling alone or in a group, emigrants who arrived at the
port of embarkation with sufficient funds, independent of ties to a newlander, and without obligations to a particular merchant had the best options.[26] Their horizons were especially open and flexible if they arrived
early, between April and June, to avoid the crowded conditions that prevailed toward the end of the season during years of heavy emigration.
Comparing different terms of transatlantic transportation was the best
way to gather information about what options were available and at what
price. At any time, there was little difference in the basic price charged for
the passage; but the kinds of services included in that quotation could
result in an economical fare, while, conversely, exclusion of some services
could entail many extra costs.[27]

After doing as much as possible to weigh the relative costs, assess the
soundness and experience of the merchants offering passage, and check the
ships and their masters, it was wisest to choose the merchant who offered
the best guarantees for certain key services: adequate supplies of good-

26. As of 1738, the Dutch authorities only let emigrants across the border who could prove
they had sufficient funds for the transshipment through the Netherlands and for the transatlantic passage. Rotterdam and Amsterdam merchants in the emigrant trade obtained free
passage and transshipment for most of the German emigrants at Schenkenschanz. Although
most merchants expected emigrants to seek transatlantic passage with them, many Germans
considered their signature on such transportation agreements nonbinding and merely a decla-
ration of intent. See Chapter 3 for details on transshipment procedures; see also "Advice to
German Emigrants, 1749," 232.

27. This is evident when the contracts of the Hopes and of Dunlop & Company in 1752
are compared. See Rattermann, "Geschichte des deutschen Elements," 14:354–57. The Hopes'
contract of 1756 is published in Yoder, *Pennsylvania German Immigrants*, 255–58. For a copy of
Daniel Harvart's contract, see Kaller, "Archivalien zur Auswanderungsgeschichte," 3; for Bodo
Wilhelm Stöcken's contract for passage from Hamburg to South Carolina in 1773, see Stadtarchiv Frankfurt/Main, Ubg A9, no. 3 (5 June–12 July 1773), LC/MD, FCP: Germany.

quality victuals and the transportation of emigrants' chests. And absolutely vital for the health of the passengers was good drinking water in sufficient quantities in casks designed only for that use. The importance of this was emphasized by virtually every immigrant who commented on the voyage. Some even recommended taking bottled water along, to be less dependent on what the freighter provided.[28] For the merchants, in turn, the logistics—the availability of enough water casks for such a large number of passengers for about two months—were formidable, although those who cut corners, miscalculated, or were cheated by their suppliers and accepted barrels that had already been used for wine, beer, or oil, received many complaints. Good provisions, such as "bread, butter, cheese, flour, peas, rice and the like as well as a third part in lightly salted meat and bacon, or instead of this, more flour, oats, peas and the like," were almost equally important for the well-being of the passengers on board. Yet the recommendation to supplement the ship's food provisions was unanimous, even though the particulars of that advice varied.[29]

The storing of the emigrants' chests and baggage in an accessible place on the same vessel was critical, because these could contain vital additional provisions, such as dried meat and fruit, spices, vinegar, medicine, wine, and brandy, besides bedding, cooking utensils, and changes of clothes. All had to be accessible for a healthy and reasonably comfortable voyage.[30] At the height of the immigrant trade, some merchants achieved very high passenger/ship ratios by shipping passengers' luggage on another vessel— toward the end of the season when late travelers did not fill an entire ship. This practice deprived passengers whose chests were on a different ship of essential items. It also led to substantial loss of property, because theft was rampant during storage whenever passengers lost sight of their baggage.

28. The author of "Sendschreiben aus Philadelphia, 14/25 September 1728" was grateful to Benjamin Furly, who had sent him "a lot of bottles filled with Bristol water," which he used with care during the voyage ("Auszug einiger Sendschreiben aus Philadelphia in Pennsylvania" [Diary of a Voyage . . . to Philadelphia in 1728], trans. Julius Sachse, "Pennsylvania: The German Influence," *Pennsylvania German Society: Proceedings and Addresses* 18 [1909]: 5–25).

29. Recommendations for extra provisions range from staples such as ham and bread (zweiback: "buy seeded bread in Magdeburg and have it sliced and baked Altona to take on shipboard") to dried fruit to mask the taste of bad water and guard against scurvy, and almost always included some form of alcoholic beverage—largely for medicinal purposes. During the voyage, some newlanders profited from selling extra provisions to passengers who had not heeded advice and had not stocked up for themselves. See "An Immigrant's Letter, 1734," Germantown, 369. Klaus Wust's summary of the diet on shipboard is based on many of the same sources that informed the outline here ("Feeding the Palatines").

30. "Advice to German Emigrants, 1749," 233–34.

Without a proper bill of lading that itemized the contents of a chest—a precautionary measure that few emigrants thought to insist on—many could not even prove, let along recoup, the loss of goods from a pilfered or stolen chest. Complaints about such abuses of passengers' property rights persisted throughout the period, despite legislation designed to curb them.[31]

The time necessary to complete all predeparture arrangements varied according to the availability of acceptable offers for passage and the speed with which the vessels could be readied for sailing. After 1739, merchants had to agree to ship emigrants within a fortnight of their arrival in port.[32] The cost of food and lodging during a long waiting period could cut into precious travel funds. Moreover, temporary quarters under crowded conditions threatened the health of emigrants, because tents on the quays and camps near the city easily became breeding grounds for contagious diseases that could be devastating to emigrants even before they boarded overseas vessels, and often also during the voyage.[33] For emigrants on tight budgets, it was therefore advisable to select a merchant who would furnish victuals at his own cost and who provided lodging aboard ship for as long as the emigrants had to await departure in Rotterdam. Additional expenses were likely to arise from the purchase of supplementary provisions for the voyage, fees for the exchange of money, for the services of stevedores, and similar items.[34] Still, while a prolonged stay at one's own expense in a city like Rotterdam, or any other port from which emigrants embarked, added to the overall cost of the trip, the freedom to choose the most suitable passage generally offset those charges. In 1749, two to three weeks of waiting in London for a suitable ship to Philadelphia required almost £8 in expenditures, which Melchior considered well spent considering that it enabled the emigrant to contract passage on a vessel whose owner or captain did not seek profits primarily from transporting pas-

31. For examples, see *Pennsylvanische Berichte*, 16 November 1749; and the Lewis Weiss memorial to John Penn, quoted in Diffenderfer, *German Immigration*, 56–61.

32. For the rules governing transshipment of emigrants across the Netherlands, see Chapter 3. Before 1739, some emigrants experienced long delays before embarkation, especially in the peak years 1732 and 1738. One of them was Andreas Gaar, who waited six weeks with his family in Rotterdam (see Letter from Germantown, 1 February 1733, in *Genealogy of the Descendants of John Gar*, 533).

33. Mortality on German emigrant ships was especially high when there were large numbers of emigrants awaiting embarkation, as in 1738 and the peak years 1749–54.

34. Former emigrants sometimes offered advice about where to buy such goods and services and about who was a trustworthy contact in port. Andrew Boni, for example, described Peter de Koker of Kornmarkt as helpful, especially for finding work when there was a long wait for embarkation (letter [16 October 1736] in Durnbaugh, *Brethren*, 40).

sengers.[35] Some emigrants, while awaiting transportation in London in 1737, were able to find well-paid work—especially the single men—and told their friends of this alternative.[36]

In Rotterdam, poor emigrants and those under previously contracted agreements with newlanders were often faced with situations more precarious than wealthier and more circumspect fellow travelers. For emigrants who had to purchase their fare "on credit" and could offer little security, it was all the more important to select a reputable merchant with a contractual passage offer that was devoid of loopholes designed to add unnecessary charges to the account or to attach unreasonable terms to the deferred payment option. Choices of that kind were difficult not only because merchants preferred paying passengers but also because the advice literature for emigrants was directed to those with some means and therefore offered little help for those who were relocating in hopes of paying for it with their labor after they arrived in the American colonies.[37] How many of these poorer emigrants actually had any choice beyond accepting the transportation contract of the first merchant who offered them shipment across the Netherlands, and then immediate accommodation and provisioning on board ship, is difficult to gauge. Since there was much competition at Schenkenschanz at the height of the migration, savvy travelers—assuming they were literate—could have compared contracts before they signed up with any merchant. It is unclear, however, whether emigrants were well-enough informed to know what to look for in such an agreement. Especially young emigrants, those who had little experience with contractual arrangements, and those who were too eager to leave or too desperate may have been unaware of how important the transportation contract was for the success of their move. For example, did they realize that a contract without a specified destination in America allowed the merchant to land his passengers anywhere—leaving some of them far from where they wanted to go or in places where there were few options for immigrants who still had to pay off their passage debts?[38] Even emigrants

35. "Advice to German Emigrants, 1749," 233.
36. Schelbert and Rappolt, *Alles ist ganz anders hier*, 96.
37. Andrew Boni, however, made the point that young and industrious persons were welcome—and well paid—in Pennsylvania and that, because they could walk to Rotterdam and needed little money during the passage, relocation was affordable (Durnbaugh, *Brethren*, 39–40). On the other hand, merchants preferred paying passengers to those traveling on credit, so emigrants with little or no means had difficulty finding space on board ships whenever demand for transatlantic transportation was high (Faust, "Unpublished Documents," 18).
38. Rotterdam firms that entered the business of transporting Germans across the Atlan-

who had already signed a contract with a particular merchant had, at least under certain circumstances, the option to withdraw from that agreement. The Hopes' revised contract stipulated the right to sign with another merchant offering a cheaper fare—provided the offer was not a competitive measure directed against the Hopes and that any costs incurred by the emigrant before his arrival in Rotterdam be paid.[39] Little evidence remains about how easy this was to accomplish and how many travelers took advantage of such a clause.[40]

A number of emigrants who had chosen a newlander as a guide found themselves abandoned by their agent at a time when they most needed expert advice and service, so that they were forced after all to make their own arrangements for the transatlantic voyage—often at additional cost. Others had second thoughts about the wisdom of their emigration plan and decided to return. While waiting in Rotterdam in the early 1740s, some emigrants decided neither to proceed to the American colonies nor to return home, but to sign up with English army recruiters who operated there.[41] At times, the Swiss authorities offered to pay their former citizens awaiting embarkation in Rotterdam for their return home, to refund the removal tax levied earlier, and to forgo formal reinstatement procedures as citizens.[42] Many followed the lead of their agent, however, and accepted his choice of merchant, contract, vessel, and captain without questioning or checking, and only later found out, in the dual crucibles of the voyage and the process of settling accounts in America, whether their dealings had been with a responsible newlander who had put his previous travel experience to good use for their sake, or whether they were to pay dearly for their blind and naive trust.

Most of the vessels engaged in the German immigrant trade to colonial America were two- or three-masted oceangoing merchantmen of various

tic at the height of the emigration in the early 1750s—Daniel Harvart, Rocquette & van Teylingen, and John Dick—offered passage "generically" to the American colonies rather than to a specific destination.

39. In light of the competition for emigrants in the early 1750s, the Hopes amended the standard contract they had used since the 1730s. See Rattermann, "Geschichte des deutschen Elements," 14:354–56.

40. Captain Hazelwood of the *Sandwich* lodged a protest against the merchant Daniel Harvart when he received only 188 freights after a wait of two months, even though he had been promised a load of 400. Harvart claimed the passengers were "spirited away" (GAR, ONA 2427/235 [22 July 1750]).

41. Rattermann, "Geschichte des deutschen Elements," 14:55.

42. Faust, *Guide to the Materials for American History,* 112.

classifications according to hull shape or rigging.[43] Most of them registered less than 150 tons, ranging on the average from about 110 registered tons in the 1720s, to 138 tons just before the Revolution.[44] Many of them carried one or two dozen cannons for defense against pirates and privateers.

The ship *Mary*, built in Philadelphia for a London merchant and registered to carry a 100-ton burden, was one of the smallest ships arriving with immigrants. She was 58 feet long, had a 10½-foot-deep hold, and a distance between decks of 4 feet, or possibly 4½ feet, scarcely adequate headroom for crew or passengers. The fore and aft parts of the vessel could provide enough headroom, at least 6 to 7 feet, by adding superstructures at either end of the ship above the spar deck in order to augment the depth of the main deck. This was probably at the time a common arrangement for crew accommodations. The caboose, just abaft the foremast, would be similarly modified. All these spaces would be entered through covered hatches and down companionways with three to four steps. In November 1743, the ship *Mary* arrived in Philadelphia from London with thirty-four passengers. Their sleeping places must have been in the four feet between decks—a space usually employed for dry storage of perishable cargo—unless they occupied areas normally reserved for the crew.[45]

The vessels London merchant John Hunt intended to use for transporting emigrants in 1750 were larger. The first measured 64 feet long at the keel, 10½ feet wide in the hold, and 4½ feet high between decks. The *Crown*, at 103 feet long, 4 feet 10 inches between decks, 25½ feet wide, with cabin and steerage 50 feet long and 5 feet 10 inches high, was larger still.[46] Her captain and crew were expected to give up the normal use of the cabin and steerage space for the passengers, which meant that the captain had to build himself a roundhouse on the quarter deck and that the sailors were to lodge in the forecastle. Modifications to relocate the captain and crew became standard features as the volume of the emigrant trade increased.[47]

43. Howard Chapelle, *History of American Sailing Ships.*

44. McCusker, "Ships Registered at the Port of Philadelphia"; and "Tonnage Duty Book [1765–75]," HSP, were the primary sources for the tonnage of German immigrant vessels (the Appendix lists the tonnage of these ships). Ships that appeared in both listings show a ratio of 0.91 *registered* tons to *measured* tons. On the difficulties of standardizing and converting eighteenth-century measurements, see McCusker, "Tonnage of Ships."

45. The description of the vessel follows L. F. Middlebrook, "The Ship *Mary* of Philadelphia," 149–51.

46. The ship *Crown* probably registered around 220 tons. See John Hunt to John Stedman, 24 January, and 14 and 24 February, 1748/9, Hunt & Greenleafe Letter Book.

47. Evidence from charterparties, contracts between captains and merchants in Rotterdam and Amsterdam. See also Chapter 3.

Some captains and crews may have resented being displaced and considered the bonuses at the end of the run inadequate compensation for the inconvenience—perhaps reason to take out their resentment in their behavior toward the passengers.

Ships were not built specifically for the German emigrant trade, but chartered and outfitted according to specific requirements for each run. The bunk space for each full freight was commonly specified to be 6 feet long and 1½ feet wide. On some ships, accommodations were fitted out to hold two passengers in an "apartment" or "cabin," with hammocks for beds.[48] Other arrangements offered firm sleeping platforms, made of a loose lattice of removable boards that was intended to accommodate four full freights in one compartment.[49] The fitting of sleeping platforms and additional bunks took advantage of, and worked around, the ship's structural elements in the cabin and steerage, such as support beams and spare masts stowed between decks. In 1765, legislation against abuses in the immigrant trade specified the height of a bunk as 3 feet 9 inches (2 feet 9 inches in the steerage), to clarify an earlier law that had stipulated only the length and width of each berth.[50] From the passenger's perspective, all such arrangements provided far too little space—an assessment that others shared, as evidenced by an anonymous proposal for regulating the shipment of Palatines.[51]

The number of people actually sharing such cabins depended on the composition of traveling groups. Families with children were usually the most cramped in their quarters, since children under the age of five had to share their parents' bunk, and children between the ages of five and fourteen were entitled to only half a bed space each. Unfortunately, nothing is known about the rationale or the actual procedure governing how cabin space was allocated. From the arrangements of passengers' financial accounts by cabin, it appears that groups of families and friends stayed together, sometimes spilling over into an adjoining compartment. Some

48. Baird, *History of the Huguenot Emigration*, 1:186–87. The Krefelders traveled on the *Concord*, a commodious ship that was 132 feet long and 32 feet broad and could carry 140 passengers. In that case, it was possible to construct cabins and private rooms for passengers. See Marion Balderston, "Pennsylvania's 1683 Ships and Some of Their Passengers," 90.

49. See passengers' financial accounts, arranged by cabin, on board the ship *Nancy*, "Redemptioners," HSP.

50. *Statutes at Large of Pennsylvania*, 5:94–97, 6:432–40.

51. "The case of the Palatine Protestants who are ship'd from Rotterdam to Philadelphia and Carolina in America in the Months of June and July [1750]," Pennsylvania Miscellaneous Papers, Penn & Baltimore, 115, HSP.

cabins were shared by single, seemingly unrelated men, some solely by women—with or without children—and many others accommodated a mix of passengers.[52] Among immigrants sharing the same general quarters between decks, in the cabin, or steerage, there was apparently no systematic segregation by sex or age. On large ships, emigrants traveling together in a group and occupying one part of the vessel seemed to get acquainted easily with fellow passengers quartered in a different area of the ship.

No matter how accommodations on board were distributed, many passengers found themselves in very crowded conditions when the vessel was ready for departure. The immigrants located between decks almost invariably lacked sufficient headroom, and where it would have been possible to stand erect, an extra tier of bunks was likely to use up that extra height by adding more people for a given deck space. Although the chests and baggage of the emigrants contributed to crowding the quarters, attempts to stow them in a place farther down below in the hold, or to ship them separately, were so disadvantageous to the passengers that everybody concerned for the immigrants' well-being advised against it. Under the living conditions on board, it was essential for immigrants to be able to get at additional provisions, medicine, and a change of clothes easily and promptly.

While arranging for contracts, making final preparations for the voyage, and awaiting departure—all in the hope of a better future in the New World—one piece of advice the emigrants were given confronted them with the possibility of total failure in their undertaking.

> Every father of a family or passenger should make an inventory and will beforehand, so that in case of death the nearest person does not become the chief heir, as often happens, and so that the nearest friends and orphans are not robbed of what they should receive; such inventories should usually be written down and declared before witnesses.[53]

The soundness of this recommendation became apparent to most passengers as soon as they encountered the open sea.

Crossing to England gave most of the emigrants their first taste of what life on board an oceangoing sailing vessel was like. Few enjoyed the experi-

52. For example, the accounts for the ship *Nancy*.
53. "Advice to German Emigrants, 1749," 234.

ence; but many seem to have adjusted in this prelude to the extraordinary conditions of even a normal sea voyage. The required stopover in England allowed for a break and some adjustments. The customs officials inspected the chests and other baggage of the emigrants—but usually in only cursory fashion, because they considered the Palatine household goods "generally not worth carrying"—and also the wines and spirits on board for the use of the passengers.[54] Occasionally trade goods were discovered and confiscated.[55] Some passengers used the stop in England to buy extra provisions; others, who thought that parts of the passage contract had not been fulfilled, looked for the corresponding merchant or English officials to seek redress for their complaints.[56] Most ships went through the necessary customs procedures for clearing and final provisioning in Cowes and Gosport and, depending on favorable wind, commenced their transatlantic voyage after about two weeks in port.[57]

It is impossible to say how many passengers dreaded setting sail for America; and it is difficult to imagine how they adjusted to weeks of life at sea. Few may have been as coolheaded about what lay ahead as Christopher Sauer, who said in retrospect: "The ship voyage is as one takes it. For my part, I maintain that it is a comfortable trip if one carries along victuals to which one is accustomed and controls one's imagination."[58] Even the most detailed accounts of the ocean crossing remain vague about many crucial aspects of daily life on an immigrant ship. What follows is a composite picture pieced together from scattered evidence about the physical features of immigrant vessels and the activities on board ship, which should help in assessing the surviving and often quite selective contempo-

54. The English consul in Rotterdam believed the Palatine household goods were of little value. "Particulars of the Trade Carried on Between the Different Ports of His Majesty's Dominions and Rotterdam and the Other Ports of the Mase and Vice Versa [consular report], 16 July 1765," PRO/CO 388/95: I(3), London (I thank Ken Morgan for copying this report for me). See also Minutes of the Board of Customs, 3 May 1765, PRO/Cust(oms) 29/3; Port Books, Plymouth (1754), *Adventure* (1 August 1754), *Halifax* (26 August 1754), PRO/Ex(chequer), 190.

55. Cowes (1749–73), *Hicks* (13 August 1755), *Polly* (19 and 23 June 1764; 16 July 1766), *Charlotte* (13 June 1764), *America* (11 January 1766), PRO/Cust(oms) 61/1–4. See also the negative account of the customs inspections in an open letter from Pennsylvania (25 November 1738) (Durnbaugh, *Brethren*, 47, 50).

56. For example, Theobald Kieffer charged that the Hope firm had not fulfilled its contract by giving the passengers bad food (Kieffer, "The Cheese Was Good").

57. The listing of immigrant voyages in the Appendix includes dates of departure in the English stopover ports.

58. Letter from Germantown, 1 August 1725, quoted in Durnbaugh, *Brethren*, 33.

rary descriptions of the voyage in terms of understanding what the typical passage was like.

Given the conditions of confinement prevailing on many immigrant ships, the ease with which passengers could adjust to the circumstances depended much on the normality of daily activities and routines on board. The captain was key in determining what rules and procedures would provide passengers with a sense of order and stability under otherwise extraordinary circumstances, and therefore captains of immigrant ships found their cargo management capabilities taxed in a special way.

Although captains found transporting immigrants to be a rather troublesome operation, most probably tried to avoid difficulties with their passengers, like captain George Wax, who was "unwilling to expose himself to mutiny on the high seas which probably would be the consequence if they [the passengers] should be like to starve."[59]

However, difficult situations often made the ships' masters seem to be unbending opponents of their passengers, even though they themselves were rarely responsible for the insufficient provisions, lack of good water, or disease brought on board—and never responsible for bad weather, which gave rise to tension and unreasonable demands by unruly passengers. Yet captains had to deal with those aggravating and threatening events in mostly unpopular fashion: by rationing, enforcing strict rules of cleanliness in an effort to curb the spread of sickness, and insisting relentlessly on the observance of certain guidelines of safety for everybody.

Leonard Melchior, a Philadelphia shopkeeper and tavernkeeper who in 1749 instructed German emigrants how best to prepare for the voyage, fully recognized the weight of the captain's responsibilities. He advised passengers not to aggravate the situation but "to conduct themselves toward the captain in a discrete and friendly manner, set forth their complaints modestly, and not to become rebellious in words and deeds, for the captain has great powers." This recommendation was much to the point, because misconceptions about the captain's use of such powers abounded and needed correction.

> Much is related of angry captains, but none can be called so angry as the one who has been provoked to wrath, for his honor, reputation, and profit demand that he treat his passengers well. The stories of kidnapping people and taking them to foreign shores are nothing but figment of the imagination of ignorant people and

59. "Report on the Petition of Theobald Kieffer," 29.

arise from the fact that often a ship is driven by contrary winds to a place to which it was not intended to go. Whoever doubts this can nevertheless enter a clause on this point in his contract in Rotterdam.[60]

The organization of life on board centered on providing food and drink; observing routines to achieve rudimentary cleanliness; and establishing order and preserving calm among passengers. The daily allowance of meat with peas, and the like, as well as the weekly rations of bread, butter, and cheese, was furnished to the passengers gathered in messes, usually in groups of five to twelve people. Responsibility for the preparation of food and drink was in the hands of some crew members, or some of the passengers who had volunteered or been hired for that task; or it was left completely up to those sharing in a mess.[61] Rationing of water and provisions seems to have been common, especially at the end of the voyage.[62] On some ships, a steward was engaged to oversee all matters concerning the passengers; and sometimes physicians and clergy were able to lend their expertise and support.[63] Caring for the sick, who required special provisions and treatment, tending to women in childbirth and to newborns, burying the dead, and consoling the survivors called for particular attention that was especially important in maintaining some sense of normalcy for the other passengers during the long weeks of confinement and danger on ship.[64]

A clause that allowed passengers to make fires on deck was usually included in the contract, which also restricted such fires to daylight hours under normal weather conditions and strictly prohibited them under all other circumstances. The fear of fire on board ship seems to have been enough to ensure utmost care by everybody.

60. "Advice to German Emigrants, 1749," 235.

61. For specific references, see Wust, "Feeding the Palatines."

62. See, for example, Faust, "Unpublished Documents," 18 (8 March 1749).

63. In 1753, Isaac and Zachary Hope granted the steward of the *Eastern Branch* 2 guineas "for the extraordinary care and trouble in serving the passengers with provisions etc." (GAR, ONA 2148/128 [12 July 1753]). Bodo Wilhelm Stöcken, who recruited settlers for South Carolina, advertised in 1773 that emigrants would find a physician and medicines on board and that a candidate of theology would tend to the passengers' spiritual needs (Stadtarchiv Frankfurt/ Main Ubg A9, no. 3 [3 June–12 July 1773], LC/MD, FCP: Germany).

64. Prudent transportation contracts specified that there would be ready access to cooking fire, extra water, and special provisions for sick passengers. Emigrants who kept records of the voyage usually reported the deaths and births that occurred en route. It was rare if nobody died during the voyage, and it was common for babies to be born on board ship.

Mice, rats, and other pests could be held in check only if food and refuse were not left around everywhere but were stored or discarded in appropriate places. Especially on crowded ships, strict enforcement of such common-sense rules were necessary.[65] This practice was accompanied most effectively by a regular and thorough cleaning of all passengers' quarters. Fumigation and twice-weekly washings with vinegar may not seem very effective by modern standards, but generally they resulted in more "sweet-smelling" accommodations and ensured a certain measure of tidiness. And the simple physical activity involved in such procedures was helpful and forced everybody to take an active interest in their situation. Personal cleanliness was equally important—lice were the main problem—but difficult to achieve under the circumstances. Yet even with restricted supplies of drinking water, experienced captains ordered rainwater to be collected and designated one day of the week as washday.[66] The image of a maze of clotheslines on deck may seem quaint; but drying and airing was also essential because of the constant problem with water penetrating everywhere.

Provisions and cooking utensils swept overboard caused considerable loss and in rare cases could result in starvation.[67] During a storm, hatches and portholes would be fastened shut and everybody had to remain below deck. Cooking was impossible under such circumstances. The threat from privateers was real when England was at war with France or Spain.[68] In case of a friendly encounter with another vessel—this might happen twice during a normal crossing of the Atlantic—the captains might not only drink to each other's health and exchange news but also barter goods for the benefit of the passengers, like fresh apples in return for cheese.[69] If prospects were good, the captain might order the seamen to fish in order to supplement provisions.

Passengers have been cast as the victims so often that it is necessary to emphasize that the immigrants themselves could significantly compound the trials of life at sea. Merchants, captains, and accompanying newlanders were all in a position to influence actively and compellingly the quality

65. On navy ships, cleanliness routines were strict because their importance in maintaining health among the seamen was well recognized. See Rodger, *Wooden World*, 107.

66. Soap does not work in saltwater, and clothing washed in saltwater attracts humidity. Rodger, *Wooden World*, 64–65.

67. Faust and Brumbaugh, *Lists of Swiss Emigrants*, 124.

68. William Hinke, ed. and trans., "Report of the Journey of Francis Louis Michel," 14; John Meurer, "From London to Philadelphia, 1742," 99.

69. Meurer, "From London to Philadelphia, 1742."

of the passengers' lives during the voyage and were responsible for many problems that occurred. They can hardly be blamed, however, for tension and general lack of cooperation and compassion among passengers. There is every indication that the hardships of the voyage frequently evoked unabashed selfishness.[70] A possible exception was in the behavior of deeply religious people, whose basic trust and belief remained unshaken by the experience.[71] Melchior's timely advice on how passengers should protect themselves is telling: "The occupants of every three or four berths should come to an understanding together at sea, first, that in case of death they will serve as executors or guardians for one another; second, that they will be quick to assist each other in sickness; third, that they will alternately keep watch for certain birds of prey (which abound at sea as well as on land) and will treat each other like brothers."[72]

Individual experiences of passengers on the transatlantic voyage from Europe to the American colonies cover a wide range. Fairly typical for one end of the scale is Mittelberger's description:

> During the journey the ship is full of pitiful signs of distress— smells, fumes, horrors, vomiting, various kinds of sea sickness, fever, dysentery, headaches, heat, constipation, boils, scurvy, cancer, mouth rot, and similar inflictions, all of them caused by the age and the highly salted state of the food, especially the meat, as well as the very bad and filthy water, which brings about the miserable destruction and death of many. Add to all that shortage of food, hunger, thirst, frost, heat, dampness, fear, misery, vexation, and lamentation as well as other troubles.[73]

Others were luckier:

> Our voyage was a very happy one, and I may say that with the exception of three days and three nights, during which we experienced a heavy storm, the time passed agreeably and delightfully,

70. A passenger in 1738—a difficult year for relocation to the American colonies—reported that emigrants behaved recklessly and that the extreme conditions of the voyage brought out the worst in everyone. See Durnbaugh, *Brethren*, 47.

71. As Cornelius Bom put it: "Those who come ought to come after Christian deliberation, with pure intentions in fear of the Lord, so that the Lord may be their support" ("Letter from Cornelius Bom [12 October 1684]," *Pennsylvania German Society: Proceedings and Addresses* 9 [1899]: 100–107, 105–6).

72. "Advice to German Emigrants, 1749," 234.

73. Mittelberger, *Journey to Pennsylvania*, 12.

every person on board enjoying himself. The women, the young girls, and the young children gathered on deck, almost every day for diversion. We did not have the pleasure of fishing on the Banks. . . .[74]

Dividing German immigration to colonial Pennsylvania into three distinctive phases—rise, peak, and decline—is also crucial for understanding the experience of German passengers who crossed the Atlantic. Most of the practices designed to maximize profits at the cost of the well-being of passengers occurred primarily during the boom period of the trade, 1749–54. During these years of peak demand for passage, it was most difficult to avoid scheming promoters and achieve flexibility in choosing terms of travel. In contrast, however, at the beginning and end of the German immigration passengers were fewer in number and often represented a valuable supplementary cargo for ships that carried dry goods or that engaged in the provisions trades or were otherwise returning from Europe in ballast.

After long weeks at sea, entry into Delaware Bay opened the final phase of the voyage for German immigrants coming to Pennsylvania. At Cape Henlopen, the commanders of transatlantic immigrant vessels engaged a pilot for the passage up the river. Since most Germans arrived in late summer or early fall, "they admired the green stands of trees along the river banks and the abundance and quality of the fruit" offered to them on the way by considerate captains and well-meaning earlier immigrants to Pennsylvania.[75] Friends who had heard about the ship's arrival in the bay rowed out to meet them, and vendors stood ready to sell their wares to passengers who had ready cash.

Arrival in Philadelphia was a big event. When the anchor was cast and the cannons were fired, a crowd gathered on shore in expectation "that the newly arrived immigrants were to be exposed for redemption sale, according to the usage of the times."[76] Many other people besides prospective masters of servants soon came on board ship, bringing apples, fresh bread, and beer, and asking for letters from and inquiring about relatives and friends. Contemporary reports made it clear that the immigrants were

74. Baird, *History of the Huguenot Emigration,* 2:378–79.

75. Adolph Benson, ed., *The America of 1750,* 1:16.

76. Meurer, "From London to Philadelphia, 1742," 104. See also "Some Account of the Life and Travel of Tho. Chalkey," 127, HSP; Johann Christopher Sauer, 1 December 1724, *PMHB* 45 (1921): 243–54, 246; and Mittelberger, *Journey to Pennsylvania,* 16.

quite relieved to be at the end of an arduous voyage. Most ignored important procedural aspects concerning the landing of the new settlers, although a number of regulations designed to monitor immigration struc-
tured the routine of arrival. After complying with the legal prerequisites of
medical inspection and registrations, the most important condition in
landing German immigrants was settling their accounts. The arrangements
for paying debts at the end of the voyage determined to a large extent the
future the immigrants would face in the New World. The resources of the
passengers, the profit-making strategies of the merchants, and the experiences of the voyage now came together in a flexible system that absorbed
the many kinds of German immigrants who had been lured by colonial
America's fame and promise.

At the very beginning of German immigration, squaring accounts was
easy, for many colonists relocated in groups of family and friends. The
vast majority of the immigrants in this early period had been able to pay
their fares in advance and imported some trade goods or even financed the
passage of a servant or two. As the migration flow from Germany increased, however, the proportion of families traveling together declined,
and the newcomers became younger and poorer. More and more passengers depended on some form of credit to finance their move across the
Atlantic. As the demand for transatlantic transportation swelled, more
immigrants found it harder and more complicated to pay off their debts
upon arrival in Philadelphia, regardless of whether they counted on relatives already in the colonies to help them, banked on the proceeds from
sales of imported goods, or relied on the willingness of Pennsylvanians to
advance money against the future labor of indentured servants. After the
immigration peaked in the early 1750s, fewer Germans—predominantly
young, unattached men—arrived in the Delaware Valley, and a substantial
number of those who came did so because of the credit merchants offered
them in exchange for indentured servitude. In short, settling up for the
voyage upon arrival in Philadelphia changed significantly over time. And
throughout, the greater options available to paying passengers compared
with those traveling on credit did much to determine the nature of the
first steps in entering colonial life, as did the difficulties that passengers
had experienced on the way.

The laws prescribing procedural and administrative requirements for
landing German immigrants and their goods grew out of a desire of the
provincial government to protect the existing order of the colony and the
health of Philadelphia's inhabitants. In the 1720s, when immigration from

both Ireland and Germany increased, registration and qualification procedures for new settlers were implemented and importation duties were
levied—but soon rescinded—in an unsuccessful attempt to control the
influx of foreigners and to prevent "impotent persons" from becoming
public charges. Furthermore, Pennsylvania authorities appointed health officers to inspect and license inward-bound immigrant ships in efforts to
bar "sickly vessels" from landing. In case of contagion, the officials had
the power to prohibit ships from anchoring or landing their cargo within a
one-mile radius of the city limits.[77]

Inspection of ship and cargo by collectors and health officers, normally a mere formality, was the Germans' first encounter with officials
representing the provincial bureaucracy. While acute outbreaks of epi-
demics traced to particular immigrant ships were rare, they never failed to
produce debates about what or who had been responsible for *previous*
neglect and failure, in attempts to master the current crisis.[78] Surviving
"health reports" for thirty-five ships indicate that a substantial proportion
of immigrant ships arrived with most of their passengers in good or at
least acceptable health.[79] Most ships carried "a few passengers" affected
with "scurvy in their gums, 6 or 7 under a low fever not of an infectious
kind," and a small minority were reported to carry immigrants affected by
"putrid Fevers and other Distempers" understood to be infectious.[80]

The qualification procedure was the next step in the landing process:

When we entered the court house, we found the government already assembled. We were told that the country belongs to the King
of England, that we were required in the first place, to take an oath
of allegiance to the King and his successors, meaning that we would

77. *Statutes at Large of Pennsylvania*, 4:135–40, 164–71, 382–88; 8:369–77.

78. The regulation proposed and the appointments made to license incoming vessels effectively—that is, to prevent those with diagnosed infectious diseases from landing in the
city—was repeatedly an issue of contention between the Provincial Assembly and the governor. See *Votes and Proceedings*, 4:2715, 2716, 2718, 2719, 2721, 2738, 2741, 2742, 2754, 2756, 2757,
2778; 5:3766, 3769. See also Schwartz, *Mixed Multitude*, 101–3, 193–96; and Horle and Wokeck,
eds., *Lawmaking and Legislators in Pennsylvania*, 2:50–51.

79. For estimates of mortality on immigrant ships, see Chapter 2.

80. "Health records by Drs. Thomas Graeme and Thomas Bond," Simon Gratz Collection, Physicians, Case 2, Box 11; Case 7, Box 29, Folder 3; Box 26, Folder 6; Box 34, Folder 3;
Ferdinand J. Dreer Autograph Collection, Physicians, Surgeons, and Chemists, vols. 1 and 2.
See also the health reports in Strassburger/Hinke, *Pennsylvania German Pioneers*, for the years
1741–55: ships no. 87, 90, 196–201, 203–11, 215–20, 222–23, 225–28, 230, 232; and those in *MPC*,
1851–53, 4:315, 570–71.

conduct ourselves as good and faithful subjects, not revolt against his Majesty, nor settle on lands not our own. In the second place, we were required to abjure all allegiance to the Pope. Then the magistrate proceeded that he was now going to read something, which we must all repeat after him with a loud voice. Finally we had to sign our names to two different papers, one of which belongs to the King of England, and the other to the Government of Pennsylvania. This done, they wished us good success, and dismissed us.[81]

Registering German immigrant men was far from being a mere formality, because it gave the newcomer certain legal rights and protections under provincial law and was also the first step toward full integration as a naturalized citizen. Properly qualified immigrants "born out of the dominions of the King of England" were granted the right to acquire, hold, sell, and pass on property, and full use of the provincial courts—an important right when seeking redress in cases of differences between immigrants and their importers.[82]

While administrative requirements determined the first two steps of the landing routine, business considerations shaped the procedures for the third stage of the debarkation process: settling outstanding debts. That scene, in which many different activities went on simultaneously, was hectic.

Every day Englishmen, Dutchmen, and High Germans come from Philadelphia and other places, some of them from very far away, . . . and go on board the newly arrived vessel that has brought people from Europe and offers them for sale. From among the healthy they pick out those suitable for the purposes for which they require them. Then they negotiate with them as to the length of period for which they will go into service in order to pay for their passage. . . .[83]

81. Meurer, "From London to Philadelphia, 1742," 105; Muhlenberg in *Hallesche Nachrichten*, 461. For the text of the oaths (or affirmations), see Strassburger/Hinke, *Pennsylvania German Pioneers*, 1:3–6.

82. James Kettner, *Development of American Citizenship*, discusses the qualification procedure as a prerequisite for full citizenship. For a description of the administrative requirements in Philadelphia, such as the magistrates present, the location, and the intricacies of recording the signatures, see Strassburger/Hinke, *Pennsylvania German Pioneers*, 1:xvii–xxix, xxxix–xlv.

83. Mittelberger, *Journey to Pennsylvania*, 17; see also Muhlenberg, *Hallesche Nachrichten*, 461.

While purchasers were making their selections, and immigrants prepared for final debarkation, Pennsylvania residents in search of relatives or
friends, or news from them, made their inquiries alongside those who had
messages to deliver or services to sell to immigrants ready to leave the ship.
Stevedores, salespeople, innkeepers, and landlords all vied for the attention
of prospective customers. In their efforts to do business, they addressed
especially newcomers who did not have friends meeting them and who
therefore needed help in transporting their baggage ashore, in finding food
and lodgings, and in establishing contacts for settling into life in the New
World. Boardinghouses and inns catering to newly arrived Germans had
their seasonal peaks in business in the late summer and early fall, and some
even took in lodgers afflicted with diseases.[84] Innkeepers were especially important to many Germans making their very first step in the New
World because they brokered critical information.[85]

Normally, landing procedures for passengers who had paid their fares
in advance were simple and quick. Immigrants who did not owe any passage money were free to have their baggage taken ashore and leave the ship.
Some were met by relatives or friends who offered immediate shelter and
guidance on where to settle. Others had to depend on strangers for a
temporary base from which they could explore and weigh opportunities
for the future. They faced a strange city and an unfamiliar language, but
this first contact with their new land was made easier because the crowd
gathered to welcome their newly anchored ship included people who spoke
both German and English and who were willing—indeed, eager—to offer
advice and help, though not all of them without cost. The services of
an interpreter were necessary during the inspection and registration procedures and were required by law.[86] Otherwise, language difficulties are
rarely mentioned in the immigrants' accounts, suggesting that German-
speaking Pennsylvanians helped new arrivals at all stages of the landing

84. Widows and former immigrants "rented" to redemptioners and merchants quartered
sick immigrants with Germans in the Philadelphia area. See *Pennsylvania Gazette*, 12 January, and
9 and 23 February 1774; Bailyn, *Voyagers to the West*, 339; "A Colonial Health Report of Philadelphia, 1754 (Thomas Graeme and Thomas Bond to the governor, 16 November 1754),"
PMHB 36 (1912): 476–77.

85. In records related to the landing of German immigrants, innkeepers appear often. See
Statutes at Large of Pennsylvania, 4:387–88; "Colonial Health Report, 1754," 476; *Philadelphische
Staatsbote*, 19 November 1769; accounts of the ships *Nancy* (1750) ("Redemptioners," HSP),
Britannia (1773) ("Munstering [*sic*] Book," HSP); "Record of Indentures of Individuals Bound
Out . . . ," *Pennsylvania German Society: Proceedings and Addresses* 16 (1907).

86. *Statutes at Large of Pennsylvania*, 6:440.

procedure.[87] In this respect, Philadelphia was quite different from other ports in the American colonies, where newly arrived immigrants could not count on a large resident population of German-speaking settlers as part of the arrival routine. This feature helped Philadelphia to remain the leading port of entry for Germans.

This regular and seasonal scene of landing immigrants was the result of favorable reports by German pioneers already settled in Pennsylvania. Since these early immigrants described the opportunities available as excellent, more and more Germans were attracted to the New World. This way, immigration from the Rhine lands swelled to a regular flow of transatlantic movement. Taking advantage of more-detailed information about the colony, widespread personal connections, better and more frequent trade links between Philadelphia and continental Europe, innovative and adventurous emigrants came up with new and various ways to get the money necessary for the relocation or to augment their starting capital once in Philadelphia. A prospective settler with enough means to "come here in this land at his own expense, and [who] reaches here in good health" was assured by his friends that "he will be rich enough, especially if he can bring his family or some man-servant, because servants are dear here. People bind themselves out here for three or four years' service for a great price. . . ."[88]

Others, interested in investing in goods rather than labor, were advised specifically about the most profitable wares to bring for resale in Pennsylvania in addition to their own household goods, tools, or farm implements.[89] The effects of such instructions about the importation of goods, and similarly of advice about the importance of family and bound labor in successful relocation plans, were far-reaching not only for immigrants and their importers. They also eventually affected many others less directly involved in the trade who wanted to purchase, or who competed with, German goods. For most of the period, there was always the potential for conflict between passengers who brought saleable goods, and merchants,

87. In one exception, Mittelberger reports a fraudulent bond agreement that suggests problems did arise because of language difficulties (*Journey to Pennsylvania*, 23).

88. "Letter from Boris Wertmüller [16 March 1684]," 102.

89. Daniel Falckner's "Curieuse Nachricht von Pennsylvania" is typical for this kind of information. Christopher Sauer's letters supported this strategy (1 August 1725): "Many of the Palatines paid the captain nothing, although they had the money. Instead they bought knives, combs of ivory and horn, steel and nails, and paid only after they had come here" (Durnbaugh, *Brethren*, 37). For a variety of items imported for resale, see Philadelphia County administration no. 116, 1773, Martin Weck (Wick), Register of Wills, Philadelphia, City Hall Annex.

in which each side claimed that the other was cheating the government out of lawful revenue. In the early years of the immigration, most new-comers were relatively affluent and brought a variety of household goods, clothing, tools, and farm implements for their own use, but also for sale— all classified as "Palatine household goods."[90] Immigrants counted on only the most cursory examination of their baggage in England and expected to carry their goods ashore with them in the colonies and to do with them as they wished. "The Palatines have brought very many goods with them so that many a man has made up to Fl 600 [about £54 sterling] by this trip, for everything was free because it was not examined."[91]

Reactions to this widely practiced and accepted custom varied. Some merchants protective of their own investment, and some zealous Phila-delphia officials, objected by decrying what they saw to be a detriment to the province as well as the empire, and seized goods suspected to be con-traband. Pennsylvanians hoping to restrict immigration cited the practice of importing trade goods in their fiscally couched argument to the Board of Trade, urging London to devise measures for curtailing the flow of Germans to Pennsylvania.[92] In the case of the seizure of the ship *Princess Augusta*, the defendants demonstrated convincingly that the Philadelphia customs official had overstepped the boundaries of his prescribed du-ties—probably to receive one-third of the value from the proceeds of the forfeiture that would have been his by law.[93]

The transatlantic transfer of considerable quantities of saleable goods, mostly in relatively small individual parcels, attracted thieves. Pilfering and theft of immigrants' chests occurred with regularity, especially at the height of the German immigration, 1749–54, and persisted until the Revo-lution. Victims generally blamed the captains, merchants, and their em-ployees, as well as fellow passengers. Immigrants and their friends sought

90. In the early years, when crowding was not a problem, David Seibt pointed out that because there were no restrictions on baggage his friends should bring an iron stove, a copper kettle, and tools ("An Immigrant's Letter, 1734," 369–70).

91. Letter by Sauer (1 December 1724), 253. John George Käsebier elaborated on Sauer's report in his letter to the ruler of Sayne-Wittgenstein (7 November 1724) and disclosed that one of the immigrants shipped 100,000 sewing needles that way (Durnbaugh, *Brethren*, 25).

92. Penn Papers, Penn & Baltimore, Penn Family, 6 December 1727, HSP.

93. *Statutes at Large of Pennsylvania*, 6:436; Philadelphia Custom House Records, vol. 1, Cad-walader Collection, HSP; Israel Pemberton to (Henry Blommart?), 22 November 1759, Pem-berton Papers, 13:112–13, HSP; *Pennsylvanische Berichte*, 1 January 1751; proceedings pertaining to the ships *Princess Augusta* (1736) and *Sandwich* (1750) in Records of the Vice-Admiralty Court Held at Philadelphia, vols. 1 and 2, LC/MD.

legal measures to curb such blatant property violations, but achieved only moderate success.[94]

Investment in goods for resale became a risky venture when immigrants gambled all their capital on future profits from imported wares without protecting themselves adequately against fraudulent business practices of merchants, captains, and newlanders whom they had trusted with the purchase, transportation, and safekeeping of goods and money. As a consequence, some immigrants lost all their capital and arrived in Philadelphia in dire financial circumstances, perhaps in debt for passage. And chances to recover their losses were exceedingly slim. Leonard Melchior, Gottlieb Mittelberger, Christopher Sauer, and Lewis Weiss reported a considerable number and variety of cases of passengers who had been cheated. The large number of complaints suggests that the proportion of immigrants who came with at least some property was substantial even after the peak of immigration around mid-century. It is difficult, however, to assess the true number of immigrants who were actually exploited, or how much of their property was diverted, embezzled, or stolen. The growing numbers of immigrants at the height of the migration seem to have involved more passengers with little experience, poor business sense, and blind trust in human nature. This accounted perhaps in part for the increase in theft and other fraudulent behavior. Meanwhile, such practices of exploiting passengers became an integral part of maritime culture. Melchior and Sauer warned immigrants that they were responsible for protecting their property and that they should arrange contractual transportation agreements, demand receipts for payments made or goods received and stored, and observe accepted business practices, including British customs regulations.[95]

Thus, what began as an informal and essentially illegal method by which German immigrants ensured an easier beginning in the New World for themselves became less attractive during the height of the immigration. Frustration and financial disaster were common as the large number of unsophisticated people participating in the migration tempted different types of thieves to extract a good share of the system's hidden profits.

94. "Advice to German Emigrants, 1749," 236–37; Sauer's letter to the governor (1755) and Lewis Weiss memorial (1774), Diffenderfer, German Immigration, 243, 250–51, 254; 58–61; Statutes at Large of Pennsylvania, 5:96; 6:435–36, 439; Votes of the Pennsylvania Assembly, 5:3647, 3770, 3780, 3794, 3795, 3800, 3803, 3804, 3807, 3808, 3839, 3840, 3850, 3851, 3878, 3880, 3889–92, 3895, 3902.

95. "Advice to German Emigrants, 1749," 226–37; Mittelberger, Journey to Pennsylvania, 11, 22; Sauer's letter to the governor (1755) and Weiss memorial (1774), Diffenderfer, German Immigration, 240–54, 58–61; Pennsylvanische Berichte, 16 September, 16 October, and 16 November 1749; 1 January 1755. See also the regulations enacted in 1750 and amended in 1765 to curb abuses in the immigrant trade, Statutes at Large of Pennsylvania, 5:94–97, 6:432–40.

Especially in the early 1750s, complaints about a wide range of property violations involving immigrants' baggage indicate that abuses were widespread and persistent, affecting many passengers who were not well equipped to cope with the loss of belongings at such a critical time.

Incidents of ill fortune, such as the loss of property, illness, and the death of family members, complicated arrival procedures even for immigrants who had already paid their fares. It was not always possible to avoid illness and accident on immigrant vessels, and misfortunes occurred throughout the period, affecting all groups without discrimination, although small children and the elderly were most vulnerable if disease attacked. Yet passengers experienced more adversity more frequently during the peak of the immigration, when the extraordinary conditions caused by serious crowding threatened health and belongings even more.

An immigrant's ability to cope with hardships depended to a large degree on the composition of the travel party to which he or she belonged. The death of an unaccompanied emigrant on a prepaid passage benefited only the merchant or managing newlander, because he had already collected the fare. In most cases, the captain shared in the spoils by seizing the deceased's effects, unless he was stopped by friends on board or ashore who insisted that correct probate procedures be followed. Very few probate records of Germans who died en route survive.[96] Those that do are few and disproportionately scattered relative to the magnitude and flow of German immigration to colonial Pennsylvania, even though probating the estates of immigrants who died on the voyage was mandated by law in 1750.[97] About thirty administrations (including several wills in German) have survived for the years 1733–73. These inventoried the estates of recent immigrants from Rotterdam, and one-third, particularly the earlier ones, were filed by fellow passengers whose relationship to the deceased remains unclear. Merchants and captains were responsible for another third. Apparently most of these individuals were not guided by a quest for passage money they had advanced, because only three administrations list freight as a debt item.[98] The remaining one-third was filed by the officers of the German Society of Pennsylvania (founded in 1764), who made it one of

96. For the year 1738, which had very high mortality rates, see Wust, "Emigration Season of 1738."

97. *Statutes at Large of Pennsylvania*, 5:96; see also Weiss memorial (1774), in Diffenderfer, *German Immigration*, 61. Immigrant probate records can be found at the Register of Wills Office, Philadelphia, City Hall Annex, although a number of records are too fragile to handle without destroying them.

98. Adm. no. 114, 1738, Daniel K(e)isling; no. 83, 1743, Anna Johanna Everly; no. 91, 1773, Martin Weck.

their regular duties to ensure that the belongings of a deceased passenger, or the proceeds thereof, went to the lawful beneficiaries.

The cumbersome and, to newly arrived Germans, unfamiliar procedures involved in probate—as well as the considerable expense—were likely to inhibit compliance with the law. There were fees for taking out letters of administration, for filing an inventory, and for other steps in connection with probating an estate, including giving a percentage of the estate value as commission to the executors. Furthermore, variable payments for a wide range of services from porterage fees to the fees charged for assessments, translations, advertising and holding public vendues, and letters home often added significantly to the price, so that only personal estates of a certain value may have justified the costs, though some of the estates were very meager.[99] If a family was struck by the death of a member, the survivors were not reimbursed for any portions of his fare. Only the decedent's belongings remained in the possession of the family. Leonard Melchior emphasized the importance of being prepared for this eventuality.[100] Greedy captains, newlanders, or self-proclaimed friends who volunteered to "look after" the baggage of surviving minors were likely to steal it and thereby leave the new arrivals destitute and compelled them to bind themselves out in search of a home and employment. Some exceedingly unscrupulous "friends" of such orphans even forced negotiations for indenture in order to pocket the proceeds from the deals.[101] Lewis Weiss reported the following case of greed that fed on the misfortune of others to Thomas Willing:

Sir, I am this moment informed that a young woman of about 17 years of age has lost her parents in the voyage of passengers in Capt. Johnson—She has had in her hands 46 french Guineas and an artful woman the wife of John Stup of this City Taylor has persuaded her to come from on board & live with her, has taken the aforesd money of her without giving her any note or Receipt for the same—I look upon this Money as belonging to the estate of Ulrich Frey the deceased father of the young woman and She is a Minor and has nothing to do with the administration thereof— and as I am informed that you have taken out or are going to take

99. For examples of administrations listing these costs, see no. 10, 1739, Hans Jacob Carn (Cern); no. 7, 1741, Johannes Brandt; no. 63, 1755, Andreas Reib (Reeb); no. 67, 1764, Philip Jacob Oukst; no. 34, 1772, Ulrich Frey.

100. "Advice to German Emigrants, 1749," 234.

101. "Two Germantown Letters of 1738."

out letters of Administration on the Estate of all the persons that have died on board of this vessel I beg the favour that you will confide the case of this young woman & take some speedy effectual remedy to recover that money from the Hands of her Inticer—who have sent already their goods on board of a Shallop to go to fair tomorrow with the money of that Girl. . . .[102]

Resources and family support determined what adjustments were made after a death or a loss of property. In the case of belongings lost through theft, fraud, or natural forces, the adjustments that had to be made depended on the extent of damage and the range of resources at hand. Family groups were typically better prepared to cope than the unattached traveler, because their property was usually distributed among several pieces of luggage, making loss of everything less likely. Furthermore, the combined financial potential of a family facilitated a speedier recovery, because as one or more members could bind themselves out as servants. In so doing, they could get room and board and immediately contribute toward housing, food, and other necessities for the family until they recovered their property or were compensated for its value. The indenture money could also serve as the basis for getting the family started on a farm or in a shop as originally planned, even though capital and labor were reduced. Without family members or friends to meet him on arrival, the passenger traveling alone had few options if his belongings were lost. Without connections, a foreigner in a strange city found it difficult to obtain credit, so indentured servitude or wage labor were the only ways to survive until lost property was restored through the slow legal process, or until new capital for a farm or shop could be accumulated.

The odds for regaining property varied. Travelers could obtain insurance from marine insurance brokers; but few immigrants knew about that procedure, and fewer still took advantage of it. None of the surviving accounts mentions baggage insurance, and neither Sauer's advice, published repeatedly in *Pennsylvanische Berichte*, nor Melchior's "Advice to German Emigrants, 1749" suggests obtaining it, although both are keen on protecting passengers against losses.[103] Consequently, few passengers could retrieve losses from natural disaster or confiscation, and none was com-

102. Enclosure to administration no. 34, 1772, Ulrich Frey.

103. Christopher Sauer also argued for appointing an effective overseer of vessels—somebody who could not be bribed—and a commission for checking and addressing immigrants' grievances concerning violations of contract and property. "Two Germantown Letters of 1755 [petitions to Pennsylvania governor by J. Christopher Sauer]."

pensated if property was stolen by someone who could evade the courts of colonial Pennsylvania (such as a newlander who stayed behind in Europe or disappeared upon arrival in Philadelphia). Immigrants could expect greater success in charging thieves and crooks among fellow passengers, seamen, and captains who stayed in Pennsylvania; but such suits were actually relatively rare until 1765. In the decade before the Revolution, the German Society of Pennsylvania provided legal aid for newly arrived Germans who were not familiar enough with the local court system and also who did not have the financial resources to file suit and see it through.

The German Society of Pennsylvania was founded in 1764, in charitable response to the need of poor, newly arrived Germans, but it was chartered and organized primarily as a legal aid society.[104] The Society's first and foremost achievement was passage of a supplementary act that regulated all aspects of the German immigrant trade. The officers of the Society visited recently arrived immigrant vessels to check compliance by captains and merchants with the regulations, initiated legal action if necessary, and supplied the immigrants with bread, blankets, medical care, and other necessities.[105]

Loss of property, and even the death of a family member, was probably easier to bear than arriving seriously, and especially contagiously, ill. In this condition, the immigrant lost all active control. Again, those who had family and friends in the new land benefited from their support and care,[106] but the independent lone or sole surviving passenger was less fortunate. If not afflicted with an infectious disease, such newcomers could be landed and brought to a boardinghouse that offered proper care, but those with sufficient funds were always better off than those who depended on their importers to provide them with the bare minimum of provisions and shelter. Care for sick passengers was required by law; but any expenses thus incurred could be added to the passengers' accounts, thereby increasing fare debts significantly. There were special boardinghouses for such cases. Commissioned by merchants, they dispensed privatized welfare.[107] For example, Catherine Weisel, the wife of John Weisel (Wiessel), who had died

---

104. Before 1764, the burden of caring for poor and sick German immigrants rested on "those Germans who still have some love for their countrymen, and often collections and charitable distributions are made by the latter to the starving, miserable people." Durnbaugh, *Brethren*, 51 (1738); see also John Wister's Mennonite alms account.

105. Beamtenratsprotokoll, vol. 1 (1770–1802), GSP.

106. "Sick, filthy, and indebted immigrants have few prospects, except friends and relatives who take care of them" stated one immigrant bluntly in 1738. Durnbaugh, *Brethren*, 48.

107. "Colonial Health Report, 1754," 476–77.

in passage, was left on the ship, having no kin or friends in Philadelphia or anywhere else. She arrived in Philadelphia ill, but with all her husband's goods and estate, and she was taken in by William Barrock, who nursed her until she died. For his trouble, she left Barrock all her belongings and money, except for one French crown to be given to the poor of her home-land.[108]

If an infectious illness was diagnosed among immigrants, chances of recovery were diminished considerably for everyone affected. In the early years, conditions for passengers remaining on board ships and banned from landing within city limits were extremely unhealthy and often aggra-vated by inadequate food, poor accommodations, and the onset of winter. Even in later years, the facilities and care available for quarantined pas-sengers on Province Island were insufficient, especially in instances when family and friends were not allowed to look after their sick. Consequently, the ill passengers left on board late-arriving immigrant vessels or landed on Province Island were exposed to increasingly wintry conditions and received less and less fresh produce among their provisions.[109] Bread and blankets were the standard items supplied to needy, newly arrived Germans by the German Society of Pennsylvania.[110] Beyond all these health prob-lems, ailing immigrants experienced an added risk of having their baggage lost or stolen during illness. And all the while, they were uncertain about the final outcome of their affliction.

A catalog of misfortunes that could befall passengers on their voyage would be incomplete without mentioning certain practices devised solely to take advantage of relatively wealthy immigrants who had paid their fare in advance. As the number of migrants increased, and among them the proportion of people traveling on credit, so did the risk of late, incom-plete, or defaults in passage payments increase. Some merchants reacted by attempting to secure their investment in human cargo by any available means, which included continuing to engage in practices that had been customary in the 1730s, when passage agreements that were contracted for an entire collective transport indemnified the leaders or heads of house-holds for those under their command and care. Under changed circum-stances at the height of the migration, a few merchants tried to extend that custom and force more-affluent immigrants to "sponsor" unrelated, poor

108. Philadelphia County administration no. 122, 1740.
109. "Advice to German Emigrants, 1749," 232, 236; "Two Germantown Letters of 1738," 12; *Statutes at Large of Pennsylvania*, 4:67, 382–88; 8:369–77.
110. Beamtenratsprotokoll, 13 September 1770; 18 January 1772; 19 December 1772, GSP.

fellow passengers in an attempt to "guarantee" payment of all fares in Philadelphia—including the passage debts of those who had died during the voyage. Other freighters took advantage of wealthier travelers by accepting advance fare payments without receipts and then claiming nonpayment upon arrival. When it was successful, that could substantially increase income from passengers' fares. Although only limited evidence of such practices survive in individual cases, the truth of charges to that effect by Sauer, Mittelberger, and others is supported by provisions in the laws designed to curb abuses in the trade.[111] Concerned friends therefore advised prospective immigrants that they might avoid such abusive and fraudulent practices by taking advantage of credit policies that merchants had already for some time offered to poorer emigrants. Thus, passengers with sufficient funds to pay their own way were nonetheless urged to remit just half of the fare in advance and the other half upon arrival—only after all particulars regulated by the written transportation contract had been fulfilled satisfactorily.[112] That insurance policy for well-off immigrants raised the price for passage, however, because some merchants reacted by charging interest on the credited portion of the fare.

The practice of splitting the fare payment, however, was devised not primarily as an insurance mechanism to protect passengers against abuses rampant at the height of the immigration, but as a means to attract more emigrants. As a result, paying for passage debts after arrival in the American colonies became an important part of the migrant experience. The options for paying up varied. Almost all counted on a network of former immigrants who had a genuine interest in assisting newcomers or who had found ways to profit from providing or facilitating the connections and services that newly arrived immigrants had to rely on in order to connect with relatives and friends or other potential purchasers of their wares and labor. Most commonly, the immigrant himself paid the credited portion of his fare—with funds he had brought or from the proceeds of the sale of goods he imported. In other cases, relatives or friends assumed the debt.[113] Another option was to have a third person, a stranger, "redeem"

111. Mittelberger, *Journey to Pennsylvania*, 22–24; *Statutes at Large of Pennsylvania*, 6:434–35, 437.

112. "Sichere Nachricht aus America"; "Advice to German Immigrants, 1749," 226–37; *Pennsylvanische Berichte*, 16 September 1749; *Statutes at Large of Pennsylvania*, 6:432.

113. Largely informal networks of credit and debt resulted from arrangements among groups of settlers with roots in the Rhine lands. Except for occasional remarks by immigrants themselves, such lines of support and obligations are difficult to trace. Most often, settlers used immigrant kin and friends as carriers for goods they "ordered" for their own use or

the freight by investing in future labor through a contract for servitude. Although "redemptioner" and "indentured servant" are terms that are often used synonymously, "redemptioner" is the more encompassing term in that it signifies the redemption of passage debts by a third person, regardless of the mode of payment or the relationship between debtor and creditor. The term "indentured servant" refers to redemption of a debt in a certain fashion: fare payment in exchange for an advance on future labor regulated by a formally contracted agreement, the indenture. One other alternative was to arrange for further credit in the form of a promissory note or long-term bond. As the immigration ebbed after the 1750s, fewer migrants had the necessary funds to finance their passage, fewer could count on family or friends to redeem them, and declining opportunities in Pennsylvania caused more to default on the payments long term. As a result, the indenture system became the most likely option for paying off highly variable amounts of passage debts.

The need to repay passage money became the distinguishing mark of the German servant trade and the basis for negotiations concerning indentured servitude, replacing the previously common service for passage, where fixed terms had been the rule.[114] The terms of transportation contracts were critical in this step—another reminder of the need to choose wisely among legally binding passage offers and not to be pressured into renegotiation during the voyage.[115] Even if most emigrants had signed passage contracts in German, the accounts were usually kept in English, and immigrants who made them legally binding with their signatures may not have fully understood what they signed. This could result in misunderstandings and added difficulties upon arrival.[116]

The pace at which decisions of consequence were made and accounts were settled during the first few days after immigrant ships arrived was

---

resale—a custom established early ("Letter from Joris Wertmüller"). A different example is Caspar Wistar, who borrowed money from an earlier immigrant in order to pay for his passage from London to Philadelphia in 1717 (Beiler, "Wistar," 189).

114. The transition began sometime in the 1720s. "Auszug einiger Sendschreiben aus Philadelphia in Pennsylvania," 19, still describes the "old" or English way of redemption.

115. The Pennsylvania law against abuses in the emigrant trade indicated that transportation agreements were not always honored; it also forbade renegotiation of passage contracts during the voyage. *Pennsylvanische Berichte*, 16 September and 16 October 1749; *Statutes at Large of Pennsylvania*, 6:437.

116. See Muhlenberg in *Hallesche Nachrichten*, 461; see also entries concerning the account of the Widow Martin in the Beamtenratsprotokoll, 24 October and 21 November 1772; 16 January 1773, GSP.

swift, possibly bewildering, and certainly crucial. This brief stage of first adjustment distinguished immigrants who actively determined what would be their first steps in life in the new land and those who, by contrast, were reduced to accepting increasingly fewer and less-desirable options as the season of arrival advanced into fall and winter and as additional expenses swelled accounts even further. The first group normally encompassed the majority of immigrants, including a wide variety of newcomers who could settle up their travel affairs with one of the simpler strategies. The second group, made up of those pressed into servitude, was usually much smaller in number and characterized by severely limited financial resources or perhaps little personal resourcefulness.

Irrespective of the particular financial and personal circumstances of passengers upon arrival, those who were welcomed by relatives or friends were lucky. The experienced, already settled immigrant verified the newcomer's account and, if necessary, suggested how to contest faulty or fabricated charges effectively. In the 1730s and 1740s, newspaper advertisements seeking "late payments" of fare debts dating back as far as five years suggest that merchants were then not too concerned with settling passengers' accounts promptly.[117] Also, absconding was relatively easy, especially for an unattached person who had little baggage. Once passengers had left the ship with the intent, or under the pretense, of obtaining the necessary cash from relatives or friends, through the sale of imported goods, or from wages for labor, they often failed to return to settle their accounts or to make binding arrangements to do so.

Toward the end of the colonial period, when the number of immigrants who had personal connections in the province had declined considerably, the officers of the German Society of Pennsylvania checked the correctness of passengers' accounts, investigated cases of alleged overcharges, and, if these were not in accord with the passage agreement, filed suit.[118] This was the last formality between immigrants and their importers, no matter how the balance was paid or whether it was in cash or short-term credit, with the exception of cases of breach of contract. Settling up allowed the newcomers finally to leave the vessel and signaled a new beginning, usually smoothed and ensured by experienced help from trustworthy people. The vast majority of payments by third persons to

---

117. *American Weekly Mercury*, 26 December 1732; *Pennsylvania Gazette*, 16 April 1739; *Pennsylvanische Berichte*, 16 May 1748 and 16 May 1751. See also "Outstanding Debts of Sundry Palatines" on the ships *Pennsylvania* (1755) and *Chance* (1756), 1761, in "Redemptioners," HSP.

118. Beamtenratsprotokoll, 20 and 24 October 1772; 2 January 1773, GSP.

balance out credited fares, including indentures, were in cash or short-term credit—that is, notes or assumptions, without interest charged. These payments were made on time in virtually all the known cases.[119]

Immigrants had limited time in which to arrange for payment of their debts to the merchant or captain. Early in the century, when ships stayed in port longer, it had been several weeks, even months.[120] Later, the contract of the ship *Pennsylvania Packet* (1773) granted passengers just two weeks for balancing outstanding fares.[121] The stipulation of the indenture of Stevann Dugman (Stephann Doechmann) on the ship *Britannia* (1773) included the important provision "void if his friends come up and pay." The wording "disappointed in their friends" in the advertisements for Germans for redemption sale can serve as yet another expression of the customary grace period immigrants had for arranging payment of passage debts.[122] Networks of kin and former neighbors were highly selective, and connections could not always be made easily.[123] Immigrants who hoped to be met upon arrival but were disappointed had to fall back on their own

119. See, for example, the accounts of the ships *Nancy* (1750) and *Britannia* (1773).

120. In February 1740, merchant Mordecai Lloyd placed a bilingual notice in the *Pennsylvania Gazette* (7 February 1739/40) warning immigrants who had arrived the previous fall but failed to settle their debts that they would be prosecuted according to law.

121. The agreement like the following one signed by the passengers of the ship *Pennsylvania Packet* reflects standard and customary usage for the decade before the Revolution: "We whose Names are hereunto annexed do hereby acknowledge that we have agreed with Capt. Peter Osborne, Commander of the good ship called Pennsylvania Packet, to pay him for our Passage from London to Philadelphia, North America, Fourteen days after our safe arrival in the said place, (the said Capt. Osborne finding us in sufficient meat & drink during the said passage) at & after the costs of eight pounds eighteen shillings Sterling per head. & in case of non performance of the said payment by any of us, that the said Captain Peter Osborne or the Owners of the said Ship shall have full Power to dispose of us for the said Money, or any of us that shall not make good the said Payment within the said fourteen Days above limited." (16 February 1773, ship no. 302; "Redemptioners," HSP.)

122. *Pennsylvania Gazette*, 1 December 1768; *Hallesche Nachrichten*, 461. Some immigrants sought out well-established and prominent Germans to redeem their debts—a bad practice, in Heinrich Muhlenberg's view (Kurt Aland, ed., *Die Korrespondenz Mühlenbergs*, 2:258).

123. For example, Maria Barbara Kober "disappeared" among the English settled in the hinterland of Philadelphia when she became an indentured servant after her arrival, and probably because she had lost her husband in 1738. For many years she had been unable to connect with the network of settlers from Schwaigern who, in turn, had "missed" her debarkation and therefore were unable to provide advice and support (Fogleman, *Hopeful Journeys*, 77–79). For Jörg Gondi, help from friends came late but freed him from a bad master to whom he was bound for his fare (Faust, "Unpublished Documents," 34–35 [c. 1753]). On the other hand, an emigrant who had taken passage on a ship from London to Maryland had much better luck in connecting with friends, who had taken a a five-week trip with five horses to meet him and his family and help him pay the outstanding fares (Faust, "Unpublished Documents," 31 [17 September 1750]).

resources. Most knew from letters to Germany or from traveling new-landers about procedures for settling up and leaving the ship. While await-ing the aid of friends, uncertainty about how to pay the balance due became more difficult to bear as time passed, as expenses owed to the ship continued to rise, and as pressures to land mounted. In this situation, indentured servitude could seem the only way out, unless the correspond-ent of the freighter would agree—upon receiving sufficient security—to extend credit for a still longer time.

The uncertainties of indentured servitude were clearly far from the high hopes emigrants harbored when they first made plans that depended on the help of local friends. One way that immigrants who still owed passage money could get off the ship to make necessary personal connec-tions or find a suitable business contact was to leave their luggage behind as surety of intent to come back. Hasty or careless negotiations at this point, however, could lead to unpleasant surprises when they returned to the ship, especially if the search for funds to pay off the credited passage money had taken a long time. As merchants were notoriously negligent in storing immigrants' baggage properly and safely, some of their employees were tempted to pilfer the chests for saleable goods.[124] And because mer-chants were also more and more interested in disposing quickly of immi-grants on credited fares, in an effort to regain their own investment in the cargo and to reduce turnaround time in port, their patience with new-comers searching for alternative methods of payment diminished, and family members staying behind on the ship were pressured into agreeing to indentured servitude when a purchaser could be found. Immigrants await-ing settlement of their accounts aboard recently landed ships had provi-sions supplied by their importer, but merchants were allowed to pass these costs on to the passengers.[125]

Delays in returning to the ship to make final arrangements for paying debts, retrieving baggage, and redeeming relatives still on board were quite likely, because making contacts in a strange city and its hinterland could be difficult and time-consuming, especially for a foreigner who did not speak the language. The regularity and seasonality of the German immi-

124. Examples of property lost or stolen during storage are in *Pennsylvanische Berichte*, 16 November 1749; "Advice to German Emigrants, 1749," 236, 237; Sauer to the governor (1755) and Weiss memorial (1774), in Diffenderfer, *German Immigration*, 243, 250–51, 254; 60–61; Beam-tenratsprotokoll, 3 April 1773. See also *Statutes at Large of Pennsylvania*, 6:435–36, for regulations meant to protect immigrants from such misfortunes.

125. See, for instance, "expenses" on the list of outstanding debts on the ship *Britannia* (1773), *PMHB* 13 (1889): 113–15.

grant trade, however, facilitated the development of many informal and formal communication lines both within the city and throughout the province. In this situation, former German immigrants living in Philadelphia and its vicinity played an important role in establishing first contacts for recently landed immigrants. Versed in both English and German, and experienced in the ways of the country, they could be—and were—of great assistance, whether out of genuine concern for fellow countrymen or lured by the business potential the immigrants represented. German store owners, innkeepers, and other prominent men with ties to the German community were especially important as relayers of information.[126] Sauer's printing shop served that function well, as the advertisements in his paper, *Pennsylvanische Berichte*, show.[127] Some networks evolved along denominational lines, while others connected people who shared the same place of origin.[128] People without any such connections found little sympathy and less assistance—a situation that could make the start of a new life in the American colonies very difficult.

The ways to debark expeditiously varied. Immigrants who had paid their fare in advance and had encountered only minor difficulties along the way were the first to go ashore, followed by those who owed part or all of their fare but whose friends or relatives in the Delaware Valley helped them balance their accounts promptly. Almost equally fast was the release from passage debts for unattached, healthy young men and women who had intended from the start to rely on their labor potential to obtain cash to settle their accounts. Such immigrants could choose between two strategies: finding wage labor or agreeing to a term of bound labor. Since the transatlantic fare for a young man was roughly equivalent to a year's wages, it was most economical to find a situation that would allow an immigrant to earn wages in the free labor market,[129] but the merchant had to agree to

126. First Germantown and then the neighborhoods in Philadelphia where German-speaking inhabitants clustered played a crucial role. See Stephanie Wolf, *Urban Village*, and Roeber, *Palatines*.

127. Edward Hocker, comp., *Genealogical Data*, is a compilation of these "lost and found" advertisements and other information pertaining to Germans in colonial Pennsylvania; see also Muhlenberg's explanation of the communication networks in greater Pennsylvania to the magistrate in Rothenburg (Aland, *Korrespondenz Mühlenbergs*, 4:159–61).

128. See, for example, the communication network based on shared former place of residence, Elsoff, evident in "Two Germantown Letters of 1738," 10–12.

129. Especially in the early decades after the founding of Pennsylvania, it was very expensive for settlers to hire servants, but indentured servants, who required room and board but generally no wages, were much easier to obtain and were considered a good deal because a bound labor contract for five years could be had for less than the wages necessary to hire a servant for

extend credit for the outstanding debt. For immigrants who had skills that
were not readily marketable or who were less inclined or prepared to accept the risks of finding suitable work in an unfamiliar market, contracting for a time of bound labor offered another option. Longer terms of
indentured servitude were necessary to pay off outstanding fares, but an
agreement that included room and board offered a security that wage labor could not give. The felicity of either choice depended much on the
particular employer with whom immigrants linked up—a relationship
that a worker who received wages could always terminate, while the bound
servant was more and longer at the whim of his master. For those who
chose bound labor, debarkation was delayed somewhat because negotiations for indentures took time even for single people with qualities in
demand for service.[130]

Throughout most of the period, contemporaries commented on the brisk-
ness of indenture sales in recently landed German immigrant vessels.[131] In
the 1770s, notices in newspapers that advertised German immigrants for
redemption sale as indentured servants probably reflect the higher proportion of immigrants who were now dependent on indentured servitude to
pay their debts and the unwillingness of merchants to extend long-
term credit more than sluggish demand, although in those years the Philadelphia market for servants generally declined in favor of wage labor.[132] In
general, German immigrants were known for hard work.[133] Evidence from
the "Record of Indentures" (1771–73) and the passenger accounts on the

one year ("Letters from the Delaware, II: Reverend Andreas Sandel"). This situation was also
advantageous for immigrants who could offer skills and experience that were sought after in
the free labor market.

130. For the early 1770s, some of those receipts for passage and servants, as well as some
indentures, survived (Cadwalader Collection, General John Cadwalader, HSP).

131. "Johannes Naas to Jacob Wilhelm Naas, 7 October 1733," in Martin Brumbaugh,
trans., History of the German Baptist Brethren, 122–23, is just one example.

132. Philadelphische Staatsbote, 28 January 1768; 24 August 1773; 5 October 1774; 1 November
1774; 3 and 10 January 1775; Pennsylvania Gazette, 1 December 1768; 24 January 1772; 5 May 1773;
19 October 1773; 14 December 1773. Sharon Salinger outlined that development (To Serve Well
and Faithfully). Muhlenberg commented on difficulties immigrants encountered in seeking redemption of their passage debts if they arrived in years when money was tight, as in 1767 and
1768 (Aland, Korrespondenz Mühlenbergs, 3:630, 635, 659).

133. Philipp Jacob Irion, who settled in Culpeper County, Virginia, made that point in a
letter to Germany (9 May 1766) (Braun, Auswanderer aus Kaiserslautern, 15). Also, advertisements
for runaway servants in the Pennsylvania Gazette make it clear that German servants were much
less likely to run away than their Irish or English counterparts.

ship *Britannia* (1773) indicate that a large number of indentures were actually negotiated in the first week after landing. Agreements for the indenture of dependent teenage children tended to require more time, because balancing the time and price of the service contract with the family's financial needs and desires was often complicated. "Many servants are purchased young—whose family comes over, sells off a couple of kids to pay the freight of all."[134] The preference for teenagers from the Rhine lands became characteristic of the Philadelphia market for indentured servants.[135] Where the family owed relatively large amounts and where many family members of different ages traveling on one account were involved, settling up could be drawn out even further. Those who had themselves either suffered loss of health or property, or were directly affected by death, sickness, or theft that afflicted one or more members of the group with whom they traveled, debarked more slowly and less auspiciously. In their circumstances, flexibility for settling accounts was lost and the landing process delayed.[136]

The order in which accounts that depended on indentured servitude for remuneration were paid up after their ship had landed reflects the complexity of the system. Predictably, young, single men and women, as well as teenage children, drew the first and best offers. Adults of advanced years and impaired health went more slowly, as did very young children. Those who had particularly large debts were at a further disadvantage because their initial price was high whatever the term that offset it. Immigrants seeking masters who would allow couples and families to stay to-

134. Benjamin Franklin to Sir Everard Fawkener, 27 July 1756, copy in Abbot E. Smith Papers, Box 1, Folder 40, College of William and Mary, Williamsburg, Va. See also the accounts of the ship *Britannia* (1773); indenture of Maria Elizabetha Braurin, who was bound out to Samuel Pleasants for five years with the consent of her father in return for £27 (more than her fare for the voyage) in 1767 (Society Miscellaneous Collection, Box HSP); Romey Blattner, also bound out by her father for one year in 1772 (Faust, "Unpublished Documents," 41).

135. Robert Morris explained this to George Washington. James Tilghman Jr. to George Washington, Philadelphia, 7 April 1774, Washington Papers, LC/MD (microfilm).

Economic historians usually limited their explorations of the German servant market to men over the age of sixteen because the ship lists rarely name younger children for easy comparison with surviving lists of indentures. See Robert Heavner, *Economic Aspects of Indentured Servitude*; Farley Grubb, "Auction of Redemptioner Servants," "Does Bound Labour Have to Be Coerced Labour?" "Immigrant Servant Labor," "Incidence of Servitude," "Long-Run Trend in Values of European Immigrant Servants," "Market for Indentured Servants," and "The Market Structure of Shipping German Immigrants." See Marianne Wokeck, "The Experience of Indentured Servants," and "Servant Migration" for a broader view.

136. Mittelberger, *Journey to Pennsylvania*, 16; Muhlenberg in *Hallesche Nachrichten*, 461; "Two Germantown Letters of 1738," 10.

gether faced similar problems. The law of 1765 mandated that husband and wife could not be separated by different indentures unless they so desired.[137] Merchants disapproved of this provision, because employers of couples were difficult to find.[138]

Strangers were unlikely to redeem such disadvantaged newcomers within the first weeks after landing in Philadelphia. First, these immigrants stayed on board, and then, when the ship was readied for departure, they were moved to boardinghouses. In both places, accommodations and provisions were generally poor.[139] Immigrants in such circumstances reportedly took to the streets to beg, and some of them appear in the records as recipients of alms: "Jacob Wolf a lusty Boy & Girl with him (that he said was his sister) were at my house begging, said he was brot in by Capn. Moore consigned to Benj. Shoemaker."[140]

The importance of flexible indentures for German immigrants is evident from the substantial proportion of passengers who, particularly in the late years, opted for or resorted to this form of temporarily bound labor in an effort to alleviate the financial burden of a new beginning or to square unmet passage debts. Indentured servants were recruited from two substantially different groups arriving from the Rhine lands. The majority negotiated their contracts willingly and accepted this system of temporary servitude either as an educational opportunity or as a rite of initiation into the New World, or they welcomed it as a means to finance an otherwise unaffordable relocation. Other newcomers were pressed into signing indentures, often on unfavorable terms, because they had experienced difficulties along the way.

The distinction between immigrants who willingly accepted and who often profited from the system of indentured servitude, and those who were forced to make use of it, is a significant one in understanding the history of the German migration. A careful reading of contemporary comments concerning the role of the system in the lives of German immigrants reveals that commentators like Sauer and Mittelberger never questioned either the existence of the system or the use of formal contracts. In fact, they pointed to the various financial and educational advantages that

137. *Statutes at Large of Pennsylvania*, 6:440.

138. *Votes*, 7:5721.

139. Beamtenratsprotokoll, GSP, mentions visits of members of the Society to such establishments (13 September and 3 December 1770; 18 January, 19 October, and 19 December 1772; 2 January and 28 September 1773).

140. From "Pocket Almanack for the Year 1755," 109. See also the alms account kept by John Wister, Wister Family Papers, HSP.

could be gained if masters were chosen wisely. Yet these commentators saw the seamier side of servitude as well, and displayed sympathy, indignation, and anger when the system was used to exploit landing Germans.[141] Their views and reactions also underscore the differentiated nature of the German immigration, among which one group could never accept servitude, except as a way for training their children, while another less well-off segment could readily expect to work, at least temporarily, as servants. Virtually all households of prominent, well-established German settlers employed servants, most of them indentured servants.[142] Moreover, many of those who had regular contact with many German settlers, especially shopkeepers, innkeepers, and land speculators—in Philadelphia and in the countryside—purchased large numbers of German immigrants on their own accounts and for their own enterprises, and also on commission for others who could not travel to Philadelphia to make their own arrangements.[143]

Sauer's overall evaluation of the indenture system is illuminating. He published his comments in December 1754, a bad year in which many immigrants arrived ill, as he reports in the same issue of *Pennsylvanische Berichte*. In the context of a discussion of the differences between Europe and America, and of explaining the reasons for emigration, he poses the question "Is there any where a city in Germany and her neighboring countries in which, when but one ship with one thousand people arrived, the inhabitants would take them as servants and pay in advance fifty to one hundred guldens [about four and a half to nine pounds sterling] for their services? And that without any security that they would stay alive for more than two days? Any body who contemplates this has to think that Pennsylvania has been granted special blessings, when every year 8, 10, 12, 16, 18, 20 to 28 ships arrive in Philadelphia late in fall and are emptied after

141. Muhlenberg was particularly concerned about children orphaned at sea and bound out to English settlers or sectarians until they reached maturity (Aland, *Korrespondenz Mühlenbergs*, 1:486, 3:410), but such concerns did not lead to concerted efforts in the German community to help those immigrants.

142. Muhlenberg, for example, needed a manservant to tend to his horses, and maids to help his wife run the household. In turn, he apprenticed his son, Johann Peter Gabriel, in Germany and the orphaned Israel Matthias Heinzelmann under his care with the son of Heinrich Keppele. See *Korrespondenz Mühlenbergs*, 3:334–36, 646.

143. This is especially evident in the lists of indentures and immigrants' accounts in merchant records. See "Record of Indentures [1771–73]," Penrose Cashbooks, 2: (entry for purchases by Caspar Wistar), 3 (entry for a large "lot" of immigrants on Curtius's account), HSP. See also Bailyn, *Voyagers to the West*, 316, 328, 334–35.

several weeks."[144] Similarly, the lack of a "German system" for contracting
indentures with variable terms in colonies other than Pennsylvania and its
neighboring provinces explains in part why their popularity as destinations
for Rhineland emigrants remained limited, compared with the persistent
attraction of the Delaware Valley as gateway to settlement in the New
World.

Mittelberger and Muhlenberg were critical of the system primarily because it threatened impecunious immigrants of some social standing and
because it broke up families. Indeed, the demands of bound labor often
separated family members from each other and placed them geographically
far apart, which meant that servitude interfered with the transmission of
traditional values passed on through the family.[145] Because of this concern,
which was heightened by their awareness of the persuasiveness of American ways, especially for teenagers, both men emphasized the more negative
aspects of contracting for indentured servitude, which they viewed as a last
resort rather than as a positive option without which relocation would
have been impossible for a substantial proportion of German immigrants.
His views, however, did not keep Muhlenberg from employing indentured
servants in his own household—another indication that dissatisfaction
with the system stemmed mostly from cases when it did not work to the
particular advantage of those making use of it.

By the middle of the eighteenth century, when the wave of German
immigration crested and the proportion of financially independent passengers began to decline significantly, more arrivals turned to indentured
servitude as their only alternative for financing the passage. As a consequence, purchasers of German immigrants assumed a substantial portion
of the risk for merchants who had extended credit in Rotterdam. It is not
surprising that under those conditions cooperating merchants in Philadelphia sought to profit from the situation by cutting back on offering
immigrants alternative options for long-term payment and instead asked
for instant cash or servitude to balance passage debts from the sale of
indentures.[146]

144. Others seconded Sauer's assessment. See Johannes Naas to Jacob Wilhelm Naas, 1733;
Jacob Seyler to Hans Jacob Birsinger, 1750, in Faust, "Documents in Swiss Archives," 120.

145. Mittelberger, *Journey to Pennsylvania*, 18; Muhlenberg in *Hallesche Nachrichten*, 461.

146. See the proviso in the contract of the passengers on the ship *Pennsylvania Packet* (1773),
quoted in note 121 in this chapter, which stipulated that the captain or the owners of the vessel
could dispose of delinquent newcomers as they saw fit after two weeks, the time in which
immigrants had to arrange the payment of their fares.

Such new accounting methods, combined with increased dependence on indentured servitude, gave immigrants and their friends reason to be concerned about abuses in the trade. After mid-century, effective political lobbying finally established rules and regulations for the immigrant trade to colonial Pennsylvania. Geared to protect the health and property of the immigrants as a way to ensure the well-being of Pennsylvania citizens who came in contact or did business with them, the laws prescribed adequate accommodations and provisions for Germans during the voyage and for some time after landing, defined responsibilities in case of death and loss of property, devised procedures for dealing with adversities, and provided measures of redress. By 1765, those regulations were comprehensive, and the experienced and respected officers of the German Society of Pennsylvania furnished the money and assistance for enforcement.[147] For the short period remaining before the Revolution, the group of truly destitute immigrants must have been relatively small, and now even the poorest and those hit by misfortune had some protection.[148]

Against the background of negotiating indentures, it is important to remember that varying the length of time to fit the size of the debt distinguished the indenture system of the German trade. However, differences in seasonal patterns of arrival that regulated the availability of servants of a particular background, variations in the predominance of certain skills and age-groups, and differences among purchasers who discriminated because of the servants' regional origins contributed also to the difference in prices for servants of various ethnic backgrounds.[149] Contracts were modified to allow for special skills or particular handicaps, such as extra debt or impaired health. Such discounting becomes apparent when debts of the same amount are matched up with the times to be served for unattached immigrants on the ship *Britannia* (1773). Thus, even though the basic price from Rotterdam to Philadelphia remained stable in real terms, variations of several months—and in extreme cases, even years—in the length of

147. Merchants realized that regulating the trade served them too in that it curbed competition and lowered the costs that accrued from importing immigrants who could neither pay their fare nor find employers to assume their debts. Henry Keppele, president of the GSP, was himself an importer of Germans.

148. The Beamtenratsprotokoll, and the Mennonite alms account attest to such charitable activities.

149. This is evident from passengers' accounts on the ship *Britannia* (1773) matched with "Record of Indentures [1771–73]."

bound service were common among German immigrants, to take into account the needs and qualifications of particular individuals.

Those who purchased servants generally settled travel accounts in cash and registered the indenture, including its specific terms, formally as the law required.[150] If the same notice advertising German freights for sale ran repeatedly, the credit terms for prospective purchases tended to become more liberal. In other words, when sales were slow, the requirement for cash payment gave way to credit arrangements.[151]

The distinctive flexibility of terms in the German indenture system occurred because the German immigration, unlike other major flows of new people to the colonies, continued to consist of a substantial proportion of families. For newly arrived Germans, indentured servitude became an option especially for dependent adolescents, who could serve until they were of age.[152] Such a term brought a price that exceeded the cost of their own fare. Employers with long-range labor needs apparently welcomed the opportunity to purchase servants for more than the two or three years customary for adults (who might also resist learning new ways more than still-untrained teenagers) and were willing to pay for that advantage. And the evidence suggests that, including the costs of schooling, training, board, clothing, and freedom dues, the long-range cost for German teenage indentured servants was high, even considering that the initial price was generous enough to pay for part of the parents' fare as well as the fare of the child bound out. Yet, the returns from such labor investment must have been promising, because adolescents commanded high prices and did not take long to find employers. The fact that merchants and other prominent men with ties to the German community appeared repeatedly as buyers of teenagers for their own use, and on behalf of customers residing outside of Philadelphia, speaks to the desirability of such servants.[153]

150. *Statutes at Large of Pennsylvania*, 6:246–49, 439–40.

151. See, for example, *Pennsylvania Gazette*, 19 October and 14 December 1773 (advertisement by Samuel Howell). According to Robert Morris, twelve-month credit was common in Philadelphia in the 1770s, especially for purchasers interested in obtaining not just one but several servants (in letter of James Tilghman Jr. to George Washington, Philadelphia, 7 April 1774).

152. Immigrants found the record of baptism—one of the several papers required for gaining manumission and permission for removal in Germany—useful in negotiating for fares and labor contracts for children and teenagers. In addition to the passport, which was critical for the European part of the trip, the only other paper that had some value for some emigrants was the minister's certificate attesting to good Christian character, without which it was impossible to get married before embarking on the voyage across the Atlantic. See also note 8 in this chapter.

153. Accounts of the ship *Britannia* (1773); "Record of Indentures [1771–73]."

Families, on the other hand, saw binding out teenage children as a way to ease the adjustment period financially for the family or, still more fundamental, as a way to make migration of the whole family possible in the first place. "There are few houses in city or country where the people are at all well off, that do not have one or two such children in them" reported an early immigrant letter home.[154] The custom obviously took hold and endured; as late as 1773, German families could still easily and regularly rely on their children to share the cost of the move to the New World by becoming indentured servants.[155] Indenture that, in the minds of German immigrants, had begun as an optional educational opportunity for dependent children that also brought an added financial advantage for the family, however, soon became a financial necessity as the flow of newcomers included more and more families that did not have sufficient funds to pay for the passage. Similarly, it became a last resort, and no longer simply an option, for those whose resources had been reduced during the voyage—a type of collateral—as the more unscrupulous merchants and newlanders devised schemes to exploit passengers and as the crowded conditions on board at the peak of the immigration increased the toll among family members who might have supported others.[156]

Another major factor responsible for the kind of first steps immigrants took toward a new beginning in America, and how successful those steps were, was the nature of the help they received upon arrival. The fact that first mostly friends and relatives, then mainly strangers, were the third parties involved in financing travel and a start in the New World mirrors the change that took place in the composition of the German migration. At the beginning of regular transatlantic emigration from Germany, newly arrived settlers coming in response to good reports of opportunities in Pennsylvania were relatively affluent and could frequently count on the support of family and friends. The prevalence of such personal assistance

154. Johannes Naas to Jacob Wilhelm Naas, 1733.

155. See, for example, the accounts of the Daagen, Eberhard, Jongh, Knor, and Reinhard families on the ship *Britannia* (1773).

156. Although Farley Grubb recognized the primary importance of financing the transatlantic passage through indentured servitude in his discussion of the reasons for the decline of bound labor ("End of European Immigrant Servitude"), his earlier explorations of the economic characteristics of the institution (for references, see n. 135, above) do not include sufficient consideration of this critical aspect. Much of the differences in length of service and the price of servants reflect the variable nature of the debt for passage, which depended not only on the port of embarkation but also, in the German case, on other circumstances, for instance, whether they relocated as members of a family or independently of kin and former neighbors.

and guidance in the transition to a new life decreased as German immigrants settled farther inland—out of the more immediate hinterland of the port of Philadelphia—and as German-speaking settlers fared less well or were less inclined to help the more recent arrivals of their compatriots in their relocation. Fewer immigrants came with the urging and aid of relatives and friends, and more who did come were dependent instead on outside help even to afford the passage. In turn, the initiation of immigrants into the ways of the new country was increasingly in the hands of strangers, who were apt to be guided by merely economic rather than largely personal considerations. The result was that protective legal measures against the exploitation of poor, newly arrived Germans became a public necessity.

The assets that emigrants could muster when they left their homelands, the resourcefulness with which they preserved their assets during the journey, the nature of their particular passage, and assistance from friends or dependence on outside help were all factors that determined immigrants' circumstances when they arrived, and augured the way in which newcomers would make their start in the New World. In the early years of the migration, the vicissitudes of the journey were tempered by relative wealth and cohesion among emigrants who ventured across the Atlantic. Many seemed vindicated in their decision to relocate, when the early struggles of settlement gave way to a decent, even comfortable, living. This was true even though for some immigrants the price for such eventual success was considerable, as they tested a range of not always fruitful opportunities in various American colonies, and as they suffered from the inexperience of the emigrant trade on which they depended for transportation overseas.[157]

In the middle of the eighteenth century, when German relocation to America peaked, the dangers of the trip affected immigrants differently. Competition for emigrants in the transatlantic transportation business swelled the ranks of movers with people who had more-limited resources and created even more crowded ships. As a result, mortality among passengers was high, but now more from greed than from inexperience in the business. As the risk of death grew, so did the likelihood of losing property. Immigrants who arrived at the height of the migration often did so in relatively poor physical and financial shape, because of the many differ-

---

157. Relatively more immigrant ships were wrecked or had disastrous voyages in the beginning phase of the German migration than later. See the Appendix.

ent interests that attempted to squeeze profits from the mass relocation. Yet quite a few of those who undertook the journey then could count on support and assistance from those who had arrived before them and whose success had encouraged them to follow suit and move too. The willingness of established German settlers to invest in immigrants of similar origin favored the stream to Philadelphia, where the custom of using bound labor to finance the relocation had developed into an integral and widely accepted part of the immigrant experience, and at the same time a valued opportunity for earlier migrants to staff their households, farms, and businesses with young country men and women.[158]

When emigration resumed after the Seven Years' War, the hazards of ocean travel with which passengers had to cope were less often the consequence of unabashed profiteering but more the result of hard-nosed and well-honed business practices of several veteran merchants with large and diversified operations and considerable experience in the trade. Passengers could still easily obtain credit for the fare, but they were less likely to suffer from crowded conditions and theft. Instead, though, they had to accept terms of transportation and credit that now favored the shipper more heavily, and that became especially limiting upon arrival in Philadelphia, where merchants increasingly pushed indentured servitude as the most acceptable means of squaring outstanding debts. As a consequence, relatively more immigrants began their life in the New World as servants and with generally more limited prospects for success. German immigrants could still bank on their reputation as good workers—which was the reason they were attractive to non-German employers and land developers— but their employment as laborers was now less often a way to solidify and extend networks among people who shared similar homeland origins, cultural and linguistic traits, or religious convictions, and primarily a well-calculated investment in this particular type of labor. Like many of the less-prosperous Rhineland immigrants who arrived around the middle of the eighteenth century, most newcomers in the 1760s and 1770s could no longer achieve the wealth and security of New World life that the early immigrants to the Delaware Valley had obtained and that had generated the dynamics to attract large numbers of German emigrants to the colonies. Without that kind of stimulus, German immigration to America slowed significantly.

158. In Georgia, it was the English rather than the Salzburgers who redeemed the debts of immigrants from Württemberg by employing them as servants. See Brinck, *Deutsche Auswanderungswelle,* 255; and Renate Wilson, "Public Works and Piety."

CHAPTER 5

Irish Immigration
to the Delaware Valley

The wave of German immigration that crested in the middle of the eighteenth century was followed by a second surge of strangers. These set out from Irish ports to settle in North America. This Irish immigration mostly repeated the dynamics established for the Germans; but it reached its peak only after the American Revolution, and its volume was considerably smaller than traditionally estimated. Unlike its German precursor, however, significant Irish immigration to the American colonies had existed well before the exodus from Ulster developed the characteristics of mass migration in the last decades of the 1700s. This mixed history created various and overlapping flows from Ireland that were distinct in the southern and northern regions from which migrants originated (see Map 3), in shifting combinations of single young men and families among the voyagers, and in a changing mix of indentured servants and fare-paying passengers.

Ireland's long-standing, close, and direct mercantile ties to colonial America formed the basis for the differences between the German and Irish migrations. These channeled where the flow went, influenced its composition, determined recruiting, shaped the migration experience, and affected chances for successful integration into life in the New World. Throughout the eighteenth century, a steady though moderate flow of emigrants from Ireland landed in the American colonies, especially in Delaware Valley ports (which were consistently the most important pre-Revolutionary destination for Irish immigrants), New York, and Baltimore.

MAP 3   Ireland

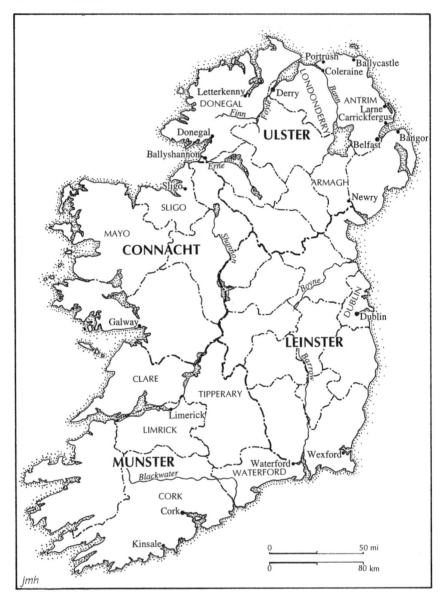

Twice, however, in the late 1720s and during the decade before the Revolution, this stream swelled significantly. In the years of relatively lighter immigration, the number of passengers on each ship was small and the proportion of indentured servants—mostly young, single men—large. During the peak periods of Irish immigration, and particularly when the tide gathered a new level of momentum in the 1760s and early 1770s, the majority of passengers embarked in Ulster, paid their fare in advance, traveled in family groups, and often disembarked in New Castle, Delaware, before the vessel made port in Philadelphia. The last decade before the Revolution was the most crucial for the Irish immigration. More than one-third of all the Irish arrived during the years when competition for work and land was stiff, when many of the best opportunities had moved well inland, and when integration into American society was partly determined by high tension between England and her North American colonies.

Irish immigration to the colonial Delaware Valley can be divided into three periods, and its pattern reveals distinct differences between streams coming from northern and southern Irish ports (see Figure 3A and Table 4).[1] The first peak came in the late 1720s, after nearly five decades of sporadic immigration, of which fewer than 500 Irish Quakers were a significant segment.[2] According to the primate of Ireland, Hugh Boulter, the buildup to this brief but severe period of famine and crisis had escalated from 1,100 migrants to all American destinations in the years 1726–27, to 3,100 in 1728 and 3,500 preparing to leave in 1729.[3] The exact number who came to America in these few years of emergency is uncertain, but the *Pennsylvania Gazette* of 6 January 1729/30, claimed that 1,155 arrived in Philadelphia and 4,500 had landed in "New Castle Government"—a figure that may be close. Another contemporary listing, "Passengers and Servants imported from Ireland from June 1729 to September 1735," put the figure for 1729 at 1,865 immigrants to Philadelphia and 3,790 immigrants to Del-

1. The Ulster ports of embarkation were Belfast, Londonderry, Newry, Larne, and Portrush; the southern ports were Dublin, Cork, Waterford, and Galway.

2. Albert Myers, *Immigration of Irish Quakers*, statistical table; Audrey Lockhart, *Some Aspects of Emigration from Ireland*, app. C.

3. This assessment by Archbishop Boulter is published in Robert Dickson, *Ulster Emigration to Colonial America*, 33. See also the more lurid report of a Londonderry merchant, published in the *Pennsylvania Gazette* (17 Nov. 1729), in which he estimated that by July 1729 about 3,500 emigrants—an average of 120–140 passengers per ship—had transported themselves and their goods to places beyond the sea from this one port, and many more from other harbors.

FIG. 3   Estimated numbers of Irish immigrants to the Delaware Valley,
1730–1774

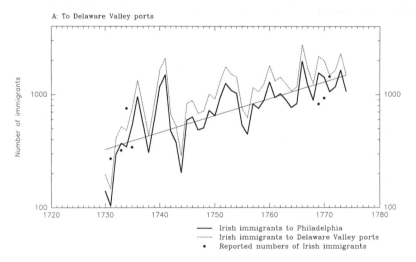

A: To Delaware Valley ports

——— Irish immigrants to Philadelphia
·········· Irish immigrants to Delaware Valley ports
•   Reported numbers of Irish immigrants

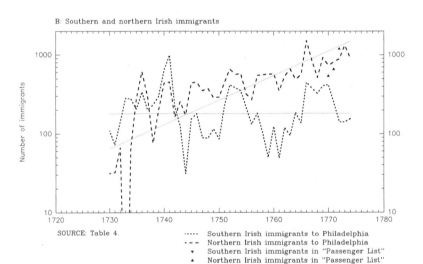

B: Southern and northern Irish immigrants

SOURCE: Table 4.

····· Southern Irish immigrants to Philadelphia
– – – Northern Irish immigrants to Philadelphia
▾   Southern Irish immigrants in "Passenger List"
▲   Northern Irish immigrants in "Passenger List"

aware.[4] Both come to a total of 5,655. They just distributed them somewhat differently between Philadelphia and New Castle. This number, however, was ten times the size of typical flows one or two decades following this crisis time, and also the general level before the late 1720s. Such a sudden surge in scale could occur in response to homeland disaster, because, unlike the German situation of the 1709 exodus, the shipping already existed, regularly plying back and forth between Ireland and the Delaware. About half the immigrants had embarked in Ulster, the other in southern Irish ports, and that proportion seems to have held over the next five years (see Table 4 and Figure 3B).

After the truly exceptional peak of 1729, the flow of Irish immigrants to the Delaware Valley apparently ebbed to about 640 immigrants per year on average (Table 4).[5] Significant fluctuations around this level were not unusual, in particular as a result of the 1740–41 famine in Ireland, and also at mid-century, when the reported number of immigrant vessels departing from southern Irish ports was high.[6] In all, though, details about the immigration from 1730 to 1763 are sketchy, because few data are available.[7] Reports about ships leaving southern Irish ports with emigrants bound for Philadelphia exist for 1730 until 1756; advertisements in the *Belfast News*

4. The list "Passengers and Servants Imported from Ireland from June 29 to Sept. 1735," Pennsylvania Miscellaneous Papers, Penn & Baltimore, Penn Family, 1725–39, 167, is undated and unsigned, so it is impossible to check for any inherent bias.

5. The number of individual years varies, but the anonymous report on "Passengers and Servants [1729–35]" lists (without numbers for 1730 and 1732) a total of 1,631 Irish arrivals in Philadelphia in the six years 1730–35, while my calculation, based on identifiable ship arrivals and typical numbers of immigrants traveling per vessel, suggests about 1,790.

6. Lockhart, *Some Aspects of Emigration*, 22, app. C. Additional information was gleaned from the customhouse notices published in the *Pennsylvania Gazette*. Those notices contain information that makes it possible to identify vessels arriving from Irish ports, to establish shipping patterns prevalent in the trade, to calculate how long ships stayed in port, and to determine where a vessel planned to sail when leaving Philadelphia. This source has several shortcomings, especially the fragmentary copies of the paper, missing listings, and incomplete transcriptions from the naval office lists.

7. Information for estimating the size of the Irish immigration includes specific reports for certain years on the number of vessels scheduled to leave Ireland for colonial Pennsylvania and, conversely, accounts of the arrival of ships from Irish ports in Philadelphia. There is one brief but inclusive listing of immigrants from Ireland registered in Philadelphia by name between August 1768 and May 1772. Dickson, *Ulster Emigration*, 33, 61, 64; Lockhart, *Some Aspects of Emigration*, 22; *Gentlemen's Magazine*, 44 (1774), 332; *Pennsylvania Gazette*, 6 January 1729/30; "Passengers and Servants [1729–35]"; "Servants and Apprentices Bound and Assign'd Before James Hamilton Mayor of Philadelphia, 1745 & 1746," HSP (published in *PMHB*, vols. 30–31 [1907–8]); "Record of Indentures [1771–73]"; "Passenger List [1768–72]"; customhouse notices in the *Pennsylvania Gazette*; Myers, *Immigration*.

TABLE 4   Estimated numbers of Irish immigrants to the Delaware Valley,
1730–1774

Year	Est. No. of Immigrants from Southern Ireland	Est. No. of Immigrants from Northern Ireland (incl. unknown)	Est. No. of Immigrants from All Irish Ports (Incl. Delaware)	Est. No. of Immigrants from All Irish Ports
1730	109	31	140	196
1731	72	32	104	146
1732	142	66	298	417
1733	281	—	371	519
1734	278	68	346	484
1735	206	280	531	743
1736	339	612	951	1,331
1737	201	296	542	759
1738	232	76	308	431
1739	295	195	580	812
1740	648	440	1,178	1,649
1741	993	451	1,489	2,085
1742	222	163	475	665
1743	125	255	380	532
1744	31	173	204	286
1745	153	442	595	833
1746	181	451	632	885
1747	89	352	486	680
1748	88	375	508	711
1749	116	287	718	1,005
1750	86	292	648	907
1751	226	446	942	1,319
1752	418	656	1,254	1,756
1753	385	565	1,085	1,519
1754	352	575	1,017	1,424
1755	214	319	533	746
1756	132	270	447	626
1757	182	549	821	1,149
1758	102	558	750	1,050
1759	50	567	887	1,242
1760	124	576	1,285	1,799
1761	49	351	940	1,316
1762	120	534	1,014	1,420
1763	95	663	893	1,250
1764	186	489	765	1,071
1765	138	558	831	1,163
1766	451	1,510	1,961	2,754

Letter for ships offering passage begin in 1750; and for one year, September 1745 to October 1746, the registration of indentures of servants from Ireland before the mayor of Philadelphia has survived.[8] When matching ship departures and arrivals, however, it becomes apparent that the listings of vessels leaving Ireland with passengers for Philadelphia are incomplete. Yet

8. Lockhart, *Some Aspects of Emigration,* app. C; Dickson, *Ulster Emigration,* app. D; "Servants and Apprentices [1745–46]"; customhouse notices published in the *Pennsylvania Gazette.*

TABLE 4   *(Continued)*

Year	Est. No. of Immigrants from Southern Ireland	Est. No, of Immigrants from Northern Ireland (incl. unknown)	Fst No of Immigrants from All Irish Ports (Incl. Delaware)	Est. No. of Immigrants from All Irish Ports
1767	377	830	1,207	1,689
1768	327	518	890	1,246
1769	407 [283]	918 [541]	1,550 [824]	2,170
1770	420 [275]	731 [658]	1,421 [933]	1,989
1771	248 [250]	809 [1,196]	1,057 [1,446]	1,480
1772	142	888	1,165	1,631
1773	142	1,314	1,641	2,297
1774	156	911	1,067	1,494
Total	10,240	21,442	36,907	51,676

SOURCE:

Customhouse notices, *Pennsylvania Gazette;* Audrey Lockhart, *Some Aspects of Emigration from Ireland to the North American Colonies Between 1660 and 1775* (New York, 1976); Robert J. Dickson, *Ulster Emigration to Colonial America, 1718–1775.* 1966. Reprint, London, 1988; "Tonnage Duty Book [1765–75]"; "Passenger List [1768–72]."

NOTES:

Numbers in brackets are reported—not estimated—numbers: "Passenger List [1768–72]."

The estimate of immigrants from southern Irish ports to Philadelphia was based on the observation that at the beginning of the migration each ship carried an average of 30 immigrants and that by the mid-1770s that number had declined to 20.

The estimate of immigrants from northern Irish ports to Philadelphia was based on the observation that at the beginning of the migration each ship carried an average of 30 immigrants and that by the mid-1770s that number had increased to 70.

The estimate of immigrants from all Irish ports to Philadelphia is the sum of immigrants from southern and northern Irish ports. An average of 45 immigrants per ship was calculated for vessels for which the exact port of embarkation in Ireland could not be determined.

The estimate of immigrants from Ireland to the Delaware Valley (Lewes, New Castle, and Philadelphia) was calculated by adding 40 percent to the number of Irish immigrants landing in Philadelphia.

these are shortcomings of relatively slight effect when compared with the omission of New Castle, Delaware, as a distinct destination in both the major data sources about departures from Ireland. Evidence for 1745–46 suggests that before mid-century more than half the Irish servants on ships ultimately bound for Philadelphia may have disembarked all or most of their human cargoes in New Castle.

All indications are that New Castle was an important port in the Irish immigrant trade before 1750. Unfortunately, none of the shipping records that would substantiate this assertion have been found.[9] In the January 6, 1729/30, issue of the *Pennsylvania Gazette*, however, it is claimed that three-quarters of the Irish immigrants to the region at this exceptional time landed in New Castle. In late summer 1736, the *American Weekly Mercury* confirmed New Castle's continued importance in the Irish immigrant trade. "On Sunday arrived a Snow from Ireland, with Passengers and Servants" (26 August 1736); "The number of Passengers and servants arrived at this Place [Philadelphia] since our last, amounts in all to 345. And we here [*sic*] from New-Castle, that in the space of about 24 hours, in the last Week, there arrived near 1000 Souls, from the same Place" (2 September 1736). Within the next two weeks, two more ships arrived: the *Neptune* from Newry with 153 passengers, and the snow *Gilbert* from Dublin, with 95 passengers and servants.[10] Table 4 estimates from identifiable shipping that 1,331 Irish passengers and servants arrived in this year, compared with 1,593 of these newspaper accounts. It attributes the bulk to Philadelphia, however, rather than to New Castle. The problem is knowing exactly where people disembarked from vessels eventually arriving in Philadelphia. In 1745–46, ships stopping over in New Castle arrived in Philadelphia with an average of twelve servants, while ships coming to Philadelphia without delay carried an average of thirty servants. This suggests that perhaps half the immigrants disembarked in Delaware.

The picture is clearer and also quite different in 1768–72, for which more data are available.[11] Now just over one-quarter of all the ships carrying almost half the immigrants registered in Philadelphia stopped first in New Castle. Less than 10 percent of those ships and immigrants came from southern Irish ports. Meanwhile, about 55 percent of the vessels sailing from Ulster with 65 percent of the northern Irish immigrants to Phila-

9. No ship or passenger lists for Delaware's ports seem to have survived. Occasional reports about ships arriving in the Delaware Valley in the *American Weekly Mercury* confirm the impression that New Castle was an important port of call for vessels from Ireland, and especially for immigrants who wanted to circumvent the 20s duty imposed on servants landed in Philadelphia. See Martin Griffin, ed., "Early Irish Immigration: Few Catholics."

10. "Passengers and Servants [1729–35]."

11. "Tonnage Duty Book [1765–75]" and McCusker, "Ships Registered at the Port of Philadelphia," allow us to determine the ownership of many ships sailing between Ireland and the Delaware Valley and to characterize vessels by type and size. The "Passenger List [1768–72]," the only source for Irish newcomers roughly comparable to the German ship lists, states the date each immigrant ship arrived, the master's name, and where it came from and enumerates the immigrants by name as a way to calculate the duty. The accuracy of the "Passenger List" and the "Tonnage Duty Book" is good, because both sets of records were kept to facilitate the collection of duties.

delphia on board anchored first at New Castle. Clearly, throughout the century there persisted a close connection between Ulster and the Lower Counties. Even though many of the ships landed first at New Castle, however, it seems unlikely that in the years 1768–72 many immigrants left the ship before the ship reached Philadelphia. During this later period, the profile of the Ulster immigrants—the proportions of men, women, and family groups—was virtually identical on ships that stopped over in New Castle and those that did not; and the average number of passengers still on board in Philadelphia was highest on ships that touched in New Castle before anchoring in Philadelphia. Thus, by the 1760s, the strong ties between Ulster and New Castle seem to have been predominantly commercial, dealing in goods, rather than forged by connections that personally linked seasoned settlers and the newcomers from northern Ireland. During the colonial period, that is, Philadelphia gradually subsumed the port-of-entry role that New Castle had played earlier in the immigrant trade with northern Ireland. This is a shift that is consistent with Philadelphia's growing importance in the North Atlantic trade in the third quarter of the eighteenth century. As a result of this change, while the level of Irish immigration into the Delaware Valley must have been higher throughout than the number of newcomers arriving annually in Philadelphia, it probably raised the total influx by two-thirds during the second quarter of the century, and by less than half in the two decades preceding the Revolution.

After the Seven Years' War, immigration from Ireland resumed and increased to levels that matched the early crisis year of 1729. During the thirteen years until the Revolution, the growth in immigration did not occur gradually, but rather shot up in two spurts, with a short-term peak of almost 3,000 newcomers in 1766, and a more extended surge of about 2,000 immigrants annually from 1769 to 1773. (See Table 4 and Figure 3A.) Compared with the earlier periods, the sources documenting this phase of the Irish immigration are relatively abundant and detailed. Yet the extraordinary character of this particular late pre-Revolutionary influx from Ireland limits the usefulness of projecting backward from these years. Combining all the available information, including comparative data on vessels leaving and arriving with Irish passengers, and records about the newly arrived immigrants who were bound as servants, suggests that the number of Irish immigrants who came was considerably lower than has been recently estimated.[12] It also reveals that the Irish arrived in two quite distinct

---

12. Dickson's estimates have been accepted by David Doyle, *Ireland, Irishmen, and Revolution-*

migration flows: one from Ulster, the other from the remaining Irish ports.[13]

Overall, the total number of immigrants from southern Ireland was small and the proportion of servants among them large, compared with a high total emigration from Ireland, of which only a relatively small percentage were redemptioners or indentured servants. Although information about the total number of Irish newcomers during the exceptional 1729 peak cannot be categorized according to ports of embarkation, indications are that emigration was significant from all parts of Ireland in reaction to widespread famine (Table 4; Figure 3B). And most of the Irish newcomers who swelled the immigration beyond previously normal levels were paying passengers, not servants. About 200 Irish servants were imported yearly (about 20 percent of the total immigration) in the late 1720s, when duties on servants landed in Philadelphia were imposed briefly to control their importation—in effect diverting their flow to New Castle.[14] In other words, the vast majority (about 80 percent) of the Irish arriving in Philadelphia in 1729 were not servants and thus readily became settlers, a fact corroborated by the settlement pattern James T. Lemon established for southeastern Pennsylvania at a time when the Delaware Valley region was indeed still the "best poor man's country."[15]

The diverse influx of up to almost 6,000 Irish immigrants to Phila-

---

ary America, and Miller, *Emigrants and Exiles*. Thomas Truxes, in his careful study *Irish American Trade*, shows an impressive command of sources from both sides of the Atlantic. Truxes also concurs with Dickson's basic assumption for estimating Irish emigration. Maurice Bric ("Ireland, Irishmen, and the Broadening of Philadelphia Polity," chap. 1), made selective use of the local Philadelphia records that are the foundation for my downward reassessment of the Irish immigration to the Delaware Valley but persisted in following G. E. Kirkham (in his introduction to the 1988 edition of *Ulster Emigration*, xvii–xviii). Leroy Eid, "No Freight Paid so Well," esp. 39–40, suggests that Dickson's figures should be revised *upward*. Aaron Fogleman, "Migrations to the Thirteen British North American Colonies," 706–7, based his estimates on the lower figures presented here.

13. "Passenger List [1768–72]"; customhouse notices in the *Pennsylvania Gazette*; "Tonnage Duty Book [1765–75]"; "Record of Indentures [1771–73]"; Lockhart, *Some Aspects of Emigration*, app. C; Dickson, *Ulster Emigration*, app. D.

14. A law imposing a 20s duty on each Irish servant imported into the province was passed in 1729; Delaware imposed a duty of £5 on the importation of convicts, a subgroup among indentured servants, in 1740. This suggests that at those times the level of Irish immigrants arriving as indentured servants was perceived to be high. The laws were intended to control the rate and composition of the immigration. See *Statutes at Large of Pennsylvania*, 4:135–40; *Laws of the State of Delaware from the Fourteenth Day of October Seventeenhundred to the Eighteenth Day of August Seventeenhundredninetyseven*, 2 vols. (New Castle, Del., 1797), 1:166–73.

15. Lemon, *Best Poor Man's Country*, 43–49.

delphia and New Castle in the crisis year of 1729 included newcomers of different economic backgrounds and of various denominational affiliations—namely, Presbyterians, Anglicans, Quakers, and Catholics.[16] The majority were of Scottish origin, and therefore mostly Presbyterians; others had become Anglicans. The sixty-four Quakers known to have arrived in 1729 were but a small number among the other immigrants from Ireland, yet this group was the single largest influx of Irish Quakers in any year during the colonial period. Catholics also constituted just a minority—estimated at about 10 percent of the overall emigration. As in the German immigration, the success of many of these immigrants as settlers fueled future immigration. It colored reports home to relatives, friends, and neighbors, who were therefore likely to choose the Delaware River ports over other destinations when they themselves decided to emigrate. In addition, as those immigrants gained success in the colonies they became employers of servants regularly imported from Ireland, and some of them even became merchants and importers of Irish servants and passengers.[17] By 1750, Philadelphia had a vibrant merchant community of expatriate Irishmen, who attracted Irish trade to the Delaware Valley; and the diverse networks that co-religionists and former neighbors had developed and expanded well into the hinterland region lured even more emigrants from Ireland to explore opportunities on the American side of the Atlantic.[18]

When Irish immigration decreased to much more moderate levels in the years 1730 to 1763, the number of indentured servants grew in proportion, while the influx of immigrants who paid their own way declined drastically. Probably only one-third of all Irish coming to Philadelphia during these years of reduced migration were capable of paying their own and their families' fares. The evidence for this is tentative but not inconsequential. The average number of free persons and servants taking passage

16. Except for the Irish Quakers, the number and proportions of the various denominations represented in the immigration from Ireland cannot be effectively determined. See Myers, *Immigration*, statistical table.

17. For the "prototypical 'Irish' interest," see Doyle, *Ireland*, 39, who uses the example of a George Croghan of Roscommon in western Pennsylvania who dealt in western lands and continued to recruit relatives from Ireland. Robert Turner, an early Quaker immigrant to Pennsylvania, brought indentured servants from southern Ireland when he relocated, and imported more after he was successfully settled. See Audrey Lockhart, "The Quakers and Emigration from Ireland," 77.

18. Evidence for distinct merchants networks is particularly rich for Quakers and also, but to a lesser degree, for Catholics. See, for example, Myers, *Immigration*, 69–71, 373; Lockhart, "Quakers," 84–86; Truxes, *Irish American Trade*, 121; Thomas Wright to Thomas Greer, 26 June 1773 (Education Facsimile No. 130, PRO of Northern Ireland); and Doyle, *Ireland*, 52, 77.

on vessels leaving from southern Irish ports to the American colonies was 30.[19] For the twelve-month period in 1745–46 for which data on the number of indentured servants from Ireland has survived, the smallest load consisted of one servant, and the largest parcel contained 60 servants, with an average number of 18 Irish servants on vessels making port in the Delaware River.[20] It is important to remember that, despite their significance for outlining the overall picture, these figures and proportions—shiploads of about 30 immigrants of whom about three-fifths were servants—obscure the considerable variations from vessel to vessel and from year to year. Some ships carried more servants than others, absolutely as well as proportionately; and at some times paying passengers may have outnumbered servants. In the Irish famine years of 1740–41, meanwhile, emigration accelerated. Although only indirect evidence is available—namely, a significant increase in the number of ships arriving from Ireland, and a new Delaware law that required passengers to be registered, as a means of controlling the influx of immigrants—it appears that immigration to the Delaware Valley swelled once again during a short period of homeland crisis.[21]

In the thirteen years before the Revolution, when Irish immigration soared, the differences between the flows originating from Ulster and the rest of Ireland became most pronounced. Especially the "Passenger List [1768–72]" allows us to delineate and specify some of those differences with more certainty than was possible for the earlier years.[22] At this time of relatively high and growing levels of Irish immigration preceding the Revolution, the very modest flow from southern Irish ports is most striking. Averaging less than 200 immigrants annually, southern Irish immigration first rose from almost 120 newcomers in 1763 to a peak of 283 in 1769, then declined to about 135 immigrants a year in the early 1770s (Table 4; Figure 3B). Meanwhile, the trade that connected southern Irish ports with Philadelphia was very active and involved many vessels (Table 5; Figures 4 and 5).[23] The volume of this shipping between southern Irish ports and

19. Lockhart, *Some Aspects of Emigration,* app. C.

20. "Servants and Apprentices [1745–46]"; customhouse notices in the *Pennsylvania Gazette.*

21. Customhouse notices in the *Pennsylvania Gazette;* Lockhart, *Some Aspects of Emigration,* 22, app. C; *Laws of Delaware,* 1:166.

22. An exhaustive nominal analysis of the "Passenger List [1768–72]" has not yet been undertaken.

23. Customhouse notices in the *Pennsylvania Gazette;* "Passenger List [1768–72]"; Lockhart, *Some Aspects of Emigration,* app. C. See also *Historical Statistics,* 2:1181; and Francis James, "Irish Colonial Trade," 582.

Philadelphia, as derived from "customhouse notices" in the *Pennsylvania Gazette*, conforms to the same basic chronological shape of peaks near 1736, 1752, and in the late 1760s (Figure 4B). Consequently, the average number of immigrants per ship remained only 20, although the range on individual ships extended from a high of 195 to only 1 or 2 passengers. It was also not unusual to have the same vessel carrying many immigrants on one voyage and just a few on another. In 1771, for example, the *Pattie* sailed from Dublin to Philadelphia with six passengers, but in 1772 the ship returned from the same city, this time carrying 105 immigrants, 73 of whom held indentures contracted in Ireland.[24] Clearly, vessels with more than 30 passengers on board were the exception, while those carrying one or two dozen immigrants were the norm. Based on last-name analysis, only 15 percent of the newcomers arriving on ships from southern Irish ports traveled in family groups, and men and boys outnumbered women and girls by two to one.[25] For the very brief period from October 1771 to May 1772, when the "Passenger List [1768–72]" could be matched with indentures registered before the mayor of Philadelphia, more than half (55 percent) of the immigrants had contracted indentures in Ireland.

The immigration from Ulster ports was quite different from the flow out of southern Ireland. This influx of northern Irish immigrants rose steadily between 1763 and 1773, when it rivaled the emergency levels of the late 1720s. That pre-Revolutionary surge in immigration was made up largely of passengers who paid their own way; and many of them came together in family groups. In this era, the numbers immigrating from Ulster ports overwhelmed the southern Irish migration. Beginning in the early 1750s at a level of about 400 immigrants a year—less than twice the scale of southern Irish immigration—the annual number of newcomers surged, especially from 1766 through 1774, to produce a total of 8,421 northern Irish immigrants arriving in Philadelphia during the last nine years before the Revolution, more than three times the number that can be identified from southern Ireland (Table 4; Figure 3B).

Yet a figure of about 11,000 northern Irish immigrants coming to Philadelphia between the French and Indian War and the Revolution is only about half of the estimate that has gained broad acceptance during the last two decades. The figure for the emigration from Ulster has been put at 37,600 in the years from 1763 to 1774, and at 19,364 for the years 1771–74

24. "Passenger List [1768–72]"; "Record of Indentures [1771–73]."
25. Immigrants with the same last name listed sequentially were considered members of a family group.

TABLE 5   Numbers of ships sailing between Ireland and the Delaware Valley, 1730–1774

Year	No. of Ships from Southern Irish Ports		No. of Ships from Northern Irish Ports		No. of Ships from All Irish Ports[e]	via Dela-ware[f]	No. of Ships to Southern Irish Ports (Gazette)	No. of Ships to Northern Irish Ports (Gazette)	No. of Ships to All Irish Ports[g]
	Gazette[a]	Lock-hart[b]	Gazette[c]	Dick-son[d]					
1730	3	1	1		4				
1731	2	3	1		4		3		3
1732	4	5	2		8	2	13		13
1733	8	2			10	2	22		23
1734	8	6	2		10	1	17	4	21
1735	6	4	8		15	1	18	2	21
1736	10	2	17		27	2	20	6	31
1737	6	2	6		13	2	17	1	18
1738	7	1	2		9	1	20		20
1739	9	3	5		16	7	18	7	25
1740	20		11		33	6	33	11	44
1741	31	2	11		43	11	35	16	52
1742	7		4		13	6	11	15	26
1743	4	2	6		10	4	12	10	23
1744	1	3	4		5	1	7	8	15
1745	5	2	10		16 (12)	6 (2)	8	15	27
1746	6	3	10		19 (19)	12 (12)	9	6	15
1747	3	3	7		11		3	13	16
1748	3	1	8		12	7	6	9	15
1749	4	5	6		15	11	12	8	22
1750	3	5	6	6	11	8	21	15	36
1751	8	6	9		28	16	22	14	36
1752	15	2	13	4	32	15	30	20	58
1753	14	3	11	6	28	14	29	14	43
1754	13	1	11	6	26	14	10	10	31
1755	8	3	6	2	14	5	29	6	35
1756	5	3	5	1	11	2	12	14	26
1757	7		10	6	19	2	15	25	40
1758	4	1	10	4	16	3	14	19	33
1759	2	1	10	3	18	8	8	18	26
1760	5		10	7	28	17	5	18	25
1761	2	1	6	7	20	17	8	12	20
1762	5	1	9	11	22	18	13	15	28
1763	4	5	11	9	18	9	11	15	26
1764	8	2	8	8	18	5	21	16	37
1765	6	4	9	6	18	6	10	18	28
1766	20	6	24	19	44	10	21	26	47
1767	17	5	13	8	30	8	24	10	34
1768	15 (7)	8	8 (3)	8	24 (10)	6	12	8	20
1769	19 (11)	19	14 (11)	11	38 (22)	4	23	10	33
1770	20 (13)	5	11 (11)	13	31 (26)	6	16	20	36
1771	12 (12)	3	13 (13)	20	25 (25)	10	17	8	25

TABLE 5   (*Continued*)

Year	No. of Ships from Southern Irish Ports		No. of Ships from Northern Irish Ports		No. of Ships from All Irish Ports[e]			No. of Ships to Southern Irish Ports (Gazette)	No. of Ships to Northern Irish Ports (Gazette)	No. of Ships to All Irish Ports[g]
	Gazette[a]	Lock-hart[b]	Gazette[c]	Dick-son[d]			via Dela-ware[f]			
1772	7 (4)		13 (2)	15	23 (6)		8	11	9	20
1773	7	7	19	20	29		17	11	17	28
1774	8	2	13	21	21		12	11	14	25
Totals	381		393		895			688	502	1,226

SOURCES:

See table footnotes, below.

NOTE:

The numbers in parentheses for 1745–46 are those for the ships known to have landed in Philadelphia with servants in 1745–46. The numbers in parentheses for 1768–72 are those for the immigrant ships in "Passenger List [1768–72]."

[a]As reported in customhouse notices in *Pennsylvania Gazette.*

[b]As gleaned from Audrey Lockhart, *Some Aspects of Emigration from Ireland to the North American Colonies Between 1660 and 1775* (New York, 1976).

[c]As reported in customhouse notices in *Pennsylvania Gazette.*

[d]As gleaned from Robert J. Dickson, *Ulster Emigration to Colonial America, 1718–1775* (1966; reprint, London, 1988).

[e]Based on combined information from all the available sources. The numbers in this column are often higher than the sum of columns one and two because customhouse notices are not always complete and the notices were not always published regularly in the years for which copies of the *Pennsylvania Gazette* have survived.

[f]Ships from Irish ports known to have stopped in New Castle or Lewes before landing in Philadelphia, according to the customhouse notices in *Pennsylvania Gazette.*

[g]Ships to all Irish ports as reported in customhouse notices in *Pennsylvania Gazette.* It is interesting that the number of ships to Ireland reported by Francis G. James ("Irish Colonial Trade") 582 differ from the numbers presented here for several years (1731 [4], 1732 [9], 1733 [17], 1734 [16], 1741 [28], 1752 [51], 1762 [25], 1768 [38], 1769 [32], 1770 [49], 1772 [24]). The differences occur in part because the notices in the *Pennsylvania Gazette* gave the dates ships "entered out" and "cleared," many of which occurred in December and January and therefore straddled two years. (Not all ships are listed in all categories either, which further complicates any count.)

FIG. 4   Numbers of ships landing in Delaware ports, 1730–1774

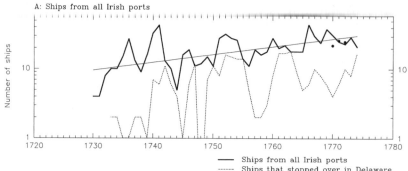

A: Ships from all Irish ports

——— Ships from all Irish ports
.... Ships that stopped over in Delaware
  •   Ships reported in "Passenger List"

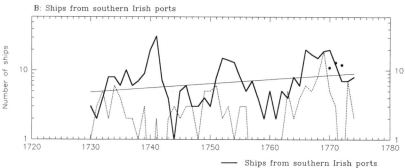

B: Ships from southern Irish ports

——— Ships from southern Irish ports
.... Ships reported by Lockhart
  •   Ships reported in "Passenger List"

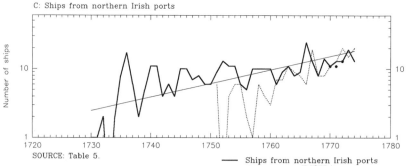

C: Ships from northern Irish ports

SOURCE: Table 5.

——— Ships from northern Irish ports
.... Ships reported by Dickson
  •   Ships reported in "Passenger List"

FIG. 5   Numbers of ships from Philadelphia to Irish ports,
1731–1774

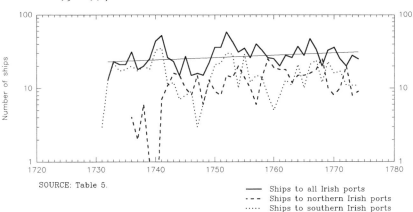

SOURCE: Table 5.

——— Ships to all Irish ports
- - - Ships to northern Irish ports
····· Ships to southern Irish ports

alone, with a little more than half of the total (roughly 20,000) destined for the Delaware Valley.[26] Even assuming that all immigrants disembarking at New Castle were from Ulster, the calculation of about 18,000 total to the Delaware Valley from northern Ireland reaches a level of only about 70 percent of current assumptions in the literature. A careful assessment of all the available evidence, however, strongly indicates that the lower figure proposed here is the more likely of the two estimates.[27]

Even more compelling than a close reading of contemporary accounts as evidence that only about 13,000 to 14,000 immigrants from northern Ireland arrived in the Delaware Valley (about 10,000 in Philadelphia) in the decade before the Revolution are the constraints imposed by the na-

26. Dickson, *Ulster Emigration*, 64, 225.

27. For the early 1770s, when pre-Revolutionary emigration from northern Ireland undoubtedly peaked, several contemporary estimates have survived: the figures reported by the linendrapers, as well as A. Young's estimate, are quoted in Dickson, *Ulster Emigration*, 61; other reports were published in the *Pennsylvania Gazette* (3 November 1773) and the *Gentlemen's Magazine* (44 [1774]: 332). Those reports basically agree that emigration from Ulster peaked at a little over 6,000 emigrants. Some of the migration was of a seasonal nature to Scotland, England, and the Newfoundland fisheries, but the majority of emigrants chose to leave for the American colonies and landed primarily in Pennsylvania and New York (B. M. Walsh, "Perspective on Irish Population Patterns," 5).

In Table 4, taking the northern Irish estimates to Philadelphia, apportioning those from unknown ports like those from known ports (76 percent for 1766–74), and allocating 76 percent to 100 percent of the non-Philadelphia (Delaware) arrivals as "northern" provides estimates of 2,000–2,150 for 1773 and 2,100–2,300 for 1766 of northern Irish coming to the Delaware Valley out of that 6,000 total—not an unreasonable proportion.

ture of the transatlantic trade between Ulster ports and Philadelphia or New Castle. The high-end estimate of about 20,000 Irish who came to the Delaware Valley in 1771–74 rests on the assumption that the number of emigrants can be roughly equated with the tonnage of ships mentioned in advertisements published to attract passengers—a measure contemporaries used to gauge the emigration flow.[28] Information from the "Passenger List [1768–72]," however, combined with details on the actual size of the vessels engaged in transporting passengers from northern Ireland, reveals that the advertised tonnage for estimating the number of emigrants is not a good measure because it significantly exaggerates the cargo capacity of ships. Ships from northern Ireland actually averaged about 100 registered tons in the years 1763–75, when slightly more than one-third of the vessels engaged in the Irish immigrant trade were built and registered in Philadelphia.[29] The registered tonnage increased in the years 1773–75, because several new ships built at that time were appreciably larger than their predecessors in the trade. The tonnage measured for the duty imposed on *all* incoming vessels by Pennsylvania, however, which was less of a builder's measure and probably reflected the stowage capacity of a vessel more adequately than the registered tonnage, averaged 134 tons, fluctuating between 60 and 200, a level considerably below the range of 250 to 500 in the advertised tonnage employed in the literature to date.[30]

28. Dickson's estimates for the Ulster emigration rest on this basic assumption (*Ulster Emigration*, 64; see also his app. B for the discrepancy in tonnage figures), which follows the reasoning published in contemporary newspapers (*Londonderry Journal*, 9 April 1773 [Education Facsimile No. 132, PRO of Northern Ireland]) and which has gained broad acceptance, most recently by Eid, "No Freight Paid So Well," 39–40.

29. McCusker, "Ships Registered at the Port of Philadelphia." By comparison, Dickson's data inflate the tonnage of vessels to a range of 250–500. It is important to remember, however, that the tonnage of eighteenth-century sailing vessels can present a variety of measures that may lead to very different tonnage figures for the same ship. Much reporting of tonnage figures was biased, depending on the purpose of the particular record and whether shipbuilders, merchants, and customs officials considered it advantageous to inflate or deflate the figures they reported. For a discussion of this important and complicated issue, see McCusker, "Tonnage of Ships." Scholars could have noted the inflation of the advertised tonnage in Irish shipping when comparing the figures with the average of 93 tons reported for the Irish trade in *Historical Statistics of the United States: Colonial Times to 1970*, 2 vols. (Washington, D.C., 1976), 2: ser. Z, 266–85.

30. Therefore the "Tonnage Duty Book [1765–75]" would yield the "best" tonnage measure for calculating the number of emigrants per ship. Compared with the actual number of immigrants reported in 1768–72, however, even that measure is too high for estimating passengers based on the tonnage of ships that carried immigrants. See also Dickson, *Ulster Emigration*, app. D.

In figuring how many emigrants left Ulster according to the carrying capacity of the ships that transported passengers, evidence of smaller ships implies that there were fewer emigrants on board, unless the ratio of passengers to tons changed.[31] The "Passenger List [1768–72]" shows that in the years 1769–70 immigrant vessels from Ulster ports averaged 60 passengers per ship or 40 passengers per measured ton. When immigration doubled according to these records in 1771, the number of immigrants per ship increased by about one-half, to 93, with more passengers sharing the available space (.66 passengers per ton). Still, the largest number of passengers reported for any one vessel was only 146 immigrants. Assuming that the rate of increase observed for the years 1769–71 continued until 1775—generally, 1773 was believed to be the absolute peak before the Revolution—the projected average number of passengers per ship would have been 140 immigrants. And allowing for a margin of variation from vessel to vessel resembling that of the earlier years, the maximum load of immigrants that any ship was likely to carry would have been 191. This was considerably less than the average of nearly 400 passengers per ship suggested by reports published in newspapers on both sides of the Atlantic in 1771–75 or by computing the number of emigrants according to advertised tonnage.[32] Weighing such sensational and imprecise reports against the parameters set by the known realities of the trade results in an overall estimate that is lower than the traditionally accepted one. It is still impressive, however, at more than 13,000 to 14,000 northern Irish immigrants landing in the Delaware Valley in the decade before the Revolution.

The evolving magnitude of the migration flow is also an important gauge of its composition. As the "Passenger List [1768–72]" helps to establish the actual numbers coming from Ulster ports during the years preceding the Revolution, it also provides information about the makeup of this influx. The most striking feature is the large proportion of families

31. Dickson, following contemporary reports, assumed that the ratio of one passenger per ton was standard, implying that it also provided adequate space even on vessels reportedly carrying 300 to 500 passengers. Dickson, *Ulster Emigration*, app. C.

32. "Passenger List [1768–72]"; Dickson, *Ulster Emigration*, app. C. Imperfect reporting mainly accounts for the inflated figures. The frequently imperfect fit of the dates and particulars of a voyage with those that were reported, in addition to the many rounded figures in those reports, suggests that vessels deviated from earlier plans and that the number of passengers was more often rumor and exaggeration than fact. The ship *Lord Dunlace* arrived in Charleston in January 1773 with 387 passengers—the highest number of Irish immigrants on board any vessel that is confirmed by a source other than a newspaper report.

traveling together.[33] More than 40 percent of the immigrants from northern Ireland were traveling as part of a family group. On average, almost
four passengers could be identified as belonging to the same family group
because they shared the same last name. (In comparison, only 15 percent of
the southern Irish immigrants landed in family groups, with not quite
three people per family.)[34] Unfortunately, the patrilineal nature by which
last names are passed on among kin imposes serious restrictions on detect-
ing other familial ties from a mere listing of names. The roster of the
Newry Pacquet (June 23, 1770) was extraordinary in its indication of groups
traveling together, because of the large number of people belonging to one
group yet not sharing the same last name. Consequently, the proportion of
Ulster immigrants who were related to someone else on the same ship may
well have been more than half. More important, this measure of kinship
networks among the immigrants cannot provide any clues about the incidents of chain migration that tied emigrants leaving from Irish ports to
immigrants already established in the American colonies. There is some
indication that all immigrants, once they were established in the New
World, were under strong family obligations to facilitate the subsequent
transfer of relatives in Ireland across the Atlantic and to assist them after
they landed.[35] A significant proportion of the single young men leaving
from Irish ports, therefore, may seem to have been traveling alone, even
though they were part of a kinship group that relocated to the American
colonies one by one over time rather than all together and all at once. In
the migration flow from Ireland, it became apparent early on that ties of
kinship and community, as well as the bonds that linked co-religionists,
were important dynamics in driving the transatlantic relocation. Resembling comparable dynamics among the Germans, these linkages were a
force that throughout the eighteenth century significantly affected the pattern of settlement.[36]

33. This is also a common pattern for the occasional lists that have survived for earlier
years. See, for example, "Extracts from the Journal of Charles Clinton." The listing of migrants on the *George and Ann* in 1929 reveals not only that families and neighbors traveled
together, but also that some of the passengers brought servants whose indentures they intended to sell upon arrival in Philadelphia.

34. If the names on the "Passenger List [1768–72]" could be linked to records in Ireland
we might gain important information about where emigrants lived and links among them
before they embarked for the Delaware Valley.

35. E. R. R. Green, "Ulster Emigrant Letters," 98.

36. The success Arthur Dobbs had settling his lands in North Carolina with Irish immigrants is an example for the strength of personal connections, especially when combined with
favorable terms for relocation and settlement (Education Facsimile No. 126: Emigration, PRO
of Northern Ireland).

Overall, the "Passenger List [1768–72]," while showing considerable variation from vessel to vessel in the years of high immigration, reveals a relatively large and consistent element of family groups among immigrants. Occasionally the compilers distinguished some individuals as "Mr." or "Mrs.," described others as servants, and mentioned specifically that several immigrants were related. Normally, the clerk listed only the first name—often abbreviated—and last name of the passenger. The listing for the *Philadelphia* was unusual, starting with Mrs. and Miss Holmes, Miss Faghenon, Mr. Holmes, and Mrs. Smith—a group that clearly seems related, although the names and their placement suggest a number of complex connections. Some immigrants brought a servant as part of their household group, as did "Tho. Hutchings" on the ship *Sally* (June 9, 1769). A common comment in the listings was "& wife & child," but the clerks used it as shorthand to save space and time, as in the list of the *Pennsylvania Farmer* (12 June 1771), rather than as a way to indicate family groups systematically.

The significance of the substantial proportion of families among newcomers arriving from Ulster ports was compounded by the relatively small number of redemptioners and indentured servants. At the height of the immigration, although not at the peak of the sailing season, only 9.7 percent of the northern Irish landed between October 1771 and May 1772 had been unable to pay their fare in advance.[37] This contrasts with about 50 percent of redemptioners for the Germans just before the Revolution, demonstrating the difference between a receding migration wave and a building one. Among this group of poor Irish newcomers, some made their own contract arrangements in Philadelphia, and thereby became "redemptioners," while others arrived with the usual four-year indenture contracted in Ireland, which was sold upon arrival to the highest or earliest bidder. Comparing the length of time of servitude, and the relative price of the two types of contractual agreements, reveals that the redemptioners had more flexibility. This was probably the result of specific skills and experience they could use as a basis for bargaining, while the servants coming already bound—who on average may have been younger than those traveling as redemptioners—had little active part in the negotiations about the price of their contract. It seems that the differences in price between indentured servants and redemptioners reflect two distinct, customary approaches to pricing what seem to have been identical services. The indentures agreed upon in Ireland mirrored primarily prices that were

37. "Passenger List [1768–72]"; "Record of Indentures [1771–73]."

traditionally and generally fixed in the Irish ports, while the servants who made their own contracts in Philadelphia could take advantage of the Pennsylvania custom that allowed masters and servants flexibility in matching the length and other particulars of the agreement with the amount of debt owed, special skills, age, and other relevant circumstances and characteristics of the redemptioner.

A comparison of the two distinctive migration flows from Ireland to Philadelphia after 1763 makes it apparent that the conventional picture of the Irish immigration has been only partly correct. The volume of Irish immigration certainly increased considerably during this period compared with most other years, but total estimates of this growth have proved to be exaggerated. Given the frequency and regularity with which moderate-size vessels made the voyage from Ireland to Delaware River ports carrying mixed cargoes of provisions, linen, passengers, and servants, the number of immigrants on board each vessel averaged closer to 100 than to the 300 previously suggested. Moreover, the proportion of servants among the Irish newcomers was significantly smaller—maybe one-quarter, at most one-third—than the conventional image has implied. In the fall of 1771 and the spring of 1772, when the "Passenger List [1768–72]" and the "Record of Indentures" overlap during the major and minor seasonal peaks of Irish immigration to Philadelphia in October and May, the proportion of servants and redemptioners among immigrants from Ireland was 24 percent. That proportion of bound newcomers became even smaller, 19 percent, when immigration from Ulster ports soared in 1773, as is evident from comparing the estimated number of Irish immigrants with Irish indentures registered in Philadelphia from 1771 to 1773.[38]

The conventional misconception about the volume and composition of the Irish immigration is due primarily to the difference between the migration streams from Ulster and southern Irish ports. Southern Irish immigration levels rose only slightly in the years before the Revolution (Table 4; Figure 3B). Passengers continued to arrive mostly in small parcels. More than two-thirds of them were single, apparently unconnected men and boys, and more than half of all the immigrants were unable to pay for their passage and therefore came as indentured servants.[39] Yet this influx from southern Ireland comprised less than a quarter of the Irish immigration during those years, and probably even less when considering that almost half the Irish immigrants arriving on ships stopping in New Cas-

---

38. "Passenger List [1768–72]"; "Record of Indentures [1771–73]."
39. "Passenger List [1768–72]"; "Record of Indentures [1771–73]."

tle—primarily those from Ulster ports—first might have disembarked there. Newcomers from Ulster ports flooded into Philadelphia in large numbers, averaging about 1,000 immigrants a year, although closer to 2,000 when those disembarking in Delaware are included. Yet in this fresh surge of migration from northern Ireland, which did not peak until after the Revolution, passengers still often traveled in extended family groups and the vast majority of individuals could pay their fares in advance.[40] These conditions were like those for the Germans a generation earlier, leading up to their peak of 1749–54.

Irish men and women, like other emigrants elsewhere, left their homes for many different reasons but rarely left records of what motivated their departure. Contemporary observers, however, tended to comment on the exodus when their own situation was affected. Landlords and employers tended to exaggerate the numbers leaving, while they lamented real and potential losses of income because of emigrating tenants and workers. In the 1770s, for example, emigration from northern Ireland was substantial and caused sufficient official concern to start a parliamentary investigation about the conditions of the linen industry and high rents. Vested interests colored the reports submitted by some of the merchants and landlords.[41] Such complaints reprised the representations of half a century earlier in the 1729 crisis: "In the mean Time Lands are every where fallen 20 or 30 per Cent. I have my self some Farm Lands but five Miles from this City [Londonderry], which were worth £45 per Annum, and now the Tenants say, they must be reduced to £24 so you may judge how it is like to be with Lands more remote from any large Town."[42] Clergy and public officials gave often strong but varied opinions about why people left but were generally ineffective in stopping a given exodus or preventing another at a later time, and the government failed to use the emigration statistics thus collected to frame future policies for regulating the migration flow.[43]

40. William Adams, *Ireland and Irish Emigration,* and Miller, *Emigrants and Exiles,* deal with emigration from Ireland in the classical era of mass migration.

41. For a listing of these reports, see Dickson, *Ulster Emigration,* 61; W. E. H. Lecky, *History of Ireland in the Eighteenth Century,* 1:245–48.

42. Account of Robert Gambie, merchant of Londonderry, to Mackey and Craighead, merchants in London, *Pennsylvania Gazette,* 17–20 November 1729.

43. Dickson, *Ulster Emigration,* 33, 61. The reports of customs officers on both sides of the Atlantic, newspaper stories about extraordinary voyages, and advertisements offering passage and freight, servants, or goods contributed only indirectly to assessments of what motivated people to leave home by providing better measure for the volume, character, and circumstances

Against the background of the enormous complexities that helped shape Irish migration patterns in the seventeenth and eighteenth centuries, several conditions that had some influence on the decision to emigrate are important to outline here.[44] In the 1600s and 1700s, religious persecution and intolerance, difficult economic conditions, and oppressive political circumstances were foremost among the reasons that prompted emigrants to move to distant places.[45] The outstanding features of the picture in Ireland are that many segments of the population suffered some form of discrimination and scarcity and had only limited opportunities open to them.[46]

The Catholic Irish—mostly tenants and laborers—who made up about 70 percent of the population (40 percent even in Ulster), were the largest constituent group of the population. They suffered not only from religious persecution but, especially, also from the effects of the penal laws that were designed to deprive them of economic and political power and social position. Estimates put their proportion at about one-quarter of the Irish immigrants to the American colonies.[47]

Presbyterians—most of them once emigrants from Scotland—lived primarily in the north, where they formed a distinct community with which isolated groups in Dublin and the southern counties maintained close links. Most of the Dissenters were tenant farmers or merchants, and, like the Catholics, they were the subjects of discriminatory legislation that caused much hardship. The Presbyterians were better off than their Catholic counterparts, however, because the security of land tenure was greater in Ulster than elsewhere and because the linen industry, as well as trade,

---

of the Irish migration. Official listings of immigrants and indentured servants, which can provide clues to the causes of emigration, have been found only for one short period of time, although both Pennsylvania and Delaware law required the registration of immigrants. *Statutes at Large of Pennsylvania*, 4:135–40, 164–71, 320–21, 360–70; 5:77–78, 94–97; 8:369–77; *Laws of the State of Delaware*, 1:166–73; "Passenger List [1768–72]."

44. Louis Cullen called attention to the broad range of different kinds of migrations that emanated from Ireland. As in the case of the Germans, the flow to the American colonies was just one among many other destinations for Irish emigrants ("The Irish Diaspora," esp. 113–14, 139–40, 143–49). The following description of Ireland in the eighteenth century is largely based on the essays by John McCracken, "The Social Structure and Social Life," and "The Ecclesiastical Structure"; and by Cullen, "Economic Development, 1691–1750" and "Economic Development, 1750–1800."

45. See Stuart Daultry et al., "Eighteenth-Century Irish Population," esp. 621–27, for general population estimates and important regional variations in population trends.

46. McCracken, "Social Structure," 32–42.

47. Miller, *Emigrants and Exiles*, 137; Doyle, *Ireland*, 70–71.

offered alternative sources of income and wealth. Religious discrimination against Presbyterians was most severe in the first two decades of the eighteenth century—part of Queen Anne's policy to promote the Church of England at home and overseas. Under those circumstances, many Presbyterian clergymen actively promoted emigration to the American colonies, likening the exodus to the biblical flight from Egypt. Although the religious motivation for emigration faded over the course of the century, the Presbyterians continued to contribute the largest proportion of Protestant emigrants (over all, about 70 percent).[48]

Irish Quakers—farmers, landowners, millers, manufacturers, and merchants in Munster, Leinster, Dublin, and Ulster—were an important minority among the emigrating Dissenters. Although their absolute numbers were small, their influence was disproportionately large because of the strong ties they had to other Quaker communities, especially with merchants in London and Philadelphia, and because of their interest and experience in providing passage for emigrants from Irish ports.[49]

Even Irish Anglicans, who were represented among rural workers and skilled urban workers of Dublin, in the professions, in public service, and in the lucrative branches of trade had little faith in the opportunities open to them at home as they watched with frustration as Englishmen took positions for which they themselves qualified. They made up one-quarter of the total Protestant emigration and one-tenth of the emigration from southern Ireland.[50]

Against this background of widespread religious intolerance and economic and political discrimination, the prospect of being unable to earn a decent living existed for nearly everyone. Repeatedly, the vagaries of climate and harvests, together with poor market conditions and low prices, resulted in crises and even devastating famines that prompted Irishmen to emigrate in large numbers. In the first half of the eighteenth century, the Irish economy experienced long-term stagnation in the volume of exports and imports, low prices, and high rents, which meant declining prosperity and vulnerability to famine in case of harvest failure, credit crunch, or

48. Miller, *Emigrants and Exiles*, 149.

49. Myers, *Immigration* (statistical table), noted that fewer than 400 Quakers emigrated from Ireland to Philadelphia in the years 1682–1750. Miller (*Emigrants and Exiles*, 151) estimated that a total of 3,000 Quakers relocated to the American colonies before 1776, mostly to Pennsylvania and New Jersey. Lockhart, "Quakers and Immigration from Ireland," does not present a total estimate of the Quaker emigration from southern Ireland, but he points out that it declined after mid-century (91).

50. Miller, *Emigrants and Exiles*, 150–51; Doyle, *Ireland*, 71.

depressed foreign markets. Crises occurred often, when factors combined
disastrously at the same time, as in 1729, when three bad harvests (1726–
28), tightening of credit (in 1727 and 1729), and poor returns in linen sales
in 1729 all coincided to bring on famine conditions. The famine of 1740–
41 was particularly devastating because poor grain and potato crops in the
previous season combined with harvest failure in 1740 and a complete lack
of available surplus grain from Europe. Near-famine conditions reoc-
curred in 1744–45, when a bad harvest and a slump in linen sales in 1744
was followed by a credit crisis in 1745.

After about mid-century, both the volume and the prices of agricultural exports increased rapidly, and advances in the linen industry provided a new source of income that enabled many to supplement their
earnings in general, and especially in crises. The remarkable growth of the
economy meant that the community was less chronically indebted and had
more resources. Because of this greater affluence, crises after 1750 were
dominated less by subsistence failure and took the form of more purely
credit problems (1767, 1770) or monetary crises tied to the sale of linen
(1759–60, 1772–73).[51] The waves of emigration in the 1760s and 1770s,
therefore, represented not so much involuntary responses to crisis as conscious reactions to new opportunities—some overseas—as the Irish economy grew in unprecedented ways.[52]

If discrimination, limited opportunity, and economic change pushed
Irish men and women to seek better opportunities and more stability elsewhere, Ireland's connections with many parts of the North Atlantic commercial community—in particular England, the West Indies, and the
middle colonies of British North America—offered considerable choice
among different destinations for starting a new life. Free from any state-
imposed sanctions that might curtail migration to the colonies, as among
the Germans, Irish emigrants could make use of diverse networks already
established in Ireland's overseas trade when weighing where and how to go.
The Irish ports were central in the process of channeling emigration.
There was no near equivalent for the Germans. These harbor towns dominated the economy and their respective hinterlands, for which they were

51. Cullen, "Economic Development," 144–59. See also *Pennsylvania Gazette*, 17 November
1729; Lecky, *History of Ireland*, 1:244–51; Dickson, *Ulster Emigration*, 70–74; Lockhart, *Some Aspects
of Emigration*, 17, 22, 52–53.

52. Cullen, "Irish Diaspora," 143–49, recently argued convincingly for this fundamental
shift in the nature of relocation to the American colonies.

the centers of banking, wholesaling, and industry.[53] They also linked virtually all of Ireland with the American colonies, because the traffic of merchants, ships, passengers, servants, officials, and soldiers was constant and regular. This generated a dependable and up-to-date flow of information—an important prerequisite in directing emigration.[54] And as in the case of the Germans, letters and visits from immigrants who were content with their new situation in America provided powerful incentives for kin, friends, and former neighbors to follow in their footsteps.[55]

Together, these two differences of regular ongoing trade and ready access to ports gave Irish passengers bound for the American colonies, as well as the merchants who transported them, a relatively large degree of flexibility in obtaining and, respectively, arranging for transatlantic passage. For Irish emigrants, the easy accessibility of the seaports meant relatively short travel times and consequently predictable and low overland transportation costs. Furthermore, the established links between seaports and their respective inland regions were based mostly on personal contacts, thus providing dependable lines of communication. Such networks allowed both promoters and prospective emigrants to react swiftly to pertinent news.[56] Irish considering migration could use this information in a number of ways. First, they could compare reports about opportunities overseas with their own personal circumstances and aspirations, whether they planned for the short term or the long term, or whether they moved alone or as part of a family or group. Second, they could use readily available information to calculate relocation costs, because for them, un-

53. See Cullen, *Economic History*, 58, on the peacetime links of the seaports and their hinterlands with overseas markets in the provision trade. See also Dickson, *Ulster Emigration*, 105 (map), app. E; Lockhart, *Some Aspects of Emigration*, app. C.

54. Doyle, *Ireland*, 22, 40; Doerflinger, *Vigorous Spirit of Enterprise*; and Truxes, *Irish American Trade*, who examined Irish-American trade and the networks that linked merchants on both sides of the Atlantic, underscore the critical importance of direct commercial connections for channeling migration. Ordinary migrants knew of these connections and used them. See, for example, Alun Davies, "As Good a Country," 317–18.

55. Evidence of the power of letters and visiting immigrants in drawing others to relocate to the American colonies has accumulated in recent years. At this point, there are many more letters to and reports about such visits to the German homelands than for the Irish migration, but the surviving documents suggest that positive news from Irish who had immigrated successfully reached Ireland throughout the century before the American Revolution. See, for example, Lockhart, "Quakers," 78; and Davies, "As Good a Country," 318, 319–20. As in the German case, however, merchants suppressed unflattering reports. *The Belfast Newsletter* (Education Facsimile No. 138: Emigration, PRO of Northern Ireland).

56. Doyle described the connections between Ireland and the American colonies as "human and prosaic" (*Ireland*, 22, 39–40).

like the Germans, the ocean fare charged to the destination of their choice made up the largest part of that expense. Irish emigrants could also make inquiries about how to obtain the most appropriate passage; they did not have to depend on middlemen, serving their own interests, for this. Correspondingly, merchants desiring to transport passengers and servants across the Atlantic took advantage of similar networks to gather information about prospective passengers and to publicize their operations in the trade. Good local knowledge permitted them to balance mixed cargoes of freight, passengers, and servants in the Irish trade with the mid-Atlantic colonies more readily than the merchants of London and Rotterdam, who ran the German emigrant trade. Both emigrants and shippers recognized the importance of personal written communications from relatives, friends, and compatriots in directing the migration flow.[57] At times, merchants who had vested interests in the emigrant trade deliberately failed to deliver unfavorable letters because they feared the impact of such reports on potential emigrants. Conversely, it became customary in the 1760s and 1770s for passengers to express their gratitude to the captain and owners of the vessel after a successfully completed voyage by writing, or signing, a letter to their friends at home for publication in the local newspaper. This was an effective advertising technique for the merchant.[58]

While Irish emigrants generally had some degree of flexibility and choice in planning their voyage, certain local factors affected their decision. Some of the points of embarkation in Ireland had special roles in the overseas trade. The majority of Irish migrants to Philadelphia left from four of the ports—Cork, Dublin, Belfast, and Londonderry—because many ships built in Philadelphia and owned and managed by Irish-American partnerships sailed frequently and regularly between those cities and the Delaware Valley.[59] Emigrants could always secure passage in those ports. Moreover, Dublin and Cork served as stopover points for vessels of

57. See Doyle, *Ireland*, 52; Miller, *Emigrants and Exiles*, 160; and Kirkham in his new introduction to Dickson, *Ulster Emigration*, xv, about the increased awareness of the critical role emigrants' letters home played.

58. Dickson, *Ulster Emigration*, 16–17, 44–45, 53, 54, 238, 255, 276.

59. The merchant networks that linked Ireland and the Delaware Valley region differed in terms of region, religion, kinship, and economic and political interests and rarely overlapped. They are detailed in Truxes, *Irish American Trade*, 38, 61, 73, 76–78, 86–87, 106–8, 117–21; Doerflinger, *Vigorous Spirit of Enterprise*, 12, 14, 15, 20, 44, 55–57, 59, 73, 76, 101, 104, 107, 121, 148–49, 152, 155–57, 173, 182, 185–88, 219, 237, 240–41, 253–55, 261, 277–78, 335, 337. Joseph Foster focuses on one prominent Presbyterian Irish merchant in Philadelphia (*The Pursuit of Equal Liberty*, 2–9).

many other origins on their way across the Atlantic. Dublin was a vital link in the commercial credit chain centered on London, while Cork specialized in victualing ships. Several ships from Ulster stopped in these southern ports for those purposes—and probably gained passengers while there. Therefore, it is not always possible to differentiate between emigrants from northern and southern Irish regions on the basis of the ship's stated port of embarkation. In addition, vessels destined for Philadelphia often stopped in more than one Irish port to take on cargo, and ships shuttling between Ireland and the middle colonies alternated among various Irish ports on different voyages. In addition, customhouse notices—the main source for this information—usually state only the last, or immediately next, port, thus obscuring any patterns wherever the links between Ireland and Pennsylvania were indirect. With the possible exception of 1729, however, there is no indication of any short supply in shipping available to emigrants. This was true even at the height of the Irish immigration in the early 1770s, when the number of ships from Ireland arriving in Philadelphia exceeded the number of vessels with Irish immigrants.[60]

In contrast, the Ulster ports of Newry, Larne, and Portrush, as well as the southern ports of Sligo, Limerick, Galway, and Waterford, sent vessels to Pennsylvania less frequently and less regularly (about one-fifth of all Irish immigrant ships destined for Philadelphia between 1750 and 1775). The commercial activity of those ports was tied less prominently to the merchant communities in the Delaware Valley.[61] Evidence on sailings from northern ports is based largely on advertisements for vessels intending to carry emigrants to Philadelphia that appeared in regional papers in northern Ireland from 1750 to 1775.[62] Ports with an average of less than two known sailings per year (Newry, Larne, Portrush) each have a unique distribution of emigration over time that does not conform to the overall pattern of sailings of emigrant ships from Ulster, which had its peak in the early 1770s. It is uncertain whether the apparent decrease in emigration from these ports in the years of otherwise heavy emigration resulted from a shift in advertising for transatlantic passage, from changes in sailing

60. In the 1770s, vessels that would make one voyage carrying passengers would carry none on the next run, as, for example, the *Hopewell* and the *Jenny* (*Londonderry Journal* 54 [4 December 1772]; 97 [4 May 1773]), both of which were identified as "passenger" ships that left Londonderry in ballast. See also Dickson, *Ulster Emigration*, 55, 115.

61. Truxes, *Irish American Trade*, 81–88.

62. Dickson, *Ulster Emigration*, app. D.

patterns due to a predominance of larger vessels and ports, or from a decline in the demands for passage to Philadelphia from those particular regions. Of the southern ports, only Waterford maintained somewhat regular ties with Delaware River ports, while the other ports sent just an occasional ship from time to time.[63] Prospective emigrants from these regions with few and infrequent sailings to the Delaware Valley therefore enjoyed less flexibility and fewer options than those emigrants living close to ports with major and constant links to Delaware River merchants. They were forced to wait for a ship bound for Philadelphia, to take another with a roughly comparable overseas destination, or to seek embarkation from a port farther away and less familiar than the one closest to their home. The observed shift toward a greater concentration of emigrant ship sailings from the larger ports, however, fits what is known about the general pattern of trade between Ireland and the Delaware Valley.

Currently available data suggest a growing importance of ties between Philadelphia and Ireland's major ports after mid-century, when the volume of trade increased, the flaxseed trade expanded, and the provision trade changed.[64] Also, merchants with interests in the transatlantic transportation of migrants were primarily concentrated in Dublin, Cork, Belfast, and Londonderry. From there, in efforts to satisfy the demands of an overseas labor market and to capture and maintain a share of the Irish passenger trade to supplement their other business, they branched out to neighboring ports by means of local agents and advertising campaigns. According to Robert Dickson's collection of advertisements for emigrant vessels in the 1770s, and his description of the operation and common and widespread use of agents in the Ulster ports and their hinterlands, two features of the Irish passenger trade stand out: the density of the network that connected merchants, ship owners, captains, and agents, and the increasingly elaborate forms of advertisement directed at potential passengers.[65] In this business, the general lack of methodical organization, long-term planning, and forceful direction was mainly the result of the availability of

63. Lockhart, *Some Aspects of Emigration,* app. C. For the importance of Waterford as a center that attracted and channeled seasonal and permanent migration to Newfoundland, see Cecil Houston and William Smyth, *Irish Emigration and Canadian Settlement,* 16–17; Bric, "Ireland, Irishmen," 35; Cullen, "Irish Diaspora," 128–31; and Truxes, *Irish American Trade,* 84–85.

64. The most comprehensive treatment of Irish-American trade is Truxes, *Irish American Trade;* see especially on the flaxseed and provisions trades, 147–58, 193–209. Doerflinger, *Vigorous Spirit of Enterprise,* deals with an important segment of the Irish-American trade from the perspective of Philadelphia's merchant community.

65. Dickson, *Ulster Emigration,* chap. 7.

shipping, which was more than ample to cope with the volume of people seeking transportation.[66] These characteristics also reflected the diversity of the networks that were in place, and the variety in the enterprise that constituted the transport of emigrants.[67]

The predominance of Philadelphia as the most common destination of vessels leaving with passengers and servants from at least four major ports in Ireland reflects both the popularity of colonial Pennsylvania for Irish emigrants and the strength of the commercial ties that linked the Delaware Valley with much of Ireland.[68] Both contributed to the distinct regional and seasonal characteristics that marked the Irish immigration to Philadelphia. Throughout the eighteenth century, the provision trade—mainly beef, pork, and butter for re-export—constituted the bulk of Irish cargoes destined for Pennsylvania.[69] Especially after mid-century, the Ulster ports and Dublin added linen to their shipments, while Cork sent wines and other re-export goods from southern Europe, the West Indies, and England. "Sailed with linen, beef, and butter" or "with beef, butter, and servants" were common descriptions in customhouse records and newspaper notices.[70] In return, Philadelphia supplied most of the flaxseed that Ireland imported in the second half of the eighteenth century, supplemented grain and flour supplies in years in which Ireland had poor harvests, and contributed to the Irish provision trade by exporting ship biscuits and barrel staves.[71]

The flaxseed trade was the most important commercial link between Ireland and the North American colonies and largely determined the rhythm of the seasonal sailing pattern—especially after 1763, when flax-

66. Dickson, *Ulster Emigration*, 115; Doyle, *Ireland*, 53.

67. Truxes, *Irish American Trade*, 139–40.

68. Large land-grant owners like Alexander McNutt, who sought settlers from Ireland for his property in Nova Scotia, found it difficult to compete for emigrants because of the good reputation Pennsylvania had gained among potential settlers. Advertisement in the *Belfast News Letter* of 21 April 1761 (no. 127 of the Education Facsimiles Series, 121–40, PRO of Northern Ireland [Department of the Environment for Northern Ireland]).

69. Cork was the center of the highly developed provisions industry. Shipping foodstuffs to the American colonies was timed to demands of the flaxseed trade, so that ships could make the run with cargo rather than in ballast to take on flaxseed in Philadelphia in early winter. Truxes, *Irish American Trade*, 147–58; Doerflinger, *Vigorous Spirit of Enterprise*, 78. R. C. Nash, "Irish Atlantic Trade," puts the trade with Philadelphia in the context of Irish trade in general and shows that the West Indies was the most important destination for Irish shipping (see esp. 344–47, 355, table 9).

70. Dickson, *Ulster Emigration*, app. D; Lockhart, *Some Aspects of Emigration*, app. C.

71. Cullen, *Economic History*, 58; James, "Irish Colonial Trade," 581; Doerflinger, *Vigorous Spirit of Enterprise*, 103; Truxes, *Irish American Trade*, 1, 38.

seed exports to start annual crops for Ireland's ever more important linen industry became strongest.[72] It also established the importance of the middle colonies—Philadelphia leading the rival ports of New York and Baltimore—albeit ranking a distant second after Ireland's trade with the West Indies.[73] In early fall, the flaxseed fleet assembled in Philadelphia to take on cargo. Usually, the ships left in December for Ireland. The choice of the particular Irish destination was variously governed by the home port of each vessel, the cargo it carried besides flaxseed, and the plans for the return voyage. Ships sailing from Ireland to Philadelphia made the trip in spring or summer and early fall. About one-quarter of all departures—evenly distributed between northern and southern regions—took place in March and April, while more than half the vessels set sail in July through September. Ships from Ulster generally preceded those originating from southern ports, although both eventually became part of the Philadelphia flaxseed fleet. In the years 1764–75, about half the ships engaged in trade between Philadelphia and Ireland shuttled directly. The remainder followed either triangular routes via southern Europe or the West Indies or, if headed to the southern mainland colonies, stopped over in Philadelphia on the first leg of the voyage and then again on their return. Whether they sailed directly or more circuitously, the majority of vessels timed the return voyage to Ireland to take advantage of Philadelphia's flaxseed trade.

The regularity and frequency with which ships sailed from Ireland to Philadelphia was a decisive advantage for prospective emigrants. Irish voyagers—unlike their German counterparts—could from the very start plan their departure according to known sailing patterns and could often choose among several different emigrant vessels. This was true whether the move was complicated or required little preparation. There is only indirect evidence that prospective immigrants to Pennsylvania were sophisticated enough to take advantage of the available choices and negotiate for the best possible fares or situations. The increasingly elaborate advertisements for vessels offering passage, including signed letters from grateful passengers of previous voyages, and the intricate networks connecting merchants of regional stature with those who had more local base, suggest that emigrants knew how to take advantage of what was essentially a buyer's market.[74] Only in ports that had no direct links to Philadelphia—

72. For a detailed description of the flaxseed trade, see Truxes, *Irish American Trade,* 193–209.
73. Nash, "Irish Atlantic Trade," 355.
74. The intricate interplay between local agents—including itinerant dealers, and firms

and in 1729, when the demand for passage apparently for once exceeded the supply of shipping—were choices more limited. The negative effects of that exceptional year for emigrants is evident from newspaper reports that describe the fate of passengers who endured disastrous voyages with high mortality on board because coastal vessels and inexperienced captains had been engaged to handle the unprecedented demand for transatlantic passage, or who were carried under false pretenses to the West Indies instead of the Delaware Valley.[75] Normally, however, emigrants from Ireland were familiar enough with the relevant aspects of the trade. The apparent absence of any contemporary advice on how to prepare for the voyage suggests that Irish emigrants did not have to rely on the reports and services of seasoned immigrants—newlanders—who played such an important role in shaping the experience of German emigrants crossing the Atlantic. Procedures that became customary for the emigrant trade were set early, mostly by Quaker captains and merchants who gained considerable experience in the transfer of passengers and their goods to the newly established middle colonies in the late 1600s, and remained standard practice for most of the eighteenth century.[76]

Passengers who could pay their fare, and indentured servants who contracted for a specified term of future service in return for the price of the passage, had various different choices. The ways in which emigrants who were too poor to pay the fare in advance secured passage apparently depended on their situation and the port of embarkation. Ann Dougherty, for example, stated that when in 1754 she could not afford the passage for her three children, she was obliged to bind them to a "certain captain Mullen, who was obligated that they should be landed and serve in the

and their overseas correspondents and partners—in arranging cargo for a ship's run from Ireland to the American colonies is detailed in Truxes, *Irish American Trade*, 133–37.

75. *Pennsylvania Gazette*, 17 November 1729; "Journal of Clinton [1729]." Reports of major shipwrecks in the Irish emigrant trade are rare: a ship from Dublin was lost in 1729, and of the 36 passengers and crew on board the *Providence* in 1769, 13 were rescued and 23 were left to drown (Education Facsimile No. 128: Emigration, PRO of Northern Ireland); 46 passengers died of starvation on the *Seaflower* en route from Belfast to Philadelphia in 1746 (Deirdre Mageean, "Emigration from Irish Ports," 11, 12); in 1762, 64 passengers died of disease on the *Sally*, which sailed from Belfast to Philadelphia (Education Facsimile No. 139: Emigration, PRO of Northern Ireland).

76. Quakers learned early to take emigrants to the American colonies. They avoided the tragedies that came from overloading and underprovisioning, which were more common in the German emigrant trade; and Quaker mariners earned a high reputation for the way they treated passengers, especially during the scramble for shipping in the peak year of 1729. See Lockhart, "Quakers," 84–86, 88.

province of Pennsylvania."[77] In Dublin, negotiations for indentured servitude took place in two inns on the quays.[78] The procedure by which indentures were legally contracted, however, was well established. Agreements for servitude that bound emigrants to merchants or captains were made before the mayor of the port of embarkation, whose responsibility it was to ensure that minors were committed only with the consent of parents or guardians and that all contracts were entered into voluntarily.[79] Most of the available evidence is for Dublin and Cork—both of which were ports of interregional importance with a large and presumably more impersonal pool of potential servants.[80] Kidnapping or "spiriting away" of emigrants occurred but was apparently not a problem of large or endemic proportions. Unfortunately, no records of indentures have been found that allow the kind of analysis so fruitfully applied to the surviving lists of servants departing from England.[81] Felons and vagrants were a distinct group among the indentured servants. Very few convicts were landed in the Delaware Valley.[82]

The general picture of recruiting Irish servants for the American colonies resembles the one we know from England; both the scale and the methods were like those of servants transported from London and Bristol to the seventeenth-century Chesapeake one hundred years earlier.[83] Skilled men and teenage boys headed the list of requests from Philadelphia merchants involved in the Irish trade. "Should thee have a mind to send a Vessel this way, . . . Stout able Labouring men & Tradesmen out of the

77. *PMHB* 58 (1934): 382.

78. Both places were called "The New York and Philadelphia Arms" and served as clearinghouses for prospective servants in 1745. See Doyle, *Ireland*, 64.

79. Dickson, *Ulster Emigration*, 89; Lockhart, *Some Aspects of Emigration*, 74–75; *Pennsylvania Gazette*, 17 Nov. 1729.

80. See, however, examples from other ports (Education Facsimiles Nos. 123–25: Emigration, PRO of Northern Ireland), which attest to a variety of arrangements that merchants and captains made for transporting indentured servants from Ireland to the American colonies in the years 1729, 1736, and 1738, respectively.

81. For some sporadic listings of indentures that have survived, see Lockhart, *Some Aspects of Emigration*, app. A, I–II. Recent examples on the English servant trade are Horn, "Servant Emigration," 51–95; Galenson, *White Servitude*; and Salinger, *To Serve Well and Faithfully*.

82. Ekirch, *Bound for America*, 25, 46, 83–85, 114–15, estimated that about 13,000 convicts were transported from Ireland. Only nine ships carried convicts to Pennsylvania. Even allowing for significant underreporting of cargoes of convicts, and assuming that the vessels were loaded to capacity with passengers, that means less than 10 percent of all convicts from Ireland landed in Philadelphia—probably somewhere around 500 in all.

83. Horn, "Servant Emigration."

Country with young Boys & Lads answer best."[84] In 1745–46—the only year for which such data is available before the peak of the Irish immigration in the early 1770s—only 13.5 percent of 546 indentures recorded for Irish immigrants were for women or girls.[85] The vast majority of servants arrived in "parcels" ranging from 1 to 60 individuals and averaging between one or two dozen per ship. Twenty-five years later, when Irish immigration soared just before the Revolution, the size of such parcels of servants had changed only slightly, increasing in range from 2 to 73, with the average about 20 bound emigrants per ship. These figures, together with evidence that protective measures against coercion of emigrants were at times called for, and that vessels repeatedly postponed their departure in hopes of obtaining a full cargo, suggest that demand for servants generally exceeded the supply.[86]

The motivations that drove poor Irishmen to relocate overseas varied widely. As for the emigrants of 1729, "the reasons those unhappy people give for their going are as various as their circumstances. . . . Their ignorance leads them," and the "poorer sort are deluded by the accounts they have of the great wages given there [in America] to laboring men."[87] There is little evidence whether poor emigrants signed on as servants because they wanted to settle in the colonies, and thereby had their passage paid, or whether they consented to indenture overseas only as a last resort, because they could not find work elsewhere. Undoubtedly, any shipload of servants had people who were leaving for both reasons. William Moraley and John Harrower are two examples of Englishmen who fell on hard

84. Benjamin Marshall to Barnaby Egan, 9 November 1765, "Extracts from the Letter-Book of Benjamin Marshall"; see also James and Drinker to Captain Enoch Story (6 May 1769), and James and Drinker to Lancelot Cowper (19 May and 7 June 1769), James and Drinker Letter Book, HSP.

85. "Servants and Apprentices [1745–46]"; "Record of Indentures [1771–73]." For an economic analysis of those records, see Farley Grubb, "Using Servant Auction Records," "The Incidence of Servitude in Trans-Atlantic Migration," and "Immigrant Servant Labor." The most detailed analysis of the 1745 indentures recorded in Philadelphia is Alfred Brophy, "Law and Indentured Servitude." Doyle (*Ireland,* 66–68) examined the names of bound servants from Ireland and found very distinct regional patterns reflected among passengers traveling on certain vessels.

86. For examples of ships unable to obtain a full load of passengers, see Dickson, *Ulster Emigration,* 66 n. 2, 115; Dickson's app. D includes planned dates of departure and actual sailing dates.

87. Ezekiel Stewart to Michael Ward, 25 March 1729 (Education Facsimile No. 122: Emigration, PRO of Northern Ireland).

times and were unable to find gainful employment, and who therefore bound themselves as servants to colonial America as a last resort.[88] Yet the extent to which overall fluctuations in the desire or need to go overseas as bound emigrants occurred is less certain. Emigration peaks that appear to be in response to local adversity, such as a bad harvest or a recession, however, point to substantial variation in the need to explore opportunities elsewhere.

The same circumstances that put immigration to Philadelphia within easy reach for Irish passengers and servants also significantly affected their experiences during the voyage. The relative frequency with which ships left Irish ports for Philadelphia, the long-standing collective experience in transporting passengers to the American colonies, and the close ties between the port of entrance and the hinterland—important factors for everyone in the trade—passengers, merchants, and captains alike—allowed Irish emigrants to gain a certain degree of familiarity with the transatlantic transportation system. This shaped their expectations about the realities of the voyage and helped them choose among available shippers and vessels. After 1763, an average of a dozen ships each sailed annually from Ulster and southern Ireland (Table 5).[89] Prospective emigrants contracted for passage on any of the vessels harbored in Irish ports, with the help of local merchants or agents or directly with the captain (who had sometimes toured the hinterland to attract passengers), or with the resident owner of the ship or local merchant to whom the ship was consigned.[90] Most of the men making contracts with emigrants had a strong incentive to deal fairly with the passengers, because the regular trade in which they were engaged would benefit from the competitive edge a good reputation

---

88. Edward Riley, ed., *Journal of John Harrower*; Susan Klepp and Billy Smith, eds., *The Infortunate.*

89. For the years 1765–75, the number of sailings shown in Table 5 reflect the number of vessels with passengers known to have arrived in Philadelphia according to the "Tonnage Duty Book [1765–75]" and the "Passenger List [1768–72]," which differ from statistics that are based on other sources. Discrepancies in the data on ships bound for Irish ports occur primarily because a significant proportion of vessels cleared port and sailed from Philadelphia late in December and early in January. Since the customhouse notices of the *Pennsylvania Gazette* reported when a vessel had cleared customs as well as when it had sailed, ships departing for Ireland could be counted in different years.

90. For the influence of local merchants and agents, see Truxes, *Irish American Trade*, 134–35; captains who recruited servants received a portion of price for which labor contracts were sold after arrival in the American colonies.

would give them.[91] From 1768 to 1772, more than two-thirds of the ships with Irish immigrants on board made the transatlantic voyage more than once—slightly more than the proportion of the Irish vessels arriving in Philadelphia between 1763 and 1775. It is not surprising that the advertisements in the Ulster newspapers in the 1770s often emphasized the length of time a ship or captain had been engaged in the trade as a feature likely to attract passengers.[92]

In the recruitment process, shippers believed firmly in the effectiveness of advertising, as is evident from the increase in announcements about passage offered to prospective travelers in the local newspapers. The advertisements focused on comfort and security during the voyage, pointing out that the "humanity" of the captain and the character of the other passengers, as well as the size of the vessel and, especially, the amount of space between decks—all of which were said to improve the chances of having an easy voyage. Consequently, the tonnage of ships seeking passengers was a prominent feature in the advertisements, The height between decks was an especially important indicator of travel comfort. The newer ships provided significantly more room than the older ones. Descriptions of the captain, and his experience as a commander and as a circumspect manager of his cargo, demonstrate the importance of a good reputation in the business. Assurances that the ship's owner would be one of the passengers and that servants were not being transported on the same vessel suggest that passengers shopped not only for comfortable accommodations but also for service and that there was a distinct difference in the way the two main classes of emigrants from Ulster—free persons and bound laborers—were treated on the voyage.[93]

The fare for the voyage was relatively inexpensive. The full-fare price fluctuated around four pounds sterling (the actual cost to the merchant was about three pounds sterling), with one guinea required as a down payment.[94] No customs restrictions applied for Irish travelers, and provi-

91. "Passenger List [1768–72]"; customhouse notices in the *Pennsylvania Gazette*; Dickson, *Ulster Emigration*, app. D.

92. This is noteworthy because Doerflinger found high turnover among vessels making port in Philadelphia in the decade before the Revolution (*Vigorous Spirit of Enterprise*, 121).

93. Dickson, *Ulster Emigration*, app. D.

94. Dickson, *Ulster Emigration*, 203. Ekirch calculated £4.7s.8d as the cost per passenger for transporting prisoners between 1737 and 1743—a price that was high because of the commission merchants received for this kind of cargo (*Bound for America*, 85). A comparable calculation for the price of transporting servants to Philadelphia was £3.12s per servant (Education Fac-

204 TRADE IN STRANGERS

sions and transportation of one chest were conventionally included in the fare price.[95] Emigrants leaving from Derry were even allowed to transport small quantities of trade goods without fear of interference from any customs officer, because of the considerable influence of the local firms involved in the trade.[96] It was also the custom to offer food and drink during the voyage in the fare—at a price for paying passengers and at the cost of smaller and coarser rations for servants. The quantity and quality of the victuals must have met most expectations, however, because explicit mention of provisions appeared only once, late in the period of heavy pre-Revolutionary emigration from Ireland.[97] Emigrants also brought food and drink of their own: oatmeal, potatoes, bacon, and tea or coffee, and sugar for the voyage.[98] Wool blankets served as bedding, which paying passengers may have brought as part of their luggage but which the shippers provided for passengers and indentured servants on board.[99]

Food rations on board were plain but adequate. Under favorable circumstances—as advertised for the ship *Britannia* in 1775—provisions for each Irish immigrant per week constituted approximately six pounds of beef, six pounds of ship bread (often imported from Philadelphia) or oatmeal, one pound of butter or a pint of treacle or molasses, and fourteen quarts of water.[100] Unless the Irish brought additional foodstuffs in their baggage, their regular diet was simple; paying passengers must have brought extra foodstuffs, or they surely would have complained about the plain, unvaried provisions on board.[101] Irish emigrants received rations that were obviously staples of the provisions trade. Since beef, butter, and the like also made up the cargo on Irish ships, there were no accusations (as

simile No. 123: Emigration, PRO of Northern Ireland). In some cases, much higher fare prices are recorded—most likely a reflection of fluctuating values of local money in relation to sterling, or the result of including the price of provisions of higher quality than usual. According to Doyle, the cost of the Atlantic voyage could range from £3.5 to £9 when provisions were included (*Ireland*, 155). Lockhart noted an average fare price of £5 that the Quaker merchants charged their passengers ("Quakers," 77).

95. Lockhart, "Quakers," 77.

96. Truxes, *Irish American Trade*, 135.

97. Dickson, *Ulster Emigration*, 206–7.

98. Green, "Ulster Emigrant Letters," 93.

99. See, for example, the "woolen blankets or bedclothes . . . for the use of all or any passengers or servants" listed besides provisions and other necessities fit for an overseas voyage in a 1736 petition (Education Facsimile No. 124: Emigration, PRO of Northern Ireland).

100. Cited in Dickson, *Ulster Emigration*, 279; see Ekirch, *Bound for America*, 100, for the less generous portions calculated for convicts.

101. Dickson, *Ulster Emigration*, app. D.

there were in the German trade) that merchants calculated provisions for passengers tightly or that they did not always allow sufficient storage space for these necessities. In the absence of detailed individual travel accounts, the silence of other sources on this point combined with the established fact that mixed cargoes of provisions and emigrants were typical on Irish ships bound for Philadelphia, suggests that hardships because of insufficient food must have been few.

Irish emigrants also generally seemed satisfied with the way the merchants and captains handled their baggage. The lack of complaints about damaged or lost property suggests that transferring the emigrants' personal belongings was easy, in part because only a small proportion of passengers (estimates range from one-tenth to one-third of all emigrants) owned goods that were valuable or plentiful enough to represent a temptation for the profiteering schemes that afflicted the German emigrant trade. If the majority of passengers traveled with bundles, rather than transporting chests filled with assorted household goods and provisions, some were too poor to even wear adequate clothing. Shirts, for example, were an item one merchant who imported servants into Philadelphia included in his calculation of expenses.[102] In contrast, reports about the emigration from northern Ireland in the early 1770s were unanimous in describing those travelers as belonging to the "middling sort" and paying their own passage.[103] Yet even at the height of the Ulster emigration, when vessels were packed with people, there is no indication of any property loss stemming from the tactics that the Rotterdam merchants, their captains, and crews employed to exploit German passengers as that migration crested in the middle of the eighteenth century.[104] The satisfactory transporting of passengers' baggage suggests either that the claim about the "middling" socioeconomic background of the emigrants was exaggerated, to emphasize the drain of capital their loss inflicted on the region of out-migration, or that emigrants could travel light because they carried cash from the proceeds of the sale of their leases, improvements, and other assets in order to buy household and other goods after they landed.[105]

102. Accountbook, Richard Neave Jr., 1773–74, HSP. This was not an isolated incident, because some Belfast merchants also provided wearing apparel (Education Facsimile No. 124: Emigration, PRO of Northern Ireland).

103. Dickson, *Ulster Emigration*, 97.

104. See Chapter 3.

105. Doyle, *Ireland*, 53. Shippers allowed emigrants from Londonderry to carry small quantities of trade goods, a practice that was apparently uncommon in other Irish ports (Truxes, *Irish American Trade*, 135).

Moreover, Irish newcomers—unlike German immigrants—could count on ready availability of familiar wares from merchants who were regularly involved in trade with Ireland.

Crowding, and the miseries resulting from it, has been one of the most powerful images evoked about the immigrant trade, but in the Irish trade, evidence for such practices is scarce.[106] Living conditions on the ships were cramped, but not unlike farmhouses at home.[107] A combination of factors was responsible for the relatively uncrowded conditions on board Irish immigrant ships. Most important was the large number of vessels employed in the Irish trade, especially at the height of the Irish immigration in the late 1760s and early 1770s, when the volume of shipping between Ireland and the colonies also peaked.[108] That is, the increasing demand for passage between 1763 and 1775, particularly in northern Ireland, was easily absorbed by ships that were already regularly engaged in trade with Pennsylvania, when an average of fourteen vessels a year sailed from Ulster to Philadelphia (Table 5).

Complaints by the Irish about overcrowding were few. As the transportation of passengers in large numbers proved profitable, merchants in Ireland increased their efforts to win emigrants. The number of ships advertising for passengers in the *Belfast News Letter* in 1771 show that there had been a significant increase in the number of vessels that solicited emigrants through the newspapers.[109] That ship owners were now more actively going after the profits to be reaped from the trade in migrants is also demonstrated by the number of fully loaded immigrant vessels that were abandoning their regular route to the middle colonies to accommodate passengers bound elsewhere— in particular, for Charleston.[110] On average,

106. Dickson, *Ulster Emigration*, app. C.

107. Green, "Ulster Emigrant Letters," 93.

108. "Number and Tonnage Capacity"; James, "Irish Colonial Trade," 582.

109. Based on a comparison of ships advertised in Ulster ports (Dickson, *Ulster Emigration*, app. D) with the "Passenger List [1768–72]" and customhouse notices in the *Pennsylvania Gazette*, 1763–75.

110. Dickson observed that the percentage of emigrant vessels leaving for Philadelphia was highest when the emigration flow ebbed—a sign of close commercial ties that existed between Philadelphia and Ireland irrespective of the emigration. Philadelphia's predominance over other destinations in the American colonies decreased when emigration from Ireland peaked (*Ulster Emigration*, 225). Newspapers in Ireland were interested in the destinations of emigrants and published their reports about emigration accordingly. *Londonderry Journal* 219 (12 July 1774), abstracted in Donald Schlegel, *Irish Genealogical Abstracts*, 34. New York and Baltimore presented strong, but regular competition for Philadelphia because, like Philadelphia, they were important ports in the flaxseed trade (Truxes, *Irish American Trade*, 5).

149 Irish immigrants per ship arrived in Charleston between 1763 and 1773. This relatively high number corroborates the observation that Philadelphia declined in popularity relative to other immigrant destinations when emigration peaked. It also supports the conclusion that vessels departing from their regular route did so because they had a full load of passengers. In the case of South Carolina, poor Protestants were attracted by the bounty act, which provided free land and payment for the passage (£4 sterling), a feature that was also attractive to the merchants who arranged these voyages and who knew—like their counterparts in the German emigrant trade earlier—that their profits rose proportionately to the number of immigrants per ship.[111] Voyages under these conditions came closest to those typical of the height of the German immigration: crowding emigrants as a way to maximize profits. Even then, however, the difference in scale remains significant. In the decade before the Revolution, the average number of Irish immigrants per ship was 40, with emigrants from Ulster averaging 67 per vessel and those embarking in southern Irish ports averaging just 20, in contrast to an average of more than 300 immigrants on vessels carrying German passengers at the peak of the migration around mid-century. For the Irish, mortality rates during the voyage were low; deaths on shipboard were confined mainly to children, who often died of measles, or to the elderly.[112]

The picture of the Irish experience during the voyage, which emerges largely from circumstantial evidence, can be characterized mainly as normal and uneventful within the general context of eighteenth-century shipping. With the exception of extraordinary circumstances on individual voyages due to adverse weather conditions or poor treatment by a captain, the years of moderate migration flow (the 1730s through the early 1760s) typically witnessed many emigrant groups of about 40 passengers per ship—including parcels of one or two dozen servants—on medium-size vessels carrying mixed cargoes of provisions and linen as well as people. Rations of food and drink on board were plain but adequate. Knowledgeable passengers arranged to supplement the rather monotonous diet provided on ship, while indentured servants with no resources of their own were probably glad to just receive provisions regularly. Quarters for immigrants were usually below deck, in a space where only children could stand

---

111. Revill, *Compilation.*

112. Green, "Ulster Emigrant Letters," 93; see also "Journal of Clinton [1729]." For a ship that landed sick Irish immigrants in Philadelphia in 1741, see Schwartz, *Mixed Multitude*, 193.

upright and where conditions were always cramped.[113] On some ships, passengers and servants were segregated. The departure from Ireland was often postponed while masters tried to complement cargoes more fully. Occasionally, stopovers along the coast to take on more cargo or provisions delayed the voyage even more.[114] Once sails were set for the transatlantic crossing—usually in spring or late summer—the voyage to Philadelphia lasted between six to eight weeks, depending on the location of the port of departure and prevailing weather conditions. Many of the ships coming from Ireland stopped in New Castle, Delaware, before anchoring in Philadelphia, and from Philadelphia the majority of ships returned directly to Ireland; the rest continued in a more circuitous pattern to southern Europe or the West Indies before making port again in Ireland.[115]

At the peaks of the Irish immigration, especially in the late 1720s and in the late 1760s and early 1770s, the normal experience of the voyage was modified. In 1729, the demand for transatlantic passenger transportation matched or even exceeded the supply of available shipping. This resulted not only in crowded conditions on ships regularly engaged in the trade between Ireland and Pennsylvania, but also in the use of vessels that were not well suited for transatlantic voyages and of captains who had no experience with that route. These circumstances were disastrous for many immigrants. Some starved, either because merchants deliberately took insufficient provisions in order to gain more room for passengers at the expense of available storage space, or because the voyage lasted longer than anticipated. Others succumbed to disease and death resulting from the close confinement of large numbers of people in a limited and unhealthful space over an extended period of time.[116]

In the later rush of the 1760s and 1770s, and particularly after 1772, ships were larger, although that did not necessarily translate into more room for passengers.[117] Merchants and captains were generally experienced

<hr />

113. For the early years, only a few ships arriving from Ireland were registered in Philadelphia. The registered tonnage ranged from 60 to 100 tons, and their dimensions were probably roughly similar to that of the ship *Mary*, described earlier. See McCusker, "Ships Registered at the Port of Philadelphia."

114. There were relatively few stopovers in Ireland, but a number of vessels, particularly those listed from Cork, started their voyages outside of Ireland, mostly from English ports. See Dickson, *Ulster Emigration*, app. D; Lockhart, *Some Aspects of Emigration*, app. C.

115. Sailing patterns are gleaned from the customhouse notices in the *Pennsylvania Gazette*.

116. *Pennsylvania Gazette*, 6 January 1729/30.

117. Between 1763 and 1775, ships in the Irish trade averaged 104 tons, with a marked

in transporting emigrants and knew what features of their vessels and operations to highlight. Judging from the advertisements during the late pre-Revolutionary peak of the migration, Irish immigrants traveled on large ships in sizable but comfortable numbers and received good treatment.[118] Even taking into account that advertising usually involves some deception, life on board Irish emigrant vessels, while probably less rosy than the promoters painted, was hardly as miserable as had been common at the height of the German immigration flow, when competition and choice among shippers were negligible and when a bad reputation of merchants or captains did not affect the profitability of the trade in immigrants. Given the circumstances that are generally characteristic of mass migration, emigrants sailing from Ulster ports were protected against the most exploitative practices that profit-seeking merchants involved in the German passenger trade had developed earlier, because the large volume of regular shipping and the close, enduring ties between the ports of embarkation and debarkation served to discourage abusive measures in the business. Worse was to come, however, after the Revolution, especially in the early 1800s, when the peaking outflow from Ulster tempted merchants carrying immigrants to various American and Canadian ports to cut corners for profit.[119]

The relatively shorter, cheaper, and less stressful voyages that brought Irish immigrants to the American colonies meant that their first steps in the New World were also likely to be easier than many of the beginnings typical for Germans who landed when the tide of their migration crested and receded near mid-century. For newcomers from Ireland, though, once again the paths to success after landing were divided according to whether immigrants arrived as debt-free passengers or as bound servants. And the respective chances that these two different kinds of immigrants would be well integrated into colonial society depended largely on the employment and settlement opportunities prevailing in the region at the time of their arrival and, for servants, after the expiration of their indentures.

The majority of immigrants embarking in southern Irish ports for

increase to 136 tons during the last three years—a reflection of a few new and larger ships that complemented the older, smaller ones already employed in the trade. "Tonnage Duty Book [1765–75]"; McCusker, "Ships Registered at the Port of Philadelphia."

118. Dickson, *Ulster Emigration,* app. D.

119. Miller, *Emigrants and Exiles;* Houston and Smyth, *Irish Emigration and Canadian Settlement.*

Philadelphia arrived as bound servants. Already in the late 1720s, the pattern of their importation conformed to that of the commodities trade between those ports. The usual parcels of one or two dozen servants complemented other cargoes (mainly provisions) and were a way to cover the costs of the westward leg of the regular flaxseed fleet.[120] From 1768 to 1772, more than two-thirds of the vessels imported emigrants from southern Irish ports to Philadelphia more than once.[121] Since virtually all the indentures were contracted in Ireland, local merchants there were the primary investors in the transportation of southern Irish servants for overseas markets. Their mode of operation probably resembled that of their better-known counterparts in England.[122] Some of the Irish merchants worked for their own accounts, while others were brokers or handled the business on a commission basis for merchants in Philadelphia.[123] In 1741, for example, Joseph W. Whitsett of Philadelphia invested in Irish servants; and in 1769 the firm James & Drinker was quite specific in instructing a captain about the kinds of servants wanted for the Philadelphia market.[124] The procurement of servants for employment across the Atlantic was risky and competitive and depended on the overflow or reserve of suitable and willing poor artisans, laborers, or adventurers resident or vagrant in the southern seaports and their hinterlands—often in consequence of bad harvests and depressed markets.[125] The original contractual agreement followed local customs and regulatory requirements in price and terms.

The demand for Irish servants generally outpaced the supply. Competition among shippers was brisk, and the numbers in individual shipments tended to be small, so that even people of marginal age, experience, or

120. Truxes, *Irish American Trade*, 39, 132.

121. "Passenger List [1768–72]"; customhouse notices in the *Pennsylvania Gazette*.

122. See Horn, "Servant Emigration," 87–94.

123. "He [William Graham, an Irish peddler] goes over to Ireland, every fall, with flaxseed &c. and returns in the spring with servants and goods, generally taking shipping and landing at New-Castle, and is said to be worth money" (*Pennsylvania Chronicle*, 22 February 1768). In the competition for servants, captains participated in the recruiting effort and received about one-third of the commission after the sale of the indentures in Philadelphia (Truxes, *Irish American Trade*, 134–35).

124. Philadelphia County administration no. 128 (1741), Philadelphia, Register of Wills, City Hall Annex; James and Drinker to Captain Enoch Story, 6 May 1769. For other examples of the business of importing servants, see Sharon Salinger, "Colonial Labor in Transition."

125. Lockhart, *Some Aspects of Emigration*, 61; Dickson, *Ulster Emigration*, 89–90. For a description of the complex context of migration from the southern counties of Ireland, see Cullen, "Irish Diaspora," 131. Servant emigration from seventeenth-century Bristol peaked at 800–900 servants a year, with fluctuations according to harvests. See Horn, "Servant Emigration," 85, 87.

skills could find masters. As the price of the indenture was the only term of the contract that was negotiable upon arrival in America, captains and merchants who had vested interests in the disposition of servants from Ireland tried to match the supply to demand as closely as possible. Acting as investors or consignees, Philadelphia merchants told their partners that the Pennsylvania market would bear skilled men and boys most profitably.[126] Yet not all servant cargoes fitted the specifications of their consignees in Philadelphia perfectly or corresponded well to the market conditions that prevailed at the time of arrival, so some individuals brought low net prices. Long delays in Ireland in order to complement cargoes further cut down on profits from indentured servants. So did weeks or months of waiting to conclude sales in Philadelphia, during which the unsold servants needed to be fed, clothed, and housed. Sales of Irish servants tended to be particularly difficult during the late summer and early fall months when they had to compete with many newly arrived German redemptioners.[127] In addition, in times of war few employers risked investing in bound labor for fear their servants would join the king's army. Most servants, however, could be sold profitably within a couple of weeks or months. Prices for four-year indentures ranged from £12 to £24 Pennsylvania money (about £7 to £14 sterling)—a range evident in 1745–46 as well as in 1771–73. The cost of transporting them was roughly £5 Pennsylvania money or £3 sterling, although we lack detailed accounts as to how provisions, fees, commissions, interest, and other charges figured into the fare and thus determined profits for captains and merchants.[128] The role of the servant in most of the negotiations was rather passive. In Ireland, the servant might have been able to choose from a number of destinations and shippers, but how to match employer and servant upon arrival in Philadelphia was the master's prerogative.

The steady influx of indentured servants in small installments from southern Ireland—at an average of just somewhat more than one hundred servants annually—was augmented, and quite likely doubled, by a similar flow originating in Ulster. The mechanisms for procuring and disposing of servants from northern Ireland were comparable to those practiced in

126. "Extracts from the Letter-Book of Benjamin Marshall"; James and Drinker to Lancelot Cowper, 19 May and 7 June 1769, James and Drinker Letter Book.

127. "Servants and Apprentices [1745–46]"; "Record of Indentures [1771–73]"; sales of servants on the ship *Dolphin*, Richard Neave Jr., Accountbook; customhouse notices in the *Pennsylvania Gazette.*

128. "Servants and Apprentices [1745–46]"; "Record of Indentures [1771–73]."

the servant trade from southern Irish ports because the commercial links
between Ulster and the Delaware Valley resembled those connecting southern Ireland and Philadelphia so much that some of the sailing patterns,
ships, and trading partners actually overlapped. The interregional role of
Dublin was one significant link between Ulster and the rest of Ireland.
The increasing number of ties that both Irish regions had with the Delaware Valley in the decade preceding the American Revolution provided
another link. The higher volume of trade was achieved largely by ships
making two voyages a year, frequently alternating between northern and
southern Irish ports.[129] Only a few Philadelphia merchants conducted
much of the trade with Ireland, and those few provided the structure for
the business of transporting emigrants and servants. The networks of mercantile partnerships often had quite distinct ties to a particular port in
Ireland, whose contacts in the colonies rarely overlapped.[130] Overall, the
labor market of colonial Pennsylvania was supplied with relatively small
shipments of a dozen or so servants from ever-changing and shifting labor
reservoirs in several Irish seaports and their hinterlands. Depending largely
on local conditions in Ireland, these sources of labor for Philadelphia
fluctuated around a trickle of perhaps two hundred bound servants a year,
which was enough to allow some specialization among shippers regularly
involved in the trade, but well below the capacity of the colonial Pennsylvania labor market.

The forces of supply and demand that shaped this labor market in the
Mid-Atlantic colonies were complex. The purchase of an indentured servant from Ireland was as much a question of choice—determined by individual needs, preferences, and financial circumstances—as a function of
supply, given the presence of servants with a variety of backgrounds and
different ethnic origins, and other types of labor as well. Only a careful
and systematic analysis of the surviving indentures will shed light on the
qualitative aspects that were likely to determine the choice among otherwise
comparable contracts. Market conditions for servants were rarely poor, but
some kinds of indentures were worth more than others. For example, men
sold better than women, skilled artisans sold better than laborers, Ger-

129. In the years 1763 to 1775, when the Irish immigration wave gained momentum, the
overall rate of repeat voyages was almost 70 percent; among ships leaving Ulster with emigrants in 1768–72, the rate was even higher: just over 78 percent. See "Passenger List [1768–
72]"; customhouse notices in the *Pennsylvania Gazette.*

130. For an analysis of Irish servants imported to Philadelphia by regional and ethnic
background and for a grouping of Irish merchants in Philadelphia and southeastern Pennsylvania in 1770 according to two distinct networks, see Doyle, *Ireland,* 66–68, 77.

mans sold better than Irish. It is impossible now to tell how homogeneous a certain group of Irish servants was, or the extent to which its composition resulted from selective processes that took place in Ireland.[131] Conversely, employment opportunities in the Delaware Valley for indentured servants who came from Ireland were not only a function of the variable demand for labor as determined by economic conditions, but also dependent on the extent and type of competition from other sources of labor and on the kinds of purchasers who were in the market. As in the German case, how did they perceive the advantages and disadvantages of buying Irish? As the potential labor pool increased and diversified throughout the colonial period, as a consequence of natural population growth, continuous immigration, and the importation of servants and slaves, opportunities for bound servants generally decreased accordingly, so that prospects for employment under indenture or otherwise were considerably poorer at the time of the extended peak of Irish immigration in 1771–73 than when the early crisis migration from Ireland occurred in 1729.[132]

The observed shift from bound labor to free labor in Philadelphia was the result not of declining imports of servants but the result of an abundance of men, women, and children qualified and willing, if not pressed, to work for wages. Employers found relative advantage in wage labor because it freed them from maintaining indentured servants when they could not be fully utilized. Conversely, many Irish avoided bound labor if they could, and appear to have placed a high premium on independence from such contracts. The reasons for this development are uncertain. It may have been easier for immigrants who came in family groups—like most of the pre-Revolutionary Ulster migrants—to opt against servitude, because making a living as a family unit allowed them economic flexibility that unconnected young men and women could not afford.[133] Another factor was undoubtedly an Irish history of subservience to English landowners and artisans that was to be avoided in the New World if at all possible.

131. "Record of Indentures [1771–73]."

132. The situation of servants in Philadelphia is discussed in Salinger, *To Serve Well and Faithfully*, although Salinger offers little analysis in terms of ethnic differences among servants bound in Philadelphia, so that the fate of Irish servants in Pennsylvania remains to be explored. Irish men, and some women, were the largest group among runaway servants whose owners advertised in the *Pennsylvania Gazette*. The lives of Philadelphia's laboring poor more generally are described and analyzed by Billy G. Smith ("The Material Lives of Laboring Philadelphians"; "The Vicissitudes of Fortune"; and *The "Lower Sort."*

133. For circumstances in the Philadelphia labor market, see Salinger, "Colonial Labor in Transition"; and B. G. Smith, "Material Lives of Philadelphians."

Indeed, most of the Irish immigration to the Delaware Valley did not consist of indentured servants or redemptioners. Passengers paying their own way were distinct from servants in two primary respects: they usually traveled in family groups, and the majority immigrated either in the late 1720s or during the decade just before the Revolution. This pattern of two distinct flows—young, single, relatively poor men, on the one hand, and families of some modest means, on the other—conforms in general to the phenomenon of eighteenth-century transatlantic migrations that Bernard Bailyn has detailed for the migration from Great Britain in the decade preceding the American Revolution, and that also characterized the earlier flow of German immigrants to colonial America.[134] Put differently, during the first or crisis peak of Irish immigration, when several thousand newcomers from all Irish ports landed on the shores of the Delaware, more than three-quarters of the immigrants were paying passengers, and the majority was connected by kinship, congregational, or community ties. As this flood ebbed in the 1730s and the immigration flow from Ireland fluctuated, mostly in response to bad harvests and general conditions of recession, around an average annual level of 640, the proportion of paying passengers among the newcomers, and the presence of families on board, at times decreased to one-third. When the tide of Irish immigration swelled once again in the 1760s and early 1770s, the overwhelming majority embarked as paying passengers in Ulster ports, and about half undertook the voyage in family groups.

The impact of this revised pattern of Irish immigration into the Delaware Valley on the development in colonial Pennsylvania was far-reaching. In the late 1720s, when Irish immigration had its early spike, land was relatively abundant and cheap—a decisive advantage to all newcomers intent on becoming landowners in the New World.[135] As settlements in the province filled up during the many years when fewer Irish came—the 1730s through the 1750s—newcomers as well as freed servants had to travel farther inland to find comparable opportunity, or had to invest more in order to set up farm or shop successfully. The Pennsylvania counties of York, Cumberland, Berks, and Northampton, including the towns of York and Reading, were established and founded in the late 1740s and 1750s, thus attesting to the extent and variety of settlement activity in the province. As spreading settlements in western Maryland and Virginia attracted

134. Bailyn, *Voyagers to the West*, chap. 5. For the German immigration, see Chapter 1, above.
135. Lemon, *Best Poor Man's Country*, 43–49.

former residents of Pennsylvania as well as newly arrived immigrants, numerous farms in the well-established counties were offered for sale or rent.

During the extended later peak of Irish immigration in the 1760s and 1770s, new settlers found the situation in Pennsylvania even more difficult and complicated than it was before the French and Indian War. This was one reason that South Carolina, which offered free passage and land, became relatively so attractive. Now Pennsylvania or Delaware may have been intended only as a stopover on the way much farther inland, where farms were still affordable. Irish newcomers with limited funds who wanted to settle as farmers, however, may have found the costs of moving on too prohibitive, and therefore remained stranded in the region much longer than they had anticipated.[136] Others, more intent on making use of their skills as artisans, traders, or professionals, had to compete in a large and diverse Delaware Valley labor market in which the balance was shifting from bound labor to wage labor. In the decade preceding the Revolution, the influx of thousands of Irish immigrants from Ulster ports accelerated these new developments and shaped what would happen to their countrymen who later relocated to the newly founded United States.[137]

Comparison of the Irish and German immigration to the American colonies reveals that the two migration flows were alike in some important ways but that certain basic differences left their marks. After sporadic and inconspicuous beginnings, immigration from both countries peaked in the late 1720s. At that time, the two streams of immigrants were about comparable in overall strength, composition, and direction. In 1727, more than 1,000 German immigrants arrived in Philadelphia. Having paid their fare in advance, they traveled mostly in family groups and relocated their entire households to farms in southeastern Pennsylvania. The influx from Ireland in 1729 exceeded this early German immigration. These people, too, came mostly as family groups, and they farmed within the same ring of settlement around Philadelphia. It is likely that they came from somewhat poorer backgrounds, however, because relocation costs from Ireland were

136. "The town of Baltimore is commodiously situated for a ready Communication with all the back parts of Pennsylvania, Maryland, and Virginia, to which most new Settlers resort. It is a hundred miles nearer than Philadelphia to Fort Pitt on the River Ohio—a new Province of vast Extent. . . ." Advertisement in the *Londonderry Journal* 106 (4 June 1773) published in Schlegel, *Irish Abstracts,* 18.

137. For the Irish migration to and community in Philadelphia during the early republic, see Bric, "Ireland, Irishmen."

considerably lower, and hence more easily met, than the expenses involved in a transatlantic move from southwestern Germany.

After the late 1720s, the two immigration streams took divergent paths. German immigration increased dramatically from an average of 400 passengers annually in the late 1720s to more than 6,000 in 1749–54, but the flow of Irish immigration ebbed for about three decades and fluctuated around somewhat more than 600 newcomers a year. As the number of Germans drawn to Pennsylvania by the promise of a prosperous life in a free country expanded, it also diversified. At the height of the immigration, around mid-century, German immigrants still traveled often in family groups, but they tended to be younger, carried less baggage, and financed the move more frequently on credit than in the early years. In the 1750s, even the promotional literature distributed in Germany acknowledged that the dream of getting rich in the New World took more newcomers longer to pursue as settlement areas in Pennsylvania filled up.[138] The favorable experiences of Irish settlers who had immigrated in 1729 across the subsequent three decades enticed others who had stayed behind to follow their example when life in Ireland was particularly difficult after bad harvests or when credit was especially tight. While some with means still sought farm settlement opportunities in the Delaware Valley and beyond, it was mostly the Irish who were too poor to pay for the transatlantic passage—or those hard-pressed by adverse circumstances and willing to accept any kind of employment, including servitude for about 200 immigrants a year—who maintained the Irish flow in the 1730s, 1740s, and 1750s. Even the servants among these people, at the expiration of their indentures joined the ranks of other recent immigrants and freedmen, in trying to carve out a decent living and searching for a farm to buy or rent, a shop in which to practice a trade, or some combination of the two.

When immigration resumed after the war in 1763, the trend of the German immigration flow was reversed downward by circumstances in both America and Europe, while the influx from Ireland, particularly from Ulster, soared to a new high. The decline of the German immigration overseas in the years preceding the Revolution was almost as dramatic as

138. Comments about the high price of land in Pennsylvania as a consequence of the increased density of settlement in the province became a standard feature in the promotional literature that land speculators from other colonies distributed among potential emigrants in Germany. See, for example, the comment in the *Lancaster Gazette* (25 March 1753), HSP; and Samuel Waldo's advertising campaign for Broad Bay, Maine; and Karl Arndt, ed. and comp., *George Rapp's Separatists*, 40, 56–58.

its spectacular rise in the second quarter of the eighteenth century. Yet as the number of immigrants decreased from above 1,000 to below 500 a year (about 12,000 total, only slightly less than the total number of Irish immigrants during the same period), the composition of the flow also altered further. The proportion of young single men traveling alone grew at the expense of women and children, and about half of all newcomers had to enter into a credit arrangement to finance their passage. In comparison, the influx of immigrants from Ireland to Philadelphia increased in the same period from more than 500 to 1,500 or so newcomers annually, to reach a total of about 14,500 during those years. If 40 percent of the passengers on board immigrant vessels that stopped first in New Castle debarked in Delaware, Irish immigration to the Delaware Valley region as a whole was more than 20,000. However, like the front edge of the German wave several decades earlier, in the second quarter of the century, the vast majority of those immigrants were capable of paying their own way and a large proportion were traveling in family groups.

Even though northern Irish migration waxed and German migration waned in the years leading up to the Revolution, most of the dynamics were similar. The history of one movement in large part echoed the history of the other. Pioneers faced with particular difficulties and possessed of particular connections to the New World blazed the way to the Delaware Valley and established local settlements in which their group became influential. Later, in response to reports of how much better New World life could be, many other homeland neighbors followed. The increased spreading of information extended the desire to emigrate not only to more men and women, but also to people with lesser means and less maturity and skills. Later, when word spread that the best opportunities had already been taken by the original pioneers, some of the immigrant flow was diverted elsewhere. At that point, younger, less well-off, and less attached immigrants characterized the migration. The remaining impulse to leave the homeland was satisfied by other destinations. Lagging by a generation or so, the northern Irish movement did not peak until after the Revolution, but in these respects, then, it very much resembled its German predecessor.

What was fundamentally different for these two migrations, however, was the nature of the transatlantic transportation system that carried them. Irish emigrants had easy access to trade, communications, and transportation channels that, for a century or more, had connected Ireland with Britain, southern Europe, the West Indies, and the American mainland colonies. The extent and diversity of this network had long offered unhappy Irish people overseas employment and settlement opportunities. Since the late 1600s, people from a variety of economic, political, religious, and regional backgrounds in Ireland and people with many different aspirations formed a steady trickle to take advantage of those opportunities. The discriminating laws of the early 1700s, and the subsistence crisis of the late 1720s, impelled Irish people to take much more advantage of the chance to better their lives in the New World—in particular, where the Penn holdings, at the time, composed the lands of greatest promise.

Under the new stimulus, the Delaware River region attracted both servants and paying passengers taking advantage of already-established transatlantic links in the provisions, linen, and flaxseed markets. Over the years thereafter, no new transportation system had to be invented. The heavy relocation of the crisis point at 1729 could come and go without stimulating a new form of business that specialized in immigrants. Indentured servants remained a regular and integral part of the Irish trade, because bound labor was in demand for most of the colonial period. The servant trade to Pennsylvania provided an alternative destination for poor Irishmen who might otherwise have been forced to go to the West Indies or the southern colonies. It yielded profits for investors on both sides of the Atlantic, and added to the returns of merchants, captains, and agents, who could thereby profitably complement their ships' mixed cargoes on the westward voyage to the American colonies, where they loaded flaxseed. Irish emigrants of sufficient means to pay their fares in advance found that passage to Philadelphia was easy to contract at reasonable terms during much of the year because sailings were frequent and regular. Shippers profited nicely from such additional loads because they contributed to the productivity of shipping.[139] These arrangements continued decade after decade, and even the surge of northern migration during the years preceding the Revolution was readily absorbed by the ample shipping plying between Ireland and the Delaware.

By contrast, the transatlantic transportation system devised for German immigrants to colonial Pennsylvania was not an integral part of an already well-established commodities trade. Arrangements for passage required the combination of many different merchants' interests along intricate lines of credit connecting Pennsylvania, England, and continental Europe. Just a few English merchants in Rotterdam played the crucial role of middlemen, matching and to some extent regulating supply and demand

139. Truxes, *Irish American Trade*, 39, 133.

for shipping and setting the terms of this specialized trade. Customers had to be found at great distances from port and transported there over many hurdles. For these reasons, compared with their Irish counterparts, German emigrants had fewer overseas destination options and less choice of shipper and ship, and they paid more for the base fare and the many services required for the journey. For most Germans, the move to Pennsylvania was irreversible; for all, it was costly. These facts affected the number and type of passengers who sought transportation in the early years: they had resources as well as determination. Later, when merchants granted new forms of credit for the passage, many more Germans of many different backgrounds and with diverse inclinations were lured to Pennsylvania—until new settlement opportunities opened up in Europe and wooed migrants eastward rather than westward.

Whatever its origin, European immigration to the American colonies was the result of many factors. Shaping and directing the flow were conditions at home, which prompted emigration; the changing promise of settlement and employment opportunities in the New World, which directed immigration flows; and the links of personal contact and trade that were forged between areas of out-migration and rapidly developing regions in the American colonies. For most of the colonial period, Pennsylvania held the promise of a better, freer life for the vast majority of German immigrants. As the province ceased to be the best poor man's country, the Germans who had immigrated in such large numbers and thus helped bring about that change, went instead to the backcountry of Maryland, Virginia, and the Carolinas—or to East Prussia, Hungary, and Russia. For the Irish, in contrast, Pennsylvania was only the most important destination among several others, so immigration from Ireland to the Delaware Valley was about half the German immigration in overall numerical strength. Because of what was happening at home, particularly in Ulster, this other flow was most heavily concentrated, and picking up momentum, in the decade before the Revolution, when settlement in Pennsylvania was relatively filled up. Since the voyage to Philadelphia was cheaper, shorter, and easier to arrange for the Irish, because of the nature of existing trade, more of them seem to have come prepared to consider Pennsylvania as a convenient gateway and acceptable interim station for newcomers to America, a function that Philadelphia, along with New York, Baltimore, and Halifax, continued to serve after the Revolution.

Conclusion

A Model for the Modern Era

In the eighteenth century, the movement of Europeans to British North America became less of a haphazard practice and more like the systematic business in migration that became so familiar in the nineteenth century and brought so many forebears of so many different types of present-day Americans across the Atlantic. It was the merchants of Rotterdam who, with their partners in Philadelphia and England, developed the system when opportunities for carrying tens of thousands of Germans to the New World opened up from the 1720s to the 1750s. Others applied that system to the new surge of Irish who wanted passage from Ulster, starting in the 1760s but peaking only near 1800. By the turn to the nineteenth century, this "trade in strangers" had become the model for transporting millions of Europeans via Liverpool, Le Havre, Hamburg, Bremen, Naples, and other ports to American harbors from Quebec to New Orleans during the nineteenth and early twentieth centuries. The system could be applied wherever interest in coming to America spread. It sustained overseas additions to the population at proportionately high levels through World War I, in spite of rapid natural demographic increase, and did much to diversify American society, keeping America indeed a "nation of immigrants."

The dynamics that shaped migration to the North American colonies, in the eighteenth century as later, were complex. Three basic components generally worked together to populate the New World: pushes, pulls, and a connecting transportation system. The "pushes" involved a variety of conditions at home that made some form of relocation, somewhere, seem desirable. The "pulls" were opportunities in America, news of which was spread by informants ranging from professional promoters to family members and personal friends. These drew potential settlers, or instead made them less eager to start a new life in the New World. These forces of "push" and "pull," however, were separated by thousands of miles of dangerous ocean and by weeks of difficult and expensive travel to reach the ocean in the first place. Thus, the third essential element in determining how migration first flowed and then ebbed, who came and when, what expectations and resources they brought to the new society, and how successfully they fitted in was a trade run by merchants who could find profit in the business of moving large numbers of people from Europe to America. These entrepreneurs exercised decisive control in shaping and directing the flow of emigrants as they took advantage of the considerable demand for settlers and servants in the colonies.

The interaction of these basic elements in continually peopling North America, decade after decade, generation after generation, has become quite clear in the intensively worked migration history of the nineteenth century. Poorly understood so far, however, is how the movement of 81,000 Germans through Philadelphia in the middle fifty years of the eighteenth century became the prototype for the later flows that made America a society that was constantly being fed by immigrants. As this study has shown, colonial German migration did establish the form for the later influx of northern Irish in the last third of the eighteenth century and the seemingly endless future waves of mass transoceanic immigration that decisively shaped American history, and indeed the history of the entire New World, on into the present.

The "push" factors in eighteenth-century Germany were many—including devastation by war, oppressive government policies, religious intolerance, harvest failures, and credit crises—and intricately interrelated. On the personal level, emigrants were pushed by fear of inescapable indebtedness and uncertainty about being able to find work to setting up a household, earn their livelihood, and provide for their families.

Modern migration studies show that those who are most likely to move tomorrow are those who moved yesterday. Indeed, the principal areas of out-migration along the Rhine and its tributaries had been experiencing population shifts almost constantly for a long time. Religious, political, and economic upheaval in virtually all of these interconnected regions had prompted many inhabitants of the Rhine lands, or family members or friends, to move temporarily or permanently from one place to another substantially before migration to North America began from this area of Europe. Throughout the region, significant numbers of newcomers, some of them originally Swiss, had recently settled in places with decimated populations. Thus, migration as reaction to increasing pressures, whether real or perceived, was not unfamiliar to many people in southwestern Germany. They had either relocated before or knew others who had.

More-detailed analysis of other, later transatlantic migrations, not possible for eighteenth-century Germany, Ireland, or England, has revealed that a strong tradition of migrating combined with one or more "push" factors has nearly always resulted in substantial levels of emigration.[1] Again and again, limited resources and limited employment opportunities for growing populations have led people to contemplate emigration. And against such background, incidents of acute distress, such as war, famine, and high prices, have prompted major exodus, but most often they are only the last straw, precipitating the final decision to leave.[2]

The early emigration from Ireland was like most English movement to the colonies after the mid-1600s. It seems to have fluctuated primarily in response to conditions at home, and it could take advantage of travel facilities that were always there, given the nature of transatlantic trade. By contrast, the trend of the German immigration to colonial Pennsylvania did not only develop directly in reaction to local difficulties, but also in accord with what temporarily seemed to be exceptional opportunities the American colonies presented relative to the much reduced opportunities to be had from staying at home or relocating within Europe instead. However, strong variations on this basic pattern show how the impact of war, famine, and other adversities resulted in significant fluctuations—such as the decline in emigration when sea travel was especially hazardous, at times of war in the 1740s or late 1750s and early 1760s, and the increase in migration in the early 1770s, when grain shortages across Europe were widespread.

Furthermore, people in the Rhine lands were unusual in that they lived in areas that had easy access to important international trade routes and

1. Carlsson, "Chronology and Composition of Swedish Emigration," 140; Sune Åkerman, "Towards an Understanding of Emigrational Processes." For the contemporary era of global migration, see Barkan, *Asian and Pacific Islander Migration*.

2. Åkerman has called that a "value added" process in the migration decision ("Emigrational Processes," 301).

lines of communication. Information about places that might be of interest to prospective settlers was readily available. Indeed, colonization was consciously promoted in this region in many different forms, ranging from personal letters and visits to widely distributed promotional pamphlets and large-scale advertising and recruiting campaigns. Yet Rhinelanders were much farther away from the gateways that offered passage across the Atlantic than their counterparts in Ireland—the other leading source of new colonists in the eighteenth century, whose close and ready access to ports with regular trade to America strongly affected the decision to relocate and greatly facilitated the move.

Throughout the eighteenth century, it must be realized, European emigrants could choose from a variety of destinations for future settlement—America was far from the only choice. When prospects at home looked dim, the "pull" factors for selecting a particular destination tended to mirror the problems they sought to escape. Land, employment, and trading opportunities were strong lures, for they promised a decent living for colonists and their families.[3] Other attractive features included exemption from taxes, conscription, and other frustrating compulsory services, as well as guarantees of religious toleration and little governmental regulation. In all those respects, the American colonies, and especially Pennsylvania, for a while compared very well with other colonizing opportunities in Europe, although only a small proportion of the total long-distance migration of the eighteenth century actually flowed across the Atlantic. As one Württemberger put it after he arrived in Philadelphia in 1754:

> Those who do not know hunger and need cannot comprehend why thousands of people undertake the voyage. The complaints about the government are legion! Work is no longer of any help in making a living—in a situation like this people become truly desperate. . . . We are told that those who want to go to Prussia will get travel money and land as in America, but what is a free man compared to a slave or serf? How much fun can a man have in a country where he has to work himself to death for his lord and where his sons are never protected from the miseries of a soldier's life?

3. Letters from immigrants and emigrants' petitions for permission to relocate provide ample evidence. It is also a theme in the recent studies that link German areas of emigration with German settlements in the American colonies. See Fogleman, *Hopeful Journeys;* Häberlein, *Vom Oberrhein zum Susquehanna,* partially published in English ("German Migrants in Colonial Pennsylvania"); Roeber, *Palatines.* German emigrants had the same goals as many English-speaking migrants, among which was the often-articulated goal of making a "decent living."

There are indeed great differences between America and Europe. . . .[4]

In the eyes of many German emigrants, Pennsylvania seemed to be "granted special blessings."[5] The lasting attraction of, first, the Delaware Valley region itself and, later, the vastly expanding backcountry of the more southern colonies—much of which could be reached readily via Philadelphia down the Great Valley—blended a variety of appealing ingredients.

The types of opportunities various areas offered newcomers determined not only what type of immigrants were most likely to be attracted there, but also the chances that they would be successfully integrated into a new life. When Germans first began to arrive in Pennsylvania in significant numbers in the 1720s, Protestants of different backgrounds and lifestyles were generally tolerated, land was relatively inexpensive, and wages were considered high. On the down side, the cost of relocation had to be paid in cash, mostly in advance. Given these circumstances, Pennsylvania attracted particularly settlers who could arrange to arrive with some starting capital (mostly in the form of European goods brought over for resale) and their own source of labor (family members or servants), and many of these were members of minority religious groups. These conditions also favored immigrants who could sell special skills and labor profitably in order to acquire the means to purchase a farm or set up shop after a few years.

As such favorable opportunities became more widely known in Germany, Pennsylvania lured relatives, friends, and neighbors of those who were already settled in the colony. Such earlier immigrants were often willing and able to help others make the same transition. The resulting rapidly accelerating rate of immigration as mid-century approached, however, could be sustained only through the initiative of enterprising merchants who sought to augment profits by providing transatlantic passage on credit. This expanded the pool of potential emigrants considerably, to reach those who did not have substantial resources or relatives to help them move. The success of this business, which counted increasingly on having passengers pay the fare after landing in the American colonies, depended to a large extent on the willingness of well-established settlers to invest in immigrants. The interest in bound immigrant laborers of partic-

4. *Pennsylvanische Berichte*, 1 December 1754.
5. Christopher Sauer's characterization in *Pennsylvanische Berichte*, 1 December 1754.

ular backgrounds thus varied significantly from one colony to another. Immigration begat immigration, so to speak. In such a chain process, the geographical spread of the migration from Germany—and likewise that from Irish ports—was funneled into certain regions, where precursors of similar background had previously settled.[6]

Another key to the increase in German immigration was the emergence of businessmen who found ways in which they could profit from transporting human cargo across the Atlantic. These merchants differed from private or government land developers who sought colonists but whose business was settlement rather than oceanic trade. In freighting emigrants onto ships bound for America, merchants in Holland expanded their role in transatlantic European networks by filling underutilized westbound shipping. For this, they capitalized both on persuasive recruiting of new settlers by former immigrants and other agents and, most important, on extending credit for passage, which broadened the pool of prospective emigrants and increased their own profits. The combination of effective recruiting and affordable transportation produced the brief but massive inflow of Germans to the colonies in the late 1740s and early 1750s.

Transporting German emigrants to colonial Pennsylvania from Rotterdam first became a regular activity in the late 1720s. Passengers embarked during the summer months of June and July, with most fares paid in advance. Once the merchants involved in the trade had worked out procedures for collecting, transshipping and freighting German emigrants and were assured that they would profit from rapidly increasing demands for transatlantic transportation, they relaxed their requirement of advance payment. First, they extended credit to young single men and women, expecting to be able to sell their labor to purchasers in Pennsylvania—a practice analogous to the long-established English custom of servant transportation. They went further, though, and adapted that practice to include families. This became the most innovative development of the mid-century German immigration. Merchants in Holland accepted a down payment on a family's fare with the portion on credit payable in Philadelphia because they were confident that children could be bound out profitably. By the height of the migration in the early 1750s, the custom of placing a substantial portion of passage money on credit was well established. Merchants had learned that cash payments of about half the ship's freight charges covered outfitting and provisioning expenses and ensured

6. The concentration of immigrant settlement is a very general phenomenon historically (Åkerman, "Emigrational Processes," 294).

some return. This more liberal credit policy allowed immigrants to delay paying all or part of their fare until they arrived in Pennsylvania, and this was a crucial temporary subsidy for the many less well-to-do Germans for whom initial relocation costs would be prohibitive. The security on which merchants extended such credit in Europe could be a specific invitation from relatives or friends already settled in the colonies who offered to help defray costs at least temporarily, or well-stocked chests of goods that could be sold, or promises to work for the unpaid portion of the fare in indentured servitude. This last was a financial guarantee often shouldered by a family's teenage children.

All those options toward paying part or all the fare upon arrival depended on certain circumstances in the American colonies that would make it possible to absorb additional settlers and their labor. In effect, the risk of financing the credit that merchants extended in European ports was passed on to those in the American colonies who were willing to invest in immigrants—primarily their labor and the German wares they had brought with them. This dynamic of German preference to employ German and buy German had a significant self-generating effect on the migration flow and distinguished Philadelphia and its backcountry regions from other colonies.[7] While many in Pennsylvania and its expanding hinterland were willing, even eager, to assume the risks that those investments presented, other colonies could not or would not, because in other colonies German settlements were few, small, and poor or because there were other, preferable sources of labor. For example, neither Nova Scotia nor South Carolina developed first a taste and then a market for German stoves, knives, and the like, or for German-speaking servants.

As the German immigration declined in the two decades before the Revolution, however, the number of financially independent newcomers— people able to provide adequate security of some kind to receive credit, decreased steadily as a proportion of the total transatlantic flow. However, because by then the custom of putting fares on credit was so firmly established that it was virtually irreversible (without losing a share of what was left of the trade), merchants instead found new ways to counteract dwindling profits, as advance payments diminished and passage debts became riskier investments. They did this by including anticipated losses in the postdelivery fare price charged in the American colonies, and they exploited to the fullest the indenture system as a guarantee for a return on

7. Åkerman argues that self-generating elements were built into most migration movements ("Emigrational Processes," 300).

their outlay. In these ways, merchants trimmed their credit policies to meet changes in the migration flow—a tactic that worked for them as long as they could count on the cooperation of their American partners, on whose knowledge of local market conditions they depended for completing their ships' runs successfully. This concerted effort yielded good returns in Philadelphia, where demand for immigrant labor was strong. In contrast, results were generally poor in ports of colonies that had no interest in or tradition of employing German immigrants. How critical such differences in the regional labor markets of the American colonies were for success in the trade in emigrants is underscored by the decision of Rotterdam merchants to consign their emigrant freights primarily to Philadelphia, although they personally had a well-established interest in the rice trade and good connections in Charleston. From their correspondents and partners, they knew that German-speaking settlement projects in the Carolinas— mostly of Swiss colonizers—had fared poorly and that slaves rather than servants provided most of the labor in southern areas. Both signals convinced them to route ships through the Delaware Valley to unload migrants before going south to take on cargoes of rice.

The mercantile specialization developed to exploit a voluntary transatlantic population movement for profit is what distinguishes the German flow to colonial America from all migrations that had preceded it. The long-established colonial transportation of mostly English servants, and the early eighteenth-century Irish passenger trade, were typically handled as a small part of regular business in commodities between the British Isles and America. The outfitting and provisioning of slave ships, becoming more active after 1700, also bore little resemblance to the immigrant trade, because profits for the slave trade were in the resale of slaves, not in the transportation demand of free people, and other uses of slave shipping were limited.

The specialization of the passenger trade, furthermore, portended the ways in which merchants later, over and over, gained from using existing underutilized shipping capacity to offer passage at reasonable terms to satisfy the demands of large numbers of people with limited means from many different parts of Europe who were willing or pressed to emigrate to the United States.[8] By then, however, transatlantic fares were relatively much cheaper, eliminating the need for indentured servitude as one important way to finance the relocation. Sending prepaid tickets had replaced

8. For a detailed analysis of the structure and organization of the Swedish immigrant trade, see Berit Brattne in cooperation with Sune Åkerman, "The Importance of the Transport Sector for Mass Emigration," in *From Sweden to America*, ed. Runblom and Norman, 176–200.

the custom of redemption by relatives and friends on arrival and became an important self-generating element for nineteenth-century migrations. In addition, vastly improved facilities for international communication and banking had made the mediating role of the newlander obsolete. He was in part replaced by the shipping agent, who could help—or exploit— emigrants who were on their way from Europe to America. This role was unambiguously defined by the profit-seeking of shippers and the agent's own personal ambitions.[9]

Developing a full-fledged business in transporting German immigrants was important for establishing a dependable link between principal areas of out-migration in the Rhine lands and what for a long time was either the "best poor man's country" itself or the first step along a path down the Great Valley and the opportunities that awaited in the Piedmont areas of the Upper South.[10] It took the growth of a specific trade in immigrants to make it possible for this transatlantic migration to expand fully, until its tide crested around 1750. Furthermore, any lasting success of merchants with regular and long-term interests in the trade depended on their recognizing and adapting to the fact that both the size and the composition of the emigration from which they profited changed over time. Cooperation among partners in England, Holland, and the American colonies then allowed them to organize the business of transporting foreign peoples, this "trade in strangers," to supplement more fully and flexibly their regular interests as ship owners or freighters in the North Atlantic dry goods and provision trades. Success depended in large part on the ability of the merchants in Holland to monitor who and how many left the Rhine lands. By skillfully exploiting the legal requirements for passage through the Netherlands, the Dutch freighters gained control of the transshipment process, which enabled them to gauge the demand for passage and tie it to circumstances in the colonies that encouraged the importation of new settlers or servants. With such information at hand, leaders in the immigrant trade could adjust their operations to deal with variations in demand and could tailor their pricing policies according to the circumstances of their passengers and, most important, to the conditions of the land and labor markets of greater Pennsylvania.

9. Dirk Hoerder described the organization of the nineteenth-century trade in German emigrants. The parallels to the eighteenth-century business in principle, if not in actual practice, are striking ("The Traffic of Emigration").

10. The continuity of a migration path that connected well-defined areas of out-migration with particular regions in which immigrants settled is recognized to have encouraged and sustained migration flows over long distances and for long periods of time. See Åkerman, "Emigrational Processes," 294.

The structure and dynamics of German immigration to and through colonial Pennsylvania, to which the merchants responded so successfully in the second and third generations of the eighteenth century, characterized later mass migrations across the Atlantic. They reveal the mechanisms that fueled flows of people across the ocean both in the colonial era and in later centuries. The most outstanding feature of the immigration of German-speaking people was the large proportion of families who relocated first together in extended, close-knit groups and then in more fragmented nuclear clusterings of husbands and wives or siblings and cousins. In contrast, the servant trade from England and Ireland that started in the seventeenth century and continued into the eighteenth evolved around the shipping of mostly single men in their teens and early twenties. The substantial later passenger trade from Ulster ports, on the other hand, began in the early 1770s to develop along lines of mass immigration that were comparable to its German predecessor. In this later wave of relocation, the major peak occurred only just before 1800. Exceptionally high numbers in the late 1710s, and again in the late 1720s and in the 1740s, represent crisis times. Irish men seem to have fled with their families to escape famine conditions after bad harvests. The sustained buildup of the wave of emigrants from Ulster ports commenced only shortly before the Revolution.

It bears repeating that starting with a relatively few, reasonably well-off pioneering immigrants is important for successful long-term settlement. Advance parties drew followers to America—from kin, from coreligionists, and from former neighbors in Europe—whether among the colonial Germans and Irish or among the many other groups that came in the nineteenth century. The pathbreaking of these pioneers created temporary migration channels that could develop into more permanent connections if circumstances of settlement proved favorable and stable. That this did not always happen is illustrated by several cases among the pre-Revolutionary Germans from Nova Scotia to Georgia, in which, in contrast to the Pennsylvania experience, settlement efforts never acquired a momentum of their own. Built on personal bonds, the recommendations of former migrants broadened the subsequent flow of newcomers and quickened its flow. It was this positive and long-term link between particular regions in the sending and receiving countries that was largely responsible for the self-generating effect of the migration flow.[11] Without sus-

11. Genealogists and historians who focus on the local level have demonstrated the lasting connections that existed among kin and neighbors in particular areas of emigration in the Rhine lands and corresponding sites of immigrant settlement in the American colonies.

tained connections between regions where immigrants had become established settlers and areas of out-migration, the attraction for emigrants was
generally short-lived—a pattern that was common from the eighteenth
century on for settlement projects that depended heavily on speculations
like those of Jean Pierre Purry and Samuel Waldo. One result of a good
reputation, however, was that the cheap farms and high wages that were
promised became more difficult to obtain—a dilution or deferral of opportunities available to newcomers that soon began to act as a braking
mechanism that slowed and stopped or redirected the immigration flow to
new localities.

In the Delaware Valley, land was being settled at a rapid rate, forcing
settlers to go farther from Philadelphia and even to leave Pennsylvania in
search of farms that were affordable. In this they were soon encouraged by
land speculators for other colonies who hoped to profit from settling
foreign Protestants but who were generally unwilling to bear the cost of
transatlantic transportation themselves—a decisive disadvantage in the
competition for immigrants, many of whom needed credit as soon as they
arrived. At the same time, the growing financial dependence of later migrants on the merchants who channeled the emigration flow to Philadelphia decreased the options for newly arrived settlers, who had to compete in ever larger numbers to find work to pay off their passage debts and
to accumulate enough capital to start out on their own. News of serious
troubles with the Indians in 1754 further undermined Pennsylvania's already waning reputation. War and a policy of distributing "headright"
lands only to free immigrants also slowed the influx to South Carolina and
prevented a major redirection of the migration flow southward. Charleston
never became a replacement for Philadelphia, because greater Pennsylvania
had the only established market for German immigrant labor.

The decline in the flow of German settlers in the 1760s and 1770s was
the combined effect of European governmental restriction on emigration
to the American colonies and the appeal of new settlement projects in
eastern Europe, which were promoted and highly subsidized by Prussia,
Russia, and Austria. Those who still chose to migrate westward usually
had some ties to people already established in the colonies. Among other
newcomers were those of only limited means, who reached the Delaware
through long-standing lines of communication, shipping, and credit among
merchants that continued to recruit and transport German passengers
across the Atlantic. Many of these immigrants were single men, probably
young, who were drawn to the Philadelphia-area labor market rather than

chance establishing new farms in the hinterlands.[12] The onset of the American Revolution virtually finished off substantial German immigration to and through Pennsylvania. Not only was Pennsylvania comparatively less attractive for German immigrants by the time of the war, but changes taking place in Europe also drew heavy numbers of settlers to the East, where relocation reached its peak in the 1780s and 1790s. The combination of American warfare (first for independence and then with various European powers) and East European redevelopment almost stopped German immigration to the newly formed Republic. When, years later, the migration to America resumed, Pennsylvania received only a small portion of the flow, because the pioneering settlements that first anchored and then extended new migration networks now were established farther west.[13]

How newcomers were integrated into life in the colonies depended not only on opportunities for immigrants in general but also on the financial circumstances of the passengers, the conditions of the voyage, and the kind of support they received from those already settled in the New World. Success was relatively easier to obtain for Rhineland immigrants who arrived in the beginning phase of the migration, who brought some capital or labor, and who could count on assistance from kin or former neighbors in learning the ways of the land and in setting up household, farm, or shop. Earning a decent living proved to be more elusive for those who came later, for those who had limited means, for those who had been exploited on their journey, and for those who had only strangers to help them gain a foothold in the new land. As the wave of immigration crested and then tapered off, German newcomers found it more difficult to realize the American dream.[14]

For a sizable portion of immigrants, indentured servitude provided a

12. Most of the German Lutheran immigrants in Philadelphia in the 1760s were poor. Roeber, *Palatines*, 277.

13. Hans-Jürgen Grabbe outlined the later migration ("European Immigration"), which extended already established migration networks and initiated new ones. Such connections between sending and receiving regions is the topic of Charles Tilly, "Transplanted Networks."

14. The leaders and "success stories" of the German communities in the two decades before the American Revolution were mostly men who had begun their careers in the 1730s and 1740s, some of them building directly on the achievements of the pioneering generation of their fathers, others breaking new paths themselves. What is remarkable, however, is the disproportionate share of the early immigrants (1720s–1740s) who left their mark on settlements along the eastern seaboard and in the Great Valley. Among the many hundreds of immigrants whom genealogists and historians have traced from the Rhine lands to North America, those who landed before the peak of immigration around mid-century had a noticeably greater impact than those who arrived in the wake of the pioneering generations.

quick initiation into the new society and determined to a large extent the way in which the immigrants could be integrated into local life. Most of the servants who were bound to a stranger in exchange for debt payment were young and therefore receptive to the new ways of their masters, whether it be in a shop or house or farm. How well they fared depended mainly on "their master's disposition, situation, and rank in society," and to some extent on the servants' ages and circumstances.[15] During the peak of the immigration, the kinds of newcomers who sought indenture became more diverse, and the masters who employed them represented a broader socioeconomic group. Under such circumstances, training was more an economic necessity—the newcomers needed the work for room and board and could not be choosy about the skills they would acquire during their time of service. Ironically, when after the 1750s at least half of all immigrants had to rely on the indenture system as the only realistic option open for defraying their passage debts, the range of prospective employers for newly arrived Germans became more limited and discriminating. Other supplies of labor—immigrants of different ethnic backgrounds, slaves, and, increasingly, free wage workers made up the bulk of the labor market in Pennsylvania.

The evolving pattern of eighteenth-century German immigration to the American colonies reflected an intricate web of many different forces that combined in changing ways over time first to generate, then to sustain, and finally to reduce the tide of about 111,000 newcomers from the Rhine lands who came to North America between 1683 and 1776. Inhabitants of southwestern Germany, where the tradition to migrate in reaction to adversities at home and opportunities elsewhere was already strong, were drawn to follow the example of successful pioneers who had been attracted by the promise of political and personal freedom, religious toleration, and plenty of land and work in the American colonies—Pennsylvania in particular— even though the relocation was difficult and the costs were substantial. Lured by the potential profits to be had from providing large numbers of emigrants with transportation to Philadelphia, merchants devised a system that enabled emigrants of limited means to undertake the voyage. This successful broadening of the pool from which immigrants to the American colonies were recruited resulted in a decline in opportunities in the immediate Delaware Valley region, as the land was taken up and the labor

15. Muhlenberg in *Hallesche Nachrichten*, 1:461.

supply expanded. These changes in turn first diffused and then reduced immigration from Germany.

This distinctive eighteenth-century German migration wave through Philadelphia foreshadowed later movements from Europe to America in three important ways. The systematic role of merchants, who somehow devised a profitable system of cheap transportation that allowed potential emigrants to take advantage of opportunities overseas while making their ocean shipping more profitable, became a standard feature of such migrations. The willingness of the pioneers of this ethnic group and their descendants to assist—and exploit—financially weak relatives and compatriots with their later relocation was another dynamic that has been crucial in generating and maintaining subsequent waves of immigration in American history. Among colonial Germans, this took the form of redeeming passage debts, while the custom in the nineteenth century became to send prepaid tickets. Both made newcomers dependent on their relatives, masters, or employers. The third characteristic feature of the German migration through Philadelphia in its early and peak phases was the large proportion of families among the newcomers.[16] This differed from most English and Irish migrations in the seventeenth century (notable exceptions being the Puritans and the first Quakers who came to the Delaware Valley) but was repeated in later transatlantic flows, which also started with family relocation before shifting toward more single young men and women. The characteristic patterns of the German immigration to the British colonies of North America—a major business relying heavily on links of ethnic identity and support, and based on migration of entire families, not just on young single adults seeking work—presages the many later mass migrations from Europe to the Americas.

The migration that came from the Ulster ports of Ireland in the last third of the eighteenth century was the first wave to echo the model established in the German immigration. Successive characteristic phases were crucial links that connected the sending and receiving regions of the network, and business interests seeking to transport passengers on underutilized shipping for profit were all factors that combined once again to produce another modern-type mass migration.

16. In the migration of the 1770s from Great Britain, two distinct migration streams are discernible: one of young, single men leaving mostly from London, and one of families leaving mostly from rural fringe regions in the north of England and the west of Scotland (Bailyn, *Voyagers to the West*, chap. 5). The first came from old sources, the latter from new recruitment areas—a distinction that similarly unfolded over time as the German migration matured.

Throughout the colonial period, however, geography, North Atlantic trade connections, and ties to the British Empire distinguished the German and Irish migrations. Residents of Ulster who, like their counterparts in the Rhine lands, were attracted to opportunities in the American colonies could relocate there much more freely and directly. In general, Irish emigrants were not legally constrained in their movement away from home and did not have a long and expensive journey to their ports of embarkation. Those were both conditions that held the relocation of Germans in America back. Moreover, emigrants leaving from Irish ports could count on regular and reliable shipping to North America, which meant that emigrants were exposed to the dangers from overcrowding only when the number of emigrants seeking transatlantic passage exceeded the cargo capacity of the vessels normally employed in the Irish commodities trade. That occurred only after the Revolution, when patterns of commerce between Ireland, Great Britain, and the United States shifted away from the mercantile connections that had been typical for the late colonial period. The extensive, routine, and frequent nature of the pre-Revolutionary trade between Ireland and North America also spread the Irish immigration more broadly across the colonies, since merchants of Irish background and with Irish connections had established businesses that created and maintained transatlantic migration networks in all major American harbors. Although the Delaware Valley port towns were again the principal gateway for Irish immigrants, significant numbers of them entered through other colonial ports. Moreover, the steady flow of servants indentured before leaving Europe, and convicts, which made up an important part of the flow of emigrants from Ireland throughout the eighteenth century, distinguished its pre-1760s migration from that of Germany.

The different nature of the Irish immigration during most of the 1700s also affected the character of settlement in the colonies and how immigrants were integrated into American society and culture. People from Ireland were scattered throughout American settlements on the eastern seaboard more broadly, because crucial connections between several colonial and Irish ports had developed in the 1600s and were extended and maintained along lines of various mercantile, religious, and regional interests throughout the eighteenth century. Most of those networks were anchored in the Irish communities of the major colonial harbors—the first stop on the way to a new life in America. Many Irish immigrants, however, settled in the rural areas of the backcountry, because most of them arrived with limited resources. Many were only in their teens and had little choice in the matter until they gained freedom from their masters. The frontier regions offered land and employment, and as settlement expanded westward Irish immigrants followed until the wave of the emigration from Ulster crested in the last quarter of the century as new land opened up beyond the Appalachian mountains.

The significance of the Delaware Valley ports as the gateway to the interior was that clusters of distinct Irish settlements developed in the greater Pennsylvania region. These settlements contributed to the religiously and ethnically mixed character of the middle colonies and the Great Valley. They also brought settlers from different European backgrounds into competition with each other as they sought to capitalize on opportunities and consolidate their gains to form a solid foundation from which their American-born and -raised children could launch their own lives successfully.

In this extension of settlement, new groups of newcomers repeatedly established communities that were different from those of their neighbors in the ways in which they organized local life and relationships and that remained distinctive even when the local mix of inhabitants changed later on.[17] These differences did much to shape the social, political, and cultural life of the region.

The "mixed multitudes" that peopled Pennsylvania more visibly than any other American colony had a profound effect on the development of life in America.[18] The diversity that non-English immigrants brought to the area became an important hallmark of American society and culture. And the mix would not have been so substantial in such a rapidly growing society without a shipping industry that could make relocation a profitable part of its business, spread the word about opportunity in America, and offer affordable transportation to Europeans as immigrants to America rippled out across the continent from 1700 to 1914.

This book has established determining generally what types of people

17. The establishment of charter cultures and the struggle for cultural dominance are themes that Jack Greene recently brought into focus (see *Pursuits of Happiness*). See also, by Greene, "Mastery and the Definition of Cultural Space" and "Search for Identity: An Interpretation of the Meaning of Selected Patterns of Social Response in Eighteenth-Century America," in Greene's *Imperatives, Behaviors, and Identities*, 1–12, 143–73. In addition, see Timothy Breen, "Creative Adaptations: Peoples and Cultures"; and Kulikoff, "Migration and Cultural Divisions."

18. Sally Schwartz made that the title of her book about colonial Pennsylvania: *"A Mixed Multitude": The Struggle for Toleration in Colonial Pennsylvania*.

came to America in this early period, when, under what conditions, into which circumstances, and with what consequences. The next step is to explore systematically the ways in which immigrants at that time adjusted to life in the New World. Whether they began new settlements themselves, or moved as newcomers to established communities, how did they become not "Germans" or "Irish" but Pennsylvanians, New Yorkers, Marylanders, or Carolinians, alongside neighbors who came from quite different origins? This next stage of investigation has to be carried out in many localities of many different types. The mix of peoples with whom Germans or Irish settled varied as widely as the other conditions they encountered for making a living and pursuing their ambitions for living in America.

In settling alongside others unlike themselves, self-perception became a central factor. "Ethnicity," as scholars of more modern migrations have called it, helped newcomers to negotiate space and acquire a sense of their contribution to the greater whole, a sense of belonging in American life. Most newcomers soon recognized and celebrated their achievements and their role in what America was becoming, not just their ability to stay apart from what was going on around them.[19] How Germans and Irish saw themselves, and how they fitted into the complex circumstances surrounding them, however, was greatly affected by how and when they came and where and how well they settled. Much of that was determined by the history of their migrations. For instance, successful transplantation of Old World traditions could occur most easily in settlements where newcomers from the same region, of the same religious background, clustered in sufficient number with adequate resources, and under competent and stable leadership. Other kinds of "success" in American terms were better achieved by quickly learning to work with others in conditions of mixed settlement and mutual interdependence.

By the late colonial period, the children and grandchildren of immigrants were no longer simply "German" or "Irish" in terms of the origins of their forebears but a complex blend of memories of the homeland,

---

19. For a recent summary of questions concerning ethnicity and assimilation, see Kathleen Conzen et al., "The Invention of Ethnicity"; Edward Kantowicz, "Ethnicity," in Mary Kupiec Cayton et al., eds., *Encyclopedia of American Social History*, vol. 1 (New York 1993), 453–66; Russell Kazal, "Revisiting Assimilation"; Ewa Morawska, "In Defense of the Assimilation Model"; Werner Sollors, ed., *The Invention of Ethnicity*; Virginia Yans-McLaughlin, ed., *Immigration Reconsidered.*

experiences in America, and re-creations of an Old World past they no longer knew firsthand but could now afford to cultivate, once they felt secure in their place in American society. Before the nineteenth and twentieth centuries arrived, it had become commonplace for the new society to develop by including and incorporating a broader and broader array of strangers.

Appendix

German Immigrant Voyages, 1683–1775

Appendix: German Immigrant Voyages, 1683–1775

I.D. No.[1]	Name of Ship[2]	Type of Ship[3]	Tons[4]	Name of Captain[5]	Port of Embark.[6]	Date of Departure[7]	Name(s) of Merchant(s)[8]	Stopover Port[9]	Date of Departure	Port of Disembark.[10]	Date of Arrival[11]	Name(s) of Merchant(s)[12]	No. of Men; Pass./Freights[13]	Best Estimate[14]
1	William & Sarah			Hill, William	R'dam			Dover		Phila	18-09-1727		104;(400)[15]	400
2	James Goodwill			Crockat, David	R'dam			Falmouth		Phila	27-09-1727		54;167(220)	167
3	Molly			Hodgeson, John	R'dam			Deal[16]	14-06-1727	Phila	30-09-1727		70;(300)	298
4	Adventure	(Galley)		Mirion, John	R'dam			Plymouth		Phila	02-10-1727		53;(220)	140
5	Friendship (Bristol)			Davies, John	R'dam			Cowes		Phila	16-10-1727		45;(190)	193
6	Mortonhouse			Coultas, John	R'dam			Deal (Dover)	15-06-1728	Phila	23-08-1728		80;205	205
7	Albany			Oxman, Lazarus	R'dam	15-06-1728		Portsmouth[17]	a08-07-1728	Phila	04-09-1728		31	100[18]
8	James Goodwill			Crockat, David	R'dam			Deal[19]	15-06-1728	Phila	11-09-1728		42	90
9	Mortonhouse			Coultas, James	R'dam			Deal	21-06-1729	Phila	17-08-1729		74;176[20]	176
10	Allen			Craiges, James	R'dam			Cowes	07-07-1729	Phila	11-09-1729		61;124	124
11	Thistle (Glasgow)			Dunlop, Collin	R'dam			Dover	19-06-1730	Phila	29-08-1730		76	260
12	Alexander & Anne			Clymer, William[22]	R'dam		Clymer Co.[21]	Deal	20-96-1730	Phila	05-09-1730	Clymer	46	130
13	Joyce			Ford, William[22]	R'dam		[Hope Co.][23]	(Boston)		Phila	30-11-1930		24;57	57
14	Samuel			Percy, Hugh	R'dam			Cowes		Phila	16-08-1731		39;109/88[24]	109
15	Pa. Merchant (London)			Stedman, John	R'dam			Dover		Phila	10-09-1731		57;172	172
16	Britannia (London)			Franklin, Michael	R'dam*	a18-07-1731		Cowes		Phila	21-09-1731		106;269	269
17	Lowther	Snow		Fisher, Joseph	R'dam			Dover		Phila	14-10-1731	Fisher	33;78[25]	78
18	Norris[26]			Loyd, Thomas	R'dam			(Boston)		Phila	15-05-1732		13	34
19	Samuel			Percy, Hugh	R'dam			Cowes		Phila	11-08-1732		106;270	270
20	Pa. Merchant (London)			Stedman, John	R'dam			Plymouth		Phila	11-09-1732		70;168	168
21	Johnson (London)	(Galley)		Crockat, David	R'dam			Deal[27]	06-08-1732	Phila	18-09-1732		112;306	306
22	Plaisance	Pink		Paret, John	R'dam		Venyloeg[28]	Cowes		Phila	12-09-1732		77;190[29]	190
23	Adventure	Pink		Curson, Robert	R'dam[*]			Cowes		Phila	23-09-1732		58;147	147
24	Loyal Judith	Pink		Turpin, Robert	R'dam			Cowes	25-09-1732[30]	Phila	25-09-1732[30]		119	325
25	Mary			Gray, John	R'dam			Cowes		Phila	26-09-1732		64;186	186
26	Dragon			Hargrave, Charles	R'dam			Plymouth		Phila	30-09-1732		70;185	185
27	Pleasant			Morris, James	R'dam*			Deal		Phila	11-10-1732		56	153
28	John & William	Pink		Tymberton, Constable	R'dam*	a08-07-1732		Dover	06-08-1732	Phila	17-10-1732		71;169[31]	169
29	Samuel			Percy, Hugh	R'dam			Deal[32]	15-06-1733	Phila	17-08-1733		90;292(300)[33]	292
30	Elizabeth (London)			Lee, Edward	R'dam			Dover	14-06-1733	Phila	27-08-1733		64;176	176
31	Hope	(Galley)		Reid, Daniel	R'dam[*]			Cowes		Phila	28-08-1733		88;231	231

No.	Ship	Rig	Tons	Master	From	Date	Consignee	Port	Cleared	Arrived	Agent	Counts	Total
32	Pa. Merchant (London)		155	Stedman, John	R'dam			Plymouth	12-07-1733 Phila	18-09-1733		71;191[34]	191
33	Richard & Elizabeth	Brig		Clymer, Christopher	R'dam			Plymouth	Phila	28-09-1733		44;138	138
34	Mary			Benn, James	R'dam			Plymouth	Phila	29-09-1733		55;171	171
35	Charming Betty			Ball, John	London			= London	Phila	11-10-1733		16;63	63
36	St. Andrew	(Galley)		Stedman, John	R'dam			Plymouth	Phila	12-09-1734	Shoemaker[36]	89;265[35]	265
37	Hope	(Galley)		Reid, Daniel	R'dam			Cowes	Phila	23-09-1734	Shoemaker	51;127	127
38	Mercury			Wilson, William	R'dam			Cowes	Phila	29-05-1735[37]		61;185	185
39	Mary	Brig	50	Marshall, James	London			= London	Phila	28-06-1735		13;39	39
40	Oliver	Billinder		Merchant, Samuel	[R'dam]			[SC]	Phila	26-08-1735		18;44[38]	44
41	Harle			Harle, Ralph	R'dam			Cowes	Phila	01-09-1736	Shoemaker	152;298(388)[39]	298
42	Princess Augusta			Merchant, Samuel	R'dam	23-07-1736	Stedman Co.[41]	Dover	Phila	16-09-1736	Shoemaker	118;(340)[40]	328
43	John	Brig	120	Fraiser, George	R'dam			Cowes	Phila	19-10-1736	Stedman	37	110
44	Samuel			Percy, Hugh	R'dam			Cowes	Phila	30-08-1737	Shoemaker	109;(300)	273
45	Molly	Snow		Howell, John	A'dam +		Clarkson[42]	Dover	09-07-1737 Phila	10-09-1737		31	78
46	Virtuous Grace			Bull [Ball], John	R'dam			Cowes	Phila	24-09-1737	Shoemaker	75;(150)	188
47	St. Andrew			Stedman, John	R'dam			Cowes	Phila	26-09-1737		142;(415)	356
48	Townsend			Thompson, Thomas	A'dam +		Clarkson	Cowes	Phila	05-10-1737		78;231	231
49	Charming Nancy (Phila)[43]		115	Stedman, Charles	R'dam	29-06-1737	Stedman Co.	Plymouth	08-07-1737 Phila	08-10-1737	Stedman Co.	117;249	249
50	William (London)			Carter, John	A'dam +			Dover	Phila	31-10-1737		68;(180,220)	178
51	Catherine	Brig	70	Phillips, Jacob	London			= London	Phila	27-07-1738		8	22
52	Winter	(Galley)		Paynter, Edward	R'dam			Deal	Phila	05-09-1738		140;253(300)	253
53	Glasgow	(Galley)	200	Sterling, Walter	R'dam			Cowes	Phila	09-09-1738	Shoemaker	120;349[44]	349
54	Two Sisters (Phila)	Snow	50	Marshall, James	R'dam	c04-06-1738	Hope Co. Marshall[46]	Cowes	04-07-1738 Phila	09-09-1738	Shoemaker	41;110	110
55	Robert & Alice			Goodman, Walter	R'dam			Dover	Phila	11-09-1738		106	289[45]
56	Queen Elizabeth			Hope, Alexander	R'dam			Deal	Phila	16-09-1738	Shoemaker	104;324	324
57	Thistle	(Galley)	240	Wilson, John	R'dam	c20-06-1738	Andrew[48]	Plymouth	Phila	19-09-1738	[Penrose][47]	95	259
58	Friendship		160	Beech, Henry	R'dam			Dover	Phila	b14-09-1738	Shoemaker	87;282	282
59	Nancy[50]			Wallace, William	R'dam			Dover	Phila	b14-09-1738		70	191[49]
60	Fox			Ware, Charles	R'dam			Plymouth	Phila	12-10-1738		47;(135)	128
61	Davy			Patton, William	A'dam			Plymouth	Phila	25-10-1738		94	257[51]
62	St. Andrew			Stedman, John	R'dam			Cowes	Phila	27-10-1738	Andrew Co.	119	328[52]
63	Thistle (Phila)	Billinder		Houston, George	R'dam			Cowes	Phila	28-10-1738	[Penrose]	42;142[53]	142
64	Elizabeth			Hodgeson, George	R'dam			Cowes	Phila	30-10-1738	[Penrose]	43	117
65	Charming Nancy (Phila)		115	Stedman, Charles	R'dam		Stedman Co.	Cowes	Phila	09-11-1738	Andrew Co.	65	177[54]
66	Enterprise			Wood, Lyonell	London			= London	Phila	06-12-1738		31	84
67	London (London)	Billinder		Pipon, Joshua	London			= London	Phila	08-01-1738/9		21	57
68	Jamaica	(Galley)	140	Harrison, Robert	R'dam*	c20-10-1738	Andrew	Cowes	05-06-1739 Phila	07-02-1738/9	Andrew	89	243
69	Samuel			Percy, Hugh	R'dam			Deal[55]	Phila	27-08-1739		111;(300)	303
70	Betsy	Snow		Budden, Richard	R'dam			Deal	Phila	27-08-1739		61;(180)	166
71	Robert & Alice			Goodman, Walter	R'dam			Deal	Phila	03-09-1739		78;218	258

I.D. No.[1]	Name of Ship[2]	Type of Ship[3]	Tons[4]	Name of Captain[5]	Port of Embark.[6]	Date of Departure[7]	Name(s) of Merchant(s)[8]	Stopover Port[9]	Date of Departure	Port of Disembark.[10]	Date of Arrival[11]	Name(s) of Merchant(s)[12]	No. of Men; Pass./Freights[13]	Best Estimate[14]
72	Friendship			Vitery, William	R'dam			Deal		Phila	03-09-1739		58;(160)	161
73	Loyal Judith			Paynter, Edward	R'dam			Deal		Phila	03-09-1739		91;(300)	248
74	Lydia (Phila)[56]		70	Allen, James	London		Stedman Co.	= London		Phila	11-12-1739	Stedman Co.	23	63
75	Friendship		160	Vitery, William	R'dam			Cowes		Phila	23-09-1740		49	134
76	Lydia (Phila)		70	Allen, James	R'dam	11-07-1740		Dover[57]		Phila	27-09-1740	[Stedman Co.]	68;(180)	186
77	Samuel & Elizabeth			Chilton, William	R'dam			Deal		Phila	30-09-1740	Stedman Co.	56;(206)	153
78	Loyal Judith			Paynter, Lovell	R'dam			Deal		Phila	25-11-1740		96	262
79	Robert & Alice			Goodman, Walter	R'dam			Cowes	14-07-1740	Phila	03-12-1740		64	175
80	Samuel			Percy, Hugh	R'dam			Dover[58]		Phila	03-12-1740		71	194
81	Francis & Ann	Snow		Coatam, Thomas	R'dam			St. Christopher		Phila	30-05-1741		15	41
82	Marlborough[59]		100	Bell, Thomas	R'dam			Cowes	08-07-1741	Phila	23-09-1741		72	196
83	St. Mark[60]		150	Wilson, William	R'dam		Hope Co.	Cowes	08-07-1741	Phila	26-09-1741		102;(300?)	278
84	Lydia (Phila)[61]		70/280	Allen, James	R'dam		Stedman Co.	Deal		Phila	29-09-1741	Stedman Co.	71	194
85	St. Andrew[62]		150/280	Stedman, Charles	R'dam			Cowes		Phila	04-10-1741		103	281
86	Friendship[63]		130/160	Thompson, Alexander	R'dam		[Percy]	Cowes	26-07-1741	Phila	12-10-1741		67;(300)	183
87	Molly[64]		100	Olive, Thomas	R'dam		Wilkins[65]	Deal		Phila	12-10-1741		76;(200)	207
88	Molly			Cranch, John	R'dam			Deal		Phila	26-10-1741		47	128
89	Thane of Fife	Snow	110	Weems, William	R'dam*	17-07-1741	Hope Co.	Aberdeen		Phila	07-11-1741		21	57
90	Europa (London)		160	Lumsden, Robert	R'dam*	20-08-1741		Lewes, Del[66]	03-09-1741	Phila	17-11-1741	[Penrose]	65	177
91	Catherine	Snow	90	Gladman, Thomas	London			New London		Phila	28-05-1742		28;44[67]	44
92	Mary	Brig		Mason, John	R'dam			Cowes		Phila	25-08-1742		29;(100)	79
93	Loyal Judith		180	Cowie, James	R'dam			Cowes		Phila	03-09-1742		90;(400)	246
94	Francis & Elizabeth		300	North, George	R'dam			Deal		Phila	21-09-1742	Strettle[68]	149	407
95	Robert & Alice			Cusack, Martly	R'dam			Cowes		Phila	24-09-1742		75	205
96	Francis & Elizabeth		300	North, George	R'dam			Cowes		Phila	30-08-1743		85	232
97	Loyal Judith			Cowie, James	R'dam			Cowes		Phila	02-09-1743	Strettle	108	295
98	Charlotta		180	Mason, John	R'dam			Cowes		Phila[69]	05-09-1743	Strettle Co.	48	131
99	Lydia		70	Abercrombie, James	R'dam			Cowes		Phila	19-09-1743	Andrew	72	196
100	Rosanna	Ship	100	Reason, James	R'dam		[Carson][70]	Cowes		Phila	26-09-1743		65	177
101	Phoenix (Phila)		200	Wilson, William	R'dam		Wilson[71]	Cowes		Phila	30-09-1743		83	226
102	Robert & Alice			Cusack, Martly	R'dam			Cowes		Phila	30-09-1743		70	191
103	St. Andrew[72]			Brown, Robert	R'dam		[Stedman Co.]	Cowes		Phila	07-10-1743	Stedman Co.	93	254
104	Endeavor	Snow		Anderson, Thomas	London			= London		Phila	10-11-1743		5	14
105	Aurora		200	Pickeman, Robert	R'dam*		Stedman	Cowes	c12-07-1744	Phila	08-10-1744	Stedman Co.	81;(390)[73]	221
106	Phoenix		200	Wilson, William	R'dam		Wilson	Cowes		Phila	20-10-1744	Wilson	110;(300)	300
107	Friendship		160	Mason, John	R'dam*	[17-06-1744]		Cowes	c25-07-1744	Phila[74]	02-11-1744	Strettle Co.	74	202
108	Carterel			Stevenson, Nicholas	R'dam			Portsmouth		Phila	11-12-1744	Shoemaker	34	93
109	Muscliffe	(Galley)	150	Durell, George	R'dam	a07-07-1744	Trimble[75]	Poole	17-09-1744	Phila	22-12-1744	Stedman Co.	79	216

No.	Ship	Type/Tons	Captain	Port	Departed	Merchant	Port of call	Arrival	Phila date	Phila merchant	Numbers	Total
110	Ann	(Galley)	Wilson, William	R'dam	17-06-1746	[Hope Co.]	Leith	00-06-1746 Phila	02-09-1746	Shoemaker	90;(250)	246
111	Neptune	Billinder 100	Wilkinson, Thomas	R'dam	21-06-1746	[Stewart][77]	Leith	Phila	25-10-1746	Strettle Co.	67;(300)	183
112	Vernon	70	Ricks, Thomas	R'dam*	12-06-1747	Stedman	Leith	Phila	c27-08-1747	Stedman Co.	55;(150)	150
113	Lydia		Tiffin, William	London			= London		27-07-1747		14	38
114	Restauration		Hall, James	R'dam	07-07-1747	[Stedman Co.]	Leith	06-07-1747 Phila	09-10-1747	Stedman Co.	134;(350)	365
115	Two Brothers		Arnott, Thomas	R'dam			Leith	Phila	13-10-1747	Shoemaker Co.[78]	96;(150)	262
116	James & Janet (Borrowstone)	140	Muir [Moor], William	R'dam*	c10-07-1747	Stedman	Leith	Phila	20-10-1747	Shoemaker Co.	44;(250)	120
117	Edinburgh		Russell, James	R'dam	19-07-1748		Portsmouth	17-07-1748 Phila	05-09-1748	Shoemaker Co.	127	347[79]
118	Hampshire (Poole)	150	Cheesman, Thomas	R'dam*	01-07-1748	Stedman	Falmouth[80]	02-08-1748 Phila	07-09-1748	Stedman	78;213	213[81]
119	Mary	(Galley)	Lawson, George	London			= London	24-07-1748 Phila	07-09-1748	Smith Co.[82]	25	68
120	Two Brothers		Arnott, Thomas	R'dam	19-07-1748	Hope Co.	Portsmouth	30-07-1748 Phila	15-09-1748	Shoemaker Co.	105	287
121	Judith		Tait, James	R'dam	19-07-1748	[Stedman Co.]	Cowes	30-07-1748 Phila	15-09-1748	Stedman Co.	52;166	166
122	Patience	80	Brown, John	R'dam	19-07-1748	[Stedman Co.]	Cowes	30-07-1748 Phila	16-09-1748	Stedman Co.	124;325	325
123	Patience & Margaret		Govan, John	R'dam		[Stedman Co.]	Leith	25-08-1748 Phila	25-10-1748	Stedman Co.	71;165	165
124	Elliot	180	Adams, James	R'dam	11-06-1749	Stedman	Cowes	20-06-1749 Phila	24-08-1749	Stedman Co.	87;240(250)/180	240
125	Crown	220	James, Michael	R'dam	12-06-1749		Cowes	09-07-1749 Phila	30-08-1749	Pemberton Co.[83]	134	395
126	Chesterfield (Phila)		Coatam, Thomas	R'dam	20-06-1749	[Searl][84]	Cowes	09-07-1749 Phila	02-09-1749		87;256	256
127	Albany (Glasgow)	220	Brown, Robert	R'dam*	20-06-1749	Brown[85]	Cowes	09-07-1749 Phila	02-09-1749	Stedman Co.	105;285	285
128	St. Andrew		Abercrombie, James	R'dam			Plymouth	09-09-1749			116;405	405[86]
129	Priscilla		Muir, William	R'dam	20-06-1749	[Stedman Co.]	Cowes	09-07-1749 Phila	11-09-1749	Stedman Co.	77;293	293
130	Christian (Glasgow)	220	Brady, Thomas[87]	R'dam*	c25-09-1749	Stedman	Cowes	08-07-1749 Phila	13-09-1749	Stedman Co.	111;300/255	300
131[88]	Two Brothers		Arnott, Thomas	R'dam	09-07-1749		Cowes	08-07-1749 Phila	14-09-1749	Shoemaker Co.	109	321
132	Edinburg		Russell, James	R'dam			Portsmouth	08-07-1749 Phila	15-09-1749	Shoemaker Co.	163; /360	445
133	Phoenix	200	Mason, John	R'dam	09-07-1749		Cowes	08-07-1749 Phila	15-09-1749	Shoemaker Co.	261; /550	674
134	Patience	80	Steel, Hugh	R'dam	15-07-1749	[Stedman Co.]	Cowes	01-08-1749 Phila	19-09-1749	Stedman Co.	137; /270	327
135	Speedwell		Creagh, James	R'dam	10-07-1749		Cowes	14-08-1749 Phila	25-09-1749	Philpot Co.[89]	85;240/215	240
136	Ranier (Ramsgate)	200	Browning, Henry	R'dam*	21-07-1749	Hope Co.	Cowes	14-08-1749 Phila	26-09-1749	[Shoemaker Co.]	127; /277	343
137	Dragon[92]		Spencer, George	R'dam*	21-07-1749	[Spencer]	Deal	09-08-1749 Phila	26-09-1749	Spencer[90]	153; /503[730±]	367[91]
138	Isaac (London)	200	Mitchell, Robert	R'dam*	c06-08-1749	Stedman	Cowes	14-08-1749 Phila	27-09-1749	Stedman	79; /206	261
139	Ann		Spurrier, John	R'dam	20-06-1749		Cowes	17-06-1749 Phila	28-09-1749	Shoemaker Co.	105; /242	301
140	Jacob		DeGrove, Adolph	A'dam			Shields, New		02-10-1749		107;249	249
141	Leslie		Ballendine, J.	R'dam	09-08-1749		Cowes	21-08-1749 Phila	07-10-1749	Kickey[93]	121;400	400
142	Lydia		Randolph, John	R'dam			Cowes		01-10-1749	Strettle Co.	154; /376	471
143	Dragon		Nicholas, Daniel	R'dam			Portsmouth	21-08-1749 Phila	17-10-1749		88;244	244
144	Fane	300	Hyndman, William	R'dam*	c03-07-1749	Stanton[94]	Cowes	21-08-1749 Phila	17-10-1749	[Shoemaker Co.]	120; /285	356
145	Good Intent	150	Boswell, Benjamin	R'dam*	c01-09-1749	Hope Co.	Cowes	09-09-1749 Phila[95]	09-11-1749		26;76	76
146	Patience	80	Steel, Hugh	R'dam		[Stedman Co.]	Cowes	23-06-1750 Phila	11-08-1750	Stedman Co.	124; /266	327
147	Bennet	(Galley)	Wadham, John	R'dam			Portsmouth		13-08-1750	Pemberton	94; /260	331
148	Edinburg		Russell, James	R'dam	22-06-1750		Cowes		13-08-1750	Shoemaker Co.	151; /314	384
149	Royal Union		Nicholson, Clement	R'dam			Portsmouth		15-08-1750		156;500/350	500
150	St. Andrew		Brown, Robert	R'dam	22-06-1750	[Stedman Co.][97]	Cowes	23-06-1750 Phila	18-08-1750	Stedman Co.	102;279	279
151	Anderson (Phila)	220/100	Campbell, Hugh	R'dam	22-06-1750	Stedman Co.[98]	Cowes	23-06-1750 Phila	21-08-1750	[Blair, Wm][96]	91; /202½	250
152	Brothers (Phila)	110	Muir, William	R'dam		Stedman Co.	Cowes	23-06-1750 Phila	24-08-1750		91;271/198	271

I.D. No.[1]	Name of Ship[2]	Type of Ship[3]	Tons[4]	Name of Captain[5]	Port of Embark.[6]	Date of Departure[7]	Name(s) of Merchant(s)[8]	Stopover Port[9]	Date of Departure	Port of Disembark.[10]	Date of Arrival[11]	Name(s) of Merchant(s)[12]	No. of Men; Pass./Freights[13]	Best Estimate[14]
153	Two Brothers		200	Arnott, Thomas	R'dam			Cowes	23-06-1750	Phila	28-08-1750	Shoemaker Co.	100	295
154	Phoenix		100	Mason, John	R'dam	22-06-1750		Cowes	23-06-1750	Phila	28-08-1750	Shoemaker Co.[99]	222;339	339
155	Nancy (Phila)[100]		100	Coatam, Thomas	R'dam	01-07-1750	Stedman Co.[101]	Cowes	25-06-1750	Phila	31-08-1750		91;270	270
156	Priscilla			Wilson, William	R'dam			Cowes	c30-06-1750	Phila	12-09-1750	Shoemaker Co.	75;210	210
157	Osgood			Wilkie, William	R'dam			Cowes	28-07-1750	Phila	29-09-1750		145;486	486[102]
158	Sally			Hazelton, William	London			Cowes	c31-07-1750	Phila	17-10-1750		25	74
159	Brotherhood			Thompson, John	R'dam	31-07-1750		Cowes	28-07-1750	Phila	01-11-1750		124;300	300
160	Sandwich			Hazelwood, Thomas	R'dam*		Harvart[104]	Cowes	24-07-1750	Phila[103]	30-11-1750		117; /200	236
161	Anderson		220/100	Campbell, Hugh	R'dam*	16-06-1751	Stedman Co.	Cowes	c04-07-1751		25-08-1751	Stedman Co.	100;(300[105]/236	294
162	Elizabeth		140	Castle [Cool], Richard	R'dam*	16-06-1751	Stedman Co.	Cowes		Phila	05-09-1751	Stedman Co.	91; /130	147
163	Shirley			Allen, James	R'dam		[Stedman Co.]	Orkneys		Phila	05-09-1751	Stedman Co.	120; /288	360
164	Patience			Steel, Hugh	R'dam	01-07-1751	[Stedman Co.]	Cowes	10-07-1751	Phila	09-09-1751	Stedman Co.	110; /255	317
165	St. Andrew			Abercrombie, James	R'dam	05-07-1751	[Stedman Co.]	Cowes	10-07-1751	Phila	14-09-1751	Stedman Co.	100; /280	357
166	Duke of Bedford		178	Jefferys, Richard	R'dam	12-07-1751	Oursel Co.[106]	Portsmouth	20-07-1751	Phila	14-09-1751	Pole[107]	139; /260	312
167	Edinburg			Russell, James	R'dam	05-07-1751		Cowes	10-07-1751	Phila	16-09-1751	Shoemaker Co.	160; /345	424
168	Nancy		100	Coatam, Thomas	R'dam	21-06-1751	[Stedman Co.]	Cowes	10-07-1751	Phila	16-09-1751	Stedman Co.	78; /200	252
169	Brothers (Phila)		110	Muir, William	R'dam			Cowes	10-07-1751	Phila	16-09-1751	Stedman Co.	94; /200	246
170	Two Brothers			Arnott, Thomas	R'dam		[Stedman Co.]	Cowes	10-07-1751	Phila	21-09-1751	Stedman Co.	112; /239	294
171	Neptune			Wier, James	R'dam			Cowes	29-07-1751	Phila	23-09-1751	Pemberton	85; /154	184
172	Neptune			Mason, John	R'dam	05-07-1751		Cowes	15-07-1751	Phila	23-09-1751	Shoemaker Co.	146; /300	366
173	Phoenix		200	Spurrier, John	R'dam*	12-07-1751	Oursel Co.[108]	Portsmouth	29-07-1751	Phila	25-09-1751	Shoemaker Co.	182; /412	511
174	Queen of Denmark		240	Parish, George	R'dam*	a08-07-1751	Stedman Co.	Cowes	29-07-1751	Phila	04-10-1751	Stedman Co.	99; /251	316
175	Janet		250	Cunningham, William	R'dam*	a13-07-1751	Stedman Co.	Cowes	10-08-1751	Phila	07-10-1751	Stedman Co.	99; /220	272
176	Duke of Württemberg		400	Montpelier, Daniel	R'dam*	a22-07-1751	Curtius[109]	Cowes	14-08-1751	Phila	16-10-1751	Curtius Co.	169; /406	508
177	Two Brothers		300	Arnott, Thomas	R'dam			Cowes	a07-07-1752	Phila	15-09-1752	Shoemaker Co.	101	298
178	Edinburg		110	Russell, James	R'dam*	24-07-1752	Dunlop Co.[110]	Cowes	13-07-1752	Phila	19-09-1752	Shoemaker Co.	104	307
179	Brothers (Phila)			Muir, William	R'dam		[Stedman Co.]	Cowes	24-06-1752	Phila	22-09-1752	Stedman Co.	83	245
180	Halifax (Phila)		180	Coatam, Thomas	R'dam[*]		Stedman Co.[111]	Cowes	a07-07-1752	Phila	22-09-1752	Stedman Co.	147	437
181	St. Andrew			Abercrombie, James	R'dam[*]		[Stedman Co.]	Plymouth	a02-07-1752	Phila	23-09-1752	Stedman Co.	111	327
182	Ann	Ship	200	Kenneway, Charles	R'dam	28-06-1752	Dunlop Co.	Portsmouth	16-06-1752	Phila	23-09-1752		75; /230	297
183	Richard & Mary			Moore, John	R'dam			Portsmouth	20-06-1752	Phila	26-09-1752		91; /219½	275
184	Anderson		220/100	Campbell, Hugh	R'dam*	30-05-1752	Dunlop Co.	Portsmouth	a19-07-1752	Phila	27-09-1752	Shoemaker Co.	85; /246	315
185	President (Glasgow)		230	Dunlop, William	R'dam*	20-06-1752	Harvart	Cowes	24-06-1752	Phila	27-09-1752	Shoemaker Co.	73; /237	307
186	Nancy		100	Ewing, John	R'dam		[Stedman Co.]	Cowes		Phila[112]	27-09-1752	Stedman Co.	85	251
187	Neptune		240	Mason, John[113]	R'dam*	05-07-1752	Rocquette[114]	Cowes	a24-07-1752	Phila	04-10-1752		169	498

No.	Ship	Captain	Emb.	Cap.	Dep. date	Merchant (Europe)	Last port	Cleared / dest.	Arrival	Merchant (America)	Passengers	Total
188	Forest	Auchterlon, Patrick	R'dam				Portsmouth	13-07-1752 Phila	10-10-1752	Hamilton, A	108; /245	304
189	Kitty[115] (Liverpool)	Barnes, Theophilus	R'dam*	200	10-07-1752	Rocquette Co.	Portsmouth	13-07-1752 Phila	16-10-1752	Curtius[116]	75	221
190	Duke of Württemberg	Montpelier, Daniel	R'dam*	400/200	20-07-1752	Curtius	Cowes	03-08-1752 Phila	20-10-1752	Howell Co.[117]	143	422
191	Rawley [Raleigh]	Grove, John	R'dam*	400/[200?]	26-07-1752	Oursel	Plymouth	Phila	23-10-1752	Howell Co.	137; /300	370
192	Phoenix	Spurrier, John	Hbg		07-08-1752		Portsmouth	03-09-1752 Phila	02-11-1752	Keppele[118]	208	614
193	Queen of Denmark	Parish, George	R'dam*			Oursel	Cowes	10-08-1752 Phila	03-11-1752	Stedman/Howell[119]	131	386
194	Louisa	Pittcaime, John	R'dam		14-08-1752		Cowes	10-08-1752 Phila	08-11-1752	Pemberton	71	209
195	Phoenix	Honor, Ruben	Hbg				Cowes	Phila	22-11-1752	Shoemaker Co.	150; /500	650[120]
196	St. Michael	Ellis, Thomas	Hbg	140			Cowes	11-06-1753 Phila	08-09-1753	Keppele	74	218[121]
197	Beulah[122] (Phila)	Richy, John	R'dam				Cowes	08-09-1753 Phila	10-09-1753	Shoemaker Co.	87	256[123]
198	Queen of Denmark	Parish, George	Hamburg				Portsmouth	10-09-1753 Phila	11-09-1753	Shoemaker Co.	101	298
199	Edinburg	Russell, James	R'dam		10-07-1752	[Stedman Co.]	Cowes	Phila[124]	14-09-1753	Shoemaker Co.	167; /352	431
200	Patience	Steel, Hugh	R'dam	80			Cowes	25-07-1753 Phila	15-09-1753	Stedman Co.	110	324
201	Richard & Mary	Moore, John	R'dam				Cowes	Phila	17-09-1753	Shoemaker Co.	108	318
202	Leathley	Lickely, John	Hamburg				Cowes	11-06-1753 Phila	19-09-1753	Stedman Co.[126]	52	153
203	Neptune	Mason, John	R'dam				Cowes	08-07-1753 Phila	24-09-1753	Okill, George	146	431
204	Peggy (Phila)	Abercrombie, James	R'dam	[250]/120		Abercrombie[125]	Plymouth	03-08-1753 Phila	24-09-1753	Stedman Co.	140	413
205	Brothers (Phila)	Muir, William	R'dam	110		[Stedman Co.]	Cowes	30-07-1753 Phila	26-09-1753	Shoemaker Co.	91	268
206	Windsor	Goad, John	R'dam				Cowes	c20-07-1753 Phila	28-09-1753	Shoemaker Co.[127]	64	184
207	Halifax (Phila)	Coatam, Thomas	R'dam	180		[Stedman Co.]	Portsmouth	18-07-1753 Phila	28-09-1753	Greenway Co.[128]	103	304
208	Two Brothers	Arnot, Thomas	R'dam				Cowes	08-07-1753 Phila	29-09-1753	Keppele	96	283
209	Rowand (Glasgow)	Tran, Arthur	R'dam*	140	c06-07-1753	Harvart	Cowes	30-07-1753 Phila	01-10-1753	Stedman Co.	109	321
210	Good Hope	Trump, John	Hamburg			Harvart	Cowes	11-06-1753 Phila	02-10-1753	Stedman Co.	53	156
211	Edinburgh	Lion, John	R'dam*	200	c26-05-1754		Cowes	28-07-1753 Phila	03-10-1753	Willing Co.[129]	104	307
212	Louisa	Pittcaime, John	R'dam			[Stedman Co.]	Cowes	30-07-1753 Phila	03-10-1753	Stedman Co.	77	227
213	Eastern Branch	Nevin, James	R'dam	180		Hope Co.	Portsmouth	31-07-1753 Phila		Stedman Co.	87; /(200)	248
214	Friendship	Seix, James	Hamburg				Cowes	Phila		Keppele	56	165
215	Nancy	Ewing, John	R'dam	100		[Stedman Co.]	Cowes	18-07-1753 Phila	14-09-1754	Shoemaker Co.	87; /200	248
216	Barclay	Brown, John	R'dam	120	02-07-1753	[Stedman Co.]	Cowes	01-08-1754 Phila	14-09-1754	Stedman Co.	116; /250	303
217	Adventure (London)	Jackson, Joseph	Hamburg				Plymouth[131]	Phila	25-09-1754	Shoemaker Co.	77;240	240
218	Richard & Mary	Moore, John	R'dam		31-07-1754	[Stedman Co.]	Cowes	Phila	30-09-1754	Keppele	90; /230	290
219	Brothers (Phila)	Muir, William	R'dam	110	22-07-1754	[Stedman Co.]	Cowes	Phila	30-09-1754	Shoemaker Co.	101;250/210	250
220	Edinburg	Russel, James	R'dam*		31-07-1754	Harvart Co.	Cowes	Phila	30-09-1754	Shoemaker Co.	190;(360)	560
221	Neptune	Wier, James	R'dam*	200	22-07-1754		Cowes	Phila	30-09-1754	Keppele	142;(400)/260	400
222	Phoenix	Spurrier, John	R'dam	200			Cowes	Phila	01-10-1754	Shoemaker Co.	239;(860)554/300	554[132]
223	Peggy (Phila)	Abercrombie, James	R'dam*	250/120	c19-07-1754	Rocquette[133]	Portsmouth	Phila	16-10-1754	[Howell Co.]	108	319
224	Friendship	Ross, Charles	A'dam+	250		Benezet	Portsmouth	Phila	21-10-1754	Benezet	118; /301	380
225	Bannister	Doyle, John	A'dam			[Benezet]	Cowes	Phila	21-10-1754	Benezet	83	245
226	Henrietta (Phila)	Ross, John	R'dam*	200/120	24-07-1754	Dunlop Co.[135]	Cowes	Phila	22-10-1754	Hillegas[134]	81	239
227	Halifax (Phila)	Coatam, Thomas[136]	R'dam	180		[Stedman Co.]	Plymouth[137]	c26-08-1754 Phila	20-10-1754	Benezet	106;(370)515/280	515
228	Good Intent	Lasley, John	R'dam+	140		Benezet	Portsmouth	Phila	21-10-1754	Benezet	81	239
229	Recovery	Jones, Amos	R'dam				Cowes	Phila	23-10-1754	Benezet	83	245[138]

I.D. No.[1]	Name of Ship[2]	Type of Ship[3]	Tons[4]	Name of Captain[5]	Port of Embark.[6]	Date of Departure[7]	Name(s) of Merchant(s)[8]	Stopover Port[9]	Date of Departure	Port of Disembark.[10]	Date of Arrival[11]	Name(s) of Merchant(s)[12]	No. of Men; Pass./Freights[13]	Best Estimate[14]
230	Mary & Sarah		240	Broderick, Thomas	A'dam +		[Benezet]	Portsmouth		Phila	26-10-1754	Benezet	90	265
231	John & Elizabeth			Hamm, Peter	A'dam		[Benezet]	Portsmouth		Phila	07-11-1754	Benezet	130;(520)/330	520
232	Friendship			MacLane, William	Hamburg			Cowes		Phila	12-12-1754	Keppele	58; /147½	186
233	Two Brothers[139]													
234	Neptune			Smith, George	R'dam			Portsmouth		Phila	07-10-1755	Shoemaker Co.	93; /226	283
235	Pennsylvania[140] (Phila)		130	Lion, Charles	London			= London		Phila	01-11-1755	Warder Co.	17; /34	41
236	Chance			Lawrence	London			Cowes		Phila	10-11-1756	James[141]	43; /109½	138
237	Squirrel			Benn, John	R'dam			Portsmouth		Phila	21-10-1761		30	91
238	Richmond			Younghusband, Charles	R'dam			Portsmouth	a21-07-1763	Phila	05-10-1763	Shoemaker Co.	86;(260)/162	260
239	Chance		150	Smith, Charles	R'dam			Cowes	13-08-1763	Phila	01-11-1763	Shoemaker Co.	92; /193	236
240	Success			Marshall, William		25-07-1763				Phila	25-11-1763	Barclay[142]	13	40
241	Pallas			Milner, Richard	R'dam*		Hope Co.[143]	Portsmouth		Phila	25-11-1763	Shoemaker Co.	65; /196½	253
242	Chance		150	Smith, Charles	R'dam		Crawford[143]	Cowes	02-06-1764	Phila	08-08-1764	Ruecastle[144]	93; /208	257[145]
243	Polly		150/140	Porter, Robert	R'dam		[Crawford][146]	Cowes	04-07-1764	Phila	19-09-1764	Ruecastle	81; /184	228
244	Sarah		160	Stanfell, Francis	R'dam		Crawford Bland[148]	Portsmouth[147]		Phila	02-09-1764	Ruecastle	108; /230	282
245	Britannia		200/170/160	Arnott, Thomas	London			= London		Phila	26-09-1764	Shoemaker Co.	112; /250	309
246	King of Prussia		90	Robinson, James	London			Portsmouth	17-06-1764	Phila	03-10-1764	James Co.[149]	53; /94	112
247	Richmond		230	Younghusband, Charles	R'dam		Manlove[150]	Portsmouth		Phila	02-10-1764	Shoemaker Co.	110; /224	273
248	Hero[151]		350/200	Forster, Ralph	R'dam			Cowes	22-09-1764	Phila	27-10-1764	Willing Co.	200; /500	629
249	Jennifer		200	Kerr, George	R'dam			Cowes	25-08-1764	Phila[152]	05-11-1764	Ruecastle	102; /247	309
250	Prince of Wales		150	Edgar, James	R'dam		Bales Co.[153]	Cowes	25-08-1764	Phila	05-11-1764	Searle, James	79; /131	153
251	Boston		150	Cat, Matthew	R'dam		Rocke[154]	Cowes	01-08-1764	Phila	10-11-1764	Rundle, Daniel	69; /203	260
252	Tryall		160	Clapp, John	A'dam			Teignmouth		Phila	04-12-1764	Searle	23; /47½	58[155]
253	Polly		150/140	Porter, Robert	R'dam		[Crawford]	Cowes[156]	03-07-1765	Phila	24-08-1765	Ruecastle	85;(250)/191½	239
254	Chance		150	Smith, Charles	R'dam		[Crawford]	Cowes	13-07-1765	Phila[157]	09-09-1765	Ruecastle	96; /216	267
255	Betsey		120	Osman, John	R'dam			Cowes	27-07-1765	Phila	19-09-1765	Gray, Thomas	75;(200)[158]	187
256	Myrtilla			Caton, James	London			= London[159]	22-07-1765	Phila	21-09-1765	Howell	40; /(c70)	83
257	Countess of Sussex			Gray, Thomas	R'dam					Phila	07-10-1765	Howell	24; /41	48
258	Chance		150	Smith, Charles	R'dam			Cowes	20-08-1766	Phila	23-09-1766	Willing & Morris	112; /200	238[160]
259	Betsey		120	Osman, John	R'dam			Cowes		Phila	13-10-1766	Howell	/154(140)[161]	179
260	Cullodian [New Culloden] (Phila)		220/150	Hunter, Richard	Lisbon/London			[Lisbon]		Phila	15-10-1766	Coyningham Co.[162]	12	27
261	Polly		150/140	Porter, Robert	R'dam		[Crawford]	Cowes[163]	20-08-1766	Phila	18-10-1766	Willing & Morris	55;(181)/128½	181
262	Sally		180/150	Davidson, John	R'dam			Portsmouth	01-09-1766	Phila	04-11-1766	Ross, John	7	16
263	Juno		130	Robertson, John	R'dam			Berwick		Phila	13-01-1767	Willing & Morris	11;(36)	36
264	Sally[164] (Phila)		148/132	Osman, John	R'dam			Cowes	03-08-1767	Phila	05-10-1767	Howell	116	255

No. & Ship	Tonnage	Captain	Origin	Agent		Port	Arrival	Date	Merchant	Passengers	Total
265 Hamilton	190/105	Smith, Charles	R'dam			Cowes	80-08-1767 Phila	01-10-1767	Willing & Morris	152; /302	366[165]
266 Britannia	200/160	Hardy, Alexander	R'dam			Portsmouth	Phila	26-10-1767	Shoemaker, Samuel	39	86
267 Minerva (Phila)	142/140	Spurrier, John	R'dam	Crawford[166]		Cowes	Phila	26-10-1767	Willing & Morris	99;(194)/182	194
268 Grampus (Phila)	120/100	Robinson, Henry	R'dam	Coburn[167]			Phila	04-11-1767	Shewell & Slater[168]	8	18
269 Sally	180/150	Brown, Patrick	R'dam			Cowes	Phila	10-11-1767	[Ross, John][169]	36; /62	73
270 Pennsylvania Packet[170] (Phila)	218/200/150	Gill, Robert	London	Neave[171]		= London	08-08-1768 Phila	03-10-1768	Howell	28;42/33½	42[172]
271 Minerva[173] (Phila)	142/140	Arnott, Thomas	R'dam	Crawford		Portsmouth	Phila	10-10-1768	Shoemaker, Samuel	108;264/247	264
272 Crawford (Phila)	220/200	Smith, Charles	R'dam	Crawford[174]		Cowes	07-09-1768 Phila	26-10-1768	Willing & Morris	98;214/c200	214
273 Betsey	120	Hawk, Samuel	R'dam			Portsmouth	06-08-1768 Phila	26-10-1768	Howell	116;224	224
274 Nancy & Suckey (Phila)	200/166	Keys, William	London	[West][175]		= London	13-07-1769 Phila	01-09-1769	Gibbs & West[176]	12;24/18½	24
275 London Packet (Phila)	200/180	Cook, James	Lisbon	[Warder]		= Lisbon	Phila	29-09-1769	Warder & Parker[177]	15;15/15	15
276 Minerva (Phila)	142/140	Arnott, Thomas	R'dam	Crawford		Portsmouth	01-08-1768 Phila	13-10-1769	Shoemaker, Samuel	93;220/193	220
277 Crawford (Phila)	220/200	Smith, Charles	R'dam	Crawford		Cowes	02-09-1769 Phila	24-10-1769	Willing & Morris	20;39/38	39
278 Neptune	110	Wallace, Thomas Edward	Lisbon			= Lisbon	Phila	27-07-1770	Wilcocks, John	8;10/8	10
279 Dolphin	110/90	Stephanson, George	London			Cowes	02-07-1770 Phila	29-07-1770	Pemberton, James	9;25/16	25
280 Rose	125	Ord, George	Lisbon					10-09-1770	Shoemaker, Samuel	7;12	12
281 Minerva (Phila)	142/140	Arnott, Thomas	R'dam	Crawford[179]		Cowes	Phila	01-10-1770	Willing & Morris	88;220/193	220[178]
282 Britannia (Phila)	120/100	White, Robert	R'dam	[White][179]		Cowes	Phila	03-10-1770	White, Robert	6;6/6	6
283 Sally (Phila)	148/132	Osman, John	R'dam			Cowes	Phila	29-10-1770	Howell	89;160/143	160
284 Crawford (Phila)	220/200	Smith, Charles	R'dam			Cowes	Phila	23-11-1770	Willing & Morris	26;72/64	72
285 Pennsylvania Packet (Phila)	218/200/150	Osborne, Peter	London	Harford Co.[180]		= London	Phila	17-06-1771	Fisher, Joshua	8;17	17
286 America	84	Lattimore, Wm Copeland	London		19-05-1771	= London	19-05-1771 Phila	27-07-1771	McCubbin, James	12;18	18
287 Minerva (Phila)	142/140	Arnott, Thomas	R'dam	Crawford		Cowes	06-07-1771 Phila	17-09-1771	Willing & Morris	99;245/204	245[181]
288 London Packet	200/180	Cook, James	Lisbon			= Lisbon	Phila	19-09-1771	Warder & Parker	9;10/9	10
289 Bull	80	Bull, William	R'dam			Cowes	Phila	31-10-1771	Willing & Morris	52;175/119	175[182]
290 Tyger[183] (Phila)	180/180	Johnson, George	R'dam			Cowes	14-09-1771 Phila	19-11-1771	Willing & Morris	130;300	300
291 Crawford (Phila)	220/200	Smith, Charles	London			Cowes	26-09-1717 Phila	25-11-1771	Willing & Morris	8;14/(16)	14
292 Betsy		Bryson, Andrew	London			= London	Phila	04-12-1771	Christie, James[184]	46;100/78	100
293 General Wolf	100	Hunter, Richard	Lisbon	[Hunter][185]		= Lisbon	Phila	10-12-1771	Gray Co.[186]	10;10	10
294 Hope[187] (Phila)	170/110	Robertson, John	London			= London	Phila	04-02-1772	Willing & Morris	23;32/26	32
295 Minerva (Phila)	142/140	Johnston, James	R'dam			Cowes	Phila	30-09-1772	Willing & Morris	48; /97	118

I.D. No.[1]	Name of Ship[2]	Type of Ship[3]	Tons[4]	Name of Captain[5]	Port of Embark.[6]	Date of Departure[7]	Name(s) of Merchant(s)[8]	Stopover Port[9]	Date of Departure	Port of Disembark.[10]	Date of Arrival[11]	Name(s) of Merchant(s)[12]	No. of Men; Pass./Freights[13]	Best Estimate[14]
296	Crawford (Phila)		220/200	Smith, Charles	R'dam			Cowes	26-09-1771	Phila	16-10-1772	Willing & Morris	145	312
297	Catherine (Phila)		170/120	Sutton, James	London	27-08-1772		= London		Phila	19-10-1772	Keppele Co.[188]	20	43
298	Phoebe		130	Castle, William	London			= London		Phila	19-10-1772	Bringhurst Co.[189]	7	14
299	Sally (Phila)		148/132	Osman, John	R'dam			Portsmouth	14-09-1772	Phila	03-12-1772	Howell Co.[190]	65	140
300	Hope (Phila)		170/110	Johnson, George	R'dam			Cowes	28-09-1772	Phila	03-12-1772	Willing & Morris	40	86
301	Morning Star		140	Demster, George	R'dam			Cowes		Phila	24-12-1772	Christie	62; /113½	136
302	Pennsylvania Packet (Phila)		218/200/150	Osborne, Peter	London			= London		Phila	30-04-1773	Fisher Co.[191]	24; /32	35
303	Catherine		170/120	Sutton, James	London	25-03-1773		= London		Phila	30-04-1773[19][2]	Keppele Co.	23; /42	50
304	Dolphin		90/90	Hill, Arthur	London			= London		Phila	21-05-1773	Neave, Richard, Jr[193]	38; /58	67
305	Carolina		180	Loxley, Benjamin	London			= London		Phila	04-06-1773	Warder Co.[194]	8; /29	38
306	Sally (Phila)		148/132	Osman, John	R'dam			Portsmouth		Phila	23-08-1773[19][5]	Howell Co.	153; /193	210[196]
307	Britannia (Phila)		280/240	James, Peter	R'dam		[Barclay][197]	Cowes	24-07-1773	Phila	18-09-1773	Fisher Co.	150; /220	292
308	Catherine		170/120	Sutton, James	London	29-07-1773		= London		Phila	21-09-1773	Keppele Co.	20	40
309	Union		180	Bryson, Andrew	R'dam			Portsmouth	26-07-1773	Phila	27-09-1773	Ritchie, Robert	107; /247	307
310	Hope (Phila)		170/110	Johnson, George	R'dam			Cowes	18-07-1773	Phila	01-10-1773	Willing & Morris	94	186
311	Charming Molly[198] (Phila)		180/164	Gill, Robert	R'dam			Portsmouth	11-08-1773	Phila	22-10-1773	Howell Co.	96	190
312	Crawford (Phila)		220/200	Smith, Charles	R'dam			Cowes[199]	21-08-1773	Phila	25-10-1773	Willing & Morris	99	196
313	Neptune		110	Wallace, Thomas Edward						Phila	23-11-1773	Wilcocks, John	5	10
314	Fame		120	Duncan, James	Lisbon			= Lisbon		Phila	24-11-1773	Coxe & Furman	3	6
315	Clementina[200]		135/124	Brown, Patrick	Lisbon			= Lisbon		Phila	07-12-1773	[Ross, John]	7	14
316	Montagne		200	Pickles, William	London			Cowes	11-10-1773	Phila	08-12-1773	Fisher Co.	27	54
317	Nancy		60	Armstrong, Thomas	Hamburg					Phila	21-06-1774	Jones, John	7	14
318	Sally	Snow	90	Jones, Stephen	London					Phila	15-08-1774	[Caldwell?] & Mease	8	15
319	Charming Molly (Phila)		180/164	Gill, Robert	London					Phila	29-09-1774	Howell Co.	15	30
320	Union		180	Bryson, Andrew	R'dam*		[Hardy]	Portsmouth		Phila	30-09-1774	Ritchie, Robert	156	309[201]
321	Patty & Peggy[202] (Phila)	Snow	120/80	Hardie, Robert	Lisbon			= Lisbon		Phila	29-10-1774		14	29
322	Sally (Phila)		148/132	Osman, John	R'dam			Cowes		Phila	31-10-1774	Howell Co.	52	103
323	Catherine		170/120	Baron, John	London			= London		Phila	16-01-1775	Keppele Co.	7	14
324	King of Prussia[203] (Phila)		150	Potts, Willliam	R'dam			Falmouth		Phila	09-10-1775	[Winey, Jacob]	72	143

I.D. No.[1]	Name of Ship[2]	Type of Ship[3]	Tons[4]	Name of Captain[5]	Port of Embark.[6]	Date of Departure[7]	Name(s) of Merchant(s)[8]	Stopover Port[9]	Date of Departure	Port of Disembark.[10]	Date of Arrival[11]	Name(s) of Merchant(s)[12]	No. of Immigrant/Freights[†]
331	America			Wasey, Joseph	R'dam			London		Phila[204]	20-08-1683		80
332	Concord[205]		500	Jeffries, [James?]	London			= London		Phila[206]	06-10-1683		33
333	Sarah Maria Hopewell			Tanner						Phila	23-06-1684		40
334	Mary Hope			Annis, John	R'dam	01-07-1710		London; Scotld		Phila[207]	23-09-1710		164
335				Richmond						Phila[208]	19-09-1717		91
336				Tower						Phila	19-09-1717		108
337				Eyers						Phila	19-09-1717		
338	Royal George			Moore, Peter	R'dam*			Plymouth		Phila	13-07-1719		200
339	Laurel			Coppel, John	Liverpool			Cork		Phila[209]	30-08-1720		242
340	John & Catherine			Oliver, James	R'dam*		Hope[210]	Boston?		Phila	21-07-1721		21
341	Ceasar			Lea, William	Holland			Dartmouth		Phila[211]	21-09-1721		140
342	Greyhound (Swansey)		50	Cupitt, Richard	R'dam*	a29-07-1722	Pillans[212]	Plymouth		Phila	02-07-1722		94
343	Globe			Mackay, John	Holland			Dover		Phila[213]	25-10-1722		120
344										Phila[214]	18-12-1722		100
345	Weerelkloot [Globe]			Mackay, John	R'dam*		Oursel			Phila	09-06-1723		39/37½
346					R'dam	06-1724				Phila[215]	01-10-1724		
347					R'dam	03-08-1724		Dover[216]	06-09-1724	Phila	02-11-1724		170[217]
348	York (Bristol)			Sweet, Henry	R'dam*		Goddard[218]	Dover		Phila	20-06-1725		24[men]
349	Adventure (Portsmouth)		120	Missing, William	R'dam*		Hope Co.	Cowes		Phila	23-06-1738		
350				Long, George	R'dam	32-08-1738				[Phila][219]	26-12-1738		[400]
351	Penelope			Beach, John	R'dam			Dover[220]	a14-07-1740	[Phila]	1740		
352	Margaret (Aberdeen)		100	Mlin, John	R'dam*		Hope Co.	Aberdeen		Phila	14-07-1741		
353	Mary[221]										1743		
354	Rupert[222] (Whitehaven)		130	Parker, Richard	R'dam		Stedman	Cowes		Phila	21-05-1744		150
355				Crosswaite	R'dam	30-08-1745	Stewart	Cowes		Phila	09-1745		230
356	John Galley	[Snow]		Hargrave, [Charles?]	R'dam	[30-08-1746?]		[London]		Lewes, Del	28-12-1746[223]		12
357	Mercury				R'dam		[Stewart?]			Phila	31-01-1747		
358	Louisbourg			Budden, [Richard?]	R'dam			Cowes; Madeira	a14-02-1747	Phila	14-02-1747		
359				Arenhouer, Johan	R'dam	24-07-1747				Phila	24-07-1747		
360	John & Alexander		180	Stevenson, David	R'dam*	a20-07-1748	Stedman [Crellius]	Leith		Phila	20-07-1748		
361										[Phila][224]	1748		
362	Patience & Margaret		180	Cassels, Robert	R'dam	a28-08-1749	Hope Co.	Cowes		Phila	28-08-1749		

†Only voyages for which numbers of immigrants or freights—that is, the number of full fares—were reported are included in this column from this point on (alternative reports of immigrants or freights appear in parentheses).

I.D. No.[1]	Name of Ship[2]	Type of Ship[3]	Tons[4]	Name of Captain[5]	Port of Embark.[6]	Date of Departure[7]	Name(s) of Merchant(s)[8]	Stopover Port[9]	Date of Departure	Port of Disembark.[10]	Date of Arrival[11]	Name(s) of Merchant(s)[12]	No. of Immigrants/Freights[225]
363	Francis & Elizabeth		180	Beck [Bock], Anthony	R'dam*	09-07-1749	Stedman	Cowes	a08-07-1749	Phila	09-1749		149/206½[225]
364	Rachel			Armstrong, John	R'dam	23-07-1749		Cowes	14-08-1749	Phila	09-1749		161/252½
365				Steward	Glasgow	c02-10-1749				Phila	02-10-1749		
366	Eastern Branch			Chevallier, [Thomas?]	R'dam	14-07-1749		Cowes[226]	a14-07-1749	Phila	1749		231
367	Patience & Margaret			Govan, John	R'dam		Hope Co.	Weymouth[227]	a13-09-1749	[Phila]	1749		
368	Friends Goodwill			Crawford, [Alexander?]	R'dam					Phila[228]	1749		
369	Good Intent			Watson	R'dam*					[Phila]	1749		[400]
370	Scarborough			Montpelier, Daniel	R'dam*		Curtius[230]	Cowes[229]		Phila	14-05-1751	Curtius	19/[200][231]
371				Watson	R'dam					Phila	05-06-1752		/165[232]
372	Swallow			Nimmo, Robert	R'dam	16-06-1752		Portsmouth	a19-06-1752	Phila[233]	25-08-1752		147
373	Halifax			Coatam, Thomas	R'dam			Cowes		Phila	1752		
374	Anne (Anna)		200	Kenneway, Charles	R'dam		Hope Co.	Portsmouth		Phila	1752	Stedman Co.	71
375	Anderson		230	Campbell, Hugh	R'dam		Dunlop Co.	Portsmouth		Phila	1752		82
376	President			Dunlop, William	R'dam		Harvart	Portsmouth		Phila	1752	Ray, Alexander	73
377	Nancy			Ewing, John	R'dam			Cowes		Phila	1752	Stedman Co.	77
378				Davis	London			= London[234]		[Phila]	11-07-1753	Plumsted, Samuel	10
379	Barclay		120	Brown, John	Holland			Cowes[235]	a18-07-1753	Phila	1753	Wolstenholme	1300
380	Sarah			Mitchell, [Robert?]				Cowes[236]	a11-08-1753	Phila	1753	Fisher	
381	Neptune			Mallum, William	Hamburg			Cowes		Phila	1754	Keppele[237]	
382										Phila	1758	Willing & Morris	
383	Pennsylvania		130	Agar	R'dam					Phila[239]	1760	Warder[238]	
384	King George		180	Campbell, Patrick	R'dam			Cowes[240]	01-11-1765	Phila	1764		
385	Charlotte		100	Jeffries, James						Phila	1765		/188
386	Britannia		120	Knox, William	R'dam*					Phila	06-09-1769	Fisher	11
387	Generous Friend		160	Osborne, Peter	R'dam*	a26-06-1773	Crawford[241]	Cowes		Phila	23-06-1773		
388	Pennsylvania Packet			Cook, John [James?]	R'dam*			Liverpool		Phila	12-1774	Fisher Co.[242]	
389	London Packet				London					Phila	12-1774	Warder Co.[243]	100
401	William & Mary		240	Spurier, John	London		Dick[245]	Portsmouth	20-07-1750	Halifax	1749	[Government]	322/228½[244]
402	Ann		405	Neale, Pandock	R'dam	06-07-1750	Dick	Portsmouth		Halifax	13-09-1750	[Government]	370
403	Alderney		150	Wilson, Joseph	London	c23-06-1750	Dick	Plymouth		Halifax	02-09-1750	[Government]	143
404	Nancy		190/170	Casson, Thomas	London	c13-07-1750	Dick	Dover		Halifax	25-09-1750	[Government]	229/162½[246]
405	Speedwell		190	Francis, Thomas	R'dam*	c18-05-1751	Dick	Portsmouth		Halifax	22-05-1751	[Government]	214/180½
406	Gale		180	Hamilton, Robert	R'dam*	05-06-1751	Dick	Portsmouth		Halifax	19-08-1751	[Government]	264/232
407	Pearl		200		R'dam*	12-07-1751	Dick	Portsmouth		Halifax	25-09-1751	[Government]	298/269
408	Murdock				R'dam*	09-07-1751	Dick	Portsmouth		Halifax	30-09-1751	[Government]	

No.	Ship	Type	Tonnage	Master	Departure date	Departure port	Agent/Note	Via	Destination	Arrival date	Sponsor	Passengers
409	Betty		140	Warden, Robert	c16-05-1752	R'dam*	Dick	Portsmouth	Halifax	12-08-1752	[Government]	161/128½
410	Sally				c30-05-1752	R'dam			Halifax	06-09-1752	[Government]	258/204½
411	Gale		190	Casson, Thomas	05-06-1752	R'dam*	Dick	Portsmouth	Halifax	06-09-1752	[Government]	249/184
412	Pearl		180	Robinson, J[ohn?]	c06-06-1752	R'dam	Dick		Halifax	21-08-1752	[Government]	251/191½
413	Speedwell		190/170		12-05-1752	R'dam	Dick		Halifax	09-08-1752	[Government]	216/160
414	Sally					R'dam	Dick		Halifax	1752	[Government]	258/204½
451	Lydia (London)	(Galley)	280/150	Abercrombie, James	25-07-1742	R'dam*	Sedgwick247	= London	New England	1742	Waldo, Samuel	150
452	Thomas			Andrews, John		[Hamburg?]			Boston	1750		
453	Priscilla			Brown					Boston	[22-08-1751]	Bowdoin, William	200
454						R'dam			Boston	06-11-1752		400
455						R'dam			Boston	06-11-1752		300
456	Integrity			Coward					New England	1752		150
457	St. Andrew			Wood, Alexander	10-07-1752	R'dam		Portsmouth	Boston	1752		300/271½
458						R'dam			New England	19-06-1753		
459	Elizabeth					Adam			Boston	1753		400
501						London			NY	1708		41
502						London			NY	13-06-1710	[Government]248	
503						London			NY	13-06-1710	[Government]	
504						London			NY	13-06-1710	[Government]	
505						London			NY	13-06-1710	[Government]	
506						London			NY	13-06-1710	[Government]	
507						London			NY	13-06-1710	[Government]	
508						London			NY	13-06-1710	[Government]	
509						London			NY	13-06-1710	[Government]	
510						London			NY	13-06-1710	[Government]	
511						London			NY	13-06-1710	[Government]	
512		Pink		Moorson		R'dam			NY	10-1722		
513		Snow							NY	12-1722250		200249
514									NY	1727		
515	Experiment	Snow		Reaves, Robert		[London?]		Dover	NY	03-1732		8051
516				Wilson, Joseph		R'dam			NY	1734		175252
517	[Prince Frederick?]	Brig		Wilson, Joseph		R'dam		Spithead	NY 06-07-1735	22-09-1735		45
518				Wilson, Joseph		R'dam			NY	1736		175
519				Wilson, Joseph		R'dam			NY	1737		175
520	Anna	(Galley)		Ratsey, Christopher		Adam +	Clarkson253		NY	1737		321254
521	Amsterdam			Wilson, Joseph		Adam*		Plymouth	NY	10-1738		300
522	Charming Polly				1738			Cowes	NY	20-04-1739		
523	Little Strength			Garrison, Nicholas	17-09-1743	R'dam	Moravians		NY	12-11-1743	Moravians	91
524	Jacob								NY	25-10-1744	Moravians	9
525									NY	06-1748	Moravians	15
526									NY	09-1748	Moravians	7
527	Irene (New York)255	Snow		Garrison, Nicholas	01-03-1749	London	Moravians		NY	12-05-1749	Moravians	111

I.D. No.[1]	Name of Ship[2]	Type of Ship[3]	Tons[4]	Name of Captain[5]	Port of Embark.[6]	Date of Departure[7]	Name(s) of Merchant(s)[8]	Stopover Port[9]	Date of Departure	Port of Disembark.[10]	Date of Arrival[11]	Name(s) of Merchant(s)[12]	No. of Immigrants/Freights
528	Irene (New York)	Snow		Garrison, Nicholas	London		Moravians	Dover	11-05-1750	NY	22-06-1750	Moravians	84
529	Sarah (Fowey)		170	Starp, Thomas	R'dam*	a22-07-1750	Hope Co.	Portsmouth		NY	22-07-1750[256]	Livingston, Philip	340
530	Indian King			Tingley, S.				Cowes		NY	[19-11-]11750		
531	Irene (New York)	Snow		Garrison, Nicholas	London		Moravians	Dover		NY	26-09-1751	Moravians	
532										NY	12-1751		7
533	Irene (New York)	Snow		Garrison, Nicholas	London		Moravians	Dover		NY	17-05-1752	Moravians	8
534	William		100	McCleon, John	R'dam*	22-07-1752	Dunlop Co.	Cowes		NY	22-07-1752		200/208[?208/200]
535	Irene (New York)	Snow		[Garrison, Nicholas]	[London]		Moravians			NY	20-11-1752	Moravians	21
536	St. Andrews			Cooper, James	R'dam*	16-08-1752	Dunlop Co.	Portsmouth		NY	c01-12-1752		150/212[?212/150]
537	Johannes			Pickeman, R[obert]	R'dam			Dover		NY	1752		230
538				Ogilvy, Aexander	R'dam[257]					[NY]			
539	Irene (New York)	Snow		Garrison, Nicholas	London		Moravians	= London	a13-06-1753	NY	09-09-1753	Moravians	32
540	Charming Sally			Heysham	Hamburg			Dover		NY	1753	Lane & Lattouch	100
541	Charming Nancy			Mallum, William	Hamburg					NY	1753	Haynes, Joseph	300
542	Fame			Seymour	Hamburg			Cowes		NY	1753	Tole, Richard	230
543	Johannes			Pickeman, W.	Holland					NY	1753	Livingston, Philip	31
544	Anne & Elizabeth			Crawford, Patrick	R'dam			Portsmouth		NY	1753		43
545	Irene (New York)	Snow		Garrison, Nicholas	London	15-03-1754	Moravians	[= London]		NY	15-04-1754	Moravians	230
546	Sarah	(Galley)		Starp, Thomas	R'dam		Hope Co.	Portsmouth		NY	10-1754		51
547	Irene (New York)	Snow		Garrison, Nicholas	London	22-09-1754	Moravians	[= London]		NY	16-11-1754	Moravians	
548	Patience			Prittcairne, John				Cowes		NY	1754	Sarley, Anthony	
549	Anne & Elizabeth			Crawford, Patrick	R'dam			Portsmouth		NY	1754		
550	Neptune			Mason, John	R'dam			Cowes		NY	1754	Livingston, Philip	
551	Irene (New York)	Snow		Jacobson, Christian	London		Moravians	[= London]		NY	02-06-1756	Moravians	14
552	Irene (New York)	Snow		Jacobson, Christian	London		Moravians	[= London]		NY	12-12-1756	Moravians	5
553	Hope (New York)[258]		120		[London]		Moravians	[= London]		NY	19-10-1761	Moravians	44
554	Hope (New York)		120		[London]		Moravians	[= London]		NY	21-10-1763		10
555										NY	09-1764[259]		
556	America			Turner, Thomas	R'dam			Cowes[260]	a11-01-1766	NY	1766		
601	Friendship		160	Lucas, James	R'dam	10-07-1752	Dunlop Co.			MD	10-07-1752	Lawson, Alexander	300/262[261]
602	Patience		200	Steel, Hugh	R'dam		Stedman Co.	Cowes		MD	1752	Snowdon, Richard	260
603	Barclay		120	Brown, John	[R'dam]			Plymouth		MD	18-10-1753	Wolstenholme	300
604	Friendship		160	Rattray, John	R'dam		Dunlop Co.	Portsmouth		MD	1753	Lawson & Johnson	300
605	Friendship		160	Rattray, John	R'dam			Portsmouth		MD	1754	Lawson & Johnson	300

No.	Ship	Pass.	Captain	Embark	Departure	Agent	Port of call	Arrival	Colony	Arrival date	Merchant	Pass.
651	Oliver	100	Wright, William	R'dam	22-06-1738	Hope Co.	Cowes; Plymouth		VA	11-1738	Byrd[262]	300
652	Hicks		Dent, Lawrence	[R'dam]			Cowes	12-09-1743 VA	VA	06-12-1743		200[263]
653			Gilpin, William	R'dam			Cowes[264]	a13-08-1755 VA	VA	1755		200
701									SC	14-07-1733[265]		
702									SC	13-07-1735[266]		
703									SC	1736[267]		
704									SC	1737[268]		
705									SC	1740[269]		
706	Lydia		Abercrombie, James	R'dam					Charleston	1744[270]		
707	St. Andrew		Brown	R'dam		Stewart	Cowes		Charleston	1744[271]		
708			Edmonds	London					SC	31-01-1747		
709			Blanchard	London					SC	31-01-1747		
710			Gould	London	09-06-1748		= London	a09-06-1748 SC	SC	09-06-1748		
711	Madeleine		Mackenzie	London	21-06-1748		Leith		SC	21-06-1748		
712	Friend's Goodwill		Crawford, A[lexander]	London					Charleston	1749[272]		400
713	Greenwich		Randolph, Edward			Hope Co.			Charleston	1750	La Roche[273]	250(200)
714	Anne		Kennaway, Charles				Cowes		Charleston	1751	Austin & Laurens	
715	Rowand	200	Tran, Arthur	R'dam*	22-07-1752	Oursel	[Cowes; Pool?]		Charleston	18-05-1752	Inglis[274]	300/220
716	Nancy	180	Curtin, Thomas	R'dam*	06-1752	Rocquette Co.			SC[275]	26-05-1752	[Dulany?]	
717	Caledonia	180	Harvey, Alexander	R'dam*	10-07-1752	Rocquette Co.	Portsmouth [Portsmouth]		Charleston	12-06-1752	Pringle & Co	/165
718	Union [Upton]	[180]	Gardner, John	R'dam					Charleston	10-07-1752	[Austin & Laurens]	[400]/291½
719	Elizabeth	140	Ross, John	R'dam	15-09-1752	Oursel	Cowes [Portsmouth; Cowes?]		Charleston	15-07-1752	McCall, John	/250
720	John & Mary	150	Robinson, John	R'dam*	07-08-1752	Rocquette Co.			Charleston	26-07-1753	McCall, John	300/150
721			Pickart, John	R'dam	c14-08-1752				SC	14-08-1752		
722			Headley[?], Andrew	R'dam	c14-08-1752				SC	14-08-1752		
723			Cooper, James	R'dam	13-08-1752				SC	14-08-1752		
724			Mantrow[?]	R'dam	24-08-1752				SC	14-08-1752		
725	Elizabeth		Rook[Ross?], Mathew	R'dam					Charleston	24-08-1752		
726	Betty		Miles, J. [MD]	R'dam					Charleston	19-10-1752		/328½
727	Minerva		Colcok, Isaac	R'dam					Charleston	19-10-1752		
728	Cunliffe		Clayton, Joseph	R'dam	20-06-1752		Portsmouth	a16-06-1752 Charleston	Charleston	1752[276]		500/308
729	Anne		Orr, John	R'dam			Portsmouth		Charleston	1753		300
730	Priscilla		Catanack, Thomas	R'dam	07-08-1754		Cowes		Charleston	1754	Inglis	200(300)
731									Charleston	1764[277]		
732	[Dragon?]								Charleston	1765[278]		
733	Frankland								SC	02-1766[279]		

I.D. No.¹	Name of Ship SU2	Type of Ship³	Tons⁴	Name of Captain⁵	Port of Embark.⁶	Date of Departure⁷	Name(s) of Merchant(s)⁸	Stopover Port⁹	Date of Departure	Port of Disembark.¹⁰	Date of Arrival¹¹	Name(s) of Merchant(s)¹²	No. of Immigrants/ Freights
734	Belfast Packet									SC	17-10-1766[280]		
735										SC	01-12-1722[281]		
736										SC	06-01-1773[282]		
801	Purrysburg			Frye, Tobias						GA	12-03-1734[283]		
802	Prince of Wales			Dunbar, George						GA	28-12-1734		10
803	Two Brothers			Thomson, William						GA	06-04-1735		
804	James			Yoakley, John						GA	01-08-1735		
805	Georgia	Pink		Daubaz						GA	27-11-1735		25
806	Simonds			Cornish, Joseph						GA	17-02-1736		
807	London Merchant			Thomas, John						GA	17-02-1736		
808	Three Sisters			Hewitt						GA	20-12-1737		
809	Two Brothers			Thomson, William						GA	07-10-1738		
810	Charles			Haeramond						GA	29-06-1739		
811	Loyal Judith			Lemon, John						GA	02-12-1741		
812	Europa			Wadham, John						GA	04-12-1741		
813	Judith			Quarme, Walter						GA	22-01-1746		
814	Charles Town			Bogg, Peter						GA	02-10-1749		
815	Charming Martha			Leslie, Charles						GA	29-10-1750[284]		
816	Antelope			McClellan, John						GA	23-10-1751[285]		
817	Oldbury		170	Brown, Henry	R'dam*	10-09-1752	Dick	Portsmouth		GA	27-11-1752	d'Harriet[286]	
818	Success			Isaacs						GA	1752[287]		/137
(851)	Les Deux-Frères				Lorient	11-1720	Co de Indes			LA	1721[288]		
(852)	La Garonne				[Lorient]	20-01-1721	Co de Indes			LA	1721		
(853)	La Charente				[Lorient]	02-1721	Co de Indes			LA	1721		
(854)	Le Portefaix				[Lorient]	07-03-1721	Co de Indes			LA	1721		
(855)	Le Saint André				[Lorient]	1721	Co de Indes			LA	1721		
(856)	La Durance				[Lorient]	1721	Co de Indes			LA	1721		
(857)	La Saône				Lorient	1721	Co de Indes			LA	1721		
901	Charming Polly[289]			Bailay, Edward	A'dam+		Clarkson			unknown	23-03-1741[290]		
902				Beach, John	[R'dam]					St. Kitts	1744		
903	Argyle			Stedman, Charles	R'dam			Portsmouth[291]		unknown	02-1745[292]		
904					R'dam					unknown	09-1745		4[293]
905										unknown	1752[294]		
906					R'dam					unknown	1753[295]		
907					R'dam					unknown	1754[297]		
908	[Flamingsche Hund?]				R'dam[296]					unknown			
909	Molly			Harvart, David	[R'dam]		Manlove & Gib			(Phila)[298]			

NOTES:

This list of German immigrant voyages for 1683–1775 summarizes information from many sources. Since research into the German-speaking migration to the American colonies is an ongoing endeavor, the list cannot be comprehensive. Readers who have information for updating or correcting the list may want to share their knowledge and improve the usefulness of the list for fellow researchers. The website for the listing of German immigrant voyages 1683–1775, can be found under the following address: php.iupui.edu/~mwokeck.

Several sources form the basis of this tabulation of German immigrant voyages: Strassburger/Hinke, *Pennsylvania German Pioneers* (hereafter S/H); the customhouse notices in the *Pennsylvania Gazette*; the ship charters contracted in Rotterdam and Amsterdam; English port books; "List of the Several Ships Clear'd Out This Year [1752] at Gosport"; and *Lloyd's Lists* and "Lloyd's Register."

Several categories of information available about German immigrant voyages were omitted from this listing because of limited space: (1) the number of women and children; (2) the number of sick and dead passengers; (3) the number of marks on the lists; (4) the places of origin of German immigrants on particular vessels; (5) the arrival dates in the stopover port in Great Britain; and (6) the destination of each ship (including the departure dates and the cargo loaded) after they had landed their human cargo in the British North American colonies.

An asterisk(*) after the name of the port of embarkation indicates that a record was found in the Gemeentelijke Archief Rotterdam, Old Notarial Archives (GAR, ONA). Although my search for those records has been extensive, it is not comprehensive, and additional records are likely to have survived. The nature of those records varies, but most often they are contracts (charterparties) between the freighter in Rotterdam and the captain of the ship chartered to carry German immigrants to the American colonies. The records are indexed by destination, date, and the names of the merchants, captains, and ships.

A cross (+) after the name of the port of embarkation indicates that a record was found in the Gemeente Archief Amsterdam, Notarial Archives (GAA, NA). Here too the search has been extensive but not comprehensive.

Information in square brackets [ ] indicates that it is based on indirect evidence.

References to particular sources are in short-title form. Complete citations can be found in the Bibliography.

[1] For ready comparison, numbers for each German immigrant voyage is the same number assigned in Strassburger/Hinke, *Pennsylvania German Pioneers* (S/H). Additional voyages have been numbered in the following way: Additional ships arriving in Philadelphia with German immigrants can be recognized by numbers 351–400 (in chronological order); ships landing in Nova Scotia are numbered 401–50; in New England, 451–500; in New York, 501–600; in

Maryland, 601–50; in Virginia, 651–700; in (South) Carolina, 701–800; in Georgia, 801–50; in Louisiana, 851–900; and at any unknown or undetermined destination 901–50.

2 The names of some ships were abbreviated to fit the column. The name of the home port, when given in the sources, was added in parentheses.

3 Ship, brig, pink, snow, galley, and billinder are the different types of ships most common in the German immigrant trade. Only some sources identify the ships that carried German immigrants by type (names are abbreviated to fit the column).

4 The tonnage of ships was variously recorded as registered, measured, or advertised (also cargo) tons, and often without any differentiation. If sources differed, the maximum (usually cargo or measured tons) and minimum (usually registered tons) values are given here.

5 The spelling of captains' names often varied, sometimes considerably. In order to identify the captains who commanded vessels loaded with German emigrants more than once, the most common form is used here. Of the 67 captains whose ships carried German passengers more than once, 34 did so twice (Ball; Budden; Casson; Cook; Cowie; Crawford, Alexander; Crawford, Patrick; Cusack; Dunlop; Govan; Hargrave; Hunter; Jacobson; Kennway; Mackay; Marshall; Merchant; North; Paynter; Penelope; Rattray; Reid; Rickeman; Robertson; Robinson, John; Strap; Thomson, William; Tran; Vitery; Wadham; Wallace; Watson; Wier; Younghusband); 15 did so three times (Brown, John; Brysan; Cooper; Crockat; Ewing; Gill; Goodman; Johnson; Montpelier; Moore, John; Osborne; Parish; Pittcairne; Porter; Sutton); 4 (Allen; Brown, Robert; Campbell; Stedman, Charles) transported Germans four times; 2 (Wilson, William; Steel), five times; 4 (Percy; Spurrier; Stedman; Wilson, Joseph), six times; 2 (Muir; Osman), seven times; 3 (Abercrombie; Coatam; Mason), eight times. Garrison sailed with Moravians nine times; Charles Smith sailed with German emigrants eleven times; and Arnott did so twelve times. In all, the 67 captains who repeated a voyage with German passengers made up less than 20 percent of all captains employed in the trade; out of all voyages, almost half (233, or 45 percent) were Atlantic crossings under a captain who was involved in the German immigrant trade at least once.

6 The names of some ports of embarkation of German emigrants are abbreviated to fit the column.

7 The date of departure is often ambiguous in the sources. The date a vessel was scheduled to sail was not always the date it actually departed. In this listing, the latest given date is recorded as the "departure" date. It is important to remember that the date given in this listing can be either the date of the contract made between shipper and captain (charterparty), which is usually indicated by "a" ("after"), "or the last of several entries in the papers that reported the sailing of ships.

Until Great Britain adopted the "new style" calendar in 1752, dates in sources originating on the continent were most often in the "new style" while dates in English and American sources usually adhered to the "old style." After 1700, that meant a difference of 11 days. For example, 21 July 1732 according to the new style translated into 10 July by the old-style calendar. Because the dates given here have not been translated, but reflect those given in the sources (which do not always indicate the style used), calculations concerning the length of the voyage, for instance, are problematical.

[8] The names of shippers, merchants, and firms listed in connection with freighting ships with German emigrants in European ports are abbreviated to fit the column.

[9] Some names of British ports in which ships with German immigrants stopped, according to the requirements of the navigation laws, are abbreviated. Ships leaving from London usually set out from Gravesend, which is not noted in this list. Ports listed in parentheses ( ) indicate other, different, information about the stopover port; ports in square brackets [ ] reflect that the evidence for the given information is indirect. The stopover ports were, from east to west: London, Deal, Dover, Portsmouth (sometimes listed under the name of the neighboring harbor Gosport), Cowes, Poole, Weymouth, Teignmouth, Plymouth, Falmouth, and also Leith in Scotland.

[10] Some of the names of the ports in which German immigrants disembarked were abbreviated to fit the column.

[11] Some dates are not precise. They are indicated with an "a" preceding, for "after"; "b" for "before"; and "c" for "circa."

[12] The names of Philadelphia merchants and firms involved in the German immigrant trade are abbreviated to fit the column.

[13] The number of men above the age of 16 is the figure most consistently reported in the records. This number reflects the maximum number of men listed in the available sources, and it is the basis for the calculations for the best estimate of passengers in the next column of the Appendix. The numbers of passengers or freights are other numbers given in the records. (Figures in boldface are totals based on listings of the immigrants' names; numbers in parentheses are from additional sources—and are generally less reliable—usually because of rounding—than the S/H ship lists.)

[14] The best estimate of the number of German immigrants arriving on ships listed in S/H is either the number reported in the records or the number that could reasonably be calculated from the imperfect, partial, or comparable data that survived for voyages without reliable reports about the number of immigrants shipped across the Atlantic.

[15] For the German immigrant voyages nos. 1–5, the memorial ("Memorial," 6 December 1727, HSP) lists 335 families and a total of 1,330 immigrants (no. 1: 110 families or 400 immigrants; no. 2: 34 families or 220 immigrants; no. 3: 72 families or 300 immigrants; no. 4: 53 families or 220 immigrants; no. 5: 49 families or 190 immigrants). In the early years of significant German immigration, the "ship lists" were also published in Colonial Records (3:282 is the publication reference of the first lists; because the references are included in the lists in S/H [through list no. 43], they are not noted in the Appendix).

[16] It is noted in the Deal Port Books that thread and linen were duty-free.

[17] The stopover port was also variably listed as Dover or Plymouth.

18 Account in Sendschreiben, 15/25 September 1728.

19 According to the port books, the vessel carried an additional cargo of thread, linen, and needles destined for Harry Alexander Primrose.

20 Four newlanders—three men and one woman from Pennsylvania—returned on this ship.

21 Richard and William Clymer, Thomas Polgreen, and Alexander Woodrup were owners of the Philadelphia-built and -registered (1726) vessel. "Company" is used loosely here, primarily as an abbreviation for a group of merchants that did not necessarily form a company in the legal sense. Among the ship's owners, Woodrup & Company, together with Dover merchant Isaac Minet Jr., were exporters of dry goods: "cloth, thread, paper, bottles, tea tables, millstones" (Port Books).

22 Hugh Blasunte was also listed as captain.

23 Over the years, the Hope Company of Rotterdam changed its composition. In the early years, Archibald and Isaac formed a firm; later the firm included Zachary Hope; then it was Isaac and Zachary; and in the 1760s the Hope and Crawford merchant houses formed a partnership in the German emigrant trade.

24 The American Weekly Mercury reported 88 Palatines on this voyage—probably the number of freights rather than passengers.

25 An advertisement in the Pennsylvania Gazette (11 November 1731) asks for payment of outstanding fares on the ship. Because this and other information concerning ships that landed with German immigrants in Philadelphia can now be retrieved easily with the help of the Accessible Archives' index to the Pennsylvania Gazette, it is not provided here.

26 The Norris brought the survivors of the ship Love & Unity, which left Rotterdam, sailed via Falmouth, and was wrecked at Martha's Vineyard after 25 weeks at sea. The newspapers reported on the incident (Pennsylvania Gazette and Philadelphische Zeitung; see also PMHB 21:124–25).

27 Henry Alexander Primrose was a merchant in Deal who dealt in cloth, thread, paper, and Rhenish wine (Deal Port Books).

28 Cornelis Venyloeg (?).

29 The American Weekly Mercury (26 December 1732) published a notice that asked German immigrants who had arrived on the Plaisance to pay their fare debts. Such notices appeared periodically in the Philadelphia newspapers; they have not been noted systematically in the Appendix.

30 Account of voyage in Gar genealogy (6 adults and 36 children died of smallpox during the voyage).

31 Large number of dead and sick migrants (44 and 11, respectively). The passengers mutinied, and some were confined to prison. The ship carried earthenware as additional goods (Dover Port Books).

32 The ship carried additional dry goods (Deal Port Books).

33 The *American Weekly Mercury* reported 300 passengers on the *Samuel*. Rounding numbers in newspaper notices about immigrants is typical.

34 The account and lists of the Schwenkfelders who traveled on the *Pennsylvania Merchant* survive and give further details.

35 The alternatively reported 300 immigrants of voyage no. 36 (like the 200 immigrants of no. 38) is a typical rounding of numbers. For further details about the voyage of the *St. Andrew*, see the Schwenkfelder lists and accounts (*Pennsylvania German Society* 9 [1908]: 367–70).

36 Benjamin Shoemaker, later Benjamin & Samuel Shoemaker.

37 Fifteen weeks at sea; many sick with scurvy.

38 According to a report in the *American Weekly Mercury* (no. 817), the immigrants who arrived on the *Oliver* were a group of "Palatines" who, together with Bernese immigrants (Faust, 2:220–24), had been transported to Charleston (26 July 1735) and had paid extra for passage to Philadelphia.

39 The 388 passengers reported in the *American Weekly Mercury* (no. 870) is probably a printing error.

40 The *American Weekly Mercury* (no. 872) reported 340 Palatines. Among them were newlanders, like Graff from Boston. Baggage and goods were seized (*Colonial Records*, 4:171; Records of the Vice-Admiralty Court at Philadelphia).

41 John Stedman, captain of the *St. Andrew*, later frequently freighted ships in Rotterdam with German emigrants. His correspondents and partners varied (Alexander Andrew [Philadelphia], George William Catanach [London], Thomas Penrose [Philadelphia], Robinson [Philadelphia], and especially, later in Philadelphia, Alexander and Charles Stedman).

42 Levinius Clarkson of Amsterdam.

43 Ship owners of the Philadelphia-built and -registered ship (1736) were John Stedman, Alexander Andrew, and George Catanach (London). Jacob Beiler probably wrote the surviving account of the voyage (*Pennsylvania Mennonite Heritage*, 2:12) and noted that 2 adults and 22 children had died at sea.

44 For the voyages nos. 53–55, a total of 1,003 Palatines was reported; 440 Palatines for the two voyages nos. 56 and 59.

45 The *Rotterdams Jaarboekje* reported that 18 died during the voyage. The report that the ships nos. 52–55 arrived with a total of 425 passengers is correct, if only men are counted.

46 Captain James Marshall and John Norris of London were owners of the Philadelphia-built and -registered (1736) ship.

47 Thomas Penrose, merchant and shipbuilder in Philadelphia, kept a cashbook for the years 1738–51 that has survived. Entries reveal that he worked for several merchants involved in the German immigrant trade (especially Alexander Andrew & Company and John Stedman & Company) on a commission basis.

48 Alexander Andrew & Company operated in Philadelphia and at times made use of ship builder Thomas Penrose as correspondent in matters concerning the importation of German immigrants.

49 The duplicate of the list of the *Nancy* (= 59A) appears as an undated list in S/H 3:103. Many passengers were sick on arrival, and the ship received a bad health report (*Colonial Records*, 4:306–7).

50 The undated list in S/H 3:103 is a duplicate of no. 59(A).

51 The *Pennsylvania Gazette* reported 160 dead. For an account of the death and sickness on the 1738 German immigrant ships, see Wust, "Emigration Season of 1738."

52 Wills, inventories, and administrations of passengers who died at sea or shortly after arrival are in Register of Wills Office, Philadelphia.

53 Many (129) sick.

54 Of the 312½ freights (447 passengers), three-quarters (250) died because of typhus on board. In Henry Keppele's diary the ship is misnamed *Charming Molly*.

55 It is noticed in the Deal Port Books that Rooth [sic] Colebran shipped additional goods (linen, silk, thread, toys, bed ticking, books).

56 Alexander Andrew (Philadelphia), George Catanach, and John Stedman of London are listed as the owners of the Philadelphia-built and -registered (1738) ship.

57 The Dover Port Books note that Rooth [sic] Colebran sent additional goods (cloth, barbers' aprons).

58 The Dover Port Books noted that George Hudson sent per master linen, silk, bed ticks, stone bottles, and paving stones.

59 According to the Ship Register 1741–42 (AM 6812, HSP), the ship carried 10 guns and was operated by a crew of 10.

60 According to the Ship Register 1741–42, the ship was owned by Isaac Hope and others; fitted with 10 guns; and had a crew of 14 men. It carried 800 (most likely a mistake for 300) Palatines and their baggage.

61 The Ship Register 1741–42 describes the *Lydia* as a vessel with 6 guns and a 9-man crew. A newspaper advertisement reported that the ship was 280 tons, although the registered tonnage was only 70 tons.

62 The ship's characteristics in the Ship Register 1741–42 are listed as 20 guns and a crew of 14. Like the *St. Mark*, the advertised tonnage of the vessel was 280, although it was registered at 150.

63 In the Ship Register 1741–42, the ship is listed with 6 guns and 11 crew. The vessel's owners were Hugh Percy, a captain in the German emigrant trade and others; it carried 300 Palatines and their baggage. In a newspaper advertisement the tonnage is given as 160 (the registered tonnage was 130).

64 The Ship Register 1741–42 reports that the vessel was owned by Michael Wilkins of London, that it carried no guns, that it operated with a crew of 9, and that it transported 200 Palatines and their baggage. This is the first ship for which a health certificate survived.

65 Michael Wilkins.

66 A report in the *Rotterdams Jaarboekje* 5 (1967): 119–20 reveals that the ship ran aground and was wrecked off Cape Henlopen. The captain and a boy drowned. All passengers were saved and transferred in three shallops to Philadelphia (the health certificates were issued for those shallops).

67 The Moravians' account of the voyage is in *PMHB* 33 (1909): 228–48. The list reflects receipt of the fee of 1s.6d levied on each male immigrant over the age of sixteen.

68 Robert Strettle and, beginning in the following year, Amos & Robert Strettle.

69 The *American Weekly Mercury* lists the ship arriving from South Carolina.

70 Samuel Carson and Henry Davy are listed as the owner of the Philadelphia-built and -registered ship.

71 Captain William Wilson and John Ritchy of London are listed as the owners of the Philadelphia-built and -registered (1742) ship.

72 John Stedman Company was the owner of the Philadelphia-built (Penrose) ship.

73 The *American Weekly Mercury* reported 390 Dutch passengers and that two ships sailed for Philadelphia, one to South Carolina; *Pennsylvanische Berichte* reported that the immigrants were mostly from Neuwied and well and healthy.

74 The ship sustained serious damage in a storm en route to Philadelphia (GAR, ONA 2340/220).

75 Francis Trimble.

76 Indentures registered before the Philadelphia mayor (September 1746). On the return voyage, the ship was taken by a French privateer (GAR, ONA 2343/78).

77 Alexander Stewart appears on the Rotterdam list of freighters of German emigrants.

78 Benjamin & Samuel Shoemaker.

79 *Pennsylvanische Berichte* reported that all immigrants were well and treated well too.

80 The stopover port was also listed as Plymouth or Pool.

81 *Pennsylvanische Berichte* reported that the immigrants were well and also well treated.

82 Smith and James. *Pennsylvanische Berichte* reported that their passengers were all well and well treated.

83 James Pemberton and John Hunt (London). The Pemberton Papers and Hunt & Greenleafe Letter Book give such details as the charter and cost for the *Crown*.

84 John Searl, John Wilcocks, and Samuel McCall are listed as owners of the Philadelphia-built and -registered ship.

85 Captain Robert Brown was owner of the ship John Stedman chartered to transport passengers and baggage to Pennsylvania.

86 Account by Hans Wyss, who was engaged as cook (Blocher, *Zürcher Auswanderer*).

87 Also listed as Andrew Bryden.

88 The listing appears as a duplicate in 1754 (S/H no. 233).

89 John Philpot, Captain James Creagh, and Graham.

90 Captain George Spencer.

91 The reported 503 freights are probably a mistake for 303; the large number of freights would translate into an estimated 653 immigrants.

92 A Greenland ship (Hunt & Greenleafe Letter Book).

93 Michael Kickey.

94 Ward Stanton.

95 *Pennsylvanische Berichte* (no. 114) reported that the immigrants' baggage was transported on a different ship, which arrived on 11 November 1749; many chests were broken open, and that delayed the delivery of passengers' belongings.

96 William Blair of Philadelphia and John and James Ritchie of Glasgow are listed as the owners of the Philadelphia-built and -registered (1748) ship.

97 William Blair (Philadelphia) and James Ritchie (Glasgow) are listed as owners of the Philadelphia-built and -registered ship.

98 Captain William Muir (Scotland) and John Stedman (London) are listed as owners of the Philadelphia-built and -registered (1750) ship.

99 Captain John Mason (London) had also an interest in the voyage.

100 Charles and Alexander Stedman and Samuel McCall Jr. of Philadelphia, together with John Stedman of Rotterdam, are listed as owners of the *Nancy* ship. An account of the passengers on board the *Nancy* survived ("Redemptioners," HSP).

101 Alexander and Charles Stedman (Philadelphia), Smauel McCall Jr. (Philadelphia), and John Stedman (Rotterdam) are listed as owners of the Philadelphia-built and -registered ship.

102 Gottlieb Mittelberger, author of *Journey to Pennsylvania*, traveled on this ship.

103 The ship was condemned and the goods were forfeited because of illegal trading by foreigners (Philadelphia Custom House Records; the report in *Pennsylvanische Berichte* [no. 127] included not only the confiscation of all chests with goods but also that the passengers had mutinied against the captain at sea; CUST[oms] 61/1, Cowes 28 July 1750, noted that the ship had goods for Madeira).

104 Daniel Harvart. The captain filed an official protest against the merchant (22 July 1750) because he had been promised a load of 400 freights but received only 188 (GAR, ONA 2427/235).

105 I *Pennsylvanische Berichte* reported that all the about 300 passengers were well.

106 The Rotterdam merchant house of Nicolas Oursel.

107 John Pole. Pole and Howell were factors for Rotterdam merchant Nicolas Oursel.

108 In the charterparty (GAR, ONA 2699/175), the Philadelphia firm of Pole & Howell is named as consignee of the merchant Nicolas Oursel; in the Philadelphia records, Benjamin and Samuel Shoemaker appear as recipients of the transport of immigrants.

109 Jacob Frederic Curtius (Philadelphia), owner and freighter of the ship, made an agreement with Ward Stanton and John Stedman, shippers in Rotterdam (GAR, ONA 2279/167; see also 2747/72, 99).

110 The Rotterdam firm John Dunlop & Company.

111 Alexander and Charles Stedman and Samuel McCall of Philadelphia, and John Stedman of London, are listed in *Lloyd's Lists* (no. 1762) that by 25 August the ship had been in a storm that caused the loss of the main topmast, shivered the main mast, and sprung two beams, but that the vessel was otherwise well.

112 *Lloyd's Lists* (nos. 1755, 1770) reported that in an encounter at sea off Philadelphia all passengers were well.

113 When merchants Rocquette & van Teylingen made a contract with John Mason, Hope stood security for the captain (GAR, ONA 2747/123).

114 Rocquette & van Teylingen.

115 For an account of voyage, see Hans Kuby, "The Ship Ketty," in Scherer, ed., *Pfälzer—Palatines.*

116 Jacob Frederic and Christian Henry Curtius (Philadelphia).

117 Howell & Pole.

118 Henry Keppele, Philadelphia merchant, was a German immigrant himself.

119 Cargo assigned to Alexander & Charles Stedman or Howell & Pole.

120 The number of freights is very high; it may well be the number of passengers.

121 After the health inspection, twelve passengers were not allowed to land. Health inspections for ships no. 195–232 survived (Simon Gratz Collection [Physicians]; Dreer Autograph Collection [Physicians], HSP). They have not been systematically noted in the Appendix.

122 Benjamin and Samuel Shoemaker of Philadelphia, and Elias Bland of London, are listed as owners of the Philadelphia-built and -registered (1747) ship.

123 Passengers in good health.

124 Lloyd's Lists (no. 1863) reported that all passengers were well in an encounter between ships at sea off Philadelphia.

125 James Abercrombie (Philadelphia) and R. Ritchie and J. Dunlap (London) are listed as owners of the Philadelphia-built and -registered (1752, 1753) ship.

126 Captain William Muir, together with Alexander and Charles Stedman.

127 Daniel Benezet and Michael Agee of Philadelphia.

128 Greenway & Rundle.

129 Thomas Willing (Philadelphia) became a major importer of German immigrants, together with Robert Morris.

130 Captain John Brown and John Stedman, both of London, are listed as owners of the Philadelphia-built and -registered (1752) ship.

131 According to the Plymouth Port Books, the Adventure carried—duty-free—120 chests and boxes that contained bedding, wearing apparel, used utensils, working tools, baggage, and other necessaries of the 240 passengers.

132 Account of voyage in letter by J. H. Schmitt. In the list, "souls" and "freights" were most likely reversed; another report of a total of 860 immigrants is too high, even if 554 freights were crammed on board; assuming 300 total freights, the likely total of immigrants would have been around 335.

133 Rocquette & van Teylingen (Rotterdam) acted as agents for Pierre Benezet (Amsterdam).

134 Michael Hillegas, Henry Elves, and Michael Hulings of Philadelphia, and John Ross of Cowes, are listed as the owners of the Philadelphia-built and -registered (1754) ship.

135 Michael Hillegas, Henry Elves, Michael Hulings of Philadelphia, together with J. Ross of Cowes, are listed as owners of the Philadelphia-built and -registered ship.

136 Also listed as John Marshead.

137 The Plymouth Port Books noted that the *Halifax* carried—duty-free—136 chests and boxes containing bedding, wearing apparel, used utensils, working tools, baggage, and other minute necessaries of 515 Palatines and passengers.

138 In Wilmington, 31 passengers went ashore.

139 The list in S/H is a duplicate of no. 133. On 25/26 July 1754, *Two Brothers* was shipwrecked (GAR, ONA 2434/50 [1 August 1754]). The *Tryal*, with Captain John Stinson, could save 80 passengers; nothing else was rescued.

140 Jeremiah Warder and James Abel of Philadelphia, together with William and Richard Neave of London, are listed as owners of the Philadelphia-built and -registered (1754) ship.

141 Abel James, who at times was in partnership with Jeremiah Warder and also with Henry Drinker.

142 Gilbert Barclay.

143 James Crawford, a substantial merchant in Rotterdam, is listed in Lloyd's Register as owner of the 1755-built ship. Crawford and his partners (Isaac and Zachary Hope and Patrick Crawford) were most influential as freighters of German emigrants in the decade before the Revolution.

144 Robert Ruecastle.

145 *Lloyd's Lists* (no. 2962) reported that the *Chance* put into Cowes (27 May 1764) with 218 Palatines for Philadelphia. It is unclear whether that count is for passengers or freights on board.

146 In Lloyd's Register, James Crawford is listed as owner of the New England-built, 150-ton ship that sailed with a crew of 12.

147 *Lloyd's Lists* (nos. 2972, 2977, 2979) reported all passengers well when another ship encountered the *Sarah* at sea off Cornwall.

148 Lloyd's Register has Elias Bland of London as owner of the 170-ton ship that sailed with a 15-man crew.

149 James & Drinker advertised in the *Pennsylvania Gazette* and the *Pennsylvanische Staatsbote* about redemptioners and also offers of travel to London. The financial account of the ship *King of Prussia* gives £1335:10:2 (Pennsylvania money) as the "neat proceeds" of the voyage.

150 Manlove and Gib; application for transshipment of 350 emigrants. In Lloyd's Register, William Gale is listed as owner of the 1748-built ship.

151 Lloyd's Register listed Thomas Willing as the owner of the 350-ton ship that sailed with a crew of thirty. Lloyd's Lists (no. 2989) reported 700 passengers on board during an extraordinarily short voyage (30 died en route, according to the Pennsylvania Gazette).

152 Lloyd's Register gives Maryland as the destination of the 200-ton ship with a 12-man crew; Lloyd's Lists (no. 2998) reported "all well" on 8 September 1764.

153 Lloyd's Register lists Bales & Company as owners of the 150-ton ship with a 10-man crew.

154 Lloyd's Register lists T. Rocke as owner of the 150-ton, Boston-built (1758) ship with a 12-man crew.

155 The Staatsbote characterizes the passengers on the Tryall as young and well.

156 CUST(oms) 61/1-4, Cowes (1749–33), PRO, London.

157 The ship encountered trouble in Delaware Bay after landing German immigrants in Philadelphia (GAR, ONA 2762/4 [10 January 1767]).

158 Staatsbote reported 200 passengers, all well.

159 Lloyd's Lists (no. 3085) reported that all passengers were well when the ship was off Scilly (ca. 9 August 1765); the Staatsbote announced that the ship arrived with several newlanders and newcomers.

160 According to the Staatsbote, most immigrants were young, all well.

161 According to the Staatsbote, the ship carried 140 freight; used to belong to John Osman, but now to Sam Hawk.

162 Nesbit & R. Coyningham of Philadelphia and R. Alexander and J. Knox of Londonderry are listed as owners of the Philadelphia-built and -registered (1760) ship.

163 CUST(oms) 61/1-4, Cowes (1749–73), PRO, London.

164 Philadelphia-built and -registered (1766) ship.

165 The Staatsbote reported "all well, none died at sea."

166 Thomas Arnott (Newburyport, Massachusetts), formerly a captain in the German immigrant trade, Crawford & Company (Rotterdam), and Willing & Morris (Philadelphia) are listed as owners of the Philadelphia-built and -registered ship.

167 Coburn, T. Slater, and J. and S. Shewell of Philadelphia are listed as owners of the Philadelphia-built and -registered (1762) ship.

168 Samuel Shewell and Thomas Slater.

169 John Ross and Preeson Bowdoin of Philadelphia are listed as owners of the ship, a prize taken from the French.

170 Huddle and P. Moore are listed as the owners of the Philadelphia-built (1759) and -registered (1770) ship.

171 Richard Neave is the corresponding merchant in London; J. Huddle and P. Moore (Philadelphia) are listed as owners of the Philadelphia-built and -registered ship.

172 Beginning of "Passenger List."

173 Thomas Arnott of Newburyport, Crawford Company of Rotternam, and Willing & Morris of Philadelphia are listed as the owners of the Philadelphia-built and -registered (1765) ship.

174 Patrick Crawford of Rotterdam and Willing & Morris of Philadelphia are listed as owners of the Philadelphia-built and -registered (1767) ship.

175 Thomas West of Philadelphia is listed as owner of the New York-built (1767) ship.

176 Benjamin Gibbs and Charles West.

177 James Warder and Richard Parker; together with Daniel Mildred and John Roberts of London they are listed as owners of the Philadelphia-built and -registered (1769) ship.

178 The *Staatsbote* reported all well.

179 Captain Robert White is listed as owner of the Philadelphia-built and -registered (1767) ship.

180 Lloyd's Register lists Harford & Company as owner of the 200-ton ship.

181 The indentures of German immigrants recorded before the mayor of Philadelphia survived for the ships no. 287–310.

182 The *Staatsbote* reported that 10 passengers died at sea.

183 Willing & Morris is listed as owner of the Philadelphia-registered (1769) ship.

184 James Christie of Baltimore.

185 Captain Richard Hunter is listed as owner of the ship.

186 John Gray & Company.

187 Willing, R. Morris, and S. Mifflin (Philadelphia) are listed as owners of the Philadelphia-built and -registered ship.

188 Henry Keppele and John Steinmetz, later Keppele & Steinmetz & Sons; Keppele & Steinmetz are listed as owners of the Philadelphia-built and -registered (1771) ship that sailed with a crew of 8; a financial account of the voyage survives and shows that only part of the income from the ship's run came from transporting German migrants across the Atlantic ("Redemptioners," HSP); difficult, 20-week-long voyage (Faust, *Unpublished Documents*).

189 Bringhurst and Mifflin.

190 Samuel Howell & Sons.

191 Joshua Fisher & Sons.

192 In the German emigrant trade, this is the only ship to make two voyages in one year (nos. 303, 308).

193 Richard Neave's account book (HSP) includes details on his trade with servants.

194 John Warder & Sons.

195 Account by J. C. Büttner.

196 According to the *Staatsbote*, several died at sea.

197 Joshua, Thomas, and Samuel Fisher of Philadelphia, J. and D. Barclay, and J. Herford of London are listed as owners of the Philadelphia-built and -registered (1770) ship. Detailed financial records survived for this voyage ("Redemptioners," HSP).

198 Samuel Howell of Philadelphia and D. Malcom and E. Nivinson of Jamaica are listed as owners of the Philadelphia-built and -registered (1770) ship.

199 CUST(oms) 61/4, Cowes (28 August 1773).

200 John Ross and William McMutrie of Philadelphia are listed as owners of the Philadelphia-built and -registered (1773) ship.

201 In an advertisement in the *Staatsbote*, the immigrants are characterized as very healthy and mostly young.

202 Margaret and William Duncan of Philadelphia and Captain Robert Hardie are listed as owners of the New Jersey–built and Philadelphia-registered (1773) ship.

203 John Winey of Philadelphia is listed as owner of the Philadelphia-built and -registered (1773) ship.

204 Passenger's account (*Pennsylvania German Society Proceedings and Addresses* 9 [1899]: 100–110).

205 Size of ship: 500 tons, 130 feet long, 32 feet wide.

206 Balderston, *Claypoole Letter Book*; "1683 Ships."

207 Passenger's account (Samuel Guldin, *Journal of the Presbyterian Historical Society* 14 [1930–31]: 28–41, 64–73).

208 Report of arrival of ships with German immigrants (nos. 334–37) published in *Colonial Records* 3:29.

209 The *American Weekly Mercury* (1 September 1720) reported "passengers here to settle."

210 Benjamin Furly vouched for Archibald Hope.

211 Customhouse notice in *American Weekly Mercury* (21 September 1721).

212 Tim Pillans.

213 Customhouse notice in *American Weekly Mercury* (25 October 1722).

214 An advertisement in the *American Weekly Mercury* (18 December 1722) noted that a ship lying in Elk River would sail in about two weeks to Philadelphia.

215 Passenger's account (Christopher Sauer, *PMHB* 45 [1912]: 243–54).

216 Stopover port also listed as Deal.

217 Two small children and 3 men died.

218 John Goddard.

219 Shipwrecked off Block Island near Rhode Island (26 December 1738); captain died; 109 landed, of whom 90 died; very high mortality attributed to bad water taken in Rotterdam (*Pennsylvania Gazette*, 1 February 1739).

220 Possibly wrecked or misrouted; left Dover the same date as *Samuel* (no. 80; Dover Port Books).

221 Description of ship (Middlebrook, "*Mary*").

222 Possibly the ship in the Penrose account.

223 Because the navigation on the Delaware River was closed, the passengers landed at Lewes, Delaware; the Moravians continued their journey by land to Bethlehem via Philadelphia (*PMHB* 33 [1909]: 235).

224 Agent John Crellius brought Germans to Philadelphia and offered them to Samuel Waldo as settlers for his lands in northern New England.

225 The *Francis & Elizabeth* and the *Rachel* were not allowed to land because of many sick passengers; almost half of the immigrants died at sea, including the captain of the former (S/H, 409; *Colonial Records* 5:410; *Pennsylvanische Berichte*). The Penrose account books provide the number of freights for both vessels and thereby demonstrate that more than half the German migrants died during the voyage.

226 Reported in *Lloyd's Lists* (no. 1422) with Philadelphia as destination; Brinck, *Auswanderungswelle* (appendix), gives Annapolis as the ship's port of arrival—with "231 Germans."

227 *Lloyd's Lists* (no. 1440) makes no mention of passengers. The ship sailed with immigrants in 1748, and it is possible that it carried few or passengers' baggage, or none, on its run in 1749.

228 *Lloyd's Lists* (no. 1471) reported that the ship passed by Charleston, damaged and with many dead, that the captain was forced along shore at Cape Fear, and he is fitting out the vessel; Brinck, *Auswanderungswelle* (appendix), lists Charleston as the destination of the "more than 400" emigrants.

229 *Lloyd's Lists* (no. 1439) does not specifically mention German immigrants on board.

230 Jacob Frederic Curtius made an agreement with Stedman and Hope to ship German emigrants to the American colonies.

231 *Pennsylvanische Berichte* (no. 145) reported that a ship with a few Germans arrived after one year: it had taken five months to reach the Delaware. Because it was frozen, the ship went on to Antigua; when it ran out of provisions, many, including the captain, became sick from scurvy and died.

232 *Pennsylvania Berichte* (no. 148) reported that most of the German and French passengers on board were single (see also Dick's 1752 list of ships; *Lloyd's Lists* [no. 1771]).

233 Lewes, Delaware.

234 In early February 1754, *Pennsylvanische Berichte* reported that the ship ran aground near Margate and capsized; the captain, his son, three sailors, three German men, four German women, and one English woman drowned.

235 From the entries in *Lloyd's Lists* (nos. 1840, 1842), it is not clear whether the vessel sailed with German emigrants or whether Cowes or Plymouth was the stopover port.

236 It is not clear from *Lloyd's Lists* (nos. 1845, 1847, 1850) whether the ship sailed with German emigrants.

237 Listed in Brinck, *Auswanderungswelle* (appendix), with 58 men.

238 "List of outstanding debts . . ." ("Redemptioners," HSP).

239 *Lloyd's Lists* (no. 2998).

240 When the ship arrived in Cowes, its goods were seized (30 June 1764), which delayed the voyage (CUST[oms] 61/3, Cowes [16 July 1766]).

241 James Crawford and Patrick Crawford, Lord Conservator of the Scotch privileges in the Netherlands.

242 Financial accounts ("Redemptioners," HSP).

243 Notice in *Staatsbote* (no. 676) asking for payment of outstanding fares.

244 For a list of names of emigrants to Nova Scotia, see C(olonial) O(ffice) 221/36; printed in T. B. Atkins, *Select Documents on the History of Nova Scotia*; the standard account of the migration is Bell, *Foreign Protestants*.

245 John Dick, English merchant in Rotterdam, obtained a commission from the English government to recruit and transport German Protestants to Nova Scotia (*Board of Trade Journal*; Bell, *Foreign Protestants*).

246 On the *Speedwell*, 17 passengers died en route; on the *Gale*, 2 died; on the *Pearl*, 32; and on the *Murdoch*, 29.

247 Sedgwick & Kilby of London; S. Züberbuhler acted as agent for Samuel Waldo.

248 On ships no. 502–11, the government shipped 3,300 Germans as redemptioners; 965 died while awaiting shipping, during the voyage, or shortly after landing (for details, see Knittle, *Palatine Emigration*; Jones, *Palatine Families of New York*; Wust, *Guardian*).

249 Immigrants returning with Ulrich Simmendinger of Reutlingen (Wust, *Guardian*, 10).

250 Ships no. 512 and 513 arrived with German immigrants (Wust, *Guardian*, 10).

251 After wandering for 30 weeks via Bermuda, only 80–90 Palatines (of the 180 who set out) arrived (*Pennsylvania Gazette* [15 March 1773]; Wust, *Guardian*, 11; *Pennsylvania Gazette*, 22 March 1732/3).

252 From 1734 to 1738 the captain regularly carried immigrants to New York, ranging from 50 to 300 per run, averaging 175 (Wust, *Guardian*, 11).

253 Levinius Clarkson, Amsterdam.

254 Another report lists about 160 passengers for the *Anna*.

255 The ship was built for the Moravians in New York in 1748 and registered in the name of Henry Antes. Like the other ships of the Moravians (*Little Strength, Jacob, Hope*) it operated out of the captain's port, New York.

256 Wust estimated that New York received 1,800 immigrants as "spillover" from Pennsylvania in 1750–54 (*Guardian*, 12).

257 The ship left Rotterdam for New York; it made it into port (Duinkerken) on 23 August 1752 with 8 feet of water.

258 The Moravians had the ship built in New Haven, Connecticut, in 1760 with four cannons and to be operated by a crew of 13; it was registered in New York.

259 Miners and ironworkers from Berg and Siegen under contract with Peter Hasenclever to develop his ironworks in the colonies (Wust, *Guardian*, 11).

260 CUST(oms) 61/3; Cowes, 11 January 1766.

261 Passengers sickly; eighty died.

262 William Byrd and J. L. Haeberlin invested in German settlers (Wust, "Emigration Season of 1738").

263 About 300 Palatines had set out; 200 arrived in Hampton Road, Virginia, 100 died during the passage.

264 Ship bound with 200 Palatines for Virginia; suspected of smuggling liquor (CUST[oms] 61/2, Cowes, 13 August 1755, PRO, London).

265 Landed with fifty Salzburgers and others in Port Royal, South Carolina, who were destined for South Carolina and Georgia.

266 Arrived with 250 Swiss immigrants (Meriwether, *South Carolina*).

267 Stephen and Joseph Crell arrived with "their people" (Meriwether, *South Carolina*).

268 John Jacob Riemensperger and twenty-nine families arrived (Meriwether, *South Carolina*).

269 John Jacob Riemensperger arrived late in the year with immigrants from Zurich (Meriwether, *South Carolina*).

270 Ship with about 170 Palatine families was bound for South Carolina but taken and plundered by French privateers (*Pennsylvania Gazette*, 11 October 1744).

271 The papers in Philadelphia (*Pennsylvanische Berichte*, *American Weekly Mercury*) reported that the captain in effect forced the German immigrants to land in Charleston rather than Philadelphia and that the ship was chased by French privateers.

272 In October, the ship was in an inlet south of Charleston, but it was put to sea again with water for only four days; no news since then (*Pennsylvania Gazette*, 23 November 1749).

273 La Roche, de la Vilette & Montaigut.

274 Inglis, Pickering & Wraxall.

275 Brinck, *Auswanderungswelle* (appendix), lists Maryland as the destination of the ship.

276 Probably the vessel listed in *Lloyd's Lists*, no. 1730 (19 June 1752).

277 All 163 immigrants who arrived were sick; 20 died during the passage; 20 died three days after landing (Meriwether, *South Carolina*).

278 Many of the 225 immigrants arrived sick; 25 died after landing (Meriwether, *South Carolina*; Revill, *Lists of Protestant Immigrants*).

279 About 200 immigrants (Revill, *Lists of Protestant Immigrants*).

280 Arrival of 283 immigrants (Revill, *Lists of Protestant Immigrants*).

281 Arrival of 32 immigrants (Revill, *Lists of Protestant Immigrants*).

282 Arrival of 53 immigrants (Revill, *Lists of Protestant Immigrants*).

283 George Fenwick Jones estimated a total of 2,661 immigrants to Georgia; for details, see *Germans of Colonial Georgia* and *Georgia Dutch*.

284 Arrived with 60 migrants from Swabia.

285 Arrived with 160 migrants from Württemberg.

286 Benjamin d'Harriet & John McCall. Brinck, *Auswanderungswelle* (appendix), lists the destination of the emigrant ship as Charleston.

287 The *Success*—with 160 emigrants from Württemberg—is listed in Brinck, *Auswanderungswelle* (appendix), but is not mentioned by George Fenwick Jones.

288 The migration of German and Swiss settlers to French Louisiana was excluded from all calculations regarding the flow of German-speaking migrants to British North America (as an indication, the numbers of the voyages appear in parentheses). Giraud, *Histoire de la Louisiane Française* (vol. 4, esp. chap. 3) estimates that 1,500 emigrants left for Louisiana (229 or 259 German and Swiss passengers on *Les Deux Frères*; 210 on *La Garonne*; 245 on *La Charente*; 300 on *Le Portefaix*; and 270 on *La Saône*). Mortality during the voyage was very high, as was the rate of death among the 2,490 migrants in port awaiting transportation from Lorient to the French colony. Usner, *Lower Mississippi*, 32–33; estimated that the Company of the Indies settled about 1,300 Germans in Louisiana in the early 1720s.

289 Possibly the same ship as 519.

290 Palatines arrived on St. Christopher's in miserable condition; 170 had died (*Pennsylvania Gazette*, 30 April 1741). The immigrants were redeemed by planters.

291 *Pennsylvanische Berichte* (nos. 55, 60) reported that the ship was captured by two Spanish men-of-war. The captain and some passengers were transferred to a Dutch ship, which landed them in England; 175 arrived in Gosport on 1 April 1745.

292 According to *Pennsylvanische Berichte* (no. 55). 350 of the ship's 400 passengers died of starvation.

293 Moravians (*PMHB* 33 [1909]: 234).

294 According to Mittelberger (*Journey*, 25), the ship was half-wrecked and driven onto the coast of Ireland. Most of the 340 passengers died of starvation.

[295] Mittelberger (*Journey*, 24) reported that the ship was wrecked in a storm in the Channel. Of the 360 passengers, only 63 survived.

[296] Shipwreck described in broadside (Broadside Collection, HSP).

[297] In a storm, the ship struck a rock off the coast of Flanders and was wrecked. Of the 700 passengers and crew, 72 survived, of whom 14 made it to America (letter of H. J. Schmitt).

[298] Directed to Philadelphia, but did not arrive.

Selected Bibliography

UNPUBLISHED MANUSCRIPTS

Canada

Public Archives of Nova Scotia
  "List of the Several Ships Clear'd out this Year [1752] at Gosport for the Several
    British Colonies in America with German Settlers" (Board of Trade, CO
    217/13, 363).

Germany

Landesarchiv Speyer
  Bestand F22 (no. 37, last folder, 43).
  Oberschultheissereirechnungen (Alsace, 1710–17).

The Netherlands

Algemeen Rijksarchief, The Hague
  College of the Admiralty of the Maas.

Gemeente Archief Arnhem
  Oud-Archief van Arnhem: Commissie- en Politieboeken der Stad Arnhem.

Gemeentearchief Nijmegen
  Oud-Archief der Gemeente Nijmegen: Schenkenschans tol.

Gemeentelijke Archiefdienst van Amsterdam
  Archief Brants (no. 88).
  Doopsgezinde Gemeenten in Nederland, 16e–20e eeuw (no. 565); Commissie voor
    de Buitenlandsche Nooten (Later: Algemeene Commissie voor Buitenlandsche
    Nooden der Doopgesinde Gemeenten) (1655), 1705–1825 en 1920–30 (partial

copies from "Gemeente Archief Amsterdam, Mennonite Amsterdam Archives,"
on microfilm at the Lancaster Mennonite Historical Society, Lancaster,
Pennsylvania; also among the Dutch West India Company Transcripts, HSP).
Gemeente Archief Amsterdam: Notarial Archives (= GAA, NA).
Samuel Hart Archief.
Hope & Company (no. 735).
Notarissen ter standplaats Amsterdam, 1578–1895 (no. 5075).

Gemeentelijke Archiefdienst van Rotterdam
Archief Doopsgezinde Gemeente.
Gemeente Archief Rotterdam: Oude Notariel Archief (= GAR, ONA).
Handschriftenverzameling (1461, 3157, 3259).
Oud Archief van der Stad Rotterdam (2783, 2218).
Archief der Gemeente Rotterdam, OSA (1769): College of the Admiralty of the
Maas.

Rijksarchief in Gelderland, Arnhem
Archief Hof van Gelre: Memorie- en Resolutien Boeken.
Archief Staten Veluwe: Kwartiersrecessen.
Gelderse Rekenkamer, 1559–1795 (702–6, 803).

United Kingdom

Public Record Office (PRO), London (Chancery Lane)
Ex[chequer]: Portbooks (Deal, Dover, Plymouth).

Public Record Office (PRO), London (Kew)
Adm[iralty].
C[olonial] O[ffice].
Cust[oms]: Copies of Counsel's Opinions; Cowes, Collector of Board; Minutes
of the Board of Customs; Plantation Commission; Reports/Accounts to
Commissioners of Ships.
T[reasury]: Extract of Advices from Amsterdam; Miscellaneous Revenue
Returns.

USA

Archives of the Commonwealth of Massachusetts, Boston
Massachusetts Archives, Emigrants (vol. 15A: Emigrants, 1651–1774).

City Archives of Philadelphia
Record of Indentures of Individuals Bound Out as Apprentices, Servants, etc., and
of Germans and Other Redemptioners in the Office of the Mayor of the City of
Philadelphia, 3 October 1771 to 5 October 1773.

College of William and Mary, Williamsburg, Virginia
Abbot E. Smith Papers.

German Society of Pennsylvania (GSP), Philadelphia

Beamtenratsprotokoll (Protocol der Beamten der incorporierten deutschen Gesellschaft [Minutes of the Officers of the Incorporated GSP]), vol. 1 (1770–1802).
Historical Society of Pennsylvania (HSP), Philadelphia
Accountbook, Richard Neave Jr., 1773–74.
Broadside Collection.
Business Collection, Benjamin Fuller Letter Book, 1762–81.
Cadwalader Collection: General John Cadwalader; Thomas Cadwalader Section; Philadelphia Custom House Records.
Church and Meeting Collection (Moravians).
James Claypoole's Letter Book, London and Philadelphia, 1681–84.
Clifford-Pemberton Papers.
Coates and Reynell Papers, John Reynell Letter Book, 1744–45; Samuel Coates Letter Book, 1763–81.
Cox-Parrish-Wharton Papers.
Ferdinand J. Dreer Autograph Collection (Physicians, Surgeons & Chemists).
Drinker Papers, James and Drinker Letter Book, 1764–66.
Dutch West India Company (Transcripts, Folder 7): 1709 Palatine Emigration; Letter Book of the Burgomasters; Letters Sent to Burgomasters, 1707–13; Resolutions and Dispositions of Burgomasters; College of the Admiralty at Rotterdam.
Simon Gratz Collection: Physicians.
John Hunt & Isaac Greenleafe, London, Letter Book, 1747–49.
List of Servants Belonging to the Inhabitants of Pennsylvania and Taken into His Majesty's Service, for Whom Satisfaction Has not Been Made by the Officers According to the Act of Parliament (21 April 1757).
John J. McCusker, "The Pennsylvania Shipping Industry in the Eighteenth Century" (1973).
John J. McCusker, "Ships Registered at the Port of Philadelphia Before 1776: A Computerized Listing."
Moravian Immigration to America, 1734–1800.
Norris Papers: Isaac Norris Sr. Letter Book, 1716–30; Isaac Norris Sr. and Jr. Letter Book, 1719–56.
Pemberton Papers: Thomas and John Clifford Letter Book, 1759–66; 1767–73; John Hunt Correspondence.
Penn Manuscripts: Official Correspondence; Thomas Penn Letter Book.
Penn Papers: Microfilm Edition; Penn & Baltimore, Penn Family.
Pennsylvania Miscellaneous Papers: Penn & Baltimore; Penn & Baltimore, Penn Family, 1725–39.
Thomas Penrose Journal (= Penrose Cashbooks, 1738–51).
Record of Indentures of Individuals Bound Out as Apprentices, Servants etc. in Philadelphia, Penna., by Mayor John Gibson, 5 December 1772–21 May 1772, and Mayor William Fisher, 1773.
Redemptioners, 1774–75, Custom House, London.

Servants and Apprentices Bound and Assign'd Before James Hamilton Mayor of Philadelphia, 1745 and 1746.

Shippen Family Papers.

Ship Register, 1741–42.

Society Miscellaneous Collection: Philadelphia; Redemptioners, 1750–1830.

Some Account of the Life & Travels of Tho. Chalkey.

Wister Family Papers: John Wister Ledger, 1748–70 (alms account: 1:476, 470).

Jasper Yeates-Brinton Collection, John Steinmetz Papers.

Lancaster Mennonite Historical Society, Lancaster, Pa.
Records of the [Mennonite] Committee on Foreign Needs in Amsterdam (partial copy on microfilm: "European Mennonites, Amsterdam Archives").

Library Company of Philadelphia, Philadelphia
Jonathan Dickinson Letter Book, 1715–21.

Library of Congress, Manuscript Division, Washington, D.C.
Foreign Copying Project: Germany, Herrenhut (Archiv der Brüder-Unität), Höchst (Preußisches Staatsarchiv Wiesbaden, Amt Höchst, Kurpfalz (Bayerisches Staatsarchiv Speyer), Neuwied (Fürstlich Weidsches Archiv); Great Britain; Netherlands, Gemeente Archief Rotterdam (s.v. landverhuizers, emigranten), "List of Palatines Who Left Rotterdam to the Various Destinations (in the English Colonies of America)" (Minutes of the Council, Archieven der Admiraliteits Colleges, XXXI, no. 239:5–18, Algemeen Rijksarchief, The Hague); Switzerland: Bern Immigraiton Records, 1705–49.

Records of the Vice-Admiralty Court Held at Philadelphia.

George Washington Papers, series 4 (microfilm).

Maryland Historical Society, Baltimore, Maryland
Dulany Papers.

Pennsylvania Historical and Museum Commission (PHMC), Harrisburg, Pennsylvania
Burd-Shippen Family Papers.

Register of Wills, Philadelphia (City Hall Annex), Pennsylvania
Philadelphia County Wills and Administrations.

NEWSPAPERS AND ALMANACS

American Weekly Mercury (1719–49), Philadelphia.

Der Ehrliche Kurtzweilige Deutsche: Americanische Geschichte und Haus Calender (1763), Chestnut Hill, Pa.

Der Gantz Neue Verbesserte Nord-Americanische Calender (1775–80), Lancaster, Pa.

Ein Geistliches Magazin (1764–70), Germantown, Pa.

Gentlemen's Magazine, London.

Der Hoch-Deutsch Americanische Calender (1739–78), Germantown, Pa.

Der Hoch-Deutsch Pennsylvanische Geschicht-Schreiber [. . .] (1739–43); after 1743 *Pennsylvanische Berichte*, Germantown, Pa.

Jahresbericht der Deutschen Gesellschaft von Pennsylvania (1764–[75]), Philadelphia.

Lancaster Gazette / Lancasterische Zeitung (1752–53), Lancaster, Pa.

Neu-eingerichteter Americanischer Geschichts-Calender (1747–51, 1759–67), Philadelphia.

Der Neuste, Verbessert- und Zuverläßige Americanische Calender (1763–79), Philadelphia.

Pennsylvania Gazette (1729–1800), Philadelphia.

Rotterdamse Courant (Rotterdam).

Die Philadelphische Zeitung (1732, 1755–57), Philadelphia.

Der Wöchentliche Philadelphische Staatsbote (1762–67); *Der Wöchentliche Pennsylvanische Staatsbote* (1768–75), Philadelphia (= *Staatsbote*).

SECONDARY LITERATURE AND PRINTED SOURCES

Abel, Wilhelm. *Geschichte der deutschen Landwirtschaft vom frühen Mittelalter bis zum 19. Jahrhundert. Deutsche Agrargeschichte, 2.* Second edition. Stuttgart, 1967.

———. *Massenarmut und Hungerkrisen im vorindustriellen Deutschland.* Göttingen, 1972.

Adams, William Forbes. *Ireland and Irish Emigration to the New World from 1815 to the Famine.* 1931; reprint ed., New York, 1960.

Adams, Willi Paul, ed. *Die deutschsprachige Auswanderung in die Vereinigten Staaten. Bericht über Forschungsstand und Quellenbestände.* Berlin, 1980.

Åkerman, Sune. "Theories and Methods of Migration Research." In *From Sweden to America: A History of the Migration.* "A Collective Work of the Uppsala Migration Research Project." Edited by Harald Runblom and Hans Norman. Minneapolis, Minn., 1976, 19–75.

———. "Towards an Understanding of Emigrational Processes." In *Human Migration: Patterns and Policies.* Edited by William H. McNeill and Ruth S. Adams. Bloomington, Ind., 1978, 287–306.

Aland, Kurt, ed. *Die Korrespondenz Heinrich Melchior Mühlenbergs aus der Anfangszeit des deutschen Luthertums in Nordamerika.* 5 vols. Berlin, 1986–96.

Allen, David Grayson. *In English Ways: The Movement of Societies and the Transferal of English Local Law and Customs to Massachusetts Bay in the Seventeenth Century.* Chapel Hill, N.C., 1981.

Alter, Willi, ed. *Pfalzatlas.* Speyer, 1963–79.

Altman, Ida, and James Horn, eds. *To Make America: European Emigration in the Early Modern Period.* Berkeley and Los Angeles, 1991.

Americana in Deutschen Sammlungen. Ein Verzeichnis von Materialien zur Geschichte der Vereinigten Staaten von Amerika in Archiven und Bibliotheken der Bundesrepublik Deutschland und West-Berlins. Compiled at the Request of the Deutsche Gesellschaft für Amerikastudien. Volume 4: Rheinland-Pfalz. Volume 5: Bayern. Baden-Württemberg, 1967.

"Zur Amerikaauswanderung aus kurpfälzischen Oberämtern (auch Heidelberg): Auswanderung von 1764–1766." *Zeitschrift für die Geschichte des Oberrheins.* Supplement, n.s., 81 (1972): 493.

"Eine Amerikareise vor 200 Jahren: Brief des Johann Friedrich Naschold aus Plattenhardt, New York, 26. Oktober 1754." *Genealogie. Deutsche Zeitschrift für Familienkunde* 15/16 (1966/67): 543–45.

Ammerich, Hans. *Landesherr und Landesverwaltung. Beiträge zur Regierung von Pfalz-Zweibrücken am Ende des Alten Reiches.* Veröffentlichungen der Kommission für Saarländische Landesgeschichte und Volksforschung, 11. Saarbrücken, 1981.

Arndt, Karl J. R., ed. and comp. *George Rapp's Separatists, 1700–1803: The German Prelude to Rapp's American "Harmony Society."* "A Documentary History." Worcester, Mass., 1980.

Assion, Peter. *Von Hessen in die Neue Welt. Eine Sozial- und Kulturgeschichte der hessischen Amerikaauswanderung mit Text- und Bilddokumenten.* Frankfurt am Main, 1987.

Assion, Peter, ed. *Der Große Aufbruch. Studien zur Amerikaauswanderung.* Marburg, 1985.

Atwood, Rodney. *The Hessians: Mercenaries from Hessen-Kassel in the American Revolution.* New York, 1980.

Auerbach, Inge. *Auswanderung aus Kurhessen. Nach Osten oder Westen?* Schriften des Hessisichen Staatsarchivs Marburg, 10. Marburg/Lahn, 1993.

———. *Hessische Auswanderer (HESAUS). Index nach Familiennamen, Volume 1: Auswanderer aus Hanau im 18. Jahrhundert.* Marburg/Lahn, 1987.

Auerbach, Inge, ed. *Auswanderung aus Hessen. Ausstellung der Hessischen Staatsarchive zum Hessentag in Lampertheim.* Second edition. Marburg/Lahn, 1986.

Auerbach, Inge, et al. *Auswanderung aus Hessen.* Exhibition handbook. Marburg/Lahn, 1984.

"Auszug einiger Sendschreiben aus Philadelphia in Pennsylvania, . . . [1729]" (Diary of a Voyage from Rotterdam to Philadelphia in 1728). In *Pennsylvania: The German Influence in Its Settlement and Development,* part 9. Translated by Julius F. Sachse. Lancaster, Pa., 1909, 5–25.

"Authentic Open Letter from Pennsylvania in America . . . [1739]." In *Brethren in Colonial America.* Translated by Donald Durnbaugh, 41–53.

Bade, Karl J. "Sozialhistorische Migrationsforschung." *Bevölkerungsgeschichte im Vergleich. Studien zu den Niederlanden und Nordwestdeutschland,* 63–74. Aurich, 1988.

Bade, Karl J., ed. *Deutsche im Ausland—Fremde in Deutschland. Migration in Geschichte und Gegenwart.* Munich, 1992.

Baier, Hermann. "Auswanderung aus dem Bodenseegebiet in den Jahren 1767–1772." *Bodensee-Chronik* 24 (1935): 6–8.

———. "Untersuchungen zur Geschichte der Auswanderung in den Jahren 1712, 1737 und 1787." *Freiburger Diözesanarchiv,* n.s., 37 (1936): 314–57.

Bailyn, Bernard. *The Peopling of British North America: An Introduction.* Madison, Wis., 1985.

———. *Voyagers to the West: A Passage in the Peopling of America on the Eve of the Revolution.* New York, 1986.

Baird, Charles W. *History of the Huguenot Emigration to America.* 2 vols. New York, 1885.

Balderston, Marion. "Pennsylvania's 1683 Ships and Some of Their Passengers." *Pennsylvania Genealogical Magazine* 24 (1965): 69–114.

Balderston, Marion, ed., *James Claypoole's Letter Book, London and Philadelphia, 1681–1684.* San Marino, Calif., 1967.

Barkan, Elliott Robert. *Asian and Pacific Islander Migration to the United States: A Model of New Global Patterns.* Contributions in Ethnic Studies, no. 30. Westport, Conn., 1992.

Barkhausen, Max. "Governmental Control and Free Enterprise in Western Germany and the Low Countries in the Eighteenth Century." In *Essays in European Economic History, 1500–1800.* Edited by Peter Earle. Oxford, 1974, 212–73.

Barrow, Thomas C. *Trade and Empire: The British Customs Service in Colonial America, 1660–1775.* Cambridge, Mass., 1967.

Becker, Albert. "Zur oberrheinischen Bevölkerungsgeschichte des 17. und 18. Jahrhunderts." *Zeitschrift für die Geschichte des Oberrheins* 95 (1943): 676–85.

Beiler, Rosalind J. "The Transatlantic World of Caspar Wistar: From Germany to America in the Eighteenth Century." Ph.D. dissertation, University of Pennsylvania, 1994.

———. "Transporting Settlers to the British Colonies: The Religious Foundations of Transatlantic Migration." ISHAW, 1996.

Bell, Raymond M. "Emigrants from Wolfersweiler Parish, Germany, to Pennsylvania Before 1750." *National Genealogical Society Quarterly* 63 (1975): 105–9.

Bell, Winthrop P. *The "Foreign Protestants" and the Settlement of Nova Scotia.* Toronto, 1961.

Bennion, Lowell C. "Flight from the Reich: A Geographic Exposition of Southwest German Emigration, 1683–1815." Ph.D. dissertation, Syracuse University, 1971.

Benson, Adolph B., ed. *The America of 1750: Peter Kalm's Travels in North America. The English Version of 1770.* 2 vols. New York, 1937.

Berkey, Andrew S., ed. and trans. *The Journals and Papers of David Schultze.* 2 vols. Pennsburg, Pa., 1952–53.

Binder-Johnson, Hildegard. "Der deutsche Amerika-Auswanderer des 18. Jahrhunderts im zeitgenössisschen Urteil." *Deutsches Archiv für Landes- und Volks-Forschung* (Leipzig) 4 (1940): 211–34.

Blickle, Peter. "Bauer und Staat in Oberschwaben." *Zeitschrift für Württembergische Landesgeschichte* 31 (1972): 104–20.

Blickle, R. "Nahrung und Eigentum als Kategorien in der ständischen Gesellschaft." In *Ständische Gesellschaft und soziale Mobilität.* Edited by Winfried Schulze. Schriften des Historischen Kollegs, Kolloquien 12. Munich, 1988.

Blocher, Andreas. *Die Eigenart der Zürcher Auswanderer nach Amerika, 1734–1744.* Zurich, 1976.

Böhme, Anton Wilhelm. *Das verlangte, nicht erlangte Canaan. . . .* Frankfurt, 1711.

Bopp, Marie-Joseph. *Die evangelischen Gemeinden und Hohen Schulen in Elsass und Lothringen von der Reformation bis zur Gegenwart.* Neustadt an der Aisch, 1963.

Boyer, Carl, III, ed. *Ship Passenger Lists: National and New England (1600–1825).* Newhall, Calif., 1977.

———. *Ship Passenger Lists: New York and New Jersey, 1600–1825.* Newhall, Calif., 1978.

———. *Ship Passenger Lists: Pennsylvania and Delaware, 1641–1825.* Newhall, Calif., 1980.

————. *Ship Passenger Lists: The South, 1583–1825.* Newhall, Calif., 1979.

Braubach, Max. "Vom Westfälischen Frieden bis zum Wiener Kongreß, 1648–1815." In *Rheinische Geschichte.* Edited by Franz Petri and Georg Droege. Volume 2: *Neuzeit.* Düsseldorf, 1976.

Braun, Fritz. *Auswanderer aus Enkenbach seit Beginn des 18. Jahrhunderts.* Schriften zur Wanderungsgeschichte der Pfälzer, 11. Kaiserslautern (n.d.).

————. *Auswanderer aus Kaiserslautern im 18. Jahrhundert.* Schriften zur Wanderungsgeschichte der Pfälzer, 17. Kaiserslautern, 1965.

Braun, Fritz, and Friedrich Krebs. "German Emigrants from Palatinate Parishes." Translated by Don Yoder. *Pennsylvania Genealogical Magazine* 25 (1968): 246–62.

Braun, Rudolf. "Early Industrialization and Demographic Changes in the Canton of Zurich." In *Historical Studies of Changing Fertility.* Edited by Charles Tilly. Princeton, N.J., 1978, 289–334.

Brecht, Martin. *Kirchenordnung und Kirchenzucht in Württemberg vom 16. bis zum 18. Jahrhundert.* Quellen und Froschungen zur Württembergischen Kirchengeschichte, Volume 1. Stuttgart, 1967.

Brecht, Martin, ed. *Der Pietismus vom siebzehnten bis zum frühen achtzehnten Jahrhundert.* Geschichte des Pietismus. Göttingen, 1993.

Brecht, Samuel Kriebel. *The Genealogical Record of the Schwenkfelder Families: Seekers of Religious Liberty Who Fled from Silesia to Saxony and Thence to Pennsylvania in the Years 1731–1737.* 2 vols. New York, 1923.

————. "Schwenkfelder Families." *PMHB* 10 (1886): 167–79.

Breen, Timothy. "Creative Adaptations: Peoples and Cultures." In Jack Greene and J. R. Pole, eds., *Colonial British America: Essays in the New History of the Early Modern Era.* Baltimore, Md., 1984, 195–232.

Bretting, Agnes, and Hartmut Bickelmann. *Auswanderungsagenturen und Auswanderungsvereine im 19. und 20. Jahrhundert.* Stuttgart, 1991.

Brewer, John. *The Sinews of Power: War, Money, and the English State, 1688–1783.* New York, 1989.

Bric, Maurice. "Ireland, Irishmen, and the Broadening of the Late Eighteenth-Century Philadelphia Polity." Ph.D. dissertation, Johns Hopkins University, 1990.

Brinck, Andreas. *Die deutsche Auswanderungswelle in die britischen Kolonien Nordamerikas um die Mitte des 18. Jahrhunderts.* Stuttgart, 1993.

Brite, John Duncan. "The Attitude of European States Toward Emigration to the American Colonies and the United States, 1607–1820." Ph.D. dissertation, University of Chicago, 1937.

Brophy, Alfred L. "Law and Indentured Servitude in Mid-eighteenth-Century Pennsylvania." *Willamette Law Review* 28 (1991): 69–126.

Brumbaugh, Martin G. *History of the German Baptist Brethren in Europe and America.* Mount Morris, Ill., 1899 (Johannes Naass to Jacob Wilhelm Naas, 17 October 1733, 108–24; Christopher Sauer to William Denny, 15 March 1755, 376–82).

Buist, Marten G. *At Spes Non Fracta: Hope & Co., 1770–1815: Merchant Bankers and Diplomats at Work.* The Hague, 1974.

Burgert, Annette Kunselman. *Brethren from Gimbsheim in the Palatinate to Ephrata and Bermudian in Pennsylvania.* Myerstown, Pa., 1994.

———. *A Century of Emigration from Affoltern am Albis, Canton Zürich, Switzerland.* Worthington, Ohio, 1984.

———. *Colonial Pennsylvania Immigrants from Freinsheim in the Palatinate.* Myerstown, Pa., 1989.

———. *Eighteenth- and Nineteenth-Century Emigrants from Lachen-Speyerdorf in the Palatinate.* Myerstown, Pa., 1989.

———. *Eighteenth-Century Emigrants, Volume 1: The Northern Kraichgau.* Breinigsville, Pa., 1983; *Volume 2, The Western Palatinate.* Birdsboro, Pa., 1985.

———. *Eighteenth-Century Emigrants from Pfungstadt, Hessen-Darmstadt, to Pennsylvania.* Myerstown, Pa., 1995.

———. *Eighteenth-Century Emigrants from the Northern Alsace to America.* Camden, Me., 1992.

———. *Emigrants from Eppingen to America in the Eighteenth and Nineteenth Centuries.* Myerstown, Pa., 1987.

———. *The Hochstadt Origins of Some of the Early Settlers at Host Church, Berks County, Pa.* Myerstown, Pa., 1983.

———. *Pennsylvania Pioneers from Wolfersweiler Parish, Saarland, Germany.* Worthington, Ohio, 1983.

———. *York County Pioneers from Friedelsheim and Gönnheim in the Palatinate.* Worthington, Ohio, 1984.

Burgert, Annette Kunselman, and Henry Z. Jones Jr. *Westerwald to America: Some Eighteenth-Century German Immigrants.* Camden, Me., 1989.

Buettner, Johann Carl. *Büttner, der Amerikaner. Eine Selbstbiographie Johann Carl Büttners, jeßigen Amts-Chirurgus in Senftenberg und ehemaligen nord-amerikanischen kriegers, mit dem Bildnisse des Verfassers.* Camenz, 1828.

———. *Narrative of Johann Carl Buettner in the American Revolution.* New York, 1971.

Campbell, Mildred. "English Emigration on the Eve of the American Revolution." *AHR* 61 (1955): 1–20.

Campbell, Red A. *The Religion of the Heart: A Study of European Religious Life in the Seventeenth and Eighteenth Centuries.* Columbia, S.C., 1991.

Canny, Nicholas, ed. *Europeans on the Move: Studies on European Migration, 1500–1800.* Oxford, 1994.

Carlsson, Sten. "Chronology and Composition of Swedish Emigration to America." In *From Sweden to America: A History of the Migration.* A Collective Work of the Uppsala Migration Research Project. Edited by Harald Runblom and Hans Norman. Minneapolis, 1976, 114–28.

Chandler, Charles Lyon, et al. *Philadelphia: Port of History, 1609–1837.* Philadelphia, 1976.

Chapelle, Howard. *History of American Sailing Ships.* New York, 1970.

Clark, Dennis. *Hibernia America: The Irish and Regional Cultures.* Contributions in Ethnic Studies, no. 14. New York, 1986.

Cohn, Raymond L. "Mortality on Immigrant Voyages to New York, 1836–1853." *Journal of European Economic History* 44 (June 1984): 289–300.

Coldham, Peter Wilson. *The Complete Book of Emigrants.* 4 vols. Baltimore, Md., 1993.

Coldham, Peter Wilson, ed. *Bonded Passengers to America.* 9 vols. in 3. Baltimore, Md., 1983.

Colonial Records (Minutes of the Provincial Council of Pennsylvania), 16 vols. Harrisburg, Pa., 1851–53.

Conzen, Kathleen Neils. "Mainstreams and Side Channels: The Localization of Immigrant Cultures." *Journal of American Ethnic History* 11:1 (Fall 1991): 5–20.

Conzen, Kathleen Neils, David Gerber, Ewa Morawska, George E. Pozzetta, and Rudolph Vecoli. "The Invention of Ethnicity: A Perspective from the U.S.A." *Journal of American Ethnic History* (Fall 1992): 3–41.

Correll, Ernst H. *Das Schweizerische Täufermennonitentum.* Tübingen, 1925.

Cressy, David. *Coming Over: Migration and Communication Between England and New England in the Seventeenth Century.* Cambridge, 1987.

Cullen, Louis M. "Economic Development, 1691–1750." In *A New History of Ireland.* Edited by T. W. Moody and W. E. Vaughan. Volume 4: *Eighteenth-Century Ireland.* Oxford, 1986.

———. "Economic Development, 1750–1800." In *A New History of Ireland.* Edited by T. W. Moody and W. E. Vaughan. Volume 4: *Eighteenth-Century Ireland.* Oxford, 1986.

———. "The Irish Diaspora of the Seventeenth and Eighteenth Centuries." In *Europeans on the Move: Studies on European Migration, 1500–1800.* Edited by Nicholas Canny. Oxford, 1994, 113–49.

———. *Merchants, Ships, and Trade, 1660–1830.* Dublin, 1971.

Curtin, Philip D. *The Atlantic Slave Trade: A Census.* Madison, Wis., 1969.

Daultry, Stuart, David Dickson, and Cormac O'Grada. "Eighteenth-Century Irish Population: New Perspectives from Old Sources." *JEconH* 41 (1981): 601–28.

Davies, Alun C. "As Good a Country as Any Man Needs to Dwell in." *Pennsylvania History* 50 (1983): 313–22.

Davis, Ralph. "Maritime History: Progress and Problems." In *Business and Businessmen: Studies in Business, Economics, and Accounting History.* Edited by Sheila Marrineer. Liverpool, 1978, 169–97.

———. *The Rise of the Atlantic Economy.* Ithaca, N.Y., 1973.

———. *The Rise of the English Shipping Industry in the Seventeenth and Eighteenth Centuries.* New York, 1962.

Debus, Karl Heinz, comp. "200 Jahre Vereinigte Staaten von Nordamerika. Pfälzische Dokumente über die Deutsch-Amerikanische Beziehung." Ausstellung des Landesarchivs Speyer in den Räumen der Stadtsparkasse Schifferstadt, 1977.

DeFoe, Daniel. *A Brief History of the Poor Palatine Refugees.* 1709. Los Angeles: Augustan Reprint Society, University of California, 1964.

Deiler, J. Hanno. "The Settlement of the German Coast of Louisiana and the Creoles of German Descent." *German American Annals,* n.s., 7 (1909): 34–102, 123–63, 179–207. Reprint ed., Baltimore, Md., 1975.

Dell, Richard F. "The Operational Records of the Clyde Tobacco Fleet, 1747–1775." Paper read at the Scottish Historians Conference, Dundee, 1980.

Deppermann, Klaus. "Pennsylvanien als Asyl des frühen deutschen Pietismus." *Pietismus und Neuzeit* 10 (1982): 190–212.

Dern, John Philip. *London Churchbooks and the German Migration of 1709.* Schriften zur Wanderungsgeschichte der Pfälzer, 26. Kaiserslautern, 1968.

Dickson, David. "An Economic History of the Cork Region in the Eighteenth Century." Dissertation, University of Dublin, 1978.

Dickson, Robert J. *Ulster Emigration to Colonial America, 1718–1775.* 1966; reprinted with a new introduction by G. E. Kirkham. London, 1988.

Diefenbacher, Karl, Hans-Ulrich Pfister, and Kurt H. Hotz, eds. *Schweizer Einwanderer in den Kraichgau nach dem Dreißigjährigen Krieg mit ausgewählter Ortsliteratur.* Heimatverein Kraichgau, Sinsheim, 1983.

Diffenderfer, Frank R. *The German Immigration into Pennsylvania Through the Port of Philadelphia from 1700 to 1775 and the Redemptioners.* 1900; reprint ed., Baltimore, Md., 1977, 1979.

Dipper, Christof. "Volksreligiosität und Obrigkeit im 18. Jahrhundert." In *Volksreligiosität in der modernen Socialgeschichte.* Edited by Wolfgang Schieder. Göttingen, 1986.

Ditz, Toby. "Shipwrecked; or, Masculinity Imperiled: Mercantile Representations of Failure and the Gendered Self in Eighteenth-Century Philadelphia." *JAH* 81 (June 1994): 51–80.

"Documents Relating to Early German Settlers in America: The Scherer Family." *German American Annals,* n.s., 4 (1906): 252–61.

Doerflinger, Thomas M. *A Vigorous Spirit of Enterprise: Merchants and Economic Development in Revolutionary Philadelphia.* Chapel Hill, N.C., 1986.

Dollinger, Robert. *Geschichte der Mennoniten in Schleswig-Holstein, Hamburg und Lübeck.* Neumünster, 1930.

Doyle, David N. *Ireland, Irishmen, and Revolutionary America, 1760–1820.* Dublin, 1981.

Dreyfus, François-G. "Beitrag zu den Preisbewegungen im Oberrheingebiet im 18. Jahrhundert." *Vierteljahrschrift for Sozial- und Wirtschaftsgeschichte* 47 (1960): 245–56.

Duffin, James M. "Germantown Landowners, 1683–1714." *Germantown Crier* 39 (Spring 1986/87): 37–41; 39 (Spring 1987): 62–67; 42 (Spring 1990): 37–39, 42, 63–65.

Duffy, John. "The Passage to the Colonies." *Mississippi Valley Historical Review* 38 (1951): 21–38.

Dunaway, Wayland F. *The Scotch-Irish of Colonial Pennsylvania.* Chapel Hill, N.C., 1944.

Dunmore, M. Walter. "A Population Study of the Pennsylvania Germans in Berks and Neighboring Counties." *Historical Reviews of Berks County* 28 (1963): 113–16.

Durnbaugh, Donald F. *Brethren Beginnings: The Origins of the Church of the Brethren in Early Eighteenth-Century Europe.* Ambler, Pa., 1992.

———. "Christopher Sauer, Pennsylvania-German Printer: His Youth in Germany and Later Relationships with Europe." *PMHB* 82 (1958): 316–39.

———. "Radical Pietist Involvement in Early German Emigration to Pennsylvania." *Yearbook of German-American Studies* 29 (1994): 29–48.

———. "Radikaler Pietismus als Grundlage deutsch-amerikanischer kommunaler Siedlungen." *Pietismus und Neuzeit* 16 (1990): 112–31.

Durnbaugh, Donald F., ed. *The Brethren in Colonial America: A Source Book on the Transplantation and Development of the Church of the Brethren in the Eighteenth Century.* Elgin, Ill., 1967.

"An Early Description of Pennsylvania: Letter of Christopher Sower, Written in 1724, Describing Conditions in Philadelphia and Vicinity, and the Sea Voyage from Europe." *PMHB* 45 (1921): 243–54.

Easterlin, Richard A. *Population, Labor Force, and Long Swings in Economic Growth: The American Experience.* New York, 1968.

Education Facsimiles: Emigration. PRO of Northern Ireland.

Edwards, Ruth D. *An Atlas of Irish History.* Second edition. New York, 1981.

Eid, Leroy V. "'No Freight Paid So Well': Irish Emigration to Pennsylvania on the Eve of the American Revolution." *Eire-Ireland* 27:2 (1993): 35–59.

Ekirch, Roger A. *Bound for America: The Transportation of British Convicts to the Colonies, 1718–1775.* Oxford, 1987.

Eltis, David. "Free and Coerced Transatlantic Migrations: Some Comparisons." *AHR* 88 (April 1983): 251–80.

Emigration from Northern, Central, and Southern Europe: Theoretical and Methodological Principles of Research. International Symposium, Cracow, November 9–11, 1981. Cracow, 1983.

Emmer, Piet C., and M. Mörner. *European Expansion and Migration: Essays on the Intercontinental Migration from Africa, Asia, and Europe.* New York, 1992.

Emmer, Piet C., et al., eds. *Wirtschaft und Handel der Kolonialreiche.* Volume 4 of *Dokumente zur Geschichte der europäischen Expansion.* Munich, 1988.

Engels, Alfred. *Die Zollgrenze in der Eiffel. Eine wirtschaftsgeschichtliche Untersuchung für die Zeit 1740 bis 1834.* Schriften zur Rheinisch-Westfälischen Wirtschaftsgeschichte, Neue Folge der Veröffentlichungen des Archivs für Rheinisch-Westfälische Wirtschaftsgeschichte, vol. 2. Cologne, 1959.

Erickson, Charlotte. "Why Did Contract Labor Not Work in Nineteenth-Century United States?" In *International Labor Migration, Historical Perspectives,* vol. 24, 34–56. Edited by Shula Marks and Peter Richardson. Hounslow, Eng., 1984.

"Extracts from the Journal of Charles Clinton, Kept During the Voyage from Ireland to Pennsylvania." *PMHB* 22 (1902): 112–14.

"Extracts from the Letter-Book of Benjamin Marshall [Benjamin Marshall to Barnaby Egan, 9 November 1765]." *PMHB* 20 (1896): 209–10.

Fabian, Monroe H. "An Immigrant's Inventory." *Pennsylvania Folklife* 25:4 (1976): 47–48.

Falckner, Daniel. "Curieuse Nachricht von Pennsylvania." Translated by Julius F. Sachse in *Pennsylvania German Society: Proceedings and Addresses* 15 (1905).

Faust, Albert B. "Documents in Swiss Archives Relating to Emigration to the American Colonies in the Eighteenth Century." *AHR* 22 (1916): 98–132.

———. *The German Element in the United States.* 2 vols. 1927; reprint ed., New York, 1969.

———. *Guide to the Materials for American History in Swiss and Austrian Archives.* Washington, D.C., 1916.

———. "Unpublished Documents on Emigration from the Archives of Switzerland." *Deutsch-Amerikanische Geschichtsblätter. Jahrbuch der Deutsch-Amerikanischen Historischen Gesellschaft von Illinois* 18/19 (1920): 9–68.

Faust, Albert B., ed. "The Graffenried Manuscripts." *German American Annals,* n.s., 11 (1913): 205–302.

Faust, Albert B., and Gaius M. Brumbaugh, eds. *Lists of Swiss Emigrants in the Eighteenth Century to the American Colonies.* 1925; reprint edition with Leo Schelbert, "Notes on Swiss Emigrants." Baltimore, Md., 1976.

Fenske, Hans. "Die Deutsche Auswanderung." *Mitteilungen des Historischen Vereins der Pfalz* 76 (1978): 183–220.

———. "International Migration: Germany in the Eighteenth Century." *Central European History* 13:31–47.

Fertig, Georg. "'Um Anhoffung besserer Nahrung willen': Der lokale und motivationale Hintergrund von Auswanderung nach Britisch-Nordamerika im 18. Jahrhundert." Verein für Geschichte und Sozialkunde (Vienna). *Beiträge zur Historischen Sozialkunde* 22 (October–December 1992): 111–20.

———. "Household Formation and Economic Autarky in the Early Modern Atlantic World: Transatlantic Migration as a Test Case for the European Marriage Pattern." ISHAW, 1996.

———. "Transatlantic Migration from the German-Speaking Parts of Central Europe, 1600–1800: Proportions, Structures, and Explanations." In *Europeans on the Move: Studies on European Migration, 1500–1800,* 192–235. Edited by Nicholas Canny. Oxford, 1994.

Filby, P. William, ed., with Mary K. Meyer. *Passengers and Immigration Lists Index: A Guide to Published Archival Records of About 500,000 Passengers Who Came to the United States and Canada in the Seventeenth, Eighteenth, and Nineteenth Centuries.* 3 vols. Detroit, 1981.

Fitzpatrick, John Clement, ed. *The Writings of George Washington* (Washington, D.C., 1931), 3:85–96.

Fogleman, Aaron Spencer. "Auswanderung aus Südbaden im 18 Jahrhundert." *Zeitschrift der Breisgau-Geschichtsvereins ("Schau-ins-Land")* 106 (1987): 95–162.

———. "Hopeful Journeys: German Immigration and Settlement in Greater Pennsylvania, 1717–1775." Ph.D. dissertation, University of Michigan, 1991.

———. *Hopeful Journeys: German Immigration, Settlement, and Political Culture in Colonial America, 1717–1775.* Philadelphia, 1996.

———. "Migrations to the Thirteen British North American Colonies, 1700–1775: New Estimates." *JIH* 12 (Spring 1992): 691–709.

———. "Review Essay: Progress and Possibilities in Migration Studies: The Contributions of Werner Hacker to the Study of Early German Migration to Pennsylvania." *Pennsylvania History* 56 (October 1989): 318–29.

———. "The Transformation of Immigration into the United States During the Era of the American Revolution." ISHAW, 1996.

Forster, Marc. *The Counter-Reformation in the Villages: Religion and Reform in the Bishopric of Speyer, 1560–1720.* Ithaca, N.Y., 1992.

Foster, Joseph. *The Pursuit of Equal Liberty: George Bryan and the Revolution in Philadelphia.* University Park, Pa., 1994.

Franz, Günther. *Der Dreißigjährige Krieg und das deutsche Volk.* Quellen und Forschungen zur Agrargeschichte, vol. 7. Edited by Günther Franz and Wilhelm Abel. Stuttgart, 1979.

Friedrichs, Christopher. *Urban Society in an Age of War: Nördlingen, 1580–1720.* Princeton, N.J., 1979.

"From London to Philadelphia, 1742." *PMHB* 37 (1913): 94–106.

Fulbrook, Mary. *Piety and Politics: Religion and the Rise of Absolutism in England, Württemberg, and Prussia.* Cambridge, 1983.

Galenson, David W. *White Servitude in Colonial America.* London, 1981.

Gemery, Henry A. "Emigration from the British Isles to the New World, 1630–1700: Inferences from Colonial Populations." *Research in Economic History* 5 (1980): 179–231.

Gemery, Henry A., and James Horn. "British and French Indentured Servant Migration to the Caribbean: A Comparative Study of Seventeenth-Century Emigration and Labor Markets." N.p., n.d.

Genealogy of the Descendants of John Gar, or More Particularly of His Son Andreas Gaar, Who Emigrated from Bavaria to America in 1732. 1894; reprint ed., Boston, 1973.

A General Treatise of Naval Trade and Commerce, as Founded on the Laws and Statutes of This Realm in Which Those Relating to His Majesty's Customs, Merchants, Masters of Ships . . . &c. Are Particularly Considered and Treated with Due Care. . . . Second edition. In the Savoy (London), 1753.

Gerber, Adolf. *Die Nassau-Dillenburger Auswanderung nach Amerika im 18. Jahrhundert.* Flensburg, 1930.

Gerhard, Dietrich, ed. *Ständische Vertretungen in Europa im 17. und 18. Jahrhundert.* Publication of the Max-Planck-Institut no. 27. Göttingen, 1969.

"The German Emigration to America, 1709–1740." *Pennsylvania German Society: Proceedings and Addresses* 8 (1897): 142.

Gillingham, Harold E. *Marine Insurance in Philadelphia, 1721–1800.* Philadelphia, 1933.

———. "Philadelphia Arrivals, 1738." *Publications of the Genealogical Society of Pennsylvania* 12 (1934): 150.

Giraud, Marcel. *Histoire de la Louisiane de française,* vol. 4: *La Louisiane après la système de law, 1721–1723.* Presses Universitaires de France, 1974.

Goebel, Julius, ed. "Neue Dokumente zur Geschichte der Massenauswanderung im Jahr 1709." *Deutsch-Amerikanische Geschichtsblätter* 13 (1913): 181–201.

Goebel, Max. *Geschichte des christlichen Lebens in der rheinisch-westphälischen evangelischen Kirche.* 3 vols. 1849; reprint ed., Giessen, 1992.

Goldenberg, Joseph A. *Shipbuilding in Colonial America.* Mariners Museum, Newport News, Virginia. Charlottesville, Va., 1976.

Gonner, Eberhard, and Günther Haselier, eds. *Baden-Württemberg. Geschichte seiner Länder und Territorien.* Geschichte der deutschen Länder, Territorien-Ploetz: Sonderausgaben. Würzburg, 1975.

Görisch, Stephan W. *Information zwischen Werbung und Warnung. Die Rolle der Amerikaliteratur in der Auswanderung des 18. und 19. Jahrhunderts.* Quellen und Forschungen zur Hessischen Geschichte, vol. 84. Darmstadt, 1991.

Grabbe, Hans-Jürgen. "European Immigration to the United States in the Early National Period, 1783–1820," *Proceedings of the American Philosophical Society* 133 (1989): 190–214.

Green, E. R. R. "Ulster Emigrant Letters." In *Essays in Scotch-Irish History.* Edited by E. R. R. Green. New York, 1969.

Greene, Jack P. *Imperatives, Behaviors, and Identities: Essays in Early American Cultural History.* Charlottesville, Va. 1992.

———. *Pursuits of Happiness: The Social Development of Early Modern British Colonies and the Formation of American Culture.* Chapel Hill, N.C., 1988.

Griffin, Martin I. J., ed. "Early Irish Immigration: Few Catholics." *American Catholic Historical Researcher* 18 (1901): 99–103.

Grubb, Farley. "The Auction of Redemptioner Servants, Philadelphia, 1709–1804: An Economic Analysis." *JEconH* 48 (1988): 583–603.

———. "Colonial Immigrant Literacy: An Economic Analysis of Pennsylvania-German Evidence, 1727–1775." *Explorations in Economic History* 24 (1987): 63–76.

———. "The Disappearance of European Immigrant Servitude in the United States: An Economic Analysis of Market Collapse, 1785–1835." Department of Economics Working Paper No. 89–3, University of Delaware, 1988.

———. "Does Bound Labour Have to Be Coerced Labour? The Case of Colonial Immigrant Servitude versus Craft Apprenticeship and Life-Cycle Servitude-in-Husbandry." *Itinerario* 20 (1997): 28–51.

———. "Educational Choice in the Era Before Free Public Schooling: Evidence from German Immigrant Children in Pennsylvania, 1771–1817." *JEconH* 52 (1992): 363–74.

———. "The End of European Immigrant Servitude in the United States: An Economic Analysis of Market Collapse, 1772–1835." *JEconH* 54 (December 1994), 794–825.

———. "German Immigration to Pennsylvania, 1709 to 1820." *JIH* 20 (1990): 417–36.

———. "Immigrant Servant Labor: Their Occupational and Geographic Distribution in the Late Eighteenth-Century Mid-Atlantic Economy." *Social Science History* 9 (Summer 1985): 249–75.

———. "The Incidence of Servitude in Trans-Atlantic Migration, 1771–1804." *Explorations in Economic History* 22 (July 1985): 316–39.

———. "Long-Run Trend in the Values of European Immigrant Servants, 1654–1831: New Measurements and Interpretations." *Research in Economic History* 14 (1992): 167–240.

———. "The Market for Indentured Servants: Evidence on the Efficiency of Forward Labor Contracting in Philadelphia, 1745–1773." *JEconH* 45 (1985): 855–68.

———. "The Market Structure of Shipping German Immigrants to Colonial America." *PMHB* 111 (1987): 27–48.

———. "Morbidity and Mortality on the North Atlantic Passage: Eighteenth-Century German Immigration," *JIH* 17 (1987): 565–85.

———. "Redemptioner Emigration to Pennsylvania: Evidence on Contract Choice and Profitability." *JEconH* 46 (1986): 407–18.

———. "Using Servant Auction Records to Study Immigration to the Delaware Valley: The Female Composition of Immigrant Servitude, 1745–1831." *Proceedings of the American Philosophical Society* 133 (June 1989): 154–69.

Grube, Walter. *Vogteien, Ämter, Landkreise in der Geschichte Süddeutschlands.* Second edition. Stuttgart, 1960.

Haag, Norbert. *Predigt und Gesellschaft. Die Lutherische Orthodoxie in Ulm, 1640–1740.* Veröffentlichungen des Instituts für Europäische Geschichte Mainz, Abteilung Religionsgeschichte, vol. 145. Mainz, 1992.

Häberle, Daniel. *Auswanderung und Koloniegründungen der Pfälzer im 18. Jahrhundert.* Kaiserslautern, 1909.

Häberlein, Mark. "German Migrants in Colonial Pennsylvania: Resources, Opportunities, and Experience." *WMQ* 50 (July 1993): 555–74.

——. *Vom Oberrhein zum Susquehanna. Studien zur Auswanderung nach Pennsylvania im 18. Jahrhundert.* Stuttgart, 1993.

Hacker, Werner. *Auswanderer vom Oberen Neckar nach Südosteuropa im 18. Jahrhundert.* Munich, 1970.

——. *Auswanderung aus dem nördlichen Bodenseeraum im 17. und 18. Jahrhundert.* Schriften des Vereins für Geschichte des Bodensees und seiner Umgebung, special vol. 6. Singen, 1975.

——. *Auswanderung aus dem südöstlichen Schwarzwald zwischen Hochrhein, Saar und Kinzig, insbesondere nach Südosteuropa.* Munich, 1975.

——. *Auswanderungen aus Baden und dem Breisgau.* Stuttgart, 1980.

——. *Auswanderungen aus dem früheren Hochstift Speyer nach Südosteuropa und Übersee im XVIII. Jahrhundert.* Schriften zur Wanderungsgeschichte der Pfälzer, 28. Kaiserslautern, 1969.

——. *Auswanderungen aus Oberschwaben im 17. und 18 Jahrhundert archivalisch dokumentiert.* Stuttgart, 1977.

——. *Auswanderungen aus Rheinpfalz und Saarland.* Stuttgart, 1987.

——. *Kurpfälzische Auswanderer vom Unteren Neckar. Rechtsrheinische Gebiete der Kurpfalz.* Stuttgart, 1983.

Ham, Hermann von. "Die Stellung des Staates und der Regierungsbehörden zum Auswanderungsproblem im 18. und 19. Jahrhundert." *Deutsches Archiv für Landes- und Volksforschung* 6 (1942): 261–309.

Hamer, Philip M., George C. Rogers Jr., and Maude E. Lyles, eds. *The Papers of Henry Laurens.* Columbia, S.C., 1970.

Handlin, Oscar. *The Uprooted: The Epic Story of the Great Migrations That Made the American People.* New York, 1951.

Hansen, Marcus Lee. *The Atlantic Migration, 1607–1860: A History of the Continuing Settlement of the United States.* Edited with a foreword by Arthur M. Schlesinger, with an introduction to the Torchbook edition by Oscar Handlin. New York, 1961.

——. "The History of American Immigration as a Field for Research." *AHR* 32 (1926–27): 500–518.

Hartmann, Gabriel. "Amerikafahrer von Dossenheim in 18. Jahrhundert." *Mannheimer Geschichtsblätter* 27 (1926): 55–58.

Haselier, Günther, ed. *USA und Baden-Württemberg in ihren geschichtlichen Beziehungen. Beiträge und Bilddokument.* Stuttgart, 1976.

Heavner, Robert Owen. *Economic Aspects of Indentured Servitude in Colonial Pennsylvania, 1771–1773.* New York, 1978.

Heinz, Joachim. *"Bleibe im Lande, und nähre dich redlich!" Zur Geschichte der Auswanderung vom Ende des 17. bis zum Ausgang des 19. Jahrhunderts.* Beiträge zur pfälzischen Geschichte und Volkskunde, vol. 1. Kaiserslautern, 1989.

Helleiner, Karl F. "The Population of Europe from the Black Death to the Eve of the Vital Revolution." In *The Cambridge Economic History of Europe, Volume 4: The Economy of Expanding Europe in the Sixteenth and Seventeenth Centuries,* 1–95. Edited by E. E. Rich and C. H. Wilson. Cambridge, 1967.

Henderson, David. *Des Landsmanns Advocat.* Philadelphia, 1761.

Henn, Volker. "Die soziale und wirtschaftliche Lage der rheinischen Bauern im Zeitalter des Absolutismus." *Rheinische Vierteljahresblätter* 42 (1978): 240–57.

Henrich, Karl. "Einwanderung nach Landau in der Pfalz im Zuge von Reformation und Gegenreformation, 1520–1830 [map provisional no. 73]." In *Pfalzatlas,* 733–59. Edited by Willi Alter. Explanatory text, vol. 20. Speyer, 1972.

Herder, Hans, ed. *Hessisches Auswandererbuch. Berichte, Chroniken und Dokumente zur Geschichte hessischer Einwanderer in den Vereinigten Staaten 1683–1983. Ein hessischer Beitrag zum 300. Jahrestag der ersten deutschen Einwanderung in Amerika.* Frankfurt am Main, 1983.

Herrick, Cheeseman A. *White Servitude in Pennsylvania: Indentured and Redemptioner Labor in Colony and Commonwealth.* Philadelphia, 1926.

Higham, John. *Strangers in the Land: Patterns of American Nativism, 1860–1925.* Corrected with a new preface. New York, 1963.

Hinke, William J. "Diary of the Rev. Samuel Guldin, Relating to His Journey to Pennsylvania, June to September, 1710." *Journal of the Presbyterian Historical Society* 14 (1930/31): 28–41, 64–73.

Hinke, William J., ed. and trans. "Report of the Journey of Francis Louis Michel from Berne, Switzerland, to Virginia, October 2, 1701–December 1, 1702." *Virginia Magazine of History and Biography* 24 (1916): 1–43, 113–37, 275–303.

Historical Statistics of the United States: Colonial Times to 1970. 2 vols. Washington, D.C., 1976.

Historischer Atlas von Baden Württemberg. Maps, Explanations, Index. Historische Kommission für geschichtliche Landeskunde in Baden-Württemberg, and Landesvermessungsamt Baden-Württemberg. Stuttgart, 1972–89.

Hochstadt, Steve L. "Migration in Preindustrial Germany." *Central European History* 16 (1984): 195–224.

Hocker, Edward W., comp. *Genealogical Data Relating to the German Settlers of Pennsylvania and Adjacent Territory.* Baltimore, Md., 1980.

Hoerder, Dirk. "The Traffic of Emigration Via Bremen/Bremerhaven: Merchants' Interests, Protective Legislation, and Migrants' Experience." *Journal of American Ethnic History* 13 (Fall 1993): 68–101.

Hoffman, William J. "'Palatine' Emigrants to America from the Principality of Nassau-Dillenburg." *National Genealogical Society Quarterly* 29 (1941): 41–44.

Hopfinger, Hans, and Horst Kopp, eds. *Wirkungen von Migrationen auf aufnehmende Gesellschaften.* Schriften des Zentralinstituts für fränkische Landeskunde und allgemeine Regionalforschung und der Universität Erlangen-Nürnberg, vol. 34. Neustadt/Aisch, 1996.

Horle, Craig W., and Marianne S. Wokeck, eds. *Lawmaking and Legislators in Pennsylvania: A Biographical Dictonary, Volume 1: 1682–1709; Volume 2: 1710–1756.* Edited by Craig Horle, Joseph S. Foster, and Jeffrey L. Scheib. Philadelphia, 1991 and 1997.

Horn, James. *Adapting to a New World: English Society in the Seventeenth-Century Chesapeake.* Chapel Hill, N.C., 1994.

———. "Servant Emigration to the Chesapeake in the Seventeenth Century." In *The Chesapeake in the Seventeenth Century: Essays on Anglo-American Society*, 51–95. Edited by Thad W. Tate and David L. Ammerman. Chapel Hill, N.C., 1979.

Horst, Irvin B. *Dutch Aid to Swiss Brethren: The Records at Switzerland.* Amsterdam, 1984.

Houston, Cecil J., and William J. Smyth. *Irish Emigration and Canadian Settlement: Patterns, Links, and Letters.* Toronto, 1990.

Huelsbergen, Helmut E. "The First Thirteen Families: Another Look at the Religious and Ethnic Background of the Emigrants from Crefeld." *Yearbook of German-American Studies* 18 (1983): 29–40.

Hull, William I. *Benjamin Furly and Quakerism in Rotterdam.* Swarthmore, Pa., 1941.

———. *William Penn and the Dutch Quaker Migration to Pennsylvania.* Swarthmore, Pa., 1935.

Hüttig, Karl-Friedrich. *Die Pfälzische Auswanderung nach Ost-Mitteleuropa im Zeitalter der Aufklärung, Napoleons und der Restauration.* Marburg/Lahn, 1958.

Hvidt, Kristian. *Flight to America: The Social Background of 300,000 Danish Emigrants.* New York, 1975.

Imhof, Arthur E., ed. *Historische Demographie als Sozialgeschichte, Gießen und Umgebung vom 17. zum 19. Jahrhundert.* Quellen und Forschungen zur Hessischen Geschichte. Darmstadt and Marburg, 1975.

Imhof, Eduard, ed. *Atlas der Schweiz.* Wabern-Bern, 1965–78.

"An Immigrant's Letter, 1734 [by David Seibt]." *Pennsylvania German* 9 (1908): 367–70.

Ingrao, Charles W. *The Hessian Mercenary State: Ideas, Institutions, and Reform Under Frederick II, 1760–1785.* Cambridge, 1987.

Inkori, Joseph E., and Stanley L. Engerman, eds. *The Atlantic Slave Trade: Effects on Economies, Societies, and Peoples in Africa, the Americas, and Europe.* Durham, N.C., 1992.

Ireland, Owen S. *Religion, Ethnicity, and Politics: Ratifying the Constitution in Pennsylvania.* University Park, Pa., 1995.

Jacobs, Henry E. *The German Emigration to America, 1709–1740.* Lancaster, Pa., 1898.

James, Francis G. "Irish Colonial Trade in the Eighteenth Century." *WMQ* 20 (1963): 574–84.

Jerome, Harry. *Migration and Business Cycles.* New York, 1926.

Jeserich, Kurt G. A., Hans Pohl, and Georg-Christoph von Unruh, eds. *Vom Spätmittelalter bis zum Ende des Reiches. Deutsche Verwaltungsgeschichte.* Volume 1. Stuttgart, 1983.

John, A. H. "The London Assurance Company and the Marine Insurance Market of the Eighteenth Century." *Economica* 25 (1958): 126–41.

Johnson, Hildegard Binder. "Der deutsche Amerika-Auswanderer des 18. Jahrhunderts im zeitgenössischen Urteil." *Deutsches Archiv für Landes- und Volksforschung* 4 (1940): 211–34.

————. "Perceptions and Illustrations of the American Landscape in the Ohio and the Midwest." In *This Land of Ours: The Acquisition and Disposition of the Public Domain.* Indianapolis, Ind., 1978.

————. "Toward a National Landscape." In *The Making of the American Landscape,* 123–45. Edited by Michael P. Conzen. Boston, 1990.

Jones, George Fenwick. *The Georgia Dutch: From the Rhine and Danube to the Savannah, 1733–1783.* Athens, Ga., 1992.

————. *The Salzburger Saga: Religious Exiles and Other Germans Along the Savannah.* Athens, Ga., 1984.

Jones, George Fenwick, ed. *Detailed Reports on the Salzburger Emigrants Who Settled in America . . . edited by Samuel Urlsperger.* Athens, Ga., 1968–.

Jones, Henry Z., Jr. *More Palatine Families.* Universal City, Calif., 1991.

————. *The Palatine Families of New York: A Study of the German Immigrants Who Arrived in Colonial New York in 1710.* Universal City, Calif., 1985.

Jordan, John J. "Moravian Immigration into Pennsylvania, 1745–1765." *PMHB* 33 (1909): 228–48.

Journal of the Commissioners of Trade and Plantations Preserved in the Public Record Office. London: His Majesty's Stationery Office, 1920, 1925, 1928, 1930–33, 1935, 1936.

Kaller, Gerhard. "Archivalien zur Auswanderungsgeschichte der Pfälzer im Generallandesarchiv Karlsruhe." In *Pfälzer—Palatines. Beiträge zur pfälzischen Ein- und Auswanderung sowie zur Volkskunde und Mundartforschung der Pfalz und der Zielländer pfälzischer Auswanderer im 18. und 19. Jahrhundert.* Edited by Karl Scherer. Kaiserslautern, 1981.

Kantowicz, Edward. "Ethnicity." In *Encyclopedia of American Social History,* vol. 1, 453–66. Edited by Mary Kupiec Cayton et al. New York, 1993.

Kazal, Russell. "Revisiting Assimilation: The Rise, Fall, and Reappraisal of a Concept in American Ethnic History." *AHR* 100 (April 1995): 437–71.

Kent, George O. "A Survey of German Manuscripts Pertaining to American History in the Library of Congress." *JAH* 56 (1970): 868–81.

Kershaw, Gordon Ernest. *The Kennebeck Proprietors, 1749–1775.* Somersworth, N.H., 1975.

Kessel, Elizabeth Augusta. "Germans on the Maryland Frontier: A Social History of Frederick County, Maryland, 1730–1800." Ph.D. dissertation, Rice University, 1981.

Kettner, James. *The Development of American Citizenship, 1608–1870.* Chapel Hill, N.C., 1978.

Kieffer, Elizabeth Clarke. "The Cheese Was Good." *Pennsylvania Folklife* 19 (1970): 27–29 (= summary of manuscript: PRO, SP 42–138).

Kirsten, Ernst. *Raum und Bevölkerung in der Weltgeschichte.* Volume 1. Bevölkerungs-Ploetz, 3d ed. Würzburg, 1965.

Kisch, Herbert. *From Domestic Manufacture to Industrial Revolution: The Case of the Rhineland Textile Districts.* Oxford, 1989.

Kiss, I. *Deutsche Auswanderung nach Ungarn aus neuer Sicht.* 1979.

Kivisto, Peter, and Dag Blanck, eds. *American Immigrants and Their Generations: Studies and Commentaries on the Hansen Thesis After Fifty Years.* Champaign, Ill., 1990.

Klein, Herbert S. "Economic Aspects of the Eighteenth-Century Atlantic Slave Trade." In *The Rise of Merchant Empires: Long-Distance Trade in the Early Modern World, 1350–1750*. Edited by James D. Tracy. Studies in Comparative Early Modern History, no. 2, 287–310. New York, 1990.

———. *The Middle Passage: Comparative Studies in the Atlantic Slave Trade*. Princeton, N.J., 1978.

———. "New Evidence on the Virginia Slave Trade." *JIH* 17 (Spring 1987): 871–77.

Klein, Thomas. "Minorities in Central Europe in the Sixteenth and Early Seventeenth Centuries." In *Minorities in History*, 31–49. Historical Studies 12: Papers Read Before the Thirteenth Irish Conference of Historians at the New University of Ulster, 1977. New York, 1979.

Klepp, Susan, and Billy G. Smith, eds. *The Infortunate: The Voyage and Adventures of William Moraley, an Indentured Servant*. University Park, Pa., 1992.

Knittle, Walter A. *Early Eighteenth-Century Palatine Emigration: A British Government Redemptioner Project to Manufacture Naval Stores*. 1937; reprint ed., Baltimore, Md., 1976.

Knodel, John E. *Demographic Behavior in the Past: A Study of Fourteen German Village Populations in the Eighteenth and Nineteenth Centuries*. Cambridge Studies in Population, Economy, and Society in Past Time, no. 6. New York, 1988.

[Kocherthal, Joshua.] *Ausführlich und Umständlicher Bericht von der berühmten Landschaft Carolina, in dem Engelländischen America gelegen*. Frankfurt am Main, 1709.

Kolb, G. "Die Siebenbürger Sachsen und die badische Einwanderung aus der Markgrafschaft Baden-Durlach im 18. Jahrhundert." *Meine Heimat* 8 (1921): 76–81.

Kollnig, Karl. *Wandlungen im Bevölkerungsbild des pfälzischen Oberrheingebiets*. Heidelberg, 1952.

Krebs, Friedrich. "Zur Amerikaauswanderung aus dem kurpfälzische Oberamtern Heidelberg (1764–66), Mosbach (1739–55) und Baden-Durlach." *Badische Heimat* 38 (1958): 303.

———. "Eine Amerikareise vor 200 Jahren." *Genealogie* 15/16 (1966–67): 534–45.

———. "Annotations to Strassburger and Hinke's Pennsylvania German Pioneers." *Pennsylvania Genealogical Magazine* 21 (1960): 235–48.

———. "Auswandererbrief von 1769 aus Amerika." *Pfälzer Heimat* 5 (1954): 26.

———. "Emigrants from Baden-Durlach to Pennsylvania, 1749–1755." *National Genealogical Society Quarterly* 45 (1957): 30–32.

———. "Studien zur Amerika-Auswanderung aus Baden-Durlach für das Jahr 1751." *Badische Heimat* 36 (1956): 155.

———. "Zur Amerikaauswanderung aus dem kurpfälzischen Oberamt Heidelberg, 1741–1748." *Zeitschrift für die Geschichte des Oberrheins* 106 (1958): 485.

———. "Zur Amerikaauswanderung aus den kurpfälzischen Oberämtern Heidelberg (1764–66), Mosbach (1739–55), und Baden-Durlach." *Zeitschrift für die Geschichte des Oberrheins* 120 (1972): 494.

———. "Zur Amerika-Auswanderung des 18. Jahrhunderts aus Altwürttemberg, hauptsächlich aus dem ehemaligen Oberamt Urach." *Südwestdeutsche Blätter für Familien- und Wappenkunde* 9 (1957): 464–65; 11 (1959): 186–89.

———. "Zur Frühauswanderung aus dem kurpfälzischen Oberamt Heidelberg nach Amerika." *Südwestdeutsche Blätter für Familien- und Wappenkunde* 10 (1958): 512.

Kriebel, Howard Wiegner. *The Schwenkfelders in Pennsylvania: A Historical Sketch.* Lancaster, Pa., 1904.

Kuby, Alfred Hans. "Die Pfarreien im Jahre 1790 [map provisional no. 19]." In *Pfalzatlas,* 828–33. Edited by Willi Alter. Explanatory text, vol. 22. Speyer, 1974.

Kuhn, Gertrud, comp. *USA-Deutschland-Baden und Württemberg: Eine Auswahl von Titeln zur Auswanderung und zur Geschichte der Deutsch-Amerikaner vor allem aus Baden und Württemberg, von den Anfängen bis zum Ende des Zweiten Weltkrieges.* Aus Anlass des 200. Jahrestages der Unabhängigkeit der Vereinigten Staaten von Amerika (Stand Mai 1976). Stuttgart, 1976.

Kuhn, Walter. "Die preußische Kolonisation unter Friedrich dem Großen." *Deutsche Ostsiedlung in Mittelalter und Neuzeit.* Cologne, 1971.

Kuhns, Levy Oscar. *The German and Swiss Settlements of Colonial Pennsylvania: A Study of the So-Called Pennsylvania Dutch.* New York, 1901.

Kulikoff, Allan. "Migration and Cultural Divisions in Early America, 1600–1860: A Review Essay." *Historical Methods Newsletter* 19 (Fall 1986): 153–69.

Küther, Carsten. *Menschen auf der Strasse. Vagierende Unterschichten in Bayern, Franken und Schwaben in der zweiten Hälfte de 18. Jahrhunderts.* Kritische Studien zur Geschichtswissenschaft, no. 56. Göttingen, 1983.

Labaree, Leonard W., et al., eds. *The Papers of Benjamin Franklin.* 25 vols. to date. New Haven, Conn., 1959–.

Lancour, Harold, ed. *Ship Passenger Lists: A Bibliography of Ship Passenger Lists, 1583–1825, Being a Guide to Published Lists of Early Immigrants to North America.* Revised and enlarged by Richard J. Wolfe. 3d ed. New York, 1978.

Landesarchivdirektion Baden-Württemberg, ed. *Das Land Baden-Württemberg. Amtliche Beschreibung nach Kreisen und Gemeinden.* Volume 4: *Regierungsbezirk Stuttgart, Regionalverbände Franken und Ostwürttemberg.* Stuttgart, 1980.

Langguth, Otto. "Pennsylvania German Pioneers from the County of Wertheim." *Pennsylvania Folklore Society* 12 (1947): 147–289.

Larsen, Grace Hutchinson. "Profile of a Colonial Merchant: Thomas Clifford of Pre-Revolutionary Philadelphia." Ph.D. dissertation, Columbia University, 1955.

Laws of the State of Delaware from the Fourteenth Day of October Seventeenhundred to the Eighteenth Day of August Seventeenhundredninetyseven. 2 vols. New Castle, Del., 1797.

Learned, Marion Dexter. *Guide to the Manuscript Materials Relating to American History in the German State Archives.* Washington, D.C., 1912.

———. *The Life of Francis Daniel Pastorius, Founder of Germantown.* Philadelphia, 1908.

Lecky, W. E. H. *History of Ireland in the Eighteenth Century.* Volume 1. London, 1913.

Lee, Everett S. "A Theory of Migration." *Demography* 3 (1966): 47–57.

Lee, W. Robert, ed. *European Demography and Economic Growth.* London, 1979.

Leemans, W. F. *De Groote Gelderse Tollen en de Tollenars in de 18de en het begin der 19de eeuw. Een bijdrag tot de geschiedenis van de Rijnhandel.* Gelderse Historische Reeks, no. 14. Arnhem, 1981.

Lehmann, Hartmut. *Pietismus und weltliche Ordnung in Württemberg vom 17. bis zum 20. Jahrhundert.* Stuttgart, 1969.

———. "Pietismus und Wirtschaft in Calw am Anfang des 18. Jahrhunderts." *Zeitschrift für Württembergische Landesgeschichte* 31 (1972): 249–75.

Lehmann, Heinz. *The German-Canadians, 1750–1937: Immigration, Settlement, and Culture.* St. John's, Newfoundland, 1986.

Lemon, James T. *The Best Poor Man's Country: A Geographical Study of Early Southeastern Pennsylvania.* Baltimore, Md., 1972.

"Letter Benjamin Marshall to Barnaby Egan, June 7, 1766." *PMHB* 20 (1896): 212.

"Letter from Joris Wertmüller [16 March 1684]" and "Letter from Cornelius Bom [12 October 1684]." *Pennsylvania German Society: Proceedings and Addresses* 9 (1899): 100–107.

"Letter from Pennsylvania Mennonites to Holland in 1773." *Mennonite Quarterly Review* 3 (1928): 224–34.

"Letters from the Delaware, II: The Reverend Andreas Sandel, June 17, 1702." *Swedish-American Historical Quarterly* 39 (July 1988): 51–63.

Leyburn, James G. *The Scotch-Irish: A Social History.* Chapel Hill, N.C., 1962.

Lloyd's Lists, 1741–1826. Reprint edition. London, 1969.

Lockhart, Audrey. "The Quakers and Emigration from Ireland to the North American Colonies." *Quaker History* 77 (1988): 67–92.

———. *Some Aspects of Emigration from Ireland to the North American Colonies Between 1660 and 1775.* New York, 1976.

Lucassen, Jan. *Migrant Labor in Europe, 1600–1900: The Drift to the North Sea.* London, 1987.

———. "The Netherlands, the Dutch, and Long-Distance Migration, in the Late Sixteenth to Early Nineteenth Centuries." In *Europeans on the Move: Studies on European Migration, 1500–1800.* Edited by Nicholas Canny. Oxford, 1994.

Mann, W. J., B. M. Schmucker, and Wilhelm German, eds. *Nachrichten von den vereinigten Deutschen Evangelisch-Lutherischen Gemeinden in Nord-Amerika, absonderlich in Pennsylvania* (= *Hallesche Nachrichten*). 2 vols. 1787; reprints 1886 and Philadelphia, 1895.

Manning, Patrick. "The Slave Trade: The Formal Demography of a Global System." In *The Atlantic Slave Trade: Effects on Economies, Societies, and Peoples in Africa, the Americas, and Europe,* 115–41. Edited by Joseph E. Inkori and Stanley L. Engerman. Durham, N.C., 1992.

Marschalck, Peter, ed. *Inventar der Quellen zur Geschichte der Wanderungen, besonders der Auswanderung, in Bremer Archiven.* Bremen, 1986.

Martin, Alfred S. "The King's Customs: Philadelphia, 1763–1774." *WMQ* 5 (1948): 201–16.

Maschke, Erich, and Jürgen Sydow, eds. *Verwaltung und Gesellschaft in der südwestdeutschen Stadt des 17. und 18. Jahrhunderts.* Veröffentlichungen der Kommission für Geschichtliche Landeskunde in Baden-Württemberg, series B: Forschungen, vol. 58. Stuttgart, 1969.

Mattmüller, Markus. *Bevölkerungsgeschichte der Schweiz.* Volume 1: *Die frühe Neuzeit, 1500–1700.* Baseler Beiträge Zur Geschichtswissenschaft 154, 154A. Edited by F. Graus, H. R. Guggisberg, H. Lüthy, and M. Mattmüller. Basel, 1987.

Mayhew, Alan. *Rural Settlement and Farming in Germany.* New York: Harper & Row, 1973.

McCracken, John Leslie. "The Ecclesiastical Structure." In *A New History of Ireland, Volume 4: Eighteenth-Century Ireland.* Edited by T. W. Moody and W. E. Vaughan. Oxford, 1986.

———. "The Social Structure and Social Life, 1714–1760." In *A New History of Ireland, Volume 4: Eighteenth-Century Ireland.* Edited by T. W. Moody and W. E. Vaughan. Oxford, 1986.

McCusker, John J. "The Pennsylvania Shipping Industry in the Eighteenth Century." Unpublished manuscript, 1973, HSP.

———. "The Tonnage of Ships Engaged in British Colonial Trade During the Eighteenth Century." *Research in Economic History* 6 (1981): 73–105.

McCusker, John J., and Russell R. Menard. *The British Economy of British America, 1607–1789.* Chapel Hill, N.C., 1991.

McDonald, John, and Ralph Shlomowitz. "Mortality on Immigrant Voyages to Australia in the Nineteenth Century." *Explorations in Economic History* 27 (1990): 84–113.

———. "Passenger Fares on Sailing Vessels to Australia in the Nineteenth Century." *Explorations in Economic History* 28 (1991): 192–208.

McNeill, William. "Human Migration in Historical Perspective." *Population and Development Review* 10 (1984): 1–18.

McNeill, William H., and Ruth S. Adams. *Human Migration: Patterns and Policies.* Bloomington, Ind., 1978.

Medick, Hans. "The Proto-Industrial Family Economy: The Structural Functioning of Household and Family During the Transition from Peasant Society to Industrial Capitalism." *Social History* 3 (1976): 291–315.

Menard, Russell R. "British Migration to the Chesapeake Colonies in the Seventeenth Century." In *Colonial Chesapeake Society,* 99–132. Edited by Lois Greeen Carr et al. Chapel Hill, N.C., 1988.

———. "Migration, Ethnicity, and the Rise of an Atlantic Economy: The Re-Peopling of British America, 1600–1790." In *A Century of European Migrations, 1830–1930,* 58–77. Edited by J. Rudolph Vecoli and Suzanne M. Sinke. Urbana, Ill., 1991.

———. "Transport Costs and Long-Range Trade, 1300–1800: Was There a European 'Transport Revolution' in the Early Modern Era?" In *The Political Economy of Merchant Empires.* Studies in Comparative Early Modern History. Edited by James D. Tracy. New York, 1991.

Meriwether, Robert L. *The Expansion of South Carolina, 1729–1765.* Philadelphia, 1974.

Meurer, John Philip. "From London to Philadelphia, 1742." *PMHB* 37 (1913): 96–106.

Meynen, Emil. *Bibliography on German Settlers in Colonial North America, Especially on the Pennsylvania Germans and Their Descendants, 1683–1933.* Leipzig, 1937.

Michel, Paul. "Täufer, Mennoniten, und Quäker in Kriegsheim bei Worms." *Der Wormsgau* 7 (1965/66): 41–52.

Middlebrook, Louis F. "The Ship *Mary* of Philadelphia, 1740." *PMHB* 58 (1934): 127–51.

Millar, John Fitzhugh. *Early American Ships.* Williamsburg, Va., 1986.

Miller, Joseph C. "The Numbers, Origins, and Destinations of Slaves in the Eighteenth-Century Angolan Slave Trade." In *The Atlantic Slave Trade: Effects on Economies, Societies, and Peoples in Africa, the Americas, and Europe,* 77–115. Edited by Joseph E. Inkori and Stanley L. Engerman. Durham, N.C., 1992, 77–115.

Miller, Kerby A. *Emigrants and Exiles: Ireland and the Irish Exodus to North America.* Oxford, 1985.

Minchinton, Walter E. "Characteristics of British Slaving Vessels, 1698–1775." *JIH* 20 (Summer 1989): 53–81.

Minchinton, Walter E., ed. *The Growth of English Overseas Trade in the Seventeenth and Eighteenth Centuries.* London, 1969.

Mitchell, James T., and Henry Flanders, comps. *The Statutes at Large of Pennsylvania from 1682 to 1801.* 18 vols. Harrisburg, Pa., 1896–1915.

Mitchell, Robert D. *Commercialism and Frontier: Perspectives on the Early Shenandoah Valley.* Charlottesville, Va., 1977.

Mittelberger, Gottlieb. *Journey to Pennsylvania.* 1756. Edited by Oscar Handlin and translated by John Clive. Cambridge, Mass., 1960.

Moch, Leslie Page. *Moving Europeans: Migration in Western Europe Since 1650.* Interdisciplinary Studies in History. Bloomington, Ind., 1992.

Moltman, Günther. "Die deutsche Auswanderung in der Kolonialzeit und das Redemptioner-System." *Zeitschrift für Kulturaustausch* 32 (1982): 318–23.

Mönchmeier, Wilhelm. *Die deutsche überseeische Auswanderung.* Jena, 1912.

Moody, T. W., and W. E. Vaughan, eds. *A New History of Ireland, Volume 4: Eighteenth-Century Ireland.* Oxford, 1986.

Morawska, Ewa. "In Defense of the Assimilation Model." *JAEH* 13 (Winter 1994): 76–87.

Morgan, Kenneth. "The Organization of the Colonial American Rice Trade." *WMQ* 52 (1995): 433–52.

Mundel, Hedwig. "A 1725 List of Wittgenstein Emigrants." Translated and edited by Don Yoder. *Pennsylvania Genealogical Magazine* 26 (1969): 133–43.

Münte, Heinz. *Das Altonaer Handlungshaus Van der Smissen, 1682–1824.* Altona, Ger., 1932.

Myers, Albert C. *Immigration of the Irish Quakers into Pennsylvania, 1682–1750.* Swarthmore, Pa., 1902.

Myers, Albert C., ed. *Narratives of Early Pennsylvania, West New Jersey, and Delaware, 1630–1707.* New York, 1912.

Nairne, Thomas, and John Norris, eds. *Selling the New World: Two Colonial South Carolina Promotional Pamphlets.* Introduction by Jack P. Greene. Columbia, S.C., 1988.

Nash, Gary B. "Urban Wealth and Poverty in Pre-Revolutionary America." *JIH* 4 (1976): 545–84.

Nash, R. C. "Irish Atlantic Trade in the Seventeenth and Eighteenth Centuries." *WMQ* 42 (July 1985): 329–56.

Neuber, Wolfgang. *Fremde Welt im europäischen Horizont. Zur Topik der deutschen Amerika-Reiseberichte der Frühen Neuzeit.* Philologische Studien und Quellen, vol. 121. Berlin, 1991.

Noble, Allen G. *To Build in a New Land: Ethnic Landscapes in North America.* Baltimore, Md., 1992.

North, Douglas C. "Sources of Productivity Change in Ocean Shipping, 1600–1850." *Journal of Political Economy* 76 (1968): 953–70.

"Number and Tonnage Capacity of Ships Outward and Inward Bound, to and from Philadelphia, by Destination and Origin, 1733–1772." In *Historical Statistics of the United States: Colonial Times to 1970.* 2 vols. Volume 2: series Z 266–85. Washington, D.C., 1976.

O'Brien, Michael J. *Irish Settlers in America: A Consolidation of Articles from the Journal of American Irish Historical Society.* 2 vols. Baltimore, Md., 1979.

"The 'Old German Letters' of Introduction" (1732). In *Genealogy of the Descendants of John Gar, or More Particularly of His Son Andreas Gaar,* 530. 1894; reprint ed., Boston, 1973.

Olson, Alison Gilbert. *Making the Empire Work: London and American Interest Groups, 1690–1790.* New York, 1992.

O'Reilly, William T. "'A Paragon of Wickedness': Newlanders and Agents in Eighteenth-Century German Migration." ISHAW, 1996.

———. "To the East or to the West? German Migration in the Eighteenth Century, a Comparative Perspective." Paper delivered to the Philadelphia Center for Early American Studies, March 1997.

Ostergren, Robert C. *A Community Transplanted: The Trans-Atlantic Experience of a Swedish Immigrant Settlement in the Upper Middle West, 1835–1915.* Madison, Wis., 1988.

Otterness, Philip Lars. "The Unattained Canaan: The 1709 Palatine Migration and the Formation of German Society in Colonial America." Ph.D. dissertation, University of Iowa, 1996.

Parker, Geoffrey. *The Thirty Years' War.* London, 1988.

Parry, M. L. *Climatic Change, Agriculture, and Settlement.* Studies in Historical Geography. Hamden, Conn., 1978.

Paul, Roland, ed. *300 Jahre Pfälzer in Amerika.* Landau/Pfalz, 1983.

Pennypacker, Samuel W. "The Settlement of Germantown." *Pennsylvania German Society: Proceedings and Addresses* 9 (1899).

Pennypacker, Samuel W., trans. "Letter from Joris Wertmüller" and "Letter from Cornelius Bom, October 12, 1684." *Pennsylvania German Society: Proceedings and Addresses* 9 (1899): 100–110.

Perkins, Edwin J. *American Public Finance and Financial Services, 1700–1815.* Historical Perspectives on Business Enterprise Series. Columbus, Ohio, 1994.

Pfälzer/Palatines. Beiträge zur pfälzischen Ein- und Auswanderung . . . Fritz Braun zu seinem 70. Geburtstag. Kaiserslautern, 1980.

Pfister, Christian. *Bevölkerungsgeschichte und historische Demographie, 1500–1800.* Volume 28 of *Enzyklopädie Deutscher Geschichte.* Edited by Lothar Gall. Munich, 1994.

Pfister, Hans Ulrich. *Die Auswanderung aus dem Knonauer Amt, 1648–1750.* Zurich, 1987.

———. *Zürcher Auswanderung nach Amerika, 1734/35. Die Reisegruppe um Pfarrer Moritz Götschi.* Separatdruck aus dem Zürcher Taschenbuch auf das Jahr 1986. Zurich, 1985.

Phayer, J. Michael. "Germans Emigrate to French Colony: An Eighteenth-Century Document." *Societas* 3 (Summer 1978): 243–47.

Ploetz, A. G., ed. *Raum und Bevölkerung in der Weltgeschichte.* 4 vols. Prepared by Ernst

Kirsten, Ernst Wolfgang Buchholz, and Wolfgang Köllmann. 3d ed. Würzburg, 1965.

"A Pocket Almanack for the Year 1755, Fitted to the Use of Pennsylvania, and the Neighboring Provinces: By R. Saunders, Philadelphia, interleaved and with Memoranda by Robert Strettel." *PMHB* 2 (1878): 109.

Pooley, Colin G., and Ian D. Whyte, eds. *Migrants, Emigrants, and Immigrants: A Social History of Migration.* London, 1991.

Post, John D. *Food Shortage, Climatic Variability, and Epidemic Disease in Preindustrial Europe: The Mortality Peak in the Early 1740s.* Ithaca, N.Y., 1985.

Postma, Johannes M. *The Dutch in the Atlantic Slave Trade.* New York, 1987.

Price, Jacob M. *Capital and Credit in British Overseas Trade: The View from the Chesapeake, 1700–1776.* Cambridge, Mass., 1980.

———. "The Emergence of the Great Quaker Business Families of Eighteenth-Century London: The Rise and Fall of a Sectarian Patriciate." In *The World of William Penn.* Edited by Richard S. Dunn and Mary Maples Dunn. Philadelphia, 1983.

———. "Transaction Costs: A Note on Merchant Credit and the Organization of Private Trade." In *The Political Economy of Merchant Empires,* 276–97. Studies in Comparative Early Modern History. Edited by James D. Tracy. New York, 1991.

Price, Jacob M., and Paul G. E. Clemens. "A Revolution in the Scale of Overseas Trade: British Firms in the Chesapeake Trade, 1675–1775." *JEconH* 47 (1987): 1–47.

Purvis, Thomas L. "Patterns of Ethnic Settlement in Late Eighteenth-Century Pennsylvania." *Western Pennsylvania Historical Magazine* 70 (1987): 107–22.

———. "The Pennsylvania Dutch and the German-American Diaspora in 1790." *Journal of Cultural Geography* 6 (1986): 81–99.

Rattermann, Heinrich Armin. "Geschichte des deutschen Elements im State Maine." *Der Deutsche Pionier. Erinnerungen aus dem Pionier-Leben der Deutschen in Amerika* 14–16 (1882–84).

———. "Die Ursachen der Massenauswanderung aus Deutschland im 18. Jahrhundert." *Gesammelte, ausgewählte Werke* 16 (1912): 99–144.

Raum, Otto F. "Die Hintergründe der Pfälzer Auswanderung im Jahre 1709." *Deutsches Archiv für Landes- und Volksforschung* 3 (1939): 551–67.

Raumer, Kurt von. *Die Zerstörung der Pfalz von 1689 im Zusammenhang der französischen Rheinpolitik.* 1930; reprint ed., Bad Neustadt a. d. Saale, 1982.

Reichmann, Eberhard, LeVerne Ripley, and Jörg Nagler, eds. *Emigration and Settlement Patterns of German Communities in North America.* Indianapolis, 1995.

"Reisetagebuch des Crefelders Johannes Naas, 1733." *Der Deutsche Pionier* 12 (1880): 340–50.

Rembe, Heinrich. *Lambsheim. Die Familien von 1547 bis 1800—für Maxdorf bis 1830—mit Angaben aus Weisenheim a. S, Eyersheim und Ormsheim.* Beiträge zur Bevölkerungsgeschichte der Pfalz, no. 1. Kaiserslautern, 1971.

"Report of the Journey of Francis Louis Michel from Berne, Switzerland, to Virginia, October 2, 1701–December 1, 1702." Translated and edited by William J. Hinke. *Virginia Magazine of History and Biography* 24 (1916): 1–17.

Resolutien von den Heeren Staaten van Holland en Westfriesland and *Resolutien von de H[oogh]* *M[ogende] H[eeren] Staaten General der Vereinigte de Nederlandsche Provincien* (States General, Resolutions). Published annually with the names of the petitioners indexed.

Revill, Janie, comp. *A Compilation of the Original Lists of Protestant Immigrants to South Carolina, 1763–1773.* Baltimore, Md., 1968.

Riley, Edward M., ed. *The Journal of John Harrower: An Indentured Servant in the Colony of Virginia, 1773–1776.* Williamsburg, Va., 1969.

Risch, Erna. "Encouragement and Aid to Immigrants, 1607–1830." Ph.D. dissertation, University of Chicago, 1931.

————. "Joseph Crellius, Immigrant Broker." *New England Quarterly* 12 (1939): 241–67.

Roach, Hannah B., ed. (Leonard Melchior). "Advice to German Emigrants, 1749." *Pennsylvania Genealogical Magazine* 22 (1962): 226–37.

Rodger, N. A. M. "The Victualling of the British Navy During the Seven Years' War." *Bulletin du Centre d'Histoire des Espace Atlantique* (Bordeaux), 1985.

————. *The Wooden World: An Anatomy of the Georgian Navy.* Annapolis, Md., 1986.

Roeber, A. G. "Erbrechtliche Probleme deutscher Auswanderer in Nordamerika während des 18. Jahrhunderts." *Zeitschrift für Neuere Rechtsgeschichte* 8 (1986): 143–56.

————. "Germans, Property, and the First Great Awakerning: Rehearsal for a Revolution." In *The Transit of Civilization from Europe to America: Festschrift in Honor of Hans Galinsky,* 165–84. Edited by Winfried Herget and Karl Ortseifen. Tübingen, 1986.

————. "In German Ways? Problems and Potentials of Eighteenth-Century German Social and Emigration History." *WMQ* 44 (1987): 750–74.

————. "'The Origin of Whatever Is Not English Among Us': The Dutch-Speaking and the German-Speaking Peoples of Colonial British America." In *Strangers Within the Realm: Cultural Margins of the First British Empire.* Edited by Bernard Bailyn and Philip D. Morgan. Chapel Hill, N.C., 1991.

————. *Palatines, Liberty, and Property: German Lutherans in British Colonial America.* Baltimore, Md., 1993.

Rolland, Susanne Mosteler. "From the Rhine to the Catawba: A Study of Eighteenth-Century Germanic Migration and Adaptation." Ph.D. dissertation, Emory University, 1991.

Roller, Otto Konrad. *Einwohnerschaft Durlach im 18. Jahrhundert.* Karlsruhe, 1907.

Rotthoff, Guido. "Die Auswanderer von Krefeld nach Pennsylvania im Jahre 1683." *Die Heimat* 53 (1983): 2–11.

Runblom, Harald, and Hans Norman, eds. *From Sweden to America: A History of the Migration.* A Collective Work of the Uppsala Migration Research Project. Minneapolis, Minn. 1976.

Rupp, Israel D., ed. *A Collection of Thirty Thousand Names of German, Swiss, Dutch, French, and Other Immigrants in Pennsylvania from 1727 to 1776.* 1856; reprint ed., 1875; reprint ed., Baltimore, Md., 1966.

Ruth, John. "A Christian Settlement 'in Antiquam Silvam': The Emigration from Krefeld to Pennsylvania in 1683 and the Mennonite Community of Germantown." *Mennonite Quarterly Review* 57 (1983): 307–31.

Sabean, David Warren. *Power in the Blood: Popular Culture and Village Discourse in Early Modern Germany.* Cambridge, 1985.

———. *Property, Production, and Family in Neckarhausen, 1700–1870.* Cambridge Studies in Social and Cultural Anthropology, no. 73. Cambridge, 1990.

Sachse, Julius Friedrich. "Literature Used to Induce German Emigration." *Pennsylvania German Society: Proceedings and Addresses* 7 (1897): 175–98.

Sachse, Julius Friedrich, ed. *Letters Relating to the Settlement of Germantown in Pennsylvania 1683–84 from the Könneken Manuscript in the Ministerial-Archive of Lübeck.* Lübeck and Philadelphia, 1903. (Copy of manuscripts interleaved in the copy of Friends Historical Library, Swarthmore, Pa.)

Sachse, Julius Friedrich, trans. and ed. *Daniel Falckner's Curieuse Nachricht von Pennsylvania.* 1707. Lancaster, Pa., 1905.

Salinger, Sharon V. "Colonial Labor in Transition: The Decline of Indentured Servitude in Late Eighteenth-Century Philadelphia." *Labor History* 22 (1981): 165–91.

———. *"To Serve Well and Faithfully": Labor and Indentured Servants in Pennsylvania, 1682–1800.* Cambridge, 1987.

Sauer, Paul. "Not und Armut in den Dörfern des Mittleren Neckarraums in der vorindustriellen Zeit." *Zeitschrift für Württembergische Landesgeschichte* 41 (1982): 131–49.

Schaab, Meinrad. "Die Anfänge einer Landesstatistik im Herzogtum Württemberg in den Badischen Markgrafschaften und in der Kurpfalz." *Zeitschrift für Württembergische Landesgeschichte* 26 (1967): 89–112.

———. *Geschichte der Kurpfalz, Volume 2: Neuzeit.* Stuttgart, 1992.

———. "Territoriale Entwicklung der Hochstifte Speyer and Worms [map provisional no. 77]." In *Pfalzatlas,* 760–80. Edited by Willi Alter. Explanatory text, vol. 20. Speyer, 1972.

Schaab, Meinrad, and Peter Moraw. "Territoriale Entwicklung der Kurpfalz (von 1156 bis 1792) [maps, provisional nos. 50, 51, 52, 53]." In *Pfalzatlas,* 393–428. Edited by Willi Alter. Explanatory text, vol. 11. Speyer, n.d.

Schaaff, Karl, ed. *Untertanenlisten des Herzogtums Pfalz-Zweibrücken aus den Huldigungsprotokollen des Jahres 1776.* Schriften zur Bevölkerungsgeschichte der pfälzischen Lande 6. Ludwigshafen/Rhein, 1977.

Schawacht, Jürgen Heinz. *Schiffart und Güterverkehr zwischen den Häfen des deutschen Niederrheins [insbesondere Köln] und Rotterdam vom Ende des 18. Jahrhunderts bis zur Mitte des 19. Jahrhunderts. 1794–1850/51.* Cologne, 1973.

Scheffer, J. G. de Hoop. *Inventaris der Archiefstukken Berusten bij de Vereenigde Doopsgezinde Gemeente te Amsterdam.* Amsterdam, 1883–84.

Schelbert, Leo. *Einführung in die Schweizerische Auswanderungsgeschichte.* Beihefte der Schweizerischen Zeitschrift für Geschichte, no. 16. Zurich, 1976.

———. "On Becoming Emigrants: A Structural View of Eighteenth- and Nineteenth-Century Swiss Data." *Perspectives in American History* 7 (1973): 439–95.

———. "People of Choice." *The Report: A Journal of German-American History* 40 (1986): 77–95.

———. "Swiss Migration to America: The Swiss Mennonites." Ph.D. dissertation, Columbia University, 1966.

———. "Von der Macht des Pietismus: Dokumentarbericht zur Auswanderung einer Baseler Familie im Jahre 1736." *Baseler Zeitschrift für Geschichte und Altertumskunde* 75 (1975): 89–199.

Schelbert, Leo, and Hedwig Rappolt. *Alles ist ganz anders hier. Auswandererschicksale in Briefen aus zwei Jahrhunderten.* Freiburg i. Br., 1977.

Scherer, Karl, ed. *Pfälzer—Palatines. Beiträge zur pfälzischen Ein- und Auswanderung sowie zur Volkskunde und Mundartforschung der Pfalz und der Zielländer pfälzischer Auswanderer im 18. und 19. Jahrhundert.* Kaiserslautern, 1981.

Scheuerbrandt, Arnold. "Die Amerikaauswanderung aus dem Kraichgau und seinen Randbereichen im 18. Jahrhundert." *Kraichgau. Beiträge zur Landschafts- und Heimatforschung* 9 (1985): 65–97.

———. "Die Auswanderung aus dem heutigen Baden-Württemberg nach Preußen, in den habsburgischen Südosten, nach Rußland und Nordamerika zwischen 1683 und 1811." In *Historischer Atlas von Baden Württemberg.* Part XII:5. Stuttgart, 1985.

Schilling, Heinz. *Vom Alten Reich zum Fürstenstaat, Deutschland, 1648–1763. Das Reich und die Deutschen.* Berlin, 1984.

Schluchter, Andre. *Das Gösgeramt im Ancien Regime. Bevölkerung, Wirtschaft, und Gesellschaft einer solothurnischen Landvogtei im 17. und 18. Jahrhundert.* Baseler Beiträge zur Geschichtswissenschaft 160. Edited by F. Graus, H. R. Guggisberg, H. Lüthy, and M. Mattmüller. Basel, 1990.

Schmidt, Erwin Friedrich. *Schweizer Familien im Zweibrücker Land.* Schriften zur Wanderungsgeschichte der Pfälzer, no. 14. Kaiserslautern, 1962.

Schoff, Wilfred H. *The Descendants of Jacob Schoff Who Came to Boston in 1752.* Philadelphia, 1910.

Schuchmann, Heinz. *Schweizer Einwanderer im frühen kurpfälzischen Streubesitz des Kraichgaus.* Schriften zur Wanderungsgeschichte der Pfälzer, no. 18. Kaiserslautern, 1963.

[Schultze, David]. "Narrative of the Journey of the Schwenkfelders to Pennsylvania, 1733." *PMHB* 10 (1886): 167–79.

Schünzel, Eva. *Die deutsche Auswanderung nach Nordamerika im 17. und 18. Jahrhundert.* Würzburg, 1959.

Schuster, Otto. "Die Auswanderung nach Pennsylvanien 1746–1772 unter Herzog Karl." In *Unsere Heimat: Die Kirche,* 127–38. Nürtingen, 1931.

Schwartz, Sally. *"A Mixed Multitude": The Struggle for Toleration in Colonial Pennsylvania.* New York, 1987.

Schwarzmeier, Hansmartin. "Auswandererbriefe aus Nordamerika. Quellen im Grenzbereich von Geschichtlicher Landskunde, Wanderungsforschung und Literatursoziologie." *Zeitschrift für die Geschichte des Oberrheins* 126 (1978): 303–69.

Selig, Robert A. "Emigration, Fraud, Humanitarianism, and the Founding of Londonderry, South Carolina, 1763–1765." *Eighteenth-Century Studies* 23 (Fall 1989): 1–23.

———. "The Idea and Practice of the *ius emigrandi* in the Holy Roman Empire from the Reformation to the French Revolution." *Yearbook of German-American Studies* 27 (1992): 15–22.

———. "The Price of Freedom: Poverty, Emigration, and Taxation in the Prince-

Bishopric of Würzburg in the Eighteenth Century." *Yearbook of German-American Studies* 26 (1991): 105–26.

———. *Räutige Schafe und geistliche Hirten. Studien zur Auswanderung aus dem Hochstift Würzburg im 18. Jahrhundert und ihre Ursachen.* Mainfränkische Studien, vol. 43. Würzburg, 1988.

Sell, Donna-Christine, and Dennis Walle. *Guide to the Heinrich A. Rattermann Collection of German-American Manuscripts.* Champaign, Ill., 1979.

Shepherd, James A., and Gary M. Walton. *Shipping, Maritime Trade, and the Economic Development of Colonial North America.* Cambridge, 1972.

"Sichere Nachricht aus America, wegen der Landschafft Pennsylvania, von einem dorthin gereissten Teutschen [Francis Daniel Pastorius], 7 March 1684." *Pennsylvania German Society: Proceedings and Addresses* 9 (1899): 133–40.

Simon, Christian. *Untertanenverhalten und obrigkeitliche Moralpolitik. Studien zum Verhältnis zwischen Stadt und Land im ausgehenden 18. Jahrhunderts am Beispiel Basels.* Baseler Beiträge zur Geschichtswissenschaft 145. Edited by F. Graus, H. R. Guggisberg, H. Lüthy, and M. Mattmüller. Basel, 1981.

Slaski, Eugene R. *Poorly Marked and Worse Lighted: Being a History of the Port Wardens of Philadelphia, 1766–1907.* Harrisburg, Pa., n.d.

Smith, Abbot E. *Colonists in Bondage: White Servitude and Convict Labor in America.* Chapel Hill, N.C., 1947.

Smith, Billy G. *The "Lower Sort": Philadelphia's Laboring People, 1750–1800.* Ithaca, N.Y., 1990.

———. "The Material Lives of Laboring Philadelphians, 1750–1800." *WMQ* 38 (1981): 163–202.

———. "The Vicissitudes of Fortune: The Careers of Laboring Men in Philadelphia." In *Work and Labor in Early America,* 221–51. Edited by Stephen Innes. Chapel Hill, N.C., 1988.

Smith, C. Henry. "The Mennonite Immigration to Pennsylvania in the Eighteenth Century." *Pennsylvania German Society: Proceedings and Addresses* 35 (1929): 1–412.

Smith, T. Lynn. *Demography: Principles and Methods.* Philadelphia, 1970, 152–57.

Smith, Warren B. *White Servitude in Colonial South Carolina.* Columbia, S.C., 1961.

Smyth, William J. "Irish Emigration, 1700–1920." In *European Expansion and Migration: Essays on the Intercontinental Migration from Africa, Asia, and Europe,* 49–78. Edited by P. C. Emmer and M. Mörner. New York, 1992.

Snyder, Martin B. *City of Independence: Views of Philadelphia Before 1800.* New York, 1975.

Soderlund, Jean R., and Richard S. Dunn, eds. *William Penn and the Founding of Pennsylvania, 1680–1684.* Philadelphia, 1982.

Sollors, Werner, ed. *The Invention of Ethnicity.* New York, 1989.

Solow, Barbara L., ed. *Slavery and the Rise of the Atlantic System.* New York, 1991.

Souden, David. "'Rogues, Whores, and Vagabonds'? Indentured Servant Emigrants to North America, and the Case of Mid-Seventeenth-Century Bristol." *Social History* 3 (1978): 23–40.

Specker, Hans Eugen. "Die Verfassung und Verwaltung der Württembergischen Amtsstädte im 17. und 18. Jahrhundert dargestellt am Beispiel Sindelfingen." In

Verwaltung und Gesellschaft in der südwestdeutschen Stadt des 17. und 18. Jahrhunderts. Protokoll über die VII. Arbeitstagung des Arbeitskrieses für südwestdeutsche Stadtgeschichtsforschung, Sindelfingen 15.–17. November 1969, 1–21. Edited by Erich Maschke and Jürgen Sydow. Veröffentlichungen der Kommission für Geschichtliche Landeskunde in Baden Württemberg, series B: Forschungen, vol. 58. Stuttgart, 1969.

Sprengel, Martina. "Studien zur Nordamerikaauswanderung in der ersten Hälfte des 18. Jahrhunderts: Nassau-Oranien." M.A. thesis, University of Cologne, 1984.

Stahl, Friedrich. "Die Einwanderung in ostpreußische Städte, 1740–1806." *Zeitschrift für Ostforschung* 1 (1952): 544–53.

Starkey, David J. *British Privateering Enterprise in the Eighteenth Century.* Exeter, 1990.

Staudt, Ricardo. "The Huber-Hoover Family of Aesch, Switzerland, and Trippstadt, Palatine." *Pennsylvania Genealogical Magazine* 12 (1935): 223–43.

Stauffer, William T., ed. "Hans Stauffer Account Books: A Study." *Publications of the Genealogical Society of Pennsylvania (Pennsylvania Genealogical Magazine)* 10 (1929): 296–302.

Steele, Ian K. *The English Atlantic, 1675–1740: An Exploration of Communication and Community.* Oxford, 1986.

Steinfeld, Robert J. *The Invention of Free Labor.* Chapel Hill, N.C., 1991.

Stopp, Klaus. *Die Handwerkers-bundschaften mit Ortansichten. Beschreibender Katalog der Arbeitsattestate wandernder Handwerksgesellen, 1750–1830. Volume 1: Allgemeiner Teil. Volume 2: Katalog.* Stuttgart, 1986.

Strassburger, Ralph B. *Pennsylvania German Pioneers: A Publication of the Original Lists of Arrivals in the Port of Philadelphia from 1727 to 1808.* Edited by William John Hinke. Volume 1: *Introduction and Lists, 1727–1775.* Volume 2: *Facsimile of Signatures.* Volume 3: *Lists, 1785–1808, and Indices.* 1934; reprint ed., Baltimore, Md., 1966.

Straub, Alfred. *Das badische Oberland im 18. Jahrhundert. Die Transformation einer bäuerlichen Gesellschaft vor der Industrialisierung.* Historische Studien, vol. 429. Husum, 1977.

Strobel, Albrecht. *Agrarverfassung im Übergang. Studien zur Agrargeschichte des badischen Breisgaus vom Beginn des 16. bis zum Ausgang des 18. Jahrhunderts.* Forschungen zur oberrheinischen Landesgeschichte, vol. 23. Freiburg, 1972.

Stumpp, Karl. *The Emigration from Germany to Russia in the Years 1763–1862.* Lincoln, Neb., 1973.

Tappert, Theodore G., and John W. Doberstein, eds. and trans. *The Journal of Henry Melchior Muhlenberg.* 3 vols. Philadelphia, 1942–48.

Taricani, JoAnn. "Musical Commerce in Eighteenth-Century Philadelphia: The Letters of Michael Hillegas." *PMHB* 113 (October 1989): 609–25.

Taylor, Philip A. M. *The Distant Magnet: European Emigration to the U.S.A.* New York, 1971.

Tepper, Michael, ed. *Emigrants to Pennsylvania, 1614–1819: A Consolidation of Ship Passenger Lists from the PMHB.* Baltimore, Md., 1979.

———. *Immigrants to the Middle Colonies: A Consolidation of Ship Passenger Lists and Associated Data from the New York Genealogical and Biographical Record.* Baltimore, Md., 1978.

———. *New World Immigrants: A Consolidation of Ship Passenger Lists and Associated Data from Periodical Literature.* 2 vols. Baltimore, Md., 1980.

Thistlethwaite, Frank. "Migration from Europe Overseas in the Nineteenth and

Twentieth Centuries." *A Century of European Migrations, 1830–1930*. Edited by J. Rudolph Vecoli and Suzanne M. Sinke, 17–49; postscript, 50–57. Urbana, Ill., 1991.

———. "Migration from Europe Overseas in the Nineteenth and Twentieth Centuries." In *XIe Congrès International des Sciences Historiques: Rapport V*, 3260. Goteborg, 1960.

Thomas, Brinley. *Migration and Economic Growth: A Study of Great Britain and the Atlantic Economy*. Cambridge, 1954.

Tilly, Charles. "Transplanted Networks." In *Immigration Reconsidered: History, Sociology, and Politics*, 79–95. Edited by Virginia Yans-McLaughlin. New York, 1994.

Todd, Vincent H., ed. *Christoph Von Graffenried's Account of the Founding of New Bern*. Raleigh, N.C., 1920.

Tomlins, Christopher L. *Law, Labor, and Ideology in the Early Republic*. Cambridge, 1993.

Tomlins, Christopher L., and Andrew J. King, eds. *Labor Law in America: Historical and Critical Essays*. Baltimore, Md., 1992.

Tracy, James D., ed. *The Political Economy of Merchant Empires*. Studies in Comparative Early Modern History, vol. 2. New York, 1991.

———. *The Rise of Merchant Empires: Long-Distance Trade in the Early Modern World, 1350–1750*. New York, 1990.

Trautz, Fritz. *Die Pfälzische Auswanderung nach Nordamerika im 18. Jahrhundert*. Heidelberg, 1959.

Trossbach, Werner. *Bauern, 1648–1806*. Volume 19 of *Enzyklopädie deutscher Geschichte*. Edited by Lothar Gall. Munich, 1993.

———. *Der Schatten der Aufklärung. Bauern, Bürger, und Illuminaten in der Grafschaft Wied-Neuwied*. Deutschlands achtzehntes Jahrhundert Studien, vol. 1. Fulda, 1991.

Truxes, Thomas M. *Irish American Trade, 1660–1783*. Cambridge, 1988.

"Two Germantown Letters of 1738 [by J. Christopher Sauer]." *PMHB* 56 (1932): 10–14.

"Two Germantown Letters of 1755 [petition to Pennsylvania governor by J. Christopher Sauer]." In Frank R. Diffenderfer, *The German Immigration into Pennsylvania Through the Port of Philadelphia from 1700 to 1775 and the Redemptioners*, 377–86. 1900; reprint ed., Baltimore, Md., 1977, 1979.

Vann, James Allen. *The Making of a State: Württemberg, 1593–1793*. Ithaca, N.Y., 1984.

———. "Politics and Society in the Holy Roman Empire, 1500–1800." *Journal of Modern History* 58 (1986): supp.

Vecoli, J. Rudolph, and Suzanne M. Sinke, eds. *A Century of European Migrations, 1830–1930*. Statue of Liberty—Ellis Island Centennial Series. Urbana, Ill., 1991.

Vierhaus, Rudolf. *Germany in the Age of Absolutism*. Translated by Jonathan B. Knudsen. Cambridge, 1988.

Volk, Stefan. "Peuplierung und religiöse Toleranz. Neuwied von der Mitte des 17. bis zur Mitte des 18. Jahrhunderts." *Rheinische Vierteljahrsblätter* 55 (1991): 205–31.

Votes and Proceedings of the House of Representatives of the Province of Pennsylvania, 1682–1776. 8 vols. (*Pennsylvania Archives*, 8th ser., 8 vols.) Harrisburg, Pa., 1931–35.

Vowinckel, Renate. *Ursachen den Auswanderung gezeigt an badischen Beispielen aus dem 18. und*

19. Jahrbundert. Vierteljahrsschrift für Sozial- und Wirtschaftsgeschichte, supplementary issue 37. Stuttgart, 1939.

Walker, Mack. *The Salzburger Transaction. Expulsion and Redemption in Eighteenth-Century Germany.* Ithaca, N.Y., 1992.

Walsh, B. M. "A Perspective on Irish Population Patterns." *Eire-Ireland* 4 (1970): 3–21.

Walter, John, and Roger Schofield, eds. *Famine, Disease, and the Social Order in Early Modern Society.* Cambridge Studies in Population, Economy, and Society in Past Time, no. 10. Cambridge, 1989.

Walton, Gary. "A Measure of Productivity in American Colonial Shipping." *Explorations in Entrepreneurial History* 21 (1968).

———. "Obstacles to Technical Diffusion in Ocean Shipping, 1675–1775." *Explorations in Entrepreneurial History* 7 (1971).

———. "Sources of Productivity Change in American Colonial Shipping, 1675–1775." *Economic History Review* 30 (1967): 67–78.

Wareing, John. "Migration to London and Transatlantic Emigration of Indentured Servants, 1683–1775." *Journal of Historical Geography* 7 (1981): 356–78.

Way, Peter. "Industrial Forge and Ethnic Melting Pot: The British Army in the French and Indian War." Paper presented to the Center for the Study of New England History, Massachusetts Historical Society, Boston, 10 September 1996.

Wedgewood, C. V. *The Thirty Years' War.* 1938. Reprint ed., Garden City, N.Y., 1961.

Wellenreuther, Hermann. "Image and Counterimage, Tradition and Expectation: The German Immigrants in English Colonial Society in Pennsylvania, 1700–1765." In *America and the Germans: An Assessment of a Three-Hundred-Year History,* 1:5–105. Edited by Trommler and Timothy McVeigh. Philadelphia, 1985.

Wicki, Hans. *Bevölkerung und Wirtschaft des Kantons Luzern im 18. Jahrbundert.* Lucerne, 1979.

Wiegand, Otto. "Ulm als Stadt der Auswanderer." *Mitteilungen des Vereins für Kunst und Altertum in Ulm und Oberschwaben* 31 (1941): 88–114.

Wilson, Charles W. *Anglo-Dutch Commerce and Finance in the Eighteenth Century.* 1941; reprint ed., Cambridge, 1966.

Wilson, Renate. "Halle and Ebenezer: Pietism, Agriculture, and Commerce in Colonial Georgia." Ph.D. dissertation, University of Maryland, 1988.

———. "Public Works and Piety in Ebenezer: The Missing Salzburger Diaries of 1744–1745." *Georgia Historical Quarterly* 77 (Summer 1993): 336–66.

Wokeck, Marianne S. "The Experience of Indentured Servants from Germany and Ireland: Guaranteed Employment, Educational Opportunity, or Last Resort?" *The Report: A Journal of German-American History* 40 (1986): 57–76.

———. "The Flow and Composition of German Immigration to Philadelphia, 1727–1775." *PMHB* 105 (1981): 245–78.

———. "Harnessing the Lure of 'the Best Poor Man's Country': The Dynamics of German-Speaking Immigration to British North America, 1683–1783." In *To Make America: European Emigration in the Early Modern Period,* 104–43. Edited by Ida Altman and James Horn. Berkeley, Calif., 1991.

———. "Irish Immigration to the Delaware Valley Before the American Revolution." *Proceedings of the Royal Irish Academy* 96, C, no. 5 (1996): 103–35.

————. "Servant Migration and the Transfer of Culture from the Old World to the New." ISHAW, 1996.

————. "Tide of Alien Tongues: The Flow and Ebb of German Immigration to Pennsylvania, 1683–1775." Ph.D. dissertation, Temple University, 1983.

Wolf, George D. *The Fair Play Settlers of the West Branch Valley, 1769–1784: A Study of Frontier Ethnography.* Harrisburg, Pa., 1969.

Wolf, Stephanie Grauman. *Urban Village: Population, Community, and Family Structure in Germantown, Pennsylvania, 1683–1800.* Princeton, N.J., 1976.

Wood, Jerome H., Jr. *Conestoga Crossroads: Lancaster, Pennsylvania, 1730–1790.* Harrisburg, Pa., 1979.

Wright, Robert E. "Thomas Willing (1731–1821): Philadelphia Financier and Forgotten Founding Father." *Pennsylvania History* 63 (Autumn 1996): 525–60.

Wust, Klaus. "Direct German Immigration to Maryland in the Eighteenth Century (a Preliminary Survey)." *The Report: A Journal of German-American History* 37 (1978): 19–22.

————. "The Emigration Season of 1738—Year of the Destroying Angel." *The Report: A Journal of German-American History* 40 (1986): 21–56.

————. "Feeding the Palatines: Shipboard Diet in the Eighteenth Century." *The Report: A Journal of German-American History* 39 (1984): 32–42.

————. "German Settlements and Immigrants in Virginia: A Bibliography." *The Report: A Journal of German-American History* 33 (1968): 47–59.

————. *Guardian on the Hudson: The German Society of New York, 1784–1984.* New York, 1984.

————. "Palatines and Switzers for Virginia, 1705–1738: Costly Lessons for Promoters and Emigrants." *Yearbook of American German Studies* 19 (1984): 43–55.

————. *The Virginia Germans.* Charlottesville, Va., 1969.

Yans-McLaughlin, Virginia, ed. *Immigration Reconsidered: History, Sociology, and Politics.* New York, 1990.

Yoder, Don. "Palatine, Hessian, Dutchman: Drei Bezeichnungen für Deutsche in Amerika." In *Der Große Aufbruch. Studien zur Amerikaauswanderung.* Edited by Peter Assion. Marburg/Lahn, 1985.

Yoder, Don, ed. *Rhineland Emigrants: Lists of German Settlers in Colonial America,* excerpted and reprinted from *Pennsylvania Folklife.* Baltimore, Md., 1981.

Yoder, Don, trans. and ed. *Pennsylvania German Immigrants, 1709–1786: Lists Consolidated from Yearbooks of the Pennsylvania German Folklore Society.* Baltimore, Md., 1980.

Index

free passage for emigrants through the
  Netherlands sought by, 64
provides for nonpaying immigrants, 101
  n. 122
recruiting agent in partnership with, 66
  n. 23, 83
as ship captain and owner, 74–75, 91, 95
stewards, 134
Stewart, Alexander, 70
Stöcken, Bodo Wilhelm, 134 n. 63
Strettle, Robert, 71
Stümpel, Johann Heinrich Christian, 121 n. 23
Swiss cantons, 5–6, 10, 14
Swiss migrants
  to the Rhine lands, 2, 5–7
  in Rotterdam, 63
Symson, Alexander, 84 n. 71

Thirty Years' War, 6
toll stations along the Rhine, 119–20, 121
trade in immigrants, system of, xx, xxvii,
  221–38. See also merchants; recruitment of emigrants; shipping of
  emigrants
transports of emigrants, 62–63, 118–21
travel accounts, 113–14
Trimbel, Francis, 64
Tschudi, Johannes, 30 n. 90
Turner, Robert, 177 n. 17

Ulster, xxi n. 2, xxx, 169, 179, 182, 185, 195–
  96, 215
  goods exported from, 197

New Castle's ties to, 174–75
religious intolerance in, 190–91
United Provinces. See Netherlands

vessels. See ships
Virginia, immigration to, 37, 40–41,
  108

Waldo, Samuel, 19 n. 60, 20–21, 33 n. 105,
  60, 76 n. 46, 103, 105,
  231
Walsem, Willem van, 64 n. 13
Warder & Parker merchant house, 71
Wars of Succession, 14, 44
Washington, George, 25 n. 71, 94 n. 100
Wax, George, 133
Weisel, Catherine, 148–49
Weiss, Lewis, 144, 146–47
Welsh immigrants, xix
Werndtlin-Göttschi, Esther, 28 n. 85
Whitsett, Joseph W., 210
Willing, Thomas, 71, 94, 106, 107 n. 137,
  146–47
Wilson, William, 70
Wistar, Caspar, 25 n. 71, 27 n. 78, 32 n. 101,
  33 n. 105, 151 n. 113
Wister, John, 30 n. 92
women and children, 44
  age distributions of migrants, 48–49
  as indentured servants, 157, 163

Zuberbühler, Bartholomus, 19 n. 59
Zuberbühler, Sebastian, 28 n. 81, 73, 76 n. 46